Confidence Games

Confidence Games

Lawyers, Accountants, and the Tax Shelter Industry

Tanina Rostain and Milton C. Regan, Jr.

The MIT Press
Cambridge, Massachusetts
London, England

MIT Press books may be purchased at special quantity discounts for business or sales promotional use. For information, please email special_sales@mitpress.mit.edu.

This book was set in Sabon by the MIT Press. Printed and bound in the United States of America.

Library of Congress Cataloging-in-Publication Data

Rostain, Tanina.
Confidence games : lawyers, accountants, and the tax shelter industry / Tanina Rostain and Milton C. Regan, Jr.
    pages cm
Includes bibliographical references and index.
ISBN 978-0-262-02713-7 (hardcover : alk. paper)
1. Tax shelters—United States—History. 2. Tax shelters—Law and legislation—United States—History. 3. Corporations—Taxation—United States—History. 4. Taxation—Moral and ethical aspects—United States—History. I. Regan, Milton C. II. Title.
HJ4653.T38R67 2014
336.2'06—dc23
                                                                                              2013034776

10 9 8 7 6 5 4 3 2 1

To the determined journalists who dug deeply to bring this story to light.

Contents

Acknowledgments and Note on Sources

Many people helped us to uncover the details of the story we tell here. Among them are the business reporters to whom this book is dedicated. Were it not for their dogged insistence on ferreting out the facts and their willingness to untangle the complexities of tax law and its application to sophisticated financial transactions, the widespread participation of major accounting firms and corporate law firms in the shelter industry would likely not have come to light. We learned much from the many journalists who wrote on this subject. We are especially grateful to Paul Braverman, Lynnley Browning, Cassell Bryan-Low, Cheryl Hall, Tom Herman, John McKinnon, Janet Novack, Rick Rothacker, and Lee Sheppard for giving generously of their time to speak with us.

Publications by Tax Analysts, a nonprofit organization devoted to providing news and analysis of tax issues, were invaluable. *Tax Notes Today* (cited in the notes as *TNT*) was an extraordinary source of detailed information about events relating to tax shelters and tax policy. The organization and its publications are a unique national resource on the vital topic of the United States tax system.

A number of lawyers who brought civil cases against law firms, accounting firms, and financial institutions involved in the shelter industry agreed to be interviewed and discuss their experiences with us. These lawyers shared a talent for recognizing that beneath the technical complexities, these organizations had perpetrated fraud not only on the government but also on their own clients. In almost all cases, the litigation was subject to a court order that prevented lawyers representing the plaintiffs from sharing documents and other discovery materials with us. The lawyers with whom we spoke did their utmost to educate us about the facts that emerged in their cases without violating their professional obligations. We would like to thank Ralph Canada, David Deary, Blair Fensterstock, Campbell Killefer, Gary Mauney, Michael Phillips, Edmundo Ramirez, Stefan Tucker, and Damon Wright for sharing their insights with us. We are also grateful to members of the U.S. Department of Justice's Tax Division who were involved in civil and criminal cases involving tax shelters for their willingness to discuss matters of public record with us.

Mike Hamersley, a former lawyer at KPMG, braved retaliation from the firm to report the wrongdoing he witnessed to governmental officials and testify about it in Congress. Mike provided us with a vivid account of his time at KPMG. He also has the rare capacity to explain clearly and in nontechnical terms the transactions about which we have written. We are grateful for his substantial assistance.

During our research for this book, we interviewed numerous firsthand observers of and participants in the events, including former government officials and partners at accounting firms and law firms. Consistent with common practice in writing on such a sensitive subject, we agreed to keep the identity of our informants confidential. In cases in which the account of an event is traceable to an identifiable source, we have obtained permission to describe the event. To keep our endnotes to a minimum, we do not cite these sources.

By the time the events described in these pages had reached their denouement, hundreds of thousands of pages of documents had become part of the public record. In writing this book, we reviewed transcripts of congressional hearings and related exhibits; documents related to government enforcement proceedings; criminal indictments and informations; settlement agreements; deferred prosecution and nonprosecution agreements; and civil and criminal trial pleadings, transcripts, and exhibits, among other materials.

Despite the wealth of documents that are now part of the public record, there are pieces of this story that we suspect we were unable to uncover. As we have noted, in almost all cases brought by clients against their former firms, the plaintiffs' lawyers were prevented by court orders from disclosing documents and discovery materials they had obtained. These orders were sought by the organizational defendants, who insisted that the shelters in question were legitimate financial transactions involving proprietary information. We believe that in most cases these orders are no longer justified—if they ever were—and that these materials should be available under the First Amendment right of access to public records. In the interest of completing this book, we decided not to challenge these orders, which would have required litigation in state courts all over the country. We also filed a number of Freedom of Information Act requests, which resulted in the acquisition of a few but not all of the documents we believed we were entitled to receive. Here too we decided not to challenge the government's responses to our requests.

Over the course of this project, numerous students at New York Law School, Harvard Law School, and Georgetown Law Center provided superb research assistance. When Tanina Rostain first started investigating the role of accounting firms in the tax shelter industry, Christine Harrington, NYLS '03, and Ilir Mujalovic, NYLS '03, obtained useful materials, wrote detailed memos, and served as helpful sounding boards. Billy Magnuson, Harvard Law School '10, offered insightful suggestions about the substance of the project and traveled far and wide to retrieve documents filed in state court proceedings. Toward the end of the drafting process, Hilary Pugmire, NYLS '12, did an excellent job of coordinating a large number of students recruited to observe ongoing criminal trials. Alice Townes, NYLS '12, kept close track of proceedings and events and wrote many helpful memos, offering frequent astute observations along the way. Zach Hutchinson, GULC '16, was invaluable in researching and helping to put the final touches on the manuscript. We are grateful to these students and many others for the time and effort they devoted to helping us with this project. Anna Selden, the Faculty Manuscripts Editor at Georgetown Law Center, engaged in a careful read of the manuscript and provided us with many useful edits.

From the beginning Roxanne Coady was an enthusiastic supporter of this project. Michael Graetz and Linc Caplan gave us helpful suggestions on our earliest efforts. Susan Silbey reminded us throughout the project to keep our eye on organizational structures and dynamics when we were tempted to see the narrative as a story about individuals. Sally Gordon was always available as a sounding board for Tanina when the problems seemed intractable.

Many tax colleagues reviewed and commented on the manuscript. Dennis Ventry reviewed the full manuscript and provided a wealth of substantive and editorial suggestions. Karen Burke, Dan Davidson,

Michael Doran, Grayson McCouch, Alan Kaden, and David Weisbach read portions of the manuscript and gave us helpful comments. Steve Cohen, Albert Lauber, Ron Pearlman, Stafford Smiley, and Ethan Yale gave generously of their time to enlighten us on many aspects of tax shelters and the tax system. Several anonymous readers also reviewed the manuscript for the MIT Press. We are grateful to these colleagues for helping us describe as accurately as we could the complex tax policy and regulatory issues involved and for sharing their recollections of the events. Any errors or omissions are, of course, our responsibility. Nancy Sachs offered the perspective of a nonspecialist who read the entire manuscript with a critical eye and an ear keenly attuned to infelicitous language.

We presented early drafts of portions of this book at workshops at Georgetown, New York Law School, and on panels at the Law and Society Association. In each instance, members of the audience provided helpful suggestions and critiques that improved the quality of the project. Parts of chapters 5, 12, and 13 were adapted from Tanina Rostain, "Travails in Tax: KMPG and the Tax-Shelter Controversy," in *Legal Ethics: Law Stories*, ed. Deborah Rhode and David J. Luban (New York: Foundation Press, 2005). Portions of chapters 8 and 12 were published by Milton Regan as "Taxes and Death: The Rise and Demise of an American Law Firm," in *Law Firms, Legal Culture, and Legal Practice*, a special issue of *Studies in Law, Politics and Society*, ed. Austin Sarat (2010).

We are grateful to our families, who offered assistance and support during the course of this project. Richard, Tanina's life partner, was a steady and supportive companion. He provided a receptive ear, encouragement, and invaluable advice in the moments when this project raised the greatest challenges. Joseph and Mila were a constant source of delight and amusement. It was a special pleasure to watch them grow into young adults during the gestation of this book. For Mitt, Nancy offered the love and encouragement of a partner and friend, while Rebecca, Ben, and Bryan furnished steady encouragement and important moments away from the economic substance doctrine. May Liam grow up in a country in which resources and burdens are shared more equally than they are today.

Last, we're deeply grateful to each other for a terrific collaboration. The companionship, conversation, and laughter were a source of ongoing sustenance; the artisanal cheeses, Mexican haute cuisine, and back-road Texas barbeque fortified us each step along the way. We could not have gone on a more enjoyable adventure together.

Introduction

In late 1999, an unmarked manila envelope arrived at the U.S. Department of the Treasury.[1] The appearance of a mysterious envelope at the Treasury was not uncommon at that time. Every once in a while, Treasury officials would receive a parcel containing the prospectus for a complicated tax evasion strategy. They assumed that the documents came from tax professionals who had been shown the materials by a client or had come across them at work. These professionals, worried that the Internal Revenue Service might never discover the tax ploy, wanted to alert the agency so that it could close down the strategy and prevent the loss of millions of dollars in tax revenue. Torn between their concern that the tax shelter would allow wealthy individuals improperly to avoid millions of dollars in taxes and their obligation to protect client or employer confidences, some professionals chose to try to protect the federal fisc. Anonymity was the fig leaf that allowed them to make peace with the fact that by sending the materials to the government they were betraying their clients' or employers' confidences.

The manila envelope that happened to arrive at the Treasury that fall contained marketing materials describing a shelter known under the acronym BOSS, which was being promoted by Big Five accounting firm PricewaterhouseCoopers. From the look of the documents, BOSS was being offered to high-wealth individuals who wanted to avoid paying any taxes on large capital gains.[2] If, as it turned out, the promotional documents described an abusive shelter—one whose claimed tax benefits were not recognized by the law—Treasury officials would be able to use the detailed description as a roadmap to shut down the shelter and find the taxpayers who were claiming tax benefits from the strategy. Government officials immediately began analyzing the documents and sharing them with other government agencies.

The timing of the envelope's arrival was propitious. In November, Congress was scheduled to hold hearings on the problem of abusive tax shelters. A year earlier, *Forbes* magazine had run a cover story on "The Hustling of X-Rated Shelters," which had described in detail questionable strategies being offered by the Big Five accounting firms.[3] According to Forbes, these shelters were being marketed under confidentiality agreements and designed to look like complex investments to avoid detection by the IRS. After the article came out, firm representatives insisted that any strategies they were selling were bona fide investments whose purpose was not solely to reduce or eliminate taxes. They were also adamant that there was no widespread abusive tax shelter problem that needed to be addressed through new legislation. Powerful members of Congress, wary of the IRS's claims that a crisis was imminent, were prone to agree. For tax officials concerned that there was a serious and spreading problem, the contents of the manila envelope were corroboration that at least one major accounting firm was actively promoting abusive tax strategies.

Earlier in 1999, KPMG, another Big Five accounting firm, had approved for sale a tax shelter known under the acronym BLIPS.[4] This tax elimination strategy turned on obtaining a loan at an above-market interest rate. Deutsche Bank, recognizing the potential for lucrative fees, agreed to provide the funds. Beginning that spring, two tax partners at KPMG involved in the review repeatedly raised concerns that the shelter would not hold up in court. When they were finally able to review the loan documentation during the summer of 1999, their fears were confirmed. The loan from the bank was a loan in name only, since the funds were not permitted to leave the bank. Despite these concerns, KPMG tax leaders pressed on, eager to get BLIPS to market because of its potential to bring in significant revenue. Before too long, the partners who had raised doubts about the shelter had been marginalized. The firm went on to make $50 million from the sale of BLIPS, which did not come to the attention of authorities until several years later.[5] When the government finally discovered BLIPS, it estimated that the shelter had cost the Treasury at least $1.5 billion in uncollected tax revenue.[6]

Meanwhile at Ernst & Young, a team of tax lawyers and accountants formed specifically to design and market tax shelters was very busy marketing a shelter similar to BLIPS. COBRA, as this shelter was known, had been developed in collaboration with Paul Daugerdas, a tax lawyer and partner at Jenkens & Gilchrist, a notable corporate law firm based in Dallas, Texas.[7] Daugerdas had joined the firm a year earlier. With two other lawyers from his old firm, he opened a Jenkens branch office in Chicago devoted to developing and promoting tax shelters. Daugerdas essentially ran his own show in Chicago with only minimal oversight from the firm. Soon the revenue began to pour in. COBRA was so successful that a small army of associates from the Dallas office periodically had to be flown up to Chicago to deal with the enormous backlog of paperwork that was generated by the sales of the shelter.

BDO Seidman, a second-tier firm, was also in the game. In early 1999, the firm had been suffering significant financial difficulties. Revenue from tax shelter activities promised to turn the situation around. Denis Field, a lawyer and charismatic leader who would shortly rise to be the firm's CEO, had formed a special group devoted to marketing tax shelters, known as the "Wolf Pack."[8] By mid-1999, the firm was enjoying almost $15 million in net profit from shelter sales. Field saw even greater wealth on the horizon. Predicting profits of more than $75 million the following year, Field exhorted tax partners with the slogan "Tax ell!" Like Ernst & Young, BDO also had turned to Daugerdas at Jenkens to help design and promote tax shelters.

Daugerdas's group was not the only one at an elite law firm that was deeply involved in tax shelter activity. The efforts of accounting firms were abetted by lawyers at several other prestigious firms. These firms included Brown & Wood (later absorbed into Sidley Austin Brown & Wood), Arnold & Porter, Locke Liddell, Proskauer Rose, Seyfarth Shaw, and LeBoeuf Lamb. Tax lawyers at these firms developed ideas for new tax strategies and worked with accounting firms, financial institutions, and investment advisory firms to implement them. They also wrote hundreds of opinion letters that were intended to induce clients to purchase shelters and protect them from liability for penalties if the IRS discovered the shelters. Even though the lawyers in many instances had helped create the shelters, their opinions purported to be the objective advice of independent legal advisors. These cookie-cutter letters, which varied only in client details, earned their law firms millions of dollars in fees.

The turn of the twenty-first century represented the high-water mark for abusive tax shelter activity at major accounting firms and elite law firms. To address the epidemic, federal tax authorities had to launch a multipronged attack. They sought new statutes and regulations to tighten the federal tax code and went after taxpayers who had used abusive tax strategies. Recognizing that they needed to shut down the problem at its source, officials trained their sights on accounting and law firms and took actions that were virtually unheard of at the time. They issued subpoenas to firms requesting documents and information about clients, launched criminal investigations, and initiated tax fraud prosecutions against professionals. By the mid-2000s, the tax shelter industry had begun to contract, but not before a significant number of tax professionals and the accounting and law firms at which they worked had been drawn into the criminal justice system.

Spanning the decade between 1994 and 2004, the abusive tax shelter crisis likely represents the most serious episode of lawyer wrongdoing in the history of the American bar. Dozens of lawyers participated, dispersed among most of the major accounting firms and many prestigious law firms. The magnitude of this episode is reflected not only in the number of lawyers involved, but also in the depth of their involvement. In the savings and loan debacle of the early 1990s and the corporate scandals a decade later, lawyers were called to task because they had enabled and covered up client wrongdoing rather than attempting to prevent it. During these earlier episodes, "Where were the lawyers?" was an oft-repeated complaint sounded by critics. In the tax shelter episode, by contrast, the lawyers were difficult to miss—if you knew where to look. Inside the firms where they worked, their fingerprints were everywhere: on the shelters they designed, the promotional materials they prepared, the client pitches they made, and the opinion letters they drafted and signed.

How did such a widespread and systemic episode of professional wrongdoing occur? In this book, we offer an account of the circumstances that gave rise to the tax shelter industry. Among the factors that contributed to the emergence of the abusive shelter market were a lax regulatory environment and a highly competitive market for professional services. At the end of the twentieth century, the IRS was struggling with outmoded collection and tracking methods, inadequate analytic tools, and severe resource constraints. It was also dealing with a hostile Congress, many of whose members were intent on rendering the agency ineffective as part of a larger antitax and antigovernment crusade.

During the same period, the American economy was booming. Numerous entrepreneurs were creating and selling off new companies, reaping millions of dollars of profits in the process. Elite lawyers and accountants were not enjoying their share of the wealth, or so they believed. Major accounting firms and corporate law firms were functioning in increasingly winner-take-all markets characterized by fierce competition. In the accounting sector, revenues from audit services—long the core service provided by the Big Five—were flat. Driven by imperatives to grow and increase profits, major firms were casting about to identify new sources of revenue. At the same time, corporate law firms were competing aggressively among themselves for lucrative client engagements, partners with substantial books of business, and greater revenue.

For tax professionals at these firms, shelters targeting the expanding number of newly minted millionaires facing substantial tax bills offered an avenue for increasing growth and profits. Tax shelters—and the supposedly independent opinion letters that accompanied them—could be marketed as products, yielding fees based on the number of virtually identical shelters that were sold. By charging a percentage of the supposed tax savings on a high volume of shelters, firms could escape the constraints on growth imposed by the hourly fee structure.

Despite the allure of lucrative fees, not all accounting firms succumbed, nor did all firms participate to the same extent. The accounting firms that were most deeply involved implemented organizational incentives that encouraged tax shelter development and marketing. Tax leaders at these firms also created organizational structures and cultures that celebrated tax shelter activities and channeled specialized expertise into devising transactions that involved hypertechnical interpretations of the tax code in order to help clients evade billions of dollars in taxes.

At law firms, tax shelter work was not institutionalized to the same degree. Loose partnership structures allowed tax shelter lawyers to work semiautonomously with little or no oversight by the rest of the firm. Whatever review and approval processes were instituted were inadequate, given the complexity and detail of the strategies involved. At Jenkens & Gilchrist, repeated failure to appreciate the risks of a tax shelter practice led eventually to the demise of the firm. Other law firms survived but ended up paying substantial penalties to government authorities and settlement awards to former clients. They also suffered significant reputational harms from government investigations and adverse publicity when their shelter activities became public.

In addition to shedding light on the environmental, organizational, and cultural dynamics that gave rise to systemic wrongdoing, the abusive tax shelter episode exposed deep vulnerabilities inherent in the American tax regime. At the highest reaches of wealth, the income tax system depends on the voluntary participation of taxpayers. Salaried employees are subject to automatic withholding, which gives them little room to avoid paying taxes. Individuals in the top 1 percent income bracket have significantly greater opportunities to structure their business affairs to minimize their tax burden. They also have the resources to enlist financial and tax advisors to devise highly complex tax-favored transactions that are very difficult for the IRS to untangle.

Traditionally, tax lawyers were expected to rein in high-wealth clients who wanted to avoid paying taxes. The U.S. tax bar has long adhered to informal professional norms under which its members advised their clients to refrain from overly aggressive strategies that improperly reduced taxes. These norms reflected an implicit agreement between the legal profession and the state. This agreement provided that lawyers enjoyed significant prerogatives, including freedom from external regulatory oversight, in exchange for a commitment to counsel clients to behave consistently with their legal obligations. Pursuant to this understanding, communications between clients and their lawyers are confidential and protected from disclosure so that lawyers can use their expertise to guide clients to comply with the law.[9]

The abusive tax shelter crisis represented a breach of this agreement. Tax lawyers not only did not advise clients against participating in questionable tax strategies, they also devoted substantial expertise and resources to designing such strategies and soliciting new clients to engage in them. One result has been erosion of the tax bar's professional autonomy, as government authorities have insisted on more expansive regulation of tax counseling and advice. More broadly, although the episode did not occasion a seismic shift in the public's views of elite lawyers, it provided grounds to distrust lawyers and the organizations in which they practice.

To address these concerns, the tax bar needs to recognize that the tax shelter episode was not the product of a handful of bad actors who hijacked the organizations in which they practiced in order to implement their nefarious schemes. Rather, it reflected the combined effects of a highly competitive market, weaknesses in the regulatory regime, and organizational environments whose structures undermined, or at least failed to encourage, traditional informal norms of tax practice. To focus on the wrongdoing of individual participants is to miss the institutional factors that contributed to the tax shelter episode.

We devote most of our attention in this book to describing the events that gave rise to the tax shelter market, and to the government's mostly successful efforts to combat it. While we discuss some measures that might reduce the likelihood of a similar episode occurring again, we do not attempt a comprehensive analysis of how to prevent the next tax shelter wave. Tax practice is especially complex, and tax lawyers inevitably must exercise considerable discretion. We believe therefore that it is up to tax lawyers to devise regulatory and organizational systems to address the weaknesses that we expose in this book. Tax professionals are not passive agents in the environment in which they work, but actors who create and maintain the institutions that structure practice. This book is an invitation to the tax bar, and elite lawyers more generally, to engage—collectively and individually—with the project of strengthening dimensions of the regulatory regime that enable them to practice at the highest level and provide their best professional advice. It is also an invitation to lawyers to create organizational structures and environments conducive to these types of practices. In our conclusion we offer some ideas for pursuing these possibilities. Ultimately, however, the responsibility lies with the tax bar, and the legal profession more broadly, to claim a space for professional norms and practices and to devise the institutions and conditions that permit them to evolve and flourish.[10]

Part I

Shelters Rising

1

The IRS under Siege

In September 1997, Senator William Roth (R, Delaware) opened Senate hearings on alleged misconduct at the IRS by announcing his outrage at what the Committee had uncovered during its investigation of the agency. "Over the course of the next days," he said, "we are going to see a picture of a troubled agency, one that is losing the confidence of the American people, and one that all too frequently acts as if it were above the law. This is unacceptable."[1]

The hearings painted a portrait of a powerful agency run amok. Senators heard from various taxpayers about abuses they claimed to have suffered at the hands of the agency. John Colaprete, owner of The Jewish Mother, a restaurant in Virginia Beach, testified that the IRS had conducted an armed nighttime raid on his home, tearing the door from its hinges, ransacking his house, and impounding his safe, his tax return records, even his dogs. During a simultaneous raid on his business manager's house, the manager was pulled from the shower at gunpoint and forcibly restrained as he tried to call his lawyer. The manager's teenage son was knocked to the floor and his fourteen-year-old daughter was forced to undress in full view of several male agents. According to Colaprete, the IRS had instigated the raid, during which it expected to find narcotics, based solely on a tip from his ex-bookkeeper, a convicted embezzler and thief, after an investigation that lasted less than forty-eight hours. "I used to believe that such things could only happen in a communistic bloc country or police state," Colaprete observed. "I do not believe that any more."[2]

A year after the hearings took place, it was clear that the most serious charges against the agency were grossly exaggerated and, in many cases, simply false. When the General Accounting Office (GAO) and other agencies subsequently conducted in-depth investigations, they were unable to substantiate any of the more egregious allegations of IRS abuse.[3] Cola-prete brought a $20 million lawsuit against the agents who raided his business, but the case collapsed when several credible witnesses contra-dicted his account. His own lawyer explained that "over time the more you go over [an unpleasant experience] in your mind, the worse it may have been."[4] By the time a more balanced appraisal emerged, however, Colaprete's story and others like it had demonized the agency in the public eye.

The Senate hearings both reflected and contributed to the fact that the IRS was a beleaguered institution in the 1990s. Antitax sentiment had gained powerful legitimacy with Ronald Reagan's election in 1980. When both Reagan and George H. W. Bush supported tax increases during their presidencies to reduce the federal deficit, proponents of tax cuts were radicalized by a sense of betrayal. They began to focus single-mindedly on pursuing tax cuts regardless of their impact on the federal budget or federal spending programs. Unlike previous conservatives, they were will-ing to tolerate high federal deficits as the price for reining in government by limiting its revenues.

Remarks by two Republican congressmen reflect the extent to which ardent hostility to taxes had entered the mainstream by the 1990s. During the midterm election campaign of 1994, Representative Bill Archer (R, Texas), who would become chair of the House Ways and Means Commit-tee in 1995, declared, "I personally would like to tear the income tax out by its roots and throw it overboard."[5] In 1995, John Kasich (R, Ohio), the Budget Committee chair in the House, said in connection with a discus-sion of the flat tax proposal that "the end game here is to strip the govern-ment of the financial means for butting into the lives of Americans, and thus returning power and responsibility to families and localities."[6] As the agency charged with federal tax collection, the IRS was a natural target of intense criticism and hostility.

The agency was also struggling to modernize its efforts to collect taxes and detect tax evasion. The IRS was and is one of the biggest fi-nancial institutions in the world. At the turn of the twentieth century, it was collecting nearly $2 trillion a year from nearly one hundred and thirty million individual and business taxpayers.[7] Financial audits con-ducted by the General Accounting Office beginning in 1992 revealed that the agency's accounting and financial control systems were in shambles.

In its first audit, the GAO found that the IRS could not account for $4.3 billion in agency spending.[8] During the following years, accounting failures continued to plague the agency. In 1998, the GAO found "pervasive weaknesses" in the IRS's financial management systems that prevented it from reliably reporting on how it spent its budget.[9] In a review of IRS collection procedures a year later, the GAO described widespread problems that "resulted in disbursements of fraudulent and other questionable tax refunds, unnecessary burden to taxpayers resulting from taxpayer receipts stolen by IRS employees, and errors or delays in posting payments to taxpayer accounts."[10] Taxpayers were required to keep careful track of their income, capital gains, deductions, and credits, yet the IRS could not account fully for the nearly $2 trillion it collected every year.[11]

In the 1990s, the IRS labored under the weight of both political hostility and its own inefficiencies and operational failures. Meanwhile, tax professionals at accounting firms, law firms, and financial institutions had started working together to create a set of sophisticated transactions that had the potential to eliminate billions of dollars in taxes owed by wealthy individuals. The IRS, constrained by limited resources and preoccupied with ensuring that it was able to perform its basic function of collecting taxes, would be slow to identify and respond to these shelters.

The Antitax Crusade

Resentment of taxes is not a new phenomenon in American politics. The founding of this nation was the culmination of events that included resistance to taxes. It is only in recent decades, however that taxes have become a central topic in the political conversation. Historian Isaac William Martin observes, "Our national obsession with tax cuts is not a timeless cultural trait. It is a new political development."[12] It may be hard to believe in the twenty-first century, but in the three decades after World War II politicians rarely fought over taxes, and the public paid little attention to tax policy when casting votes. By the late 1970s, however, taxes became a more salient concern for a larger portion of the electorate.

A significant impetus for this shift in attitudes was a change in how property taxes were assessed at the local government level. A set of informal practices historically had resulted in the assessment of property at a fraction of its value. This buffered citizens, especially homeowners, from the full financial effect of increases in property value due to inflation and economic growth. In the 1970s, however, state officials took steps to end this system to centralize and standardize property tax assessment, depriving "local assessors of the discretion that they had used to grant informal privileges."[13]

Assessments based on the full market value of property resulted in significant property tax increases for many homeowners. This prompted a backlash that helped create a political movement focused on reducing taxes. The most prominent early success in this effort was the passage of Proposition 13 in California in 1978, which amended the state constitution to sharply limit increases in property taxes. This measure prompted a host of initiatives across the country that aimed to limit taxes and spending, supported not only by those concerned about tax rates but also by conservatives who hoped to limit the scope of government. The success of these campaigns in turn influenced electoral politics, as many politicians concluded that "big tax cuts were good politics."[14] The "permanent tax revolt" was born.

The tax revolt gained significant momentum as part of a backlash against the civil rights movement, affirmative action, and their association with the expansion of government benefits for minorities, particularly African Americans. As Tom Edsall and Mary Edsall have shown, the battle over Proposition 13 reflected a deep racial divide. For whites, who supported the referendum by a margin of two to one, property taxes became connected with busing decrees, racial preferences in hiring, and a slew of entitlements, supported by taxes, whose main beneficiaries appeared to be blacks. The tax revolt mapped a division "along lines of taxpayers versus tax recipients" that coincided with racial divisions. African Americans were "disproportionately the recipients of government programs for the poor, disproportionately the beneficiaries of government led efforts to redistribute rights and status, and the black middle and working classes were far more dependent on government programs and jobs than their white counterparts."[15] The antitax movement provided a compelling logic around which the conservative movement could mobilize white populist sentiment against the liberal agenda that was successfully advanced by the Democratic Party in the 1960s and 1970s.[16]

Among the politicians who seized on reducing taxes was the then governor of California Ronald Reagan. Reagan made tax cuts a central part of his 1980 presidential campaign, a position that survey data indicated resonated with a large portion of voters. As political scientists Jacob Hacker and Paul Pierson suggest, "[a]lthough it is hazardous to speak of elections producing mandates for specific policy initiatives, it seems appropriate to consider the 1980 election results a mandate for lower taxes."[17] Reagan came into office with the desire to cut taxes across the board by 10 percent every year for three years. The Economic Recovery Tax Act of 1981 cut the top marginal rate of the personal income tax from 70 percent to 50 percent, indexed personal income tax rates to protect against tax increases reflecting inflation, and provided deep rate cuts and tax benefits for corporations.[18]

Ultimately, Reagan's tax-cutting fervor collided with his and other conservatives' concerns about fiscal prudence and the federal deficit. The 1981 cuts and an economic recession increased the deficit, and the Reagan administration's desired increases in defense spending threatened to widen it considerably more. In response, Reagan supported 1982 legislation that rolled back corporate tax breaks and imposed new excise taxes. In 1984, the administration again supported tax increases as a response to concerns about a mounting deficit. A comprehensive tax bill, the Tax Reform Act of 1986, reduced tax rates but also eliminated many deductions, resulting in a revenue-neutral impact. As a consequence, while Reagan's election made tax cutting a mainstream political issue, antitax forces were disappointed overall with his administration's unwillingness to make tax cuts a priority that trumped other considerations.

That disappointment boiled over into outright revolt when President George H. W. Bush in 1990 reneged on his earlier pledge—captured in his infamous phrase "read my lips"—not to raise taxes. Bush supported tax increases as part of a budget package that was designed to address the growing federal deficit. In response, Representative Newt Gingrich (R, Georgia) and his allies persuaded more than half the Republicans in the House to oppose their party's ostensible leader. While Bush ultimately obtained passage of a package that included tax increases, the conflict marked the beginning of intensified conservative focus on tax cuts regardless of their fiscal consequences. As Hacker and Pierson observe, "the new-line Republicans reversed the priority between fiscal conservatism and tax cuts. For this generation of politicians, reducing taxes was absolutely central."[19]

The intensity with which Republicans pursued this mission was reflected in the party's response to President Clinton's proposal in 1993 to confront the deficit by passing a budget that included a combination of tax increases and spending cuts. His plan received not a single Republican vote in the House or the Senate, the first time in modern history that a federal budget passed without any support from the minority party. When Republicans regained control of the House in the 1994 elections, they claimed that it was a mandate to implement the policies set forth in the Contract with America, a set of principles that Gingrich had played a prominent role in developing. The Contract pledged to bring about changes that would result in "the end of government that is too big, too intrusive, and too easy with the public's money." It promised that Republicans on the first day of the next Congress would "immediately pass" eight major reforms, including the requirement of "a three-fifths majority vote to pass a tax increase."[20]

The Republicans made no secret of their agenda to eliminate the income tax.[21] In 1996, the House voted to repeal it. Without an alternative method to collect revenue, the measure did not get very far in the Senate.[22] A year later, Congressmen Dick Armey (R, Texas) and Bill Tauzin (R, Louisiana) launched a "Scrap the Code" tour. The two traveled to several cities to speak at anti-income tax rallies, attracting crowds numbering in the thousands.[23]

The single-minded focus on tax cuts was further reflected in the growing prominence of Grover Norquist's organization, Americans for Tax Reform (ATR). The roots of the organization lay within the Reagan administration, with a White House effort headed by Norquist to generate support for the 1986 tax legislation. The centerpiece of ATR's strategy was the Taxpayer Pledge that it asked all candidates for Congress to sign. Candidates promised to "oppose any and all efforts to increase the marginal tax rates for individuals and/or businesses," and to "oppose any net reduction or elimination of deductions and credits, unless matched dollar for dollar by further reducing tax rates."[24] Over time, signing the pledge became a fundamental requirement for a growing percentage of Republican politicians.

The broader aim of the antitax crusade was to shrink government to a size where, in Norquist's words, it could be "drowned in a bathtub." The IRS was a prime target for this campaign. Its difficulties in performing its most basic functions reinforced this resentment toward the agency and fueled the growing belief that the tax system was arbitrary and unjustified.

The Tax Collection Dinosaur

It was not as if operations were running smoothly at the Internal Revenue Service in the 1990s. A big source of the problem was the agency's inability to upgrade its data collection and analysis systems. Through most of the last decade of the twentieth century, the agency still relied almost exclusively on paper returns to obtain taxpayer information.[25] During tax season, thousands of employees visually scanned more than a hundred million returns, looking for obvious errors. Other employees, hired seasonally by the IRS, typed hurriedly around the clock to input data from forms into the IRS computer system.[26] With so many returns being processed at breakneck speed, mistakes were inevitable.[27] One study showed a 20 percent error rate in the IRS's data, half of which was attributable to the transcription process.[28] It didn't help that the agency was using software from the 1960s, storing taxpayer information on magnetic tapes.[29] Data transcription was charged by the line to the IRS unit seeking the information, creating an incentive to capture less rather than more information.[30] Although Congress made piecemeal allocations to various IRS projects to modernize its computers and establish an electronic filing system, the funds were not enough to permit the agency to hire top-flight information technology expertise. The result was several failed efforts to computerize, a total of $4 billion gone to waste, and a huge public embarrassment for the IRS.[31]

So much money was consumed transporting, unloading, transcribing, sorting, filing, and storing paper returns that the IRS had few resources left to analyze the data it did obtain.[32] As a result, the methodology it used to identify suspect returns was simplistic and outdated. To determine which returns to scrutinize more closely, the IRS used a rudimentary statistical method that analyzed the relationships among amounts entered on a return and compared those numbers to returns with similar incomes. This technique was developed based on large-scale comprehensive audits of taxpayers that were intended to identify indicators of inflated deductions, understated income, and other methods of tax evasion. The last time the IRS had conducted such a study was in 1988.[33] When the IRS sought funding to update its data in 1995, Congress refused to allocate the $400 million it requested.[34]

For obvious reasons, the IRS kept the methods it used to identify questionable returns secret, but the technique was so crude that a statistician figured out which factors functioned as red flags by conducting regression analyses on a sample of returns, comparing those that had been selected for audit with those that had not. The statistician, author of *How to Beat the I.R.S. at Its Own Game*, advised taxpayers claiming large deductions that they could avoid being audited by doing things such as including an explanation of the deductions on the return and writing neatly.[35]

The difficulty of verifying the accuracy of taxpayer filings was especially acute when it came to returns from high-wealth individuals and businesses. Salaried employees in the United States are subject to mandatory withholding of income tax. They also fall under a third-party reporting regime that constrains their ability to evade taxes: employers report earnings to the IRS, banks report interest earned and mortgage payments, and companies report dividends. Taxpayers earning less than a million dollars a year derive three-quarters of their income from wages so opportunities to fudge numbers are limited. In contrast, corporations and wealthier taxpayers—typically business owners, landlords, and partnership investors—have much greater control over how their gains and losses are reported. They generate and oversee the information included in partnership and other business-related forms, which provides them with much more leeway to evade taxes.[36] The IRS plan to update data that Congress declined to fund in 1995 would have focused on these types of taxpayers.[37]

Despite the greater opportunities for evasion enjoyed by wealthy taxpayers and businesses, the IRS could do little with the data it did collect. Congress refused, for instance, to allocate funds to permit the IRS to match partnership filings to individual and corporate tax returns. As a result, there was no simple mechanism to pull up a partnership return, filed under one name and taxpayer identification number, and the corresponding individual or corporate return, filed under another name and identification number.[38] In addition, the design of the original partnership returns did not correlate with specific entries on individual and corporate returns.[39] The agency's inability to compare the information from these returns was especially significant since partnerships were a favored vehicle for the creation of tax shelters.

The difficulty of catching tax evasion among high-wealth individuals and businesses was compounded by a significant brain drain at the agency during the 1990s. One problem was compensation. The IRS had inadequate resources to offer competitive salaries to the experienced and highly trained tax professionals that it needed to recreate and untangle the sophisticated transactions that underlie complex returns. Partnership returns can run into the hundreds of pages; corporate returns into the thousands. IRS salaries were set at 50 percent of salaries in the private sector, which made it difficult to attract people with the expertise to analyze this information effectively. Another issue was the lack of prestige connected with employment at the IRS in the 1990s. In an earlier period, working at the agency was considered an opportunity for career advancement and a source of professional pride. As the IRS's failures mounted, however, it became increasingly embarrassing to be associated with it.[40] Meanwhile large accounting and law firms were aggressively courting top IRS talent to staff their rapidly expanding tax practices.

In the 1990s, the IRS had few resources and even fewer incentives to audit wealthy taxpayers. Under a tracking method imposed by Congress, the agency's success was measured in great part by how many cases it resolved, not by how much money was brought in by tax collection. As a result, agents tended to be concerned more with moving cases through the pipeline than with spending time deciphering complex filings that might yield more tax revenues. In addition, since 1995, the IRS had been under a specific mandate from Congress to focus on audits of poor working people who may have improperly claimed the earned income tax credit available to taxpayers with income below a certain threshold.[41]

The agency's poor performance showed in its audit rates. In the late 1970s the overall individual audit rate was about 2.5 percent. By 1996, it had declined to 1.67 percent, falling below 1 percent in 1999. Partnership returns were audited even less frequently, at a rate of half a percent.[42] Corporations with assets over $100 million, which had been audited in 1980 at a rate of 77 percent, were audited in 1997 at a rate of 35 percent.[43] The overall audit rate for corporations fell by nearly a third, from 2.9 percent in 1992 to 2.0 percent in 1998.[44] In the late 1990s, there was as great a likelihood for a person earning less than $25,000 to be audited as a person earning more than $100,000.[45]

Although Congress regularly excoriated the IRS for its inadequacies, since the mid-1990s it had denied the agency the resources needed to improve performance. Resentment toward the agency and dissatisfaction with its operation culminated in the Senate hearings in 1997 and 1998. While the hearings revealed shortcomings in the IRS's operations, they mainly provided a highly visible forum for antitax forces to levy sensational charges about outrageous agency behavior.

The IRS on Trial

Convening the Senate hearings in the fall of 1997, Senator William Roth declared, "There is no other agency in this country that directly touches the lives of more Americans, nor is there any agency which strikes more fear into their hearts. The threat of an audit, the awesome power of the IRS, looms like the Sword of Damocles over the heads of taxpayers. As Chairman of the Senate Finance Committee, I want to know why. I wanted to understand where this fear came from. I wanted to know if it was justified."[46]

Several IRS agents offered testimony to the Finance Committee that described examples of ineptitude and corruption at the agency. Ostensibly fearing for their jobs and even their physical safety, they had been given permission to testify anonymously, sitting behind screens and with their voices electronically altered to prevent identification. Jennifer Long, a long-time IRS employee, testified that IRS agents fabricated evidence against taxpayers they had targeted. The agency, she said, wanted to "stick it to people who couldn't fight back." Other witnesses described harrowing dealings with the agency that ended in divorce, homelessness, and even suicide.[47]

Congressional leaders decried the IRS's "SWAT team" raids and "Gestapo-like" tactics.[48] The news media grabbed the story and ran with it. Sound bites from the proceedings were broadcast on the evening news. Hearing witnesses appeared on Sunday morning talk shows to elaborate on their horror stories.[49] *Newsweek* even ran a cover article coauthored by former IRS Commissioner Fred Goldberg describing how rogue auditors abused taxpayers.[50]

The IRS's Criminal Investigation Division (CID) was a prominent focus in this avalanche of criticism. A year after the last Finance Committee hearing, however, an independent commission charged by Congress to study the CID concluded that it was "an organization of dedicated, talented, and hardworking individuals who carry out their law enforcement responsibilities in a professional manner."[51] During the testimony, representatives of the IRS had sat silently by, limited by statutory confidentiality obligations that prohibited the disclosure of taxpayer information and concerned that any response to counter the charges against the agency would only serve to escalate the accusations.

The hearings also revealed useful, but much less publicized, information about the deleterious impact of insufficient resources and counterproductive incentives. IRS employees and outside experts testified that poor taxpayers "were pursued because their cases were more easily brought to a close," which resulted in better statistics for performance reports, "while those with money to fight back sometimes were allowed to slip away without paying."[52] In addition, "[p]rocedures were not always followed, sometimes because of corner cutting to meet productivity demands, more often due to lack of training, which was continually cut because Congress did not pay for it."[53] There were also complaints that "high-level managers took care of friends and made life difficult for those they disliked."[54]

On May 7, 1998, in a surprising display of bipartisanship, the Senate passed the IRS Restructuring and Reform Act by a vote of 97 to 0.[55] After the bill was reconciled with an earlier House version, President Clinton signed it into law that summer. The legislation provided that the IRS's mandate was to restructure and revise its procedures and operations to become a more user-friendly agency. The statute also created a new oversight board, imposed new reporting obligations on the IRS, and granted taxpayers enhanced rights and protections against harassment and other misconduct by IRS employees.

The statute, in addition, contained a little-noted section that accounting firms had long favored. Riding the anti-IRS momentum, the organized accounting profession persuaded Congress to include a provision under which communications between taxpayers and tax practitioners, including tax accountants, would receive the same confidentiality protection as traditionally afforded communications between clients and their lawyers.[56] By expanding the universe of material that tax accountants could keep from the IRS, the statutory tax accountant privilege gave accounting firms a boost in competing with law firms for tax advice business.

The 1998 IRS Restructuring and Reform Act's emphasis on greater solicitude for taxpayers was consistent with the new IRS Commissioner's agenda. Charles Rossotti, appointed in late 1997, was the founder of a successful computer consulting company. He was the first commissioner without a tax background, but was regarded as someone who could help modernize the agency and improve its relationship with taxpayers. After passage of the 1998 Act, Rossotti revised the agency's mission statement.

The stated purpose of the IRS had been "to collect the proper amount of tax revenue at the least cost" in a manner "warranting the highest degree of public confidence in our integrity and fairness."[57] The revised statement emphasized helping Americans "to understand and meet their tax responsibilities."[58] The IRS, mindful both of the need to modernize its operations and the beating that it had taken in Senate hearings and in the media, was required to put enforcement activities on the back burner, at least for the time being.

From Tax Collection to Customer Service

Under Rossotti's leadership, the IRS initiated a massive restructuring and modernization. One hundred thousand employees were reassigned to divisions organized according to taxpayer types, retrained on their new job obligations, and educated about the importance of customer satisfaction.[59] Simultaneously, the agency began shifting to new computer systems to strengthen its information tracking capabilities and expand electronic filing mechanisms, an urgent imperative given the technological fiascos earlier in the decade.

There was no question that taxpayer service was a widespread problem. The agency was doing a poor job of educating taxpayers about their filing and payment responsibilities and explaining collection procedures. One telling statistic: In 1995, taxpayers heard 400 million busy signals when they tried to call the IRS. When callers did get through, they often encountered employees who did not have sufficient knowledge—or much inclination—to assist them.[60] Addressing these problems was a priority, but it came at significant cost. Despite its new mandate for the agency, Congress refused to increase funding. According to one source, the IRS's budget, adjusted for inflation, actually declined 5 percent between 1992 and 1999, while the number of tax returns and the amount of tax collected grew.[61]

The reorganization significantly strained agency resources. To assist in the restructuring, the IRS hired Booz Allen, a management consulting firm, paying it $100 million for its services. A smaller-ticket item was a million-dollar advertising campaign emphasizing the friendlier tone at the agency.[62] Without new funding, enforcement personnel had to be reassigned to address customer service needs. During filing season, for example, many collection employees were shifted to answering taxpayer queries.[63] Revenue agents also had to devote many hours to participating in the reorganization process. According to Commissioner Rossotti, a year after the IRS Restructuring and Reform Act's passage, the number of staff available for audits and collections was 19 percent lower than in 1997.[64]

Other provisions in the 1998 bill slowed collection efforts. New procedures that provided stronger taxpayer rights with regard to levies and property seizures made these processes more costly and time consuming. Training employees about new procedures took up time and resources. As Rossotti testified a year after the act was passed, taxpayer rights provisions required the equivalent of nearly 3,000 person years of staff time to comply with procedural requirements.[65] Under the statute, the IRS was also curtailed from using lifestyle audits—targeting people who appeared to be living well beyond their means, at least as they reported on their tax returns. These had been a helpful technique to reveal tax evasion among high-wealth individuals.[66]

The 1998 statute's disabling effects on tax collection were magnified by the inclusion of a provision known colloquially as the "Ten Deadly Sins," a list of prohibitions that would result in the dismissal of an IRS agent. The list included some clearly serious conduct, such as lying under oath; it also included other misconduct—harassing or retaliating against a taxpayer—that left broad room for interpretation.[67] Under this provision, a taxpayer complaint could entangle an employee in a drawn-out process in which the employee had to justify her actions or risk losing her job.[68] Appointed to be a watchdog over the agency, the new inspector general for tax administration pursued complaints aggressively.[69] The benefit of complaining about revenue agents was not lost on taxpayers, who began to threaten and use complaints to derail the cases against them. A later investigation confirmed the widespread use of complaints as a dilatory tactic, concluding that nearly 90 percent of those brought in 2001 were meritless.[70] One group of tax resisters filed nearly 2,000 false misconduct complaints against revenue agents as part of a fraudulent scheme to avoid paying taxes.[71]

Given the risks of taking a hard line with recalcitrant taxpayers, the best strategy for enforcement agents was to be nice and keep their heads down.[72] "Don't aggravate taxpayers," one agent was instructed by his manager. Another was told, "Don't probe too deeply. Just find three or four items and close the case."[73] Talking to a reporter, one collection agent said: "Please don't call us tax collectors in the newspaper. We don't collect taxes anymore. We aren't allowed to."[74]

The effects showed up in enforcement statistics. In the 1999 fiscal year, property seizures dropped 98 percent from the year before.[75] Bank account levies and wage garnishments were at one quarter of the level they had been two years earlier.[76] In 1999, the overall audit rate for individuals was less than 1 percent.[77] Face-to-face audits declined by 40 percent.[78] At the same time, the IRS continued to focus its audits on poorer Americans. In 1999, for the first time, taxpayers earning less than $25,000 were more likely to be audited than those earning more than $100,000. Since 1988, the audit rate for wealthier Americans had fallen 90 percent, from 11.4 to 1.15 percent.[79]

During the 1980s, the agency had been perceived as doing an adequate job enforcing the tax laws, but by the late 1990s, it was behind the eight ball. Attempting to respond to the difficulties posed by limited resources, obsolete technology, and new legal constraints, it was unable to keep pace with sophisticated new schemes and techniques that might emerge to avoid paying taxes. At the same time, agency officials had little appetite to engage in aggressive enforcement activity that might risk triggering the type of public denunciation that the IRS had received on Capitol Hill and in the media.

In the meantime, wealthy individuals and corporations—with assistance from large financial institutions, state-of-the-art computer systems, and the emerging Internet—were engaging in increasingly complex business transactions. The United States was experiencing an economic boom that lifted the wealth of corporations and large numbers of entrepreneurs to new heights. In the meantime, accounting firms and law firms, under intense competitive pressures, were anxiously seeking to identify new sources of revenue. Tax strategies, sold as products to multiple clients, offered a new avenue to fuel growth and increase profits. The problem was that the profitable strategies were abusive tax shelters—transactions resulting in tax benefits that were not recognized under the law.

2

Why Tax Shelters Matter

Abusive tax shelter activity at the turn of the twenty-first century cost the U.S. Treasury billions of dollars and sent a number of lawyers and accountants to prison. To appreciate the complexity of the problem of abusive shelters, it is important to understand what a tax shelter is and what in principle distinguishes a legitimate shelter from an abusive one. Understanding this fundamental distinction is critical to appreciating exactly what happened in the most recent tax shelter wave and in assessing the extent to which the tax system remains vulnerable to new types of abusive tax shelters. A basic difficulty is that such shelters are often more easily recognized after the fact than precisely defined in advance. Nonetheless, this theoretical distinction—as difficult as it is to apply in practice—separates transactions that constitute permissible tax avoidance, approved by Congress, and those that can serve as the basis for civil or even criminal liability.

Legitimate and Abusive Tax Shelters

An important goal of the income tax system is to measure a taxpayer's economic income and tax that income at specified rates. Consistent with this goal, the Internal Revenue Code contains an expansive definition of gross income—"all income from whatever source derived"—and lists a range of items to be included in it. It then permits "ordinary and necessary" business expenses to be deducted from gross income to arrive at a lower figure. Known as "taxable income," or net income, this is the amount of income actually subject to income taxation. Determining net income thus requires numerous judgments about which expenditures can be deducted from income because they are associated with earning it.

The concept of net income also comes into play when a taxpayer buys and later sells an asset. For tax purposes, the income that the taxpayer receives from the sale is reduced by the cost that he or she incurred in originally purchasing it. This is known as the "basis." Although the basis of an asset may be adjusted upward or downward after purchase, the concept of basis is intended to limit taxable income to the net economic gain that the taxpayer enjoyed from buying and then selling the asset. The higher the basis, the lower the taxable income from the sale.

Tax shelters reflect the fact that many provisions in the tax code seek to influence taxpayers by treating income and expenses connected with certain types of behavior more favorably than other income or expenses. The law does this by taxing some income at a lower rate or not at all, and by allowing deductions for certain types of outlays but not others. The tax laws encourage savings for retirement, for instance, by exempting certain contributions to retirement plans from taxation until the taxpayer withdraws the money upon reaching retirement age. They seek to promote home ownership by making most home mortgage interest deductible. They encourage charitable giving by making many such gifts deductible. They provide for employment "cafeteria plans" that allow employees to pay certain medical expenses from pretax dollars. Participation in these activities enables taxpayers to "shelter" some portion of their income from taxes. The government is willing to forgo revenues from taxing the sheltered income because it wants to use the incentive of lower taxes to encourage people to engage in certain socially useful activities.

Legitimate shelters are those that involve the kinds of activities that Congress wants to encourage. Because Congress intends to benefit taxpayers who participate in these activities, the fact that an individual might be motivated by a desire to lower taxes is not a concern. On the contrary, that's the point of these types of provisions: harnessing the desire for lower taxes to promote valuable economic and social behavior.

A useful way to distinguish legitimate from abusive tax shelters is to ask the question: Does the shelter in which the taxpayer is engaging involve the kind of socially useful behavior that Congress wants to encourage by creating a tax incentive? Would Congress have considered this type of taxpayer behavior valuable enough to incur the loss of tax revenues? If the answer is no, then a taxpayer is seeking tax-favored treatment for activities that Congress did not intend to subsidize and is engaging in an abusive tax shelter. There is no reason in this instance to allow taxpayers to pay lower taxes. Indeed, permitting this would be counterproductive. Tax policy experts generally agree that behavior like this is wasteful and does not contribute to social welfare. In other words, the resources invested in abusive tax shelters represent a deadweight loss to society. Professor Michael Graetz famously described such a tax shelter as "a deal done by very smart people that, absent tax considerations, would be very stupid."[1]

In some cases, statutory requirements and external checks curtail the extent to which taxpayers can receive unintended tax benefits. In the retirement savings context, for instance, laws limit the amount that can be sheltered for this purpose, require the monies to be contributed to special accounts—employer-sponsored retirement plans or IRAs—and impose penalties if the monies are withdrawn before a specific age. Retirement savings contributions are confirmed by third parties, such as banks and employers. These mechanisms, which are written into the law and enlist the verification of third-party institutions, prevent taxpayers from using tax-favorable provisions to avoid paying taxes in ways that are not consistent with their purpose.

But there is a limit to the constraints that Congress can build into legislation, and a clever taxpayer and her tax advisor can often seek to take advantage of interactions among various Code provisions to obtain a benefit inconsistent with Congressional intent. The facts of *Knetsch v. Commissioner*, a case that made it to the United States Supreme Court, provide a good example.[2] In 1953, Karl Knetsch was a successful sixty-year-old businessman who earned $200,000 a year, equivalent to more than $1.5 million in 2010. Knetsch purchased $4 million dollars' worth of thirty-year term annuities from the Sam Houston Insurance Company. Under the terms of the annuities, Knetsch would earn 2.5 percent interest, or $100,000 a year, until his ninetieth birthday. When Knetsch reached ninety, the annuities would begin to pay him $43 a month until his death.

Knetsch funded the purchase of the annuities with a loan from Sam Houston Life Insurance Company at an interest rate of 3.5 percent a year. As a consequence, the interest rate on his debt was higher than the interest rate on his return. Knetsch was paying $140,000 a year, or $40,000 more than he was receiving from the annuities. Given his outlay over the thirty-year maturity period, it would take more than 2,000 years for him recoup his investment once he began receiving annuity payments.

It is hard to imagine that Knetsch, or anyone else for that matter, would find such a deal attractive. Who would be willing to pay $40,000 a year until he reached age ninety for the right to receive $43 a month thereafter? Not surprisingly, the transaction had other benefits that explained its appeal. The interest income that Knetsch earned from the annuities was not taxable. In addition, the loan was non-recourse—secured only by the cash value of the insurance policy and not his personal assets—so Knetsch was not at risk of losing his property if he defaulted on the loan.

Most important, under the language of tax laws then in effect, Knetsch could deduct from his taxable income the interest on the loan that he was paying the insurance company each year. In the 1950s, marginal tax rates—the amount of tax paid as income rises—were very high. By deducting the interest on the loan against his income, Knetsch believed that he could reduce his tax liability by more than $110,000 per year. Assuming tax rates remained the same, his yearly $40,000 pretax investment (making $140,000 in interest payments minus the $100,000 income he received from annuities) would produce a $70,000 after-tax profit for the next thirty years. Without considering the tax benefits, the transaction made no economic sense. But when the tax consequences were factored in, Knetsch had every reason to think he had a very good deal.

At the time Knetsch bought his annuities, there was no language in the Code explicitly stating that he could not deduct his loan interest payments in this type of arrangement. To the contrary, the Code stated that interest paid on indebtedness could be deducted, and did not indicate that debt incurred to buy this type of insurance should be treated differently from any other debt.[3] Nonetheless, when the Supreme Court decided the case, it inquired into whether the interest payments that the taxpayer made to the insurance company "constituted 'interest paid . . . on indebtedness' within the meaning of" the tax laws. The Court observed that "Knetsch's transaction with the insurance company did "not appreciably affect his beneficial interest except to reduce his tax." Thus, the Court concluded, "there was nothing of substance to be realized by Knetsch from this transaction beyond a tax deduction."[4]

Couldn't Knetsch argue that the ability to deduct interest payments on his annuity reflected Congressional desire to encourage people to save for retirement? The response is that Congress intended only to benefit people who were "really" saving for retirement. Even though Knetsch purchased a retirement annuity, the transaction as a whole was not genuinely designed to provide retirement savings. As the Court put it, Knetsch's savings plan for retirement was "a sham."[5] No economically rational person would pay $40,000 a year in order to receive $43 a month when he reached age ninety. Given this fact, the Court concluded that Knetsch's only reason for engaging in these activities was to gain tax benefits that Congress had not intended to confer. His conduct therefore constituted an abuse of the tax law. In *Knetsch,* the Court reaffirmed the principle that even if taxpayers comply with the letter of a provision that provides tax benefits for certain activity, they will not receive those benefits if their behavior is not the type of activity the provision is designed to reward.

In *Knetsch*, as in earlier and later cases, the Court did not rely solely on the literal language of the statute. Rather, it determined that in permitting the deducting of interest on loans, Congress had intended only to cover actual indebtedness. Because the Court did not have a statement of purpose or specific wording on which to rely, it was articulating what it understood to be Congress's intent. There was no reason to reward Knetsch under the tax code for spending the time and money to engage in these transactions because he wasn't doing so to save for retirement in any meaningful sense. Without the tax benefits he sought, neither Knetsch nor society would be better off from him engaging in these transactions. Society, in fact, would be worse off—Knetsch would have wasted assets for no good reason. Why then, should the government reward him for doing so?

Anti-Abuse Doctrines

Overview

Because determining Congress's intent can be difficult, courts over the years have developed what are known as "anti-abuse" doctrines to help distinguish legitimate from abusive shelters when Congressional intent is unclear. These doctrines reflect the idea that the costs associated with a transaction that is genuinely intended to produce income should be respected for the purpose of reducing taxable income. This is consistent with the principle of taxing net income. By contrast, unless they result from an activity that clearly falls within a category that Congress intended to favor, costs that are incurred only to obtain tax benefits cannot be used to reduce taxes. The fundamental issue underlying these doctrines is whether a claimed tax loss corresponds to an actual economic loss that makes the taxpayer worse off.

In disallowing the tax treatment Knetsch sought, the Court applied an anti-abuse doctrine that has become known as the "economic substance" doctrine. The origin of the doctrine is generally attributed to the 1935 U.S. Supreme Court case *Gregory v. Helvering*.[6] In that case, a taxpayer owned an interest in a corporation that owned 1,000 shares of stock in another company. The taxpayer created a third corporation and transferred shares to it. Six days later, she dissolved this corporation and received the 1,000 shares. The taxpayer claimed for tax purposes that she had received the shares as a result of a corporate reorganization that resulted in taxation at a lower rate than had the shares been distributed to her via a dividend payment. The Supreme Court rejected the taxpayer's claim that the shares were transferred to her as part of a reorganization, despite the fact that the steps taken conformed to the terms of the tax code. The Court empasized,

The whole undertaking, though conducted according to the terms of subdivision (B), was in fact an elaborate and devious form of conveyance masquerading as a corporate reorganization, and nothing else. . . . [T]he transaction upon its face lies outside the plain intent of the statute. To hold otherwise would be to exalt artifice above reality and to deprive the statutory provision in question of all serious purpose.[7]

As tax scholar Leandra Lederman has noted, the economic substance doctrine requires that where a taxpayer claims tax-favored treatment for a transaction, if that transaction is not one that Congress obviously intended to encourage, it must have economic substance to obtain the taxpayer's desired treatment.[8] That is, the taxpayer's economic position must change in a meaningful way as a result of the transaction. Over the years, the doctrine has received various formulations that have emphasized different factors. Among the factors the courts have considered are: whether a transaction holds a reasonable possibility for pretax profit,[9] whether a transaction involves meaningful financial risk to the taxpayer,[10] whether there is a reasonable ratio between a taxpayer's investment and the tax benefit sought, and whether a taxpayer's sole or primary purpose is to avoid taxes.[11]

The economic substance doctrine and other anti-abuse doctrines flow from the focus of the income tax system on measuring net income. Consistent with this idea, costs associated with transactions that are intended, based on objective and subjective criteria, to produce income, are respected for purposes of taxation. By contrast, costs incurred as a result of transactions that are not designed to produce income—and which have not been singled out by Congress for favorable treatment—are not respected for tax purposes.

Anti-abuse doctrines created by the courts have engendered a great deal of controversy. Applying these doctrines involves difficult judgments and courts often seem to arrive at inconsistent results based on highly nuanced contextual differences. Determining Congress's intent regarding an unanticipated situation often seems like guesswork, especially when the transaction in question has the same form as the category of transactions Congress has identified for favorable tax treatment. As a result, courts have produced a large body of cases with no easily discernible coherent thread, and no scholar has succeeded in coming up with a unifying account that has commanded general acceptance among tax specialists. These difficulties give rise to a reasonable objection: If divining some hypothetical legislative intent is such a challenge, wouldn't it be preferable for courts to recognize the tax benefits claimed by a taxpayer in a given case and allow Congress to make its purpose explicit by amending the Code? Courts adopt this strategy all the time in other regulatory contexts.

As an alternative, why not at least require the IRS to identify those shelters that it regards as abusive? The agency has the authority to issue notices that describe those transactions for which taxpayers will not be permitted to claim tax losses. Until that occurs, why not permit taxpayers to claim benefits based on their literal compliance with the Code?

Judicial doctrines that are hard to define and apply raise deeper normative issues as well. Isn't it unfair to taxpayers like Knetsch to disallow the tax benefits they claim when they relied on the language of a statute in planning their affairs? Don't taxpayers have a right to try to minimize the taxes they owe? Disallowing the tax benefits Knetsch claimed on the ground that his transaction lacked economic substance—it didn't involve actual "indebtedness" in the sense intended by Congress—was one approach to deal with his clever tax planning technique. Another approach would have been to allow Knetsch to prevail and invite Congress to make its intent clear by amending the statute. Indeed, by the time the Knetsch case had reached the Supreme Court, Congress had already changed the law—closed the loophole—to bar prospectively the technique Knetsch used. One can argue that such an approach is preferable because it defers to Congress to clarify its intent by enacting a provision that applies to the type of transaction at hand.

Notwithstanding their imprecision, however, doctrines that aim to prevent the use of abusive tax shelters play a critical role in limiting the vulnerability of the tax system to taxpayers' efforts to avoid their obligations. While deference to Congress is often an appropriate approach in other regulatory contexts, in the tax shelter area economic substance and other anti-abuse judicial doctrines are necessary to safeguard the income tax system. This is true because the complexity of the tax law creates nearly limitless opportunities for taxpayers to structure their transactions to take advantage of formal features of the law, and because the income tax relies on a "self-assessment" system in which taxpayers are expected to calculate how much tax they owe.

Rules, Complexity, and Judicial Doctrines

The tremendous complexity of the Internal Revenue Code reflects in part the fact that it represents tradeoffs among several different considerations. In addition to the goals of taxing net income and encouraging certain behaviors, these considerations include economic efficiency, ease of administration, and horizontal and vertical equity—equity among taxpayers at the same income level and across income levels, respectively. The more complex a given law, the more finely it distinguishes among different individuals or transactions and the better it may be tailored to achieve its underlying objectives. As legal scholar David Weisbach notes, in tax "complex law reduces under- or over-taxation of particular activities relative to the desired amount as compared to simple law," which uses broader categories.[12] In attempting a nuanced approach, the tax laws end up with a bewildering number of classifications and categories that cover the full spectrum of personal, professional, and business transactions and relationships that exist among U.S. taxpayers.

As Weisbach emphasizes, the complexity of the Code is also a function of taxpayers' capacity to change the form of their transactions to obtain favorable tax treatment without changing the underlying economics. In this regard, the income tax differs significantly from other regulatory schemes. In most areas of law, it makes sense to draft the law to fit the most common circumstances rather than to attempt to devise a rule for every possible situation. As Weisbach observes, "If the law fits only common circumstances, rare and unusual facts might be mis-regulated, but under- or overdeterrence in these cases is not costly because the transactions are unusual." That is, at some point, the costs of fitting the law to rare circumstances exceed the benefits of doing so. "More importantly," Weisbach notes, "the uncommon transactions will remain uncommon . . . so one may be confident in the assessment of the costs and benefits" of the amount of specificity in the law.[13]

In tax law, in contrast, as Weisbach suggests, "uncommon transactions that are taxed inappropriately become common as taxpayers discover how to take advantage of them."[14] Congress therefore can't afford to ignore the fact that these transactions will receive tax treatment that it regards as undesirable. The response to this situation in tax law typically is for Congress to draft additional rules to apply to the once uncommon transaction that has now become more common.

Weisbach describes one example of this dynamic. Taxpayers A and B each own properties that they would like to exchange with one another. If they do so, however, the exchange would constitute a "realization" event that would trigger tax liability for each. Put simply, were they just to exchange properties, the exchange would be considered essentially a sale and each taxpayer would have to pay tax on his or her profit. Therefore, instead of making that exchange, they each contribute their properties to a partnership, which then distributes to them each other's property. Under now-repealed partnership tax rules, the contribution of the properties and their distribution in this "mixing bowl" transaction were both tax-free events. Thus, as Weisbach notes, A and B could avoid taxation "by using a partnership to do indirectly what would have been a realization event had it been done directly."[15]

In response, Congress amended the partnership rules to specify precisely which transactions would be treated as contributions and distributions and which would not. The result, as Weisbach observes, is "a highly complex set of rules that distinguishes between partnership transactions and 'mixing bowl' sales, with safe harbor periods, presumptions, exceptions, required risk allocations, allowable preferred returns, accommodation partner rules, and dozens of examples."[16] These rules serve to classify transactions with various characteristics as equivalent either to a tax-free partnership transaction or a taxable sale or exchange.

Tax law makes hundreds of such distinctions, such as between debt and equity, sale and lease, and independent contractors and employees. In doing so, the tax law generally "must, on some basis, choose between the two extremes rather than characterize transactions in the middle as part of each." This inevitably provides for significantly different treatment of activities just on each side of the dividing line. This discontinuity creates incentives for taxpayers to change the features of a transaction only enough to gain desirable tax consequences—to move the transaction just over the line to obtain tax preferred treatment. This type of arbitrage occurs to some extent under any regulatory scheme. It may be especially pronounced in tax law, however, because taxpayers can receive tax benefits by changing the form of a transaction without significantly changing its underlying economics.[17]

Given the vast and unforeseeable number of transactions that conceivably can occur, any system of rules that aims to classify these activities will tend to evolve toward ever-greater complexity. One feature of this complexity will be what Weisbach calls "interaction costs," which "are the costs of ensuring that the various provisions of the law work together—that they do not conflict or have unintended gaps or loopholes."[18] As the number of rules increases, interaction costs rise dramatically. "[I]n the tax law context[,]" Weisbach notes, "the law must anticipate all of the interactions, even for rare transactions. Otherwise, rare transactions will become more frequent as taxpayers discover the tax benefits. Thus, as tax rules become complex, interaction costs increase rapidly and rules quickly become unmanageable."[19] Furthermore, as "technical complexity yields greater ambiguity," this "creates more planning opportunities for those inclined to operate in the gray area of the law."[20]

Weisbach focuses on the theoretical reasons that adding rules gives rise to new opportunities for tax arbitrage. In practice, Congress's frequent amendments to the rules have, if anything, exacerbated the problem. Typically, Congress focuses on fixing one problem at a time. As a result, tax authorities try "to shore up current law with thousands of stopgap measures,"[21] and new provisions are often drafted with less than ideal clarity.[22] In the meantime, other sections of the Code lie undisturbed for long periods, waiting for a creative shelter designer to mine their potential.[23] New abusive tax shelter opportunities pop up routinely.

Given these near limitless opportunities, relying on Congress or the Treasury to enact more rules is not a solution each time a new tax shelter comes to light. Anti-abuse doctrines are necessary to prevent taxpayers who want to take advantage of tax benefits that Congress has not expressly ruled out in the law. Otherwise, every year before Congress has a chance to act, well-off taxpayers who can afford sophisticated tax planning will be able to reduce or erase their tax liabilities. Consider again the transaction in *Knetsch*, likely the earliest mass-marketed abusive tax shelter on record. The total number of taxpayers who bought the transaction is not known, but we do know that Sam Houston Life Insurance regularly advertised the transaction in the Wall Street Journal and the business press and sent out unsolicited direct mailings to potential customers.[24] Sam Houston, moreover, wasn't the only insurance company offering the same deal. Depending on how far and how fast these transactions spread, the Treasury was at risk of losing enormous amounts in tax revenue if it had to wait for Congress to amend the Code to disallow these shelters.[25]

Self-Assessment and the Role of Opinion Letters

One other characteristic of the U.S. tax system contributes to tax shelter activity—the self-assessment nature of the regulatory scheme. It is a "self-assessment" system because the government relies on taxpayers to sort their transactions into the appropriate categories and determine how much tax they owe, rather than doing the work for the taxpayer. The IRS rarely audits tax returns to verify that these calculations are correct. In assessing their own taxes, taxpayers have strong incentives to understate what they owe.

In the United States and most other countries, it is the taxpayer's responsibility to organize receipts and expenditures into the appropriate categories, determine their tax treatment, and calculate the amount of tax that is due. Taxpayers have much more information about their activities than does the government, which makes self-assessment cost-efficient as long as taxpayers provide honest information about their obligations. In addition, self-assessment can be seen as consistent with the principle of political self-determination, under which citizens impose obligations on themselves that the government generally trusts them to honor.[26] Although audit rates of wealthy Americans have risen since the late 1990s, at the turn of the twenty-first century the IRS reviewed less than one percent of returns to evaluate their accuracy. Then as now, in the overwhelming majority of cases, a taxpayer's return was treated as presumptively accurate. Yet, as Professor Michael Doran observes, "[t]he federal government collects more than $1 trillion each year through the federal income tax, and those collections are premised on the notion that, for the most part, taxpayers will determine how much they owe and will remit those amounts to the government."[27]

Under this scheme, taxpayers are not simply passive objects of regulation whose obligations are determined by government officials. Rather, they play a crucial role in ensuring that the system functions by determining their own obligations themselves. When the taxpayers signs their return, they make the following statement: "Under penalties of perjury, I declare that I have examined this return, including accompanying schedules and statements, and to the best of my knowledge and belief it is true, correct, and complete."[28] The statement expresses the idea that the government ultimately is heavily dependent upon taxpayers to act in good faith when they submit their returns.

Despite the expectation that taxpayers will honestly calculate their liability, tax law reflects a considerable amount of tolerance for self-serving behavior. Taxpayers are subject to minimal disclosure obligations and are given wide latitude to take positions that favor themselves at the expense of the government. They are not required, for instance, to disclose information that may weaken their self-assessment unless failure to do so would be fraudulent. Instead, the law simply imposes a higher penalty for substantial understatement of taxes if relevant information has not been disclosed. This gives taxpayers an opportunity to submit returns that reflect an interpretation of facts that best promote their interests without alerting the government to facts that may undermine that interpretation.

Contrast this with, say, environmental regulation, which imposes detailed reporting requirements on companies and subjects them to periodic inspections. If environmental law were structured like tax law, companies would submit conclusions about their compliance with the law to the government, but without necessarily providing information necessary to evaluate those conclusions. We would effectively have an "honor system" for pollution control—which, for the most part, is how the tax system works. Such a system makes the government vulnerable to taxpayers who are not willing to act in good faith in calculating their tax liabilities.

Although taxpayers are subject to penalties for understating the taxes they owe, these are generally believed to be too low to be effective deterrents. Taxpayers who engage in transactions whose primary purpose is to shelter income can avoid penalties if they satisfy certain objective and subjective criteria. Taxpayers must have "substantial authority" in the law for their claims that their assessment of their taxes is correct. This standard has been interpreted to mean that their legal position has at least a 35 percent chance of prevailing on the merits.[29] As a general rule, to avoid penalties for understating their taxes, taxpayers must act in good faith and their belief in the accuracy of their return must be reasonable.[30]

Under regulations in effect in the late 1990s, the requirement that a taxpayer's belief be "reasonable" was satisfied if a taxpayer relied in good faith on an opinion from a professional tax advisor who analyzed the pertinent facts and legal authorities and concluded unambiguously that "there [was] a greater than 50 percent likelihood that the tax treatment of the item will be upheld" if challenged by the IRS. The penalty provisions shifted the onus of determining whether a shelter was legitimate from the taxpayer to a legal advisor.

In a world in which tax professionals gave independent, well-researched, and thoughtful advice, this penalty scheme would function to prevent many abusive transactions. But financial incentives can easily distort the market for legal opinions. During the tax shelter boom, it was widely believed among tax practitioners and government officials that an opinion from any law firm protected a taxpayer from understatement penalties (as well as other civil and criminal liability). In tax shelter promoter circles, opinion letters became known as "get out of jail free cards."

The tax self-assessment regime, which relies on the good faith of taxpayers and the objectivity of their advisors, is highly vulnerable to abuse. When shelters were widespread during the 1990s, the risk of penalties from participating in an improper shelter was minimal. To begin with, although it is not permissible to take into account the chance of audit in determining whether to take a position on a return, a sophisticated taxpayer was well aware that there was a very small likelihood that the return would be audited. Even if the return was audited and the shelter discovered, a taxpayer could avoid penalties by producing an opinion letter from a law firm that argued that a court would more likely than not uphold the transaction. In the highly unusual situation where an opinion letter was deemed inadequate to provide penalty protection, the taxpayer would be subject to, at most, a 20 percent penalty on the understatement of taxes. So taxpayers who used an abusive tax shelter to understate their taxes by $100,000—if caught and found not to have reasonable cause— would owe the government $120,000 plus the interest that had accrued on the amount due.[31]

Fairness and Other Normative Considerations

Arguments based on the distinctive features of the income tax laws explain how tax shelters arise and why judicial anti-abuse doctrines are necessary to combat them. They do not, however, address the fairness of applying these doctrines to taxpayers who rely on the language of a particular tax provision when they enter into transactions, only to discover after the fact that the tax benefit they counted on receiving has been disallowed, they will have to pay interest on the taxes due, and in the occasional case they may be subject to penalties.

The response is that tax is not the only regulatory scheme in which courts do not rely solely on the language of statutes but interpret them with a view to their purpose. Since Congress first began to legislate, federal courts have been required to apply its mandates to unforeseen circumstances. The issue of fair notice is no different in the tax context than in other regulatory contexts where courts have looked beyond the terms of a statute to determine how it might apply to a situation that Congress had not anticipated.[32]

In addition, as in other regulatory contexts, in arranging their affairs, taxpayers are expected to determine not only what statutes say but also how courts have interpreted them. A taxpayer contemplating a transaction whose sole purpose is to avoid taxes—and which confers no economic benefits apart from its tax benefits—is presumed to be on notice that courts have invoked the economic substance doctrine to deny tax-favored treatment to those types of transactions. *Knetsch* and cases like it that apply the economic substance doctrine are "an inescapable part of the tax landscape."[33]

It is, of course, a fiction that taxpayers will be able on their own to determine how courts might treat a transaction for tax purposes. Penalties for understatement of tax are intended to encourage taxpayers who are unsure about their obligations to consult with tax practitioners to obtain advice about how courts are will likely treat shelter transactions if challenged by the IRS. If taxpayers rely on professional advice that their position more likely than not will be upheld, they won't be subject to penalties. The worst that can happen to taxpayers who acted in good faith is that their lawyer was wrong and they owe interest and more taxes than they originally paid. Not a pleasant prospect for taxpayers who discover this long after the fact, but not a particularly unfair result, either.

Some commentators nonetheless might object that the tax system is different from other regulatory regimes and that taxpayers are entitled to use the formal categories provided in the tax laws to engage in transactions that minimize their taxes, regardless of their underlying economics.[34] This claim is captured in the oft-repeated quote from *Gregory v. Helvering* that "[t]he legal right of a taxpayer to decrease the amount of what would otherwise be his taxes, or altogether avoid them, by means which the law permits is not to be doubted."[35]

It is not clear what exactly the Court meant in stating that a taxpayer had "a legal right" to minimize her taxes. Immediately following this sentence, the Court went on to observe that: "the question for determination is whether what was done, apart from the tax motive, was the thing which the statute intended." In addition, no right to minimize one's taxes exists in the Constitution; nor has Congress created a right to avoid paying taxes subject to special solicitude or protection. As the Supreme Court's subsequent decisions suggest, it was not identifying a specific right or entitlement; rather, it was simply noting that the motive to avoid taxes by itself does not render a transaction legally (or morally) suspect.[36] Indeed, as discussed earlier, many provisions in the Code seek to induce certain behaviors by enlisting taxpayers' desire to avoid paying taxes. Anti-abuse doctrines are important to prevent major tax revenue losses and do not present particularly worrisome fairness concerns. They are also important from a social welfare perspective. If anti-abuse doctrines motivate tax professionals to give conservative advice that steers wide of the line between legitimate tax planning and abusive transactions, nothing valuable to society is lost.[37]

Curbing abusive transactions therefore is an important social objective and anti-abuse doctrines can play a major role in accomplishing it. In the late twentieth century, however, tax shelters arose on an unprecedented scale. The first wave of shelters in the 1970s and 1980s had distinctive characteristics, and eventually were thwarted by new legislation. The wave that followed involved more varied and complex shelters that presented a more difficult challenge.

Tax Shelters Grow Up

While taxpayers undoubtedly have found ways to shelter income from taxation since the income tax was established in the early twentieth century, tax shelters became a widespread and more prominent activity in the 1970s and 1980s. One reason was the growing complexity of the tax law as a result of the cumulative effect of additional rules. Another was an increase in the use of the tax code to favor certain activities, as tax law became more popular as a way for Congress to promote social purposes while limiting budgetary outlays. This popularity continues to this day. As one experienced tax practitioner comments, "It is amazing how many things we are running through the Internal Revenue Code and through the Internal Revenue Service. We're running education, we're running energy, we're running health care, we're running retirement and I can go on and on."[38] The result, according to one tax scholar, is "a variety of subsidies and economic stimuli that are unrelated to the administration and collection of taxes."[39] This can create confusion about which tax benefits Congress has or has not intended to provide, as taxpayers structure their activities to comply with the formal requirements for receiving benefits.

In the early years of the tax shelter industry, promoters designed products mainly for high-wealth investors facing high marginal tax rates. From the end of World War II until 1981, individuals were subject to federal income tax rates that could reach 70 percent or more. Indeed, the taxpayer in the *Knetsch* case was subject to a marginal federal income tax rate exceeding 90 percent. As more taxpayers became interested in sheltering income, promoters expanded their market to upper middle-class taxpayers by syndicating tax-favored investments for groups of investors. That is, the shelter promoter formed a limited partnership to engage in these investments in which the taxpayers were limited, or passive, investors who did not participate in the business operations. The partnership invested in activities such as oil and gas exploration, real estate, and equipment leasing, as well as more exotic enterprises like llama breeding. Syndicators marketed these partnerships "largely to self-employed professionals such as medical doctors, dentists, architects, lawyers, and others who had substantial income from their professional services."[40]

These investments often produced deductions that taxpayers could use to defer taxation but not completely eliminate it. When the deferral ended and the time came to pay the tax, the income that had been sheltered could be treated not as so-called "ordinary income" but as capital gains, which is taxed at a lower rate. In a real estate investment, for instance, investors made modest contributions to a building project and the partnership borrowed the rest of the money. As two journalists described, "By deducting the interest and taking rapid depreciation write-offs, the partnership was able to show huge paper losses, which the investors divided among themselves and wrote off on their income tax returns."[41] Thus, for an investment of $10,000, a person in the 50 percent marginal tax bracket might acquire paper losses of $20,000 or more, thereby saving $10,000 in taxes. When the building finally was sold, the income from the sale would be taxed at the capital gains rate.

Taxpayers gained tax advantages not only from investments that deferred taxation and eventually taxed income as capital gains. They also took advantage of the growth in tax-exempt products such as state and local bonds, as well as opportunities to exclude from taxation earnings on the invested cash value of life insurance policies.[42] As a result, "[d]emand for tax advantaged investment structures grew rapidly through the 1970s and 1980s as tax avoidance began to displace investment quality as a primary investment goal."[43] In 1980, IRS Commissioner Jerome Kurtz reported that nearly 200,000 returns representing 18,000 shelters were involved in the examination and IRS appeals process. These returns, Kurtz maintained, involved almost $5 billion in "questionable deductions."[44] Indeed, between 1979 and 1986, the annual number of tax shelter returns under examination by the IRS increased from 182,731 to 426,634.[45] Kurtz warned, "The great abuse we are finding in this area could result in a serious decline in taxpayers' perception of the fairness and evenhandedness of our administration of the tax system and consequently in the level of voluntary compliance."[46]

The level of tax shelter activity during this period is reflected in data presented by Professor George Yin. From 1975 to 1986, the amount of net losses reported by individual taxpayers from their partnership and subchapter S corporation[47] investments grew by more than 525 percent, while the amount of reported net income increased by only a little over 136 percent.[48] Consistent with this, the number of individual income tax returns reporting net losses from such investments increased during this period by about 171 percent, while the number reporting net income grew by only 36 percent. As Yin observes, "The increase in the number of returns reporting losses is contrary to normal market expectations and suggests that some amount of the losses may have been non-economic or tax shelter losses."[49]

The government used every weapon in its arsenal to combat the shelters that arose in the 1970s and 1980s. It disallowed them on the ground that they had no economic substance or were not otherwise allowed under the tax regulations. It imposed new reporting and record-keeping requirements for tax shelters, adopted more stringent constraints on tax practitioners giving advice on tax shelters, and amended the tax law to change the treatment of certain activity associated with many of the shelters. The consensus, however, seems to be that tax shelter activity abated only when Congress adopted the "passive activity loss" and at-risk rules in the Tax Reform Act of 1986. This legislation addressed a characteristic common to most of the shelters, which was using passive investment losses to shelter ordinary income. Under those rules, losses from passive investments could only be used to offset income from those same investments, not other types of income.[50] In addition the rules required certain claimed losses to be limited to amounts a taxpayer had at risk in a transaction.[51] The rules were "a major factor, if not the single most critical factor," in curbing tax shelter activity. Data indicate that after 1986, increases in net income from investment in entities traditionally used to shelter income increased dramatically while increases in net losses were much smaller.[52]

Congress seemed to have figured out how to stop the widespread abusive tax shelter activity of the 1970s and 1980s with the passive loss rules and other reforms in the 1986 Act. The Act also significantly lowered the highest marginal tax rate. As a consequence, tax policy analysts believed that high-bracket taxpayers would have much less of an incentive to engage in shelter transactions. For several years afterward, shelters existed on a much smaller scale than they had before. Many observers assumed that the government had shut down the tax shelter industry for all practical purposes.

But conditions were brewing for a revival. Intensified global economic competition, stunning wealth from the Internet boom, and greater business demands on law and accounting firms all helped create a new wave of shelters in the 1990s and early 2000s. These forces intersected to bring forth sophisticated abusive shelters on a scale unlike anything anyone had seen before.

Gimme Shelters

The need for the IRS to focus more on collection and less on enforcement in the late 1990s could not have come at a worse time. Corporate taxpayers had growing incentives to eliminate or at least reduce tax liabilities as much as possible, while an emerging class of the superrich expanded individual demand for shelters. At the same time, accounting firms, financial institutions, and law firms all faced intensified competitive pressures that made the development of mass-marketed tax shelters a very attractive line of business. Unlike the 1980s, tax promoters could now rely on sophisticated financial instruments to construct shelters of forbidding complexity. The result was a major surge in abusive shelter activity, to which the IRS was slow to respond. While the demand for tax shelters had increased by the 1990s, the tax shelter boom of that decade was mainly a supply-driven phenomenon orchestrated by some of the major professional institutions in American society.

Demand

Corporate Taxpayers

At mid-twentieth century, corporations treated their tax departments as cost centers. Under this approach, the focus was on minimizing costs while meeting a company's tax obligation. By the end of the century, however, many corporations had shifted to treating their tax department as a profit center. This latter model emphasized the tax department's contribution to reported income through its minimization of the corporation's tax liabilities. This encouraged tax departments to focus actively on tax planning activities that contributed to the company's bottom line.

This shift in focus reflected increasing economic competition for U.S. companies in the last two decades or so of the twentieth century. In the three decades after World War II, many U.S. corporations held dominant positions in markets characterized by oligopoly rather than vigorous competition. In 1950, the United States produced about 60 percent of the manufacturing output of the seven largest capitalist countries.[1] Large-scale production created economies of scale that established formidable barriers to entry in many markets, limiting competition to large vertically integrated firms. In the decades immediately following the war, as L. G. Thomas notes, "transportation costs were high, there was little foreign competition, communication and data processing costs were high, and information moved slowly. Under these conditions strategic assets were very durable."[2] Companies subject to relatively mild competitive pressures maintained profitability by raising prices, with little incentive to trim costs and operate more efficiently. The list of leading firms in various industries was relatively stable. A firm that was in the top fifth of its industry, for instance, had only a 10 percent chance of losing that position within five years.[3]

Reflecting the advantages of large-scale production, fewer than five hundred companies in the United States were responsible for almost half of the country's total industrial output. These companies employed more than a fifth of all nonfarm workers in the United States.[4] They owned about three-quarters of the country's industrial assets and earned about 40 percent of its profits. Given their large capital investments, these firms had to be able to plan production with confidence that goods could be sold at a specific price. To accomplish this, they relied on a mixture of strict planning processes and collusion with other leading firms in their markets. The result was that "[t]he giant corporation of mid-century America necessarily possessed vast discretion and economic power."[5]

In the 1970s, however, several developments began to emerge that reduced the importance of economies of scale, weakened barriers to entry, and intensified competition in many formerly stable industries. Communications and information technology made it possible for potential rivals with minimal vertical integration to compete with long-established companies. Instead of organizing the production process within a single firm, companies began to contract with suppliers around the globe to obtain the resources and services they needed at each stage of the process for the lowest cost and highest quality. With the appearance of computer systems, companies could use software for billing, procurement, inventory controls, and other operational functions. Within a few decades they were performing these functions and contacting current and prospective customers using the Internet. Traditional vertically integrated firms had high fixed costs and used large-scale production to minimize the cost per unit of the items they sold. Technology made it possible for newer firms to reduce fixed costs by constructing supply chains that could be adjusted based on fluctuations in demand and production. The old production system could now be segmented and assigned to a variety of suppliers in diverse locations. As a result, entry into many markets no longer required massive capital investment to minimize the costs of production.

Heightened competition at the global level became more feasible with the emergence of transportation and communications technologies such as satellites, overseas cables, and steel shipping containers.[6] Companies used these technologies to move facilities abroad, contract with suppliers around the world, and launch enterprises in low-cost locations. Anyone could use software "to create a virtual company consisting of little more than a chain of supply contracts with an auction held at each link in the chain designed to get the best deal every step of the way."[7] Potential market entrants then began to lobby to dismantle the regulatory regime that had served to reinforce the oligopolistic markets of the postwar period. They argued that deregulation would spur competition that would provide better goods and services to consumers faster and more cheaply. This led many industries to eliminate the intricate network of cross-subsidies that was created to respond to the needs of various economic interests. Firms that once had been able to assure profitability by establishing predictable prices now had to maintain their margins by focusing more intently on reducing costs and operating more efficiently.

The result has been the appearance in many industries of "hypercompetition."[8] This condition is characterized by unstable competitive advantages that are continually at risk of being eroded by more innovative or efficient competitors. In such markets, "competitors must move quickly to build [new] advantages and erode the advantages of their rivals."[9] Any competitive advantage is temporary; financial returns are volatile, and firms must continually innovate throughout their supply chains to develop new sources of advantage. The effects of hypercompetition can be seen in the greater volatility of competitive position among firms in many industries. While a firm had only a 10 percent chance of falling out of the ranks of the top fifth in its industry in the immediate postwar period, by 1998 that risk had increased to 25 percent.[10] Between 1970 and 1990, the rate at which companies exited the Fortune 500 quadrupled.[11] By 2000, the average U.S. company was losing more than half its customers every four years.[12] Scholars also have noted increasing volatility in recent years among firms in the same industry, as success depended less on the characteristics of the industry and more on the internal capacity of the firm to create new strategic assets as old ones rapidly depreciate.[13] Indeed, the boundaries that defined particular industries themselves became increasingly fluid in the last two decades of the twentieth century as products and services were combined in different ways and competitors could emerge from any existing market.

These developments, which had their roots in the 1970s, coincided with the emergence of what economic sociologist Neil Fligstein has called the "financial conception" of corporate control.[14] As firms became more diversified among product lines, markets, and industries in an effort to spread their risks, they evolved toward a multidivisional form in which decision making was more decentralized than in previous years. To the extent that firms became less vertically integrated, this prompted movement from a command and control authority structure to flexible production systems that granted more authority to persons at lower levels in the organization.

Since top management did not necessarily have production or marketing experience with all the fields in which a given company competed, corporations needed to develop a new conception of managerial control to coordinate their diverse activities. The financial conception of control treated multidivision companies as a collection of assets competing for internal investment from top management on the basis of their comparative rates of return. As Fligstein remarks, "the financial conception of control viewed the central office as a bank and treated the divisions as potential borrowers. The central office would invest in divisions that showed great potential and divest those in slow-growing markets."[15] The firm's central goal was to "allocate capital across product lines in order to increase short-term rates of return."[16] The industries in which a company operated thus matter less than the relative profitability of its various units, which management could determine by using standard financial criteria.

By the 1990s, the prevalence of hypercompetition and the financial conception of control led many companies to treat their tax liabilities as costs of business that could be minimized through the use of sophisticated financial techniques. As one observer suggests, "modern corporate strategists perceive income tax liabilities as another cost of business that can and should be managed, like inventory costs or environmental regulations."[17] The "active management of corporate tax liabilities" became a common phenomenon unlikely to recede in light of the growing refinement of financial planning strategies.

Given this approach to tax obligations, corporate tax departments had an incentive to engage in tax planning activities up to the point at which the marginal cost of doing so equaled the marginal increase in reported income resulting from the tax decrease that they achieved. The focus on contribution to reported income provided a metric to evaluate a tax department's performance by managers who might have lacked the tax expertise otherwise to assess the quality of the department's activities. Firms that adopted a profit-center performance standard for their tax departments ended up with lower effective tax rates.[18]

The notion that "tax departments are increasingly counted on as innovative profit centers and that tax managers are increasingly provided incentives to produce profit"[19] was well established by the turn of the twenty-first century. In a 2001 survey of corporate tax departments in manufacturing companies, the measure used most often to evaluate department performance was the tax savings it provided.[20] More than half indicated that this metric affected the compensation of tax department employees. In a survey of Fortune 1000 tax directors, 46 percent ranked the effective tax rate as the most important consideration in pursuing the tax department's goals, compared to 16 percent who ranked compliance first.[21] As one prominent tax practitioner concluded in 1999, the "senior corporate managers now perceive a corporation's tax liability not as an inelastic and inevitable misfortune, but rather as a necessary cost that responds to aggressive management, just like other corporate expenses."[22]

Individual Taxpayers

The growing concentration of wealth in the United States also created demand from individuals for tax shelters at the turn of the twenty-first century. From 1970 to 2000, the share of income going to the bottom 90 percent of all Americans decreased from almost 67 percent to a little over 52 percent.[23] The share held by the top 10 percent rose from 33 percent to almost 48 percent. Furthermore, the share held by the top 1 percent increased from a little under 9 percent in 1975 to more than 21 percent in 2000, a rate of increase of almost 143 percent. The concentration of income is even more pronounced when we consider that by 2000 the share of income held by the top 0.1 percent was almost 11 percent, compared to about 2.5 percent in 1975, an increase of 337 percent.[24]

The wealthiest Americans enjoyed significant increases not only in their share of the nation's income, but also in the amount of income that they commanded. Adjusted for inflation, the average income of the top 10 percent of United States taxpayers rose from $130,327 in 1970 to $185,136 in 1995. By contrast, average income among the other 90 percent fell from $31,470 in 1970 to $30,171 in 1995. The average after-tax income of the wealthiest 1 percent of households rose from $322,733 in 1970 to $617,882 in 1995, an increase of more than 91 percent.[25]

A substantial reason for the large spike in income among the wealthiest households was a huge increase in executive compensation over the last few decades of the twentieth century. The percentage of income based on wages, salary, and pensions for the top 1 percent increased from just under 53 percent in 1975 to a little over 63 percent in 2000, while the percentage of income from dividends dropped during that period from almost 13 percent to about 5 percent. The change in source of income from 1975 to 2000 was especially dramatic for the top 0.01 percent of Americans. The percentage based on compensation increased from just under 26 percent to almost 61 percent, while the percentage from dividends declined from 40 percent to about 5.5 percent.[26] Between 1992 and 2000, the average pay of the CEO of Standard & Poor's 500 companies increased from $3.5 million to $14.7 million.[27] A comprehensive study of executive compensation from 1936 to 2003 indicates that for the period 1970 to 1979, the average CEO received about forty times the pay of an average worker. By 2003, the ratio was 367 to 1.[28]

At the same time that executive compensation was rising sharply, entrepreneurs in the Internet technology sector were also reaping large financial rewards. The Internet boom of the last years of the 1990s resulted in especially outsized gains in wealth for persons who cashed in shares of technology companies. What venture capitalist John Doerr described as "the greatest legal wealth creation in history"[29] generated a potentially lucrative market for transactions that would shield this income from taxation.

The increase in share price on the opening day of initial public offerings (IPOs) for just a few companies illustrates the broader phenomenon. Priceline opened at $16 a share and closed the day at $69.[30] The founders' stake in the company was worth $4.3 billion. Netscape's opening price was $28 per share; it closed at $58.25, with trading of 14 million shares. Founder Jim Clark's shares were worth $565 million, venture capital firm Kleiner Perkins's stake was worth about $260 million, the company's new CEO's shares were worth almost $245 million, and the programmer who had developed the browser held shares worth $58 million.[31] Trading in EarthWeb began at $14 a share and spiked to almost $49 a share; the founders' stake in the company was worth $65 million each. Pre-offering shares of TheGlobe.com were $9 a share; the company closed at a price of $63.50 per share. The founders' shares were each worth about $50 million.[32] Webvan issued shares at $15 each, which moved to almost $25 dollars apiece by closing. As a result, the founder was worth more than $2 billion and the new CEO's recruitment package rose to almost $300 million.[33] In April 1999, *The Industry Standard* featured a cover with the founders of Priceline.com and Broadcast.com and the headline "THIS WEEK'S BILLIONAIRES."[34] The magazine noted that someone who had invested $100,000 in American Online eighteen months earlier would now be worth $1.3 million.

In the height of the frenzy, from October 1998 to April 2000, more than three hundred Internet companies had initial public offerings, with a good number enjoying comparable bounces in share price. Those who cashed in their shares before the market collapsed enjoyed huge paydays and were prime customers for shelters to shield that income.

The fact that some Internet fortunes were made without satisfying standard requirements for demonstrating business viability to potential investors may have made the paper losses generated by shelters seem a plausible basis for tax savings. In August 1999, for instance, Webvan saw a first-day increase of 66 percent in its share price despite the fact that it projected losses of $78 million in 1999, $154 million in 2000, and $302 million in 2001—or half a billion dollars in its first three years. Investors gave little weight to such projections on the view that the Internet was the basis for a "new economy" in which "time-honored methods of valuing stocks no longer worked and should be discarded."[35]

Supply

Traditionally, accounting and law firms were dedicated to providing individualized services to clients. This conception of professional service, which dated back to the early twentieth century in the United States, was animated by the view that human problems arise under conditions of uncertainty and are not subject to mechanical solutions. Instead, these problems called for expert judgment.[36] Historically, professional firms were organized to enhance the capacity for professional judgment. New hires worked under the close supervision of more senior professionals and were given greater responsibility over time over increasingly important matters. The partnership structure of firms, meanwhile, created a discretionary zone for experienced professionals to apply their expertise.

The rise of the tax shelter industry, which involved developing and marketing tax products to multiple clients, offers a window into how this traditional conception of professionalism came under strain at the end of the twentieth century. In particular, the episode illustrates how financial incentives, filtered through organizational mandates, distorted the exercise of professional expertise.

At a macro perspective, the tax shelter market is one example of how professional firms have become vulnerable to intensified market forces in the last quarter of the twentieth century. As commentators have noted, the emergence of the tax shelter market is part of a larger transformation in which professional service firms have become more explicitly self-conscious business ventures. While claiming the trappings of professionalism, these firms conduct their day-to-day operations like any other business, driven mainly by the goal of profit maximization.[37] In this account, the assumption is that the incentive to increase revenue has supplanted professional judgment. Applied to the shelter market, this approach implies that shelter promoters, rather than assessing the legitimacy of the transactions they were promoting, were single-mindedly devoted to marketing them as widely as possible before enforcement agencies got wind of them and shut them down.

There is no doubt that among market participants, many of those involved wanted to make a quick return regardless of legal constraints. In addition, many nontax partners, who were not involved in promoting shelters, turned a blind eye to increased revenues from tax services. But the effects of market pressures on professional judgment turn out to be more complex. Many individuals swept up in the shelter market were highly regarded tax professionals with lengthy experience in practice. They spoke and acted as if professional standards and legal requirements mattered. Despite efforts to apply their best professional judgments, however, they often allowed the firms to approve and market abusive tax shelters. In these instances, organizational pressures and business rationalizations did not so much displace professional judgments as distort them. The rise of the shelter industry reflects the vulnerability of professional judgment to organizational imperatives in a period of intense market competition.

Accounting Firms in the Late Twentieth Century

By the second half of the twentieth century, the major accounting firms in the United States had risen to prominence by providing services to large corporations that involved audits of corporate financial statements and attesting to the reliability of various company representations. With the securities acts in the 1930s, outside accountants were given the responsibility for certifying that the financial statements of publicly traded companies were consistent with generally accepted accounting principles. As their corporate clients grew in size and expanded their activities, accounting firms grew and expanded with them. By the 1930s, the major firms had come to be known as the "Big Eight."[38] Prohibited by ethics rules from engaging in competitive bidding or advertising, each firm developed an industry specialty. Based in Chicago, Arthur Andersen focused on traditional manufacturing industries, while Price Waterhouse was the auditor of choice for blue chip companies. Accountants also had been involved in tax return preparation since the enactment of the income tax laws. At major accounting firms, tax services—which included, in addition to return preparation, tax planning and representing clients in controversies before the IRS—were ancillary to audit services, which were the bread and butter (and jam) on which major accounting firms subsisted and thrived. Until the 1980s, the Big Eight earned most of their fees from audit services.

While not a dominant source of firm income, tax services fit comfortably with accounting services. With the enactment of the tax laws in the early twentieth century, businessmen had suddenly been required to maintain written records to support the determination of taxable income.

CPAs were pressed into service to assist in preparing financial records. Tax accounting became an important subspecialty of the field.[39] Arthur Andersen led the way in providing tax services, developing a specialty in income tax in the 1910s, which it subsequently parlayed into audit and consulting engagements.[40]

By the 1930s, all of the Big Eight accounting firms had specialized tax departments and provided tax-planning advice. A client might be contemplating a business deal, for example, and a tax specialist might suggest ways to structure the transaction to take advantage of available tax benefits and then assist with implementation. Tax professionals at accounting firms were also available to represent clients in controversies with the IRS. With the exception of tax return preparation, which was the bailiwick of accountants, the tax services offered by major accounting firms were not all that different from services offered by tax lawyers at corporate firms.[41]

The provision of audit, tax, and management advisory services—or consulting services as they were later known—fell under the traditional model of professional services, which were organized around the application of specialized expertise to the unique problems of individual clients.[42] The hallmark of tailored or "bespoke" services was the billable hour. Calculating fees based on time expended was premised on the assumption that it was not possible to predict how much total time a matter might take up, since unforeseen circumstances—requiring additional research and investigation—could arise in any matter.[43] Not only were hourly fees favored in the provision of tax services, but until the 1990s contingent, or result-based, fees were banned.[44]

In addition to the billable hour, accounting firms adopted other characteristics of the traditional professional model. Firms were organized to encourage the development and exercise of professional judgment. Despite their much greater size, accounting firms were set up as loose bureaucratic-professional partnerships, much like law firms. Individual partners had the final say on matters entrusted to them.[45] Accounting firms also instituted training and promotion protocols similar to those of law firms. Entry-level accountants were put through a rigorous multi-year training program during which they learned to apply technical rules and became familiar with the unwritten norms of their particular firms and the larger profession. Like lawyers in corporate firms, accountants at major firms were also subject to an up-or-out rule: if they were not promoted to a senior position in the partnership after a specified period of time, they were assisted in finding alternative placements.[46]

Beginning in the 1960s, audit services began to experience pressure from different directions. Suits against firms proliferated as liability for the failure to detect fraud expanded.[47] When businesses failed during the economic downturn of the next decade, audit services came under increased scrutiny from the Securities and Exchange Commission (SEC), which threatened to take a more aggressive regulatory stance. In the meantime, anticompetitive barriers inside the industry began to break down under the threat of antitrust liability. In 1973, the American Institute of Certified Public Accountants (AICPA) was forced to lift its ban on competitive bidding for audits and, a few years later, its prohibition against advertising. Major firms, which had once enjoyed an informal agreement that they would not compete for each other's clients, were now in audit price wars. In the decade that followed, competition increased as the number of corporate mergers and acquisitions surged and corporate consolidations left fewer companies to audit.[48]

In the meantime, the audit process itself was undergoing changes, becoming increasingly rationalized. With the routinization of audit, the space for the exercise of discretionary judgment narrowed. Beginning in the 1960s, the AICPA began to issue regular research bulletins that sought to articulate the principles that were to guide the audit process. These principles were ultimately codified in accounting rules. At the same time, corporate clients began to use computers for data processing and storage. Automated systems reduced the need for auditors to play a role in gathering information and detecting fraud.[49] By the 1980s, audits had become commoditized. Nothing distinguished an audit provided by one Big Eight accounting firm from another and firms were no longer able to compete on the basis of quality or specialized industry expertise in the provision of audit services.

As revenues from audits flattened out, the major firms began to search for new service areas and business strategies. They turned to consulting, which appeared to provide a solution.[50] Having long offered management advisory services, accounting firms launched systematic efforts in the 1980s to build their consulting practices. These efforts, however, soon met with roadblocks. Led by SEC chair Arthur Levitt, that agency began to voice concerns that consulting presented a conflict of interest with the provision of audit services.[51] Within the next decade, firms were forced to divest themselves of their consulting divisions because of ongoing pressure from the SEC. In Arthur Andersen's case, the differences in its audit and consulting cultures eventually created insurmountable tensions.[52]

When major accounting firms' foray into consulting failed, the only competitive advantage left was their size and capacity, enhanced by computer networks, to audit their clients' operations across geographically dispersed sites. With the increasing importance of size, major accounting firms, anxious that second-tier firms would overtake and displace them as the auditors for large multinational corporations, launched a series of mergers. In the late 1990s, the Big Eight became the Big Six and then the Big Five.

In the 1990s, accounting firms began to grow their tax practices, emphasizing the development of standardized tax strategies. Until this period, firms had offered individualized tax advice to clients on how to structure transactions to minimize tax liability along the same model as their provision of audit and consulting services. Tax advice focused on counseling clients about specific deals, and the strategies proposed arose in the context of clients' individual business needs. In the 1990s, firms began to recognize the significant efficiency gains that would result from developing turnkey tax products for immediate use that they could sell to many similarly situated clients.

The impetus to create standardized products accelerated when the AICPA in response to regulatory pressure amended the rules governing tax advice to permit contingent fees. In the mid-1980s, the Federal Trade Commission initiated an investigation of accounting firms, contending that certain ethical prohibitions, including a ban on contingency fees, constituted unlawful restraints of trade. The investigation culminated in a settlement in 1990 under which the AICPA narrowed the prohibition of contingent fees to services provided to audit clients and the preparation of original tax returns.[53] Several years later, the AICPA issued rulings that made clear that a percentage fee was not, in any case, a contingent fee, since its payment did not depend on achieving a particular result.[54] The door was now open to firms to design and market tax products to multiple clients, charging fees based on the anticipated tax deduction generated by the transaction. In effect, accounting firms were able to earn percentage-based commissions for their tax strategies. So long as fees were structured so that they were due regardless of whether the client's position would ultimately be upheld by the IRS or in court, a firm could escape the characterization of its fees as contingent on obtaining a particular outcome.[55]

The focus on standardized products and the loosening of fee restrictions could not have come at a more propitious moment. During the late 1990s, the United States was enjoying the dot.com boom and its economy was surging. A large group of newly minted millionaires emerged who were ideal prospects for tax product sales. The major accounting firms ramped up their tax practices and went on a tax lawyer hiring spree, engaging in extensive entry-level recruitment at law schools and offering highly lucrative compensation packages to lure away senior tax partners from well-established corporate firms.[56] Between 1995 and 2001, the U.S. tax practices of KPMG, Deloitte & Touche, Ernst & Young, and PricewaterhouseCoopers more than doubled their revenue, from $ 2.4 to 5.6 billion.[57]

Law Firms

The Guilded Age   Until the last two decades of the twentieth century, corporate law firms made up the segment of the legal profession that was most successful in organizing itself as a guild that enjoyed significant insulation from both market pressures and government regulation. The legal departments of corporate clients typically were quite small and focused on the most routine work. Clients therefore used outside firms for most of their legal needs. For much of the century, especially in the period following World War II, a company typically used one firm for most of its work. The relationship tended to be long term; a company rarely replaced a firm or shopped around to generate competition. This arrangement provided a firm with a regular work flow and a predictable income stream. The steady work served as an opportunity to train younger lawyers and generally minimized the need for partners to spend significant time attempting to generate business. Clients were institutionalized, passed on from senior to junior lawyers in due course. The benefit of having a firm familiar with its operations made a client reluctant to switch to a new firm that it would have to educate about its business.

Under these conditions, a law firm was able to develop what economists call firm-specific capital.[58] That is, a firm had unique assets that provided its lawyers with the opportunity to earn more by practicing in that firm rather than elsewhere. Lawyers in the firm gained access to regular work from clients and became familiar with their needs over the course of their careers at the firm. They also acquired professional training that imparted the particular ways in which the firm approached, organized, and performed legal work for its clients. In addition, they developed relationships with colleagues to whom they could turn for assistance and advice, which enhanced their productivity. If lawyers were promoted to partner, the availability of such firm-specific capital created powerful incentives to commit them to the firm for the course of their entire careers. Furthermore, clients regarded themselves as retaining the firm rather than individual lawyers. This made leaving the firm an unattractive option because lawyers would not be able to take clients with them.[59]

Relative insulation from competition for both clients and lawyers gave law firms considerable control over their environment and afforded them the opportunity to structure their operations around their internal needs and their partners' understanding of professional norms. They were able to bill clients at rates that they regarded as reasonable without having to account in detail for their charges. They decided how their work should be organized and their services delivered without the need for serious attention to efficiency. Indeed, the typical corporate law firm would have regarded concerns for efficiency as antithetical to the standards of professional quality by which work should be evaluated. The implicit model of service was the professional craftsman who was willing to spare no effort or expense in providing customized service. The scarcity of financial information about law firms reinforced the notion that pecuniary considerations were secondary to the pursuit of professional excellence as determined by one's peers.[60]

A firm's internal organization typically reflected and reinforced lawyers' sense of allegiance to the collective welfare of the entity. Partners were compensated mainly on the basis of seniority rather than calculations of each partner's contribution to revenues. Decisions of any significance were made by the partnership as a whole, with limited reliance on formal lines of management authority. Every partner was personally liable for the obligations of the partnership. This meant that in theory any partner could be called upon to pay damages resulting from the negligence or misconduct of a colleague if the firm's assets were insufficient to satisfy a claim. Partners were drawn from the ranks of associates who had spent the first several years of their legal career at the firm becoming socialized in its norms and values. Those associates who were not promoted to partner received assistance from the firm in finding positions in client legal departments or smaller firms to which the firm might refer business. Finally, for a good part of the twentieth century, members of major corporate law firms tended to have a common outlook because they recruited only white Protestant men from elite social backgrounds and a small number of colleges and law schools.

In a profession that was largely self-regulated until the latter part of the twentieth century, corporate law firms enjoyed even more freedom from external oversight than most other lawyers. State bar authorities generally concentrated their efforts on responding to complaints about lawyers who represented individuals, either in small firms or solo practice.[61] Common law standards of liability were relatively protective of lawyers, and relationships with clients were such that any dissatisfaction with performance was likely to be addressed informally.

There were few regulatory provisions during this period that imposed obligations on lawyers engaged in specific areas of practice. Under the Internal Revenue Code, the Treasury Department had long had the authority to issue and enforce rules of conduct for tax practitioners, but there was minimal activity on that front. To a considerable degree, therefore, corporate firms' independence from client influence was matched by their independence from oversight by the bar or the state. The conventional wisdom was that this absence of meaningful external control was not a problem. To the contrary, it was thought to be a precondition for adherence to the highest ethical standards.[62] The relative economic security that the corporate law firm lawyers enjoyed ostensibly meant that they were subject to fewer pressures to engage in behavior that was regarded as problematic because it was overtly commercial. By contrast, lawyers in less stable practices with less wealthy clients were supposedly vulnerable to more temptation and client pressures to violate ethical rules.[63]

These features of the corporate law firm enabled it to serve as an effective socializing agent until the latter decades of the twentieth century. Firms regulated behavior through a system of informal peer control that operated with minimal formal layers of authority. Partners regarded themselves as autonomous professionals with equal claims to participate in decision making and viewed hierarchical organization as ethically suspect. None of this necessarily meant that lawyers in corporate firms were more ethical than lawyers in other practice settings or that this was a golden age for the legal profession. Firms openly discriminated on the basis of race, sex, religion, class, and ethnic origin. While enjoying some measure of independence from immediate commercial imperatives, corporate lawyers' close association and identification with long-term clients may have led them unthinkingly to assimilate their clients' world views, compromising their independence in more subtle ways.[64] Nonetheless, firms committed to a particular vision of professional practice were in a position to instill that vision in the lawyers who worked in them.

Elite Tax Bar Practice   The relative insulation of law firms from market forces during most of the twentieth century created conditions that nurtured a relative consensus on how tax lawyers should approach the task of providing advice to clients on their tax obligations. Lawyers in elite firms during this period held a monopoly on furnishing tax advice for major corporations and high-wealth individuals. These lawyers were integrated into the transactional practice of their firms. They typically were consulted when corporate partners approached their tax colleagues about a business objective that a client of the firm wanted to achieve. Equipped with knowledge of the client's goals, the tax lawyer then sought to structure a transaction that minimized the client's tax liability. The value to clients of a lawyer's advice rested on the lawyer's capacity to provide independent judgment about how a court would treat the tax benefits claimed for a transaction. This judgment was informed by a sense of the internal coherence of the provisions at issue, the salience of judicially created standards, and an understanding of at least a general set of basic principles that animated the Internal Revenue Code. Close association with corporate transactional partners made tax lawyers familiar with the types of deals that were being done by corporate clients, which helped inform an assessment of the business purpose and economic substance of a given transaction.

Elite practitioners regarded the exercise of such professional judgment as the feature of their practice that distinguished them from mere technocrats who provided advice based simply on the literal terms of the tax code.[65] The lawyer's aim was for the client to take a position that didn't raise concerns with tax authorities, rather than a position that on balance would be financially advantageous even if challenged by the government. Because work came to the tax advisor from corporate partners whose clients had already decided to engage in some activity for business reasons, the issue of business purpose rarely tended to be contentious. In addition, because these transactions were intertwined with clients' business affairs, courts were likely to defer to them on this subject.

Elite tax lawyers during this period tended to take a view of a tax advisor's professional obligations that was sensitive to society's interest in a well-functioning tax system. There was not complete unanimity on the scope of an advisor's obligations and various practitioners formulated their responsibilities in different ways. Nor was it possible to express practitioner norms in the form of explicit rules; expectations represented more of a general approach to how a good tax lawyer was supposed to counsel a client in particular situations. Nonetheless, there was a broad consensus within the elite bar that professional judgment that drew on multiple considerations beyond the literal terms of the tax code imposed a limit on how far a lawyer should go to minimize a client's tax liability. This view persists today among many members of the elite tax bar, but there was an especially strong agreement on it until the last two or three decades of the twentieth century.

The organized tax bar consistently insisted on the distinction between tax advisor and tax advocate in its struggles over the years with the American Bar Association regarding the professional responsibilities of tax lawyers. In various pronouncements, the ABA characterized advocacy as the lens through which to view a tax lawyer's obligations, regardless of context. It declared that the lawyer owes "entire devotion to the interest of the client" and has described the IRS as the client's adversary.[66] By contrast, the ABA's Section of Taxation maintained that "a tax return is not a submission in an adversary proceeding," and that lawyers who provide guidance to taxpayers in determining their liability were not simply advocates. Rather, they advised their clients on how best to determine their tax obligations.[67]

Many influential members of the elite tax bar in the mid-twentieth century suggested that the tax advisor's distinctive role involved a dual responsibility to the client and to the tax system as a whole. Prominent tax practitioner Seymour Mintz observed in 1963 that while a sizable segment of the tax bar believed that the tax lawyer owed undivided loyalty to the client, a "considerably larger group" would say that there was something "special and peculiar" about tax practice.[68] Similarly, Randolph Thrower, a private practitioner who served as IRS Commissioner, emphasized that tax lawyers "are vested with a professional responsibility to the public for both the law and its administration. One who recognizes no such responsibility is not a professional."[69]

Henry Sellin, a tax lawyer and former academic, emphasized the complex responsibilities of the tax lawyer by identifying four different functions that he or she performs: "(1) business/tax planner, (2) tax return preparer, (3) Internal Revenue Service practitioner, and (4) litigator/advocate."[70] Only when "the administrative procedures of the Service have been completed and the case is in the courts," he argued, does the tax lawyer become the litigator/advocate who has "only one obligation, to his client." At that point, "his only obligation to the Service is that of one litigator to another—to abide by the rules of litigation."[71]

Randolph Paul, who served in the Treasury Department and was a founder of the law firm Paul, Weiss, also expressed a conception of the tax advisor that reflected both devotion to the client and acknowledgment of special responsibilities. Although Paul never hesitated "to make any argument that I think will advance the client's financial interest even though I may feel that acceptance of the argument in an opinion which is not carefully narrowed to the facts may create a precedent unfriendly to the best interests of the revenue,"[72] he noted that tax advisors had certain obligations as a result of the particular nature of tax disputes. "One peculiar responsibility of tax advisers," he observed, "derives from the fact that tax controversies are between the client and the Government, rather than between two private litigants. Our established procedures make the Government more dependent upon the taxpayer than is the private litigant upon the other side in an ordinary controversy."[73]

As some elite tax lawyers saw it, it was misguided to regard the relationship between government and the taxpayer as inherently adversarial. "The distinction between taxpayers and their government is wrong," Henry Sellin declared in 1974, "for the government is the taxpayers, just as the taxpayers are the government. We are they and they are we."[74] The citizen's obligation to pay her fair share of taxes was a duty not only to the government but to other taxpayers.[75] Similarly, Merle Miller, founder of what is now the law firm Ice Miller, noted the "moral obligations owing by taxpayers to one another, because of their reciprocal positions as taxpayers."[76]

From this perspective, clients were part of a larger community whose survival required cooperation among its members. They might obtain a short-term benefit by not paying their fair share of taxes, but they and their fellow citizens would suffer substantial long-term injury if this became the dominant strategy for all taxpayers. The elite tax bar's traditional norms therefore included some responsibility to further a client's enlightened self-interest as a citizen in providing advice about tax obligations.

Members of the elite bar also suggested that tax advisors should foster respect for the tax system among their clients. An important responsibility of tax advisors, claimed H. Brian Holland of Ropes & Gray, was to explain the reasons for rules that to an uninitiated client might seem arbitrary or unreasonable. The lawyer "should not curry favor" with the client who complained by saying that the entire tax law is arbitrary. Explaining the rationale for rules provided for a "better understanding of tax laws and less friction between the public and the tax administrator."[77] Similarly, Merle Miller urged lawyers against "aiding and abetting taxpayers in their suspicion, distrust and even animosity toward those who are writing and enforcing our tax laws." The lawyer "must do his best to maintain in his fellow citizens a proper respect for the methods we have set up under a democratic system for the collection of each citizen's share" of taxes.[78]

To this day members of the elite tax bar have been especially notable for their skepticism, if not downright hostility, toward aggressive tax shelters. Elite lawyers have regarded themselves as working on "real transactions" aimed at "making money in the short-run or the long-run by increasing revenues or reducing (nontax) expenses," as well as on "business-based financings" designed to raise capital. Their role is to "cast a desired business transaction in a form that is most beneficial from a tax perspective. The basic business purpose is a given but there may be choices as to form."[79]

By contrast, elite lawyers have regarded tax shelters as transactions driven mainly by the desire to reduce tax liability. As Wall Street tax lawyer Peter Canellos puts it, "The investment in a tax shelter is a fee paid for tax benefits. The investor either expects to lose it or expects a return with an economic yield that is below market on a risk-adjusted basis."[80] Rather than responding to the tax concerns of a client who desires to enter into a business transaction, a "tax shelter professional" works to "create an artificial transaction to take advantage of a loophole. Such a transaction cannot be real—no one wanted to do the transaction before the loophole was discovered—it can only be made to appear real."[81] In such an instance, "only the lawyer's wisdom and self-restraint stand between the client and the artful construction of transactions."[82] This aversion to aggressive shelters is premised on "the distinction between legitimate economic activity, which is assumed to be a social good, and pure tax planning, which is not."[83] The elite bar traditionally has seen itself as policing this boundary, which it has regarded as essential to the integrity of the tax system.[84] Members of "the tax bar" and "the tax shelter bar" thus effectively operate in different worlds.[85]

Members of the elite tax bar have been averse to recommending or providing opinions on tax shelters because of what Canellos describes as "concern about the systemic effects of shelters and the pressures on conscientious advisers to support questionable deals."[86] As one practitioner suggested, tax avoidance plans that are doubtful are presented to lawyers daily. There can be a powerful temptation to accept them "because the administrative process is long in developing a technique for overcoming a specific tax-avoidance device." As a result, "a tremendous amount of restraint on the part of the tax bar is required in order not to create [an] inequitable shifting of the fair load from your high-bracket taxpaying client to the low-bracket taxpayer."[87]

The elite tax bar's traditional attitude toward shelters is expressed especially clearly in a 1980 law review article that features an exchange of fictitious memos between a senior partner at a law firm and a young tax associate who offers suggestions for reducing the tax liability of a new client.[88] The centerpiece of the associate's recommendations is a "tax straddle" arrangement under which the client will buy and sell Treasury bill futures. "Due to a quirk in the law,"[89] the associate writes, the loss on a T-bill itself is treated as an ordinary loss that can be offset against the taxpayer's income, while the gain on a T-bill future is treated as capital gain taxed at a lower rate. The client would follow through on the losing portion of the transaction so as to suffer loss on an actual bill, while structuring the gain part of the transaction so as to close it out before maturity. The result is that the taxpayer would be able to use the losses to shelter ordinary income, while enjoying capital gains treatment on any income from the transactions. The associate acknowledges some risk that the scheme will be disallowed, but suggests that the client engage in transactions masking the tax straddle that will decrease the likelihood that it will be detected on a return even if there is an audit.

The partner reviewing the memo disapproves of the associate's approach: "There is in your memo no quest to sort out right from wrong, much less any attempt to determine the correct legal result under complex provisions. Instead your stance seems to be: let's find an argument for the taxpayer and, having found it, let's carry it as far as we can, so long as the downside risk is not too bad, while freely factoring in the possibility of nondiscovery into the risk assessment." The result is a proposal that "corrupts the fabric of the tax system, destroying distinctions between ordinary income and capital gain." The partner doubts that the courts will accept it, but even if they do, "it is surely mad to allow it," since it would produce a system "where the rich, who could afford to go into these manipulations, could freely convert ordinary income to capital gain and move income around from year to year as they see fit."[90] This would require Congress to respond with legislation to address the situation, which would add to the complexity of the tax system. The partner notes that when he was actively involved in tax practice, "I thought there was some mix in my duty. It was not unalloyed avoidance-seeking, but had at least a measure of allegiance to the fisc and to higher principle. Some things were wrong, even if they worked."[91]

The elite tax bar thus traditionally formulated a conception of the tax advisor's role that stopped short of the unqualified devotion to the client that characterized the advocate. Elements of the advisor model were neither as explicit nor as categorical as those of the adversarial model, and there was some variation in the intensity with which tax lawyers embraced them in different situations. Nonetheless, there was a relative consensus for most of the twentieth century that the tax advisor occupied a distinct role that involved different responsibilities from those of the advocate. This role required that lawyers rely on a sophisticated understanding of their professional obligations, as well as an understanding that the client was both a taxpayer and a citizen, to determine how far they would go in helping their clients minimize their tax liabilities.

Law Firms under Pressure   Beginning in the late 1970s, increasing competitive pressure on United States businesses from companies abroad and from accelerating technological innovation, compounded by the emergence of hostile corporate takeover activity in the mid-1980s, led to intensified efforts to increase productivity and control costs. Corporate legal expenses had been steadily increasing as business operations became more complex, global, and subject to greater regulation. Companies sought to rationalize their use of legal services by bringing more functions within their legal departments and by increasing the status, responsibilities, and sophistication of inside counsel. Faced with pressure to reduce legal costs, general counsel began to loosen ties with outside law firms, encouraging competition for their company's legal work.

With these changes, a company was less likely to rely on a single law firm for most of its legal work, and individual law firms had less opportunity to gain intimate familiarity with a company's operations. This made it less costly for a client to switch from one law firm to another, and easier to consider several firms when deciding who would represent the client on which matters. As firms gradually lost assurance of a steady stream of business from particular clients, they began to lose some of the firm-specific capital that helped tie lawyers to the firm. It became less certain that lawyers at a given firm would be able to rely on the firm for enough work to keep them busy, which made an increasing number of lawyers consider whether another firm might offer more attractive opportunities. The attachment between firm and lawyer weakened even further as general counsel began to claim that their relationships ran between themselves and individual lawyers rather than specific firms. Clients, in other words, had become less institutionalized.

As the relationship between corporate clients and law firms evolved, law firms began to make clear to their lawyers that they were responsible for generating enough work for themselves and the firm. As lawyers became more entrepreneurial, they began to build their own "books of business" that were independent of the particular firm in which they practiced. The result was the emergence of fiercely competitive markets for both clients and lawyers. Most law firms perceived an imperative to grow and diversify to compete in the newly competitive market for corporate legal services. Acquiring partners from other firms or merging with entire firms was the quickest way to increase the scale and scope of services that a firm could provide.

Success in these efforts was dependent on steadily increasing profits per partner, a metric that became the dominant way of evaluating the financial health and prospects of a law firm. High profits per partner gave a firm the opportunity to lure away partners and their clients from firms with lower figures. All this became more feasible with an explosion of financial information about law firms spearheaded by the magazine *The American Lawyer* beginning in the early 1980s. Increasing mounds of information became available on matters such as revenues, profits, billing rates, partner compensation, and associate salaries as the veil was lifted on aspects of practice that traditionally had been secret and opaque.

As law firms became less insulated from market forces, their internal structure and procedures began to change. The risk of losing partners to other firms, as well as the desire to lure partners from competitors, led most firms to abandon partner compensation based on seniority. Most firms devised compensation systems that gave substantial weight to the revenues that the firm earned from the clients that a lawyer brought in. A growing percentage of partners no longer came from associates who had worked their way up in the firm, but from lateral partners from other firms who brought profitable books of business. The desire to keep profits per partner high also led some firms to "de-equitize" partners who were not generating sufficient revenues so that they no longer were entitled to a share of the firm's profits.

The scope of the work that law firms performed and the fees that they charged gradually became subject to closer client scrutiny, with many general counsel demanding a larger decision-making role on matters that previously had been the province of outside counsel. Some clients went so far as to hire companies to audit their legal bills, while others were not shy about asking for discounts in return for a certain amount of business. In the early 1990s, the multinational company Dupont launched a "preferred provider" program to contain its legal costs. Reducing its outside firms from about 350 to 40, Dupont required the outside lawyers in the program to collaborate, take measures to minimize litigation costs, consider alternatives to hourly billing, and provide more cost-effective legal services.[92] Other large corporations soon followed suit. These new arrangements all underscored that corporate law firms no longer had unfettered discretion to decide how to organize, deliver, and bill for legal services based mainly on internal considerations. General counsel made it increasingly clear that they would evaluate law firm services by how much they enhanced corporate clients' ability to meet business objectives, not simply by professional craft standards.

With law firms subject to increasing competition, a distinct hierarchy of practice areas began to emerge in the last three decades of the twentieth century. This hierarchy reflected the fact that as law firm consultant Joel Henning put it, "different legal services command different market values."[93] Moving up this hierarchy, the stakes for the client were higher and the price of the legal work involved was less important. Moving down, the work became more routine and clients were more sensitive to its price.

At the top of the "services value pyramid" were cutting-edge legal practices customized to the needs of a particular client. This work involved crafting novel transactions, devising creative responses to regulatory requirements, or representing the client in "bet the company" litigation. Clients placed a high value on this kind of work and were willing to pay premium fees for it. The second level on the pyramid was work for clients who "rather than needing the profession's most creative talent, wanted [. . .] to find a firm that accumulated experience in handling certain types of problems" and didn't need to start from scratch.[94] Clients were more sensitive to price here than they were at the top of the service value pyramid, but tended to select firms mainly on the basis of experience and past performance. Finally, the bottom level of the pyramid involved relatively routine work that could be divided into discrete tasks performed according to standard procedures. Clients selected firms for bottom-tier work mainly on the basis of price and reliability. The pyramid thus extended from cutting-edge work at the top to commodity work at the bottom.

As clients began in the 1980s and 1990s to differentiate more aggressively among the types of work that they needed, the legal services market had to respond in kind. Not only did legal work become more segmented, but the types of work that fell into various segments also became less stable. The legal services found at each level of the pyramid continued to change over time, as competitive pressures constantly pushed work downward. The result over the past few decades was a rapidly accelerating life cycle for legal work. Often, what began as cutting-edge, high-margin work done by a small number of firms matured into more standard services that many firms could provide at decreasing cost. Law firms therefore had to become sensitive to their position on the pyramid, and to consider when and to what extent the services they provide were likely to become commodities. While they responded to this likelihood in different ways, most major firms attempted to increase their proportion of high-end work and reduce the amount that was price-sensitive.

As law firms grew larger and faced more intense competitive pressures as the twentieth century drew to its close, they moved toward more centralized management structures with more formal departments and lines of responsibility. In many firms, the managing partner and executive committee assumed greater authority for making decisions that the full roster of partners had previously made. Firms began to hire professional nonlawyer managers in high-level positions. They often added another layer of management by creating a larger number of practice groups and departments to handle increasingly specialized work.

Firms' greater reliance on centralized management and more formal organizational features arose in response to loosening, informal norms and weakening peer control. As firms eventually dismantled various discriminatory hiring practices, their lawyers no longer came from a relatively homogeneous, narrow segment of society with a common outlook and experience. In addition, increasing specialization meant that larger numbers of lawyers focused on narrower areas of the law, with less common ground with colleagues who might serve as the basis for informal guidance and review of their work. As an active lateral market arose, lawyers within firms increasingly worked with other lawyers who had grown up in different professional cultures. Firms also moved from general partnerships to limited liability partnerships, which meant that each partner was responsible only for his own actions and those of the lawyers he directly supervised.

At the same time, law firms moved toward promotion and compensation systems that emphasized the need for lawyers to be entrepreneurial in generating revenue. Individual lawyers recognized that their stature and tenure within the firm, as well as their opportunities elsewhere, depended on the book of business they developed. The result was periodic struggles between formal and informal authority systems within firms on a variety of matters, including firm-wide conflict-of-interest policies, the institution of uniform engagement letters, the determination of fees, and the staffing of matters. Many powerful "rainmakers" jealously guarded their authority to set the specific terms of their relationships with clients and often successfully resisted firms' attempts to impose standard policies that would minimize risk to the firm. As one leading scholar put it, "[A] position of managerial authority in the firm . . . will always be subordinate to the power of the lawyers controlling the largest bloc of clients."[95]

For all these reasons, law firms had less assurance that lawyers would exercise discretion in uniform ways and in the interests of the firm. The managerial systems they instituted, however, could only partially compensate for the weakening of shared professional norms. Potentially mobile rainmakers with portable books of business comprised an informal power structure that limited managers' formal authority.[96]

As their relationships with clients loosened in the late twentieth century, law firms were transformed from organizations with substantial firm-specific capital to aggregations of mobile individual capital that could be only imperfectly integrated into the firm. The corporate law firm sought to hold its dynamic parts together with more centralized management, but the practical realities of revenue generation inevitably limited the extent it could do so. As a result, firms became "exquisitely fragile and unstable businesses."[97]

Tax Practice: The Consensus Erodes   Increasing competitive pressures on law firms left their mark on tax practice. As corporate clients began to devote more attention to managing their taxes like other costs, the nature of what they asked of tax advisors began to change. They began to seek out transactions that took advantage of various provisions in the tax code to reduce taxes, only afterward formulating plausible business purposes for the transactions that might pass muster with the IRS. If lawyers in elite firms failed to give their blessing to a transaction, clients were prepared to shop around to find a lawyer who would. With increasing competition in the market for legal services, the number of lawyers and law firms that were willing to provide an opinion in support of aggressive transactions began to grow. This in turn placed pressure even on lawyers in elite firms, who knew that they were losing business to other firms who were ready to stray from the consensus that had earlier guided the tax bar.

Accounting firms posed an even more significant competitive threat. As they moved more aggressively into tax and consulting services, accounting firms began to increase their market share of tax work at the expense of law firms. By 2001, a tax scholar would write, "Tax work is now much more likely to go to an accountant than a lawyer."[98] The orientation in accounting to focus on rules rather than standards made accounting firms receptive to client demand for designing transactions that would reduce taxes by virtue of their compliance with the literal terms of the Internal Revenue Code. Accountants' professional training tended to make them less burdened than lawyers by concerns about statutory purpose or spirit, an approach reinforced by, as Tanina Rostain put it, "a fundamental lack of fit between the core concepts of accountancy and their counterparts in tax law." Methods of computing taxable and financial income increasingly diverged since inception of the income tax, "as tax concepts developed to further social and political goals that were foreign to accountancy's aim of measuring income."[99]

Accounting firms competed with law firms not only for clients but also for lawyers. They began recruiting heavily at law schools, increasing salaries to make themselves more competitive. They also began to lure away partners from major law firms, with the promise of higher compensation and a client base and organizational infrastructure that made it unnecessary for lawyers to generate business on their own. Vice chairman John Lanning of KPMG wrote in 1999 that the firm hired 175 professionals with law degrees in the previous year, more than a hundred of them right out of law school. Lanning declared that "the commitment of the firm to our new law school hires is seen in the firm's $125 million annual budget for training and orientation programs."[100] Even more striking was an arrangement in which Ernst & Young lured three prominent tax partners away from King & Spalding in 1999 to establish a new law firm, McKee Nelson Ernst & Young, that received financial backing and shared office space with the accounting firm in Washington, D.C.[101]

The complexity of the new wave of tax shelters meant that promoters such as accounting firms needed to enlist the services of members of the elite tax bar. Their pitch to many lawyers with respect to tax shelter work was that tax law was starting to focus on products rather than particular solutions crafted for individual clients and that clients were migrating to large global firms that could provide one-stop shopping for legal, tax, financial, and business advice. In addition, lawyers could avoid increasing client resistance to hourly billing by moving to a practice in which they were compensated based on a percentage of the tax savings that they achieved for clients. Lawyers who failed to heed these trends, they warned, were going to be left behind in the emerging new economics of tax practice.

To the extent that lawyers were inclined at the turn of the century to respond to these competitive pressures by being more receptive to client demands for tax reduction transactions, they could invoke the increasing authority of textualism—in applying a statute, focusing on its terms rather than its underlying purpose—as an interpretive method in law in general and in tax law in particular. In the words of one proponent "strict statutory construction is crucial to achieving the Rule of Law" because it achieves "equality, uniformity, and predictability."[102] In tax law, the elite of the bar had begun their careers when tax law had fewer rules and practitioners could be generalists. This made them comfortable with looking to standards rather than simply rules as sources of authority. In addition, as tax scholar Joseph Bankman observed, "[t]his group attended law school at a time during which textualism was associated with long-vanquished formalism."[103] By contrast, with the resurgence in the academy of strict constructionism, the new generation of tax specialists had imbibed more of a textualist orientation in law school than their predecessors. In addition, junior tax lawyers came into practice when the law had become more specialized and structured around rules. These lawyers confronted the need to "learn and explain rules which their more senior partners hoped to retire without mastering."[104]

As a result of this trend, junior lawyers were more skeptical of judicial doctrines based on contextual standards such as business purpose or economic substance that did not rely on the literal words of legal texts. This trend was reflected in practitioners' attitudes to *ACM Partnership v. Commissioner* (1998), which disallowed claimed tax benefits from a transaction even though the transaction complied with the literal terms of the tax code. As Bankman noted in 2001, "[v]irtually everyone I've ever heard from or spoken with over the age of 60 supports the government's position in such cases. The level of support drops directly, and dramatically, with age."[105] One prominent practitioner and former government tax official noted that when he started practicing law in the 1960s he "really believed that the tax law was a coherent set of rules to help people who were doing real investing—who were working in real business transactions—to decide how to report those transactions for purposes of determining the amount of tax they had to pay." In the late 1990s, he observed, "you've got a group of people that believes it's just a bunch of rules and if you can figure out a way to satisfy the rules then you can let the rules drive the transaction. [They think] you can sit in your office and read the rules and come up with ways to do things and then go out and convince people to do them, and that's okay."

By the end of the twentieth century, two trends in law practice had converged. The first was intensifying competition that led law firm leaders to believe that growth and continuously higher profits per partner were necessary for survival. In this quest, firms coveted high-value services for which the firm could charge a premium fee untethered from hourly rates. The second trend was the erosion of a consensus about the norms of tax practice and the emergence of a division within the elite tax bar concerning where to draw the line between aggressive and improper tax advice. This trend had important implications for judgments about the difference between legitimate and abusive tax shelters.

At this time several forces and events combined that would result in an explosion of abusive tax shelter activity. Monitoring tax shelters was not a priority for the IRS, which was preoccupied with responding to the withering criticism that it had received on Capitol Hill in 1997. Corporate and individual taxpayer demand for shelters increased, while competitive pressures gave professional organizations strong incentives to invest in developing shelters that relied on the interaction of complex financial instruments to eliminate or reduce taxes. These organizations played a crucial role in the wave of abusive tax shelters unleashed in the first years of the new century.

Part II

Accounting Firms

4

The Skunk Works

The emergence of KPMG paralleled that of the other major accounting firms. Its predecessor firm, Peat Marwick, was founded in 1911 and specialized in providing audit and tax services to banking and financial institutions. During the 1950s, the firm was the most aggressive and innovative of the Big Eight, emerging as the largest and highest grossing accounting firm in the United States.[1] The firm grew by rapidly buying up small firms and expanding its consulting services. In 1987, Peat Marwick joined forces with a second-tier firm to become KPMG Peat Marwick, at the time the biggest accounting firm in the world.[2] This was the first in a series of consolidations that turned the Big Eight into the Big Six by the late 1990s.[3] (The merger between Price Waterhouse and Coopers & Lybrand in 1998 then brought the number down to five; Arthur Andersen's bankruptcy in 2001, to four.) Over the next ten years, tax services continued to expand at KPMG.[4]

During most of its history, the firm had been organized according to different geographic areas. Under this structure, tax professionals in a particular office reported to the tax partner in charge of that office, who in turn reported to a tax partner higher up in the organizational hierarchy. In the early 1990s, the firm was reorganized along industry groups. After the reorganization, tax professionals reported to tax partners within their industry group. The reorganization increased each group's capacity and incentives to develop specialized services to suit the needs of clients in particular sectors. It also facilitated the capacity to cross-sell services and products through audit services that served the same industry. The reorganization gave rise to new performance measures under which revenue goals were established for different industry groups. Revenue targets had earlier been deemphasized, but now became an important focus of the tax practice.[5] With the shift to industry groups, a tax professional's compensation benefits and advancement became tied to the success of his or her group.

In the 1990s, tax leaders at the firm also began to rethink their fee structure. Like corporate law firms, accounting firms had traditionally charged for their services based on a billable hour. At some point in the 1990s, partners at KPMG became aware that competing firms had moved to value-based fees, typically calculated as a percentage of the tax savings obtained. This move could significantly increase the revenue potential of accounting firms.[6] Under the leadership of John Lanning, who was named head of Operations Tax Services in 1996 and vice chair of Tax Services in early 1998, the firm began to emphasize designing tax products that could be sold to numerous similarly situated clients and priced on this basis. Jeff Stein, the partner in charge of International Tax Services and next in line to become vice chair after Lanning retired, was an equally enthusiastic proponent of generating fees by focusing on tax products.

"A Brilliant Tax Strategy"[7]

The tax product bug caught on quickly at KPMG. Spearheaded by partners in the Washington National Tax (WNT) office, the firm's technical headquarters and think tank, several colleagues formed a group they called the "Skunk Works."[8] The group drew its name from the original Lockheed Corporation Skunk Works, which worked secretly to develop stealth fighter planes to deploy against the Axis powers during World War II.[9] Members of KPMG's Skunk Works met informally every few months to discuss ideas for tax strategies that would reduce or completely eliminate their clients' tax liability.[10] As tax scholar Calvin Johnson notes, "A 'skunk works' operation was once a secret research lab for developing planes to defeat the Nazis and the Communists. The KPMG tax skunk works dreamed up transactions against our United States."[11]

One tax stratagem that seized the group's imagination involved a transaction designed by Seagram and Dupont, two Fortune 500 multinational companies, that had generated considerable attention a few years earlier. In April 1995, Seagram needed cash because it wanted to acquire MCA, Inc., a media company valued at several billion dollars. A source of potential cash was about 160 million shares of Dupont that Seagram owned, which Dupont was interested in buying back. If the transaction was treated as a sale, however, the proceeds would be taxable at a 35 percent rate. Seagram's tax advisors designed a sophisticated transaction under which Seagram could, for tax purposes, treat the proceeds as the distribution of a dividend by Dupont. As a result, the proceeds of the transaction were taxed at an effective tax rate of 7 percent.

This aggressive tax avoidance transaction saved Seagram more than $1 billion in taxes and was widely reported in the business and tax press.[12] The transaction was the subject of heated debate in the tax bar, with several observers concluding that the tax savings, which were premised on a literal reading of the statutes and regulations, were legitimate. Shortly after the transaction became public, Congress amended the tax provision on which the tax benefits were premised.[13]

The KPMG Skunk Works members became excited when they read about the Dupont-Seagram strategy. By taking advantage of the interaction of two provisions of the Internal Revenue Code, Seagram's ingenious transaction made a very substantial capital gain all but disappear for tax purposes. In 1995 Stan Wiseberg, a partner in KPMG's WNT office, expert in corporate reorganizations, and convener of the Skunk Works, held freewheeling discussion sessions to develop a transaction that would take advantage of some of the same regulations to convert taxable into nontaxable gains.[14] Several other WNT partners were active participants, including Joel Resnick, considered an elder statesman in the office, and Richard Smith, a partnership tax specialist who had been recruited from the IRS earlier that year.[15] Another regular attendee was John Larson, a manager in KPMG's San Francisco office and member of the International Services practice.

Shortly after the group began discussing a strategy based on the Seagram-Dupont ploy, Larson ran into David Lippman and Michael Schwartz, two other members of the International Services practice, at an internal KPMG tax conference. Lippman and Schwartz worked from KPMG's New York office, where some of the most technically sophisticated tax professionals at the firm outside of WNT were located. In the course of their cocktail party conversation at the conference, Larson explained the idea for the strategy to Lippman and Schwartz. As the three colleagues spoke, they realized that the strategy might have huge potential. After the conference, the three continued to exchange ideas and drafts. Robert

Pfaff, a partner in the Denver office and occasional participant in the Skunk Works, also began to provide regular suggestions and feedback.

The transaction designed by Lippman, Schwartz, and Larson exploited the same tax regulations as the Seagram-Dupont deal. The goal of the KPMG strategy, however, was not to structure an actual sale to minimize tax effects. Instead, the collaborators' purpose was to design a transaction that created capital losses that an individual taxpayer could use as deductions to offset gains from an unrelated transaction. The target clients were entrepreneurs who had a one-time gain from the sale of their business and needed a loss to shelter that gain from taxation. In the mid-1990s, many business owners in the San Francisco, Denver, and New York areas fit this description. The goal of the transaction was to create a large artificial loss.

The strategy was intended to exploit a rule that applies in what are termed "incomplete redemptions." This rule, reflected in a Treasury regulation, states that if an amount received in a redemption is treated as a dividend (as opposed to the proceeds of a sale) then "a proper adjustment of the basis of the remaining stock will be made."[16] The fundamental idea underlying this rule was that when the sale of stock back to the company is deemed to be a dividend distribution, the seller of the stock should not lose all of his or her basis in it—that is, the amount paid for the stock at purchase that would be deducted from the proceeds of the sale to determine taxable gain if the transaction were treated as a sale. In this way, the basis is shifted to any remaining stock owned by the shareholder.

A second set of rules provides that a party is entitled to this shift in basis can apply it to any property held by a "related party." The Seagram-Dupont transaction partly relied on these rules. The rationale underlying these rules is that property held by related parties is attributed to both. Thus, for instance, a wife's ownership of stock is attributed to her husband and vice versa. If one spouse has no stock to which to apply the basis, the basis can be applied to the stock of the other spouse.

Under the transaction designed by the Skunk Works team, the taxpayer who was seeking the loss would purportedly be able to take advantage of the basis shifted from a related party—in this case a foreign corporation. It was essential that the corporation not be subject to taxation either in the United States or in the country where it was incorporated. The strategy involved setting up a shell company incorporated in the Cayman

Islands, a tax haven. The transaction was designed so that the basis that shifted to the taxpayer was the same amount as the loss she wanted to claim. That way, when the transaction was unwound, the taxpayer could claim a loss equivalent to the adjusted basis, which could be used to offset capital gains.

The Foreign Leveraged Investment Program or FLIP, as it came to be known, worked something like this: Assume the client had a $100 million gain she wanted to shelter. The shelter's promoters would set up a corporation in the Cayman Islands; call it Cayman. The client would buy options to purchase 85 percent of Cayman at a premium. This payment was the mechanism through which the taxpayer paid her fees for the transaction, which were set at 7 percent of the tax loss desired. Having purchased these options, the client and Cayman were now "related": The client was deemed to own Cayman under the ownership attribution rules in Section 318 of the Code—just as Seagram was deemed to own a part of Dupont by virtue of continuing to hold warrants to purchase Dupont stock after the Dupont stock redemption. Next, Cayman bought $100 million worth of a foreign bank stock, which it purchased with $100 million borrowed from that same bank. Meanwhile, the client bought a modest amount of the foreign bank stock.

The next steps were a little more complicated. The foreign bank redeemed its stock from Cayman at the same time that the client bought options to purchase the equivalent number of shares in the bank. Cayman used the proceeds of the redemption to pay back the foreign bank. In actuality, while there were ledger entries to indicate that the foreign bank loaned the money for the original stock sale to Cayman, the money never left the bank. Since Cayman and the client were supposedly related, the client's options to purchase were constructively owned by Cayman. Cayman therefore had no reduction of its ownership interest in the foreign bank—just as Seagram's ownership of warrants to buy Dupont prevented a reduction of its ownership interest in Dupont. And just as Dupont's redemption of Seagram's shares was treated as a dividend distribution to which no basis attached, so the foreign bank's redemption of its shares was, supposedly, a dividend distribution to Cayman. Cayman was not especially concerned that the dividends would be taxable under U.S. law since the company was not subject to U.S. law, nor, for that matter, to tax laws in its home jurisdiction.

Having had all its shares redeemed by the foreign bank, Cayman had no remaining shares that could be adjusted to reflect the $100 million basis of the shares that were redeemed. The taxpayer, however, still had a small number of foreign bank shares. As a party related to Cayman, the taxpayer could apply that basis to these shares. In other words, the basis in the tiny amount of foreign bank stock that had been purchased was adjusted by $100 million. Now all the client needed to do was sell these shares at market price, and—voila—under a literal reading of the rules, the taxpayer could claim a $100 million loss. At the 1998 capital gains rate of 20 percent, the transaction according to its promoters enabled the client to avoid $20 million in taxes.

When the transaction finally came to light years later, tax scholars who reviewed it doubted that it met the technical requirements of the applicable tax provisions. The transaction was also invalid under several equitable doctrines, including the step transaction doctrine. Under this judicial doctrine, courts can determine the tax implications of a transaction by collapsing and then ignoring interim steps. As Johnson explains, "If we collapse the steps between [the foreign bank] and Cayman, there is no borrowing, no purchase of stock, and no redemption and repayment, only the $100 million staying in the [foreign bank] vaults. Nothing rode on the Cayman purchase and sale back of foreign bank stock, except the generation of a claimed $100 million loss that didn't really happen."[17]

The transaction, in addition, lacked economic substance. Although its developers tried to camouflage the absence of economic reality by adding a series of trading maneuvers, at bottom, the taxpayer did not have a "reasonable expectation" of pretax profit. Cayman typically held its foreign bank shares for two months. Having paid 7 percent for its options to buy Cayman, the taxpayer would have had to reap an annual return greater than 150 percent—not impossible, but certainly not reasonable to expect either.[18] Unlike the Seagram-Dupont arrangement, the only reason for entering into the transaction was to generate a tax loss.

FLIP Goes to Market

As Lippman, Schwartz, and Larson developed the transaction, they realized they needed an investment advisory company to execute the steps of the transaction and bring in a bank to provide the loan. In May 1996, Larson got in touch with Jeff Greenstein, the principal of Quadra

Investment, whom he knew had contacts at Union Bank of Switzerland (UBS). Greenstein was soon on board and a few months later approached the bank about participating in the transaction.

During the spring, the FLIP team also realized that a concurring opinion from an outside law firm would strengthen the marketability of their product. Bob Pfaff thought of R. J. Ruble, a young tax partner at the law firm Brown & Wood, whom he had heard give a talk. Beginning in the late 1990s, Ruble was a featured speaker at prestigious Practicing Law Institute lectures on the ethics of corporate tax lawyers. Tax professionals in the New York area regularly attended these sessions to comply with statewide bar requirements for continuing education in ethics. A self-described "tax shelter lawyer," Ruble argued in one lecture that a tax lawyer's responsibility in advising a client was solely to further the client's interests. Tax lawyers, he insisted, had no separate obligation to the tax system. Decrying the "shrillness" of the public response to the tax shelter problem, Ruble reminded his audience that the tax system was an "adversary system." Whatever problem existed, he contended, was the government's fault for having drafted too many rules. "If we are able to use these rules to our clients' benefit and the government's detriment, we are merely doing our job," he concluded.[19] Pfaff liked Ruble's approach.

Ruble discussed the strategy with Pfaff and the KPMG team and agreed to provide a concurring "independent" legal opinion to clients who purchased FLIP. He also began providing suggestions on the opinion letter the firm was drafting, that is, effectively writing the draft himself. Over the next year, he established an alliance between his firm and the tax products group at KPMG to "jointly develop and market tax products and jointly share in the fees."[20] He also worked out an agreement with KPMG so that every time Brown & Wood's name was mentioned during a sales pitch, the firm would earn a $50,000 fee regardless of whether it had provided an opinion letter in connection with the transaction.[21]

By fall 1996, KPMG had finalized a draft opinion letter concluding that FLIP, if challenged by the IRS, would "more likely than not" be upheld in court. Schwartz and other KPMG colleagues began to introduce clients to the strategy.[22] The shelter's designers also prepared a "pitch" book, entitled "Generating Capital Losses," which explained the steps of the transaction.[23] FLIP was priced at 7 percent of the anticipated tax savings and was intended to be marketed to clients who were seeking a minimum $10 million loss.

The Perez brothers, from McAllen, Texas, were early purchasers of FLIP. Sons of migrant workers, the three brothers had developed a successful business providing ambulatory health services which they planned to sell to a large corporation. As they were finalizing the sale, they were contacted by a line partner in KPMG's Dallas office. This partner had no prior contact with the family, but had obtained the Perez name from an advisor to the brothers who was subsequently paid a large finder's fee. When they first heard about the strategy, the Perez brothers asked to consult with their lawyer, but were told that the strategy was proprietary. In a pattern that was repeated in subsequent FLIP cases, they were asked to—and did—sign a confidentiality agreement. They were also told that the strategy was legal and would not be audited by the IRS. As they discussed the strategy among themselves, one of the brothers observed: "I guess that's how rich people do it." Overcoming their initial reservations, the Perez brothers purchased the strategy.

The Perez transaction was not the only FLIP case where methods such as finder's fees were used that raised questions about the independence of the advisors involved. First Union Bank, based in North Carolina, entered into an agreement with KPMG under which the bank provided marketing assistance for the firm's tax products and earned $100,000 for each client referred. The close relationship that developed between the bank and the accounting firm mirrored the relationship between Carolyn Branan, a partner in KPMG's Charlotte office and an enthusiastic promoter of FLIP,[24] and her husband, Ralph Lovejoy, who managed First Union's Personal Financial Consulting Group. Neither Lovejoy nor Branan thought it necessary to inform clients of their personal connection, even though it might have raised a question about whether either was able to provide independent advice to the clients they shared.

With revenue from the first half dozen FLIP transactions flowing in, KPMG tax leaders began to appreciate the enormous profit potential of charging value-added fees for commoditized tax strategies to wealthy individuals. At the same time, they recognized that the tax product sales process was disorganized.[25] Line partners were using different versions of a client engagement letter, which did little to protect the firm against being sued if the strategy went bad. Occasionally too the strategy was implemented in a manner that made it difficult for the taxpayer to claim any tax benefits.[26]

Recognizing that lack of centralization and organization could put the firm at significant legal risk, Lanning, the firm's head of Tax Services Operations, created a new Department of Professional Practice for Tax (DPP) in February 1997.[27] Although such departments already existed in consulting and attest services, no firm-wide compliance and risk management system existed for tax strategies. Lanning asked Richard ("Larry") DeLap to head the department. DeLap, who was based in Silicon Valley, had developed expertise in the taxation of technology start-ups and was the national partner in charge of the firm's tax practice for high-tech companies after the firm's reorganization in 1993. Within the firm, DeLap had a reputation as a thoughtful and independent professional. Although the newly created DPP was located in the WNT office in Washington, D.C., Lanning agreed to let DeLap run the group from KPMG's Silicon Valley office.

The DPP's first order of business was to review the draft opinion letter for FLIP, which had never been formally vetted by an independent group inside KPMG. The need for review was all the more pressing because in March of that year, the U.S. Tax Court issued a very important decision exhibiting newfound skepticism about tax shelters. In *ACM Partnership v. Commissioner*, the Tax Court in 1997 set aside a complex series of transactions engaged in by Colgate Palmolive to create a $98 million tax loss.[28] In ruling against the company, the court revived the business purpose doctrine, which in recent years had been somnambulant. Because the court concluded that there was no genuine business purpose served by the transactions other than to reduce taxes, it disallowed Colgate Palmolive's claimed loss.

DeLap requested several tax partners by email to evaluate the technical merits of the strategy as well as how it was being marketed.[29] During a conference call in early April, the review group concluded that the firm could continue to market FLIP despite the *ACM* decision, but requested Pfaff and Larson to "beef up" the opinion letter. During the following months, DeLap tried to impose some modicum of order on the marketing and implementation process, insisting that line partners who were selling FLIP not deviate from the approved form letters, obtain appropriate waivers of liability from clients, and make sure to obtain signed engagement letters from clients before implementation.[30] All of these procedures were intended to protect the firm in what was recognized as "clearly a high-risk practice."[31]

DeLap's appointment to head the newly created DPP coincided with firm-wide efforts to emphasize products over individualized services. Under Lanning's leadership, the firm committed significant resources to designing and marketing generic tax "solutions."[32] Eager to become the industry leader in this area, the firm established the Tax Innovation Center (TIC) inside the KPMG WNT office, the technical support center for its tax services nationwide. The TIC was charged with encouraging tax professionals throughout the firm to submit ideas for new tax strategies and shepherding the more promising ideas through the development process. To this end, the TIC awarded "light bulb" prizes—specially designed paperweights—and cash prizes to tax professionals who submitted ideas that were developed successfully.[33] To disseminate information about new tax products across the firm, the TIC regularly issued Tax Product Alerts that explained the new product, its "target" audience, its pricing structure, and the steps to be taken to deliver it. The notice also included access to a product "tool kit" that contained sample letters, a sample product, and a client "Q &A" that anticipated questions a prospective client might ask.

An early Tax Product Alert even went so far as to propose selling more-likely-than-not opinions as products to clients who were contemplating transactions that might be challenged as tax shelters. The 1997 Taxpayer Relief Act expanded the definition of tax shelters subject to underpayment penalties, but preserved a safe harbor for taxpayers who had reasonably relied on the well-reasoned opinion of a tax advisor in entering the transaction. With the broadening of potential taxpayer liability, the TIC apparently saw a new marketing opportunity. "Because of the tax law change," it underscored, "this product potentially has a huge market and can generate high margin (and in many cases large fee) engagements when priced on a value-added fixed-fee basis." Potential targets for the product were clients who planned to engage in transactions with "significant federal tax risk." As a fee, the Tax Product Alert suggested 10 percent of the penalty exposure that the opinions purportedly prevented from being assessed.[34]

To enhance its tax products focus, the firm engaged in a lawyer-hiring spree, recruiting aggressively at law schools and attracting partners away from traditional corporate law practices with multimillion-dollar deals.[35] One ad that ran in the *ABA Journal* depicted a rock climber rappelling down a sheer cliff face. In bold letters, it urged tax lawyers "to choose their own path" "in a changing landscape." Clearly intended to lure young tax associates from traditional—read "staid"—corporate practice, the advertisement promised exciting work at the firm's WNT office working alongside the "nation's leading tax authorities." It also offered the opportunity to work with the TIC, "ground zero for the identification, analysis, packaging and distribution of new high-growth tax products and services."[36] In 1999, John Lanning, vice chair of Tax Services, a position that put him directly below the firm's chair, applauded the firm's success in recruiting tax lawyers, noting that the firm had hired 175 professionals with law degrees in the previous year, more than half of them right out of law school.[37]

To obtain greater penetration among current clients and attract new ones, the firm hired a sales force that would focus exclusively on promoting tax products. In December 1998, Lanning announced the firm's new "Tax Sales Organization" which, he predicted, would produce $200 million in revenue by the end of the year. Business Development Managers (BDMs), as they were called, were not recruited based on their tax expertise, but on their substantial sales experience. Paid a base salary and a substantial commission on each product sold, BDMs were expected to "hel[p] create an aggressive sales culture" at the firm.[38] In the same announcement that described the creation of the BDM force, Lanning informed the tax partners that the firm had made a significant investment in telemarketing resources, which would be deployed in connection with products where they could "add significant value.[39]

Moving on to Greener Pastures

By spring 1997, KPMG had sold ten FLIP deals, earning the firm over $6 million in fees. Another four deals with potential fees of $1.5 million were in the works. FLIP's original developers, however, were already moving on to other firms. In early 1997, David Lippman, now going by the last name Smith, left KPMG for Quadra, the "investment advisory" firm involved in implementing FLIP. (He was soon joined by Larry Scheinfeld, another tax partner at KPMG, and Ralph Lovejoy, who had been at First Union.)[40] Schwartz, in the meantime, moved over to the accounting firm Coopers & Lybrand, the predecessor firm to PricewaterhouseCoopers. Smith and Schwartz may have left because they felt that the bureaucratization of the tax product process at KPMG stifled their creativity; perhaps they also had personality conflicts with Pfaff and Larson, who insisted on being present at every sales presentation and were very secretive about the financial aspects of FLIP.[41] Smith and Schwartz were also probably in search of higher income—the management fees paid to investment advisory firms implementing shelters were more than double those earned by KPMG, and the firms were much smaller. Shortly after their departure, Smith and Schwartz began to market a version of FLIP with Coopers & Lybrand and, after the merger with Price Waterhouse, with PricewaterhouseCoopers (PwC), ultimately closing approximately fifty FLIP transactions. Back at KPMG, Larson and Pfaff believed that the strategy was proprietary to the firm and that it had been stolen.

Soon Pfaff and Larson also left KPMG. Although they had no professional investment expertise, they formed their own investment advisory firm under the name "Presidio" whose principal—if not sole—purpose was to collaborate in designing and implementing tax shelters with the tax shelter group at KPMG. Pfaff and Larson anticipated a lucrative long-term relationship between the two firms. Pfaff enjoyed a close friendship with Lanning, dating back to their time together in KPMG's Denver office. In KPMG, Lanning was known for his confrontational management style, said to reflect his time at the United States Naval Academy. Years earlier, Pfaff became friends with Jeff Stein when they both worked in KPMG's Paris office, providing tax services to wealthy American expats living in Europe. Stein, a self-confident and abrasive figure—who in the words of one colleague would "sell his mother for the bottom line"—would soon be succeeding Lanning to head KPMG's tax practice and was putting his full weight behind the firm's efforts to expand its tax product activities.

To ensure that the process inside the firm progressed smoothly, Pfaff sent Lanning and Stein a lengthy memo setting forth his vision for KPMG's Tax Advantaged Transaction practice, as the tax shelter group was known, and its relationship going forward with Presidio. According to Pfaff, the goal was to create a "true" turnkey product—a tax solution that worked directly out of the box—on which the firms could earn royalties on sale. To succeed in this endeavor, KPMG needed to forge alliances with the international banking and leasing communities and the small number of law firms that were "skilled and respected in this area." Pfaff expected that KPMG's highly respected name would open the necessary doors.

Pfaff noted that marketing tax shelters had become more problematic with the U.S. Tax Court decision in *ACM* because the firm could no longer "openly market" the tax results of an investment.[42] Pfaff's takeaway from the opinion was that KPMG had to develop a stealth approach to sales, in which the firm publicly insisted that any tax-advantaged product was an investment opportunity and privately told clients that the real point was tax elimination.

To increase consistency in client engagements and product implementation, Pfaff urged KPMG's tax leaders to entrust sales and implementation to a handful of tax experts who had the aptitude and interest for tax-advantaged products. "The ideal candidate," he said, "would be someone who knows the product cold, is flexible, decisive, and has reasonably good sales skills." Although going with "technicians" was advisable, it was important that "he or she not be a 'waffler.'" Pfaff identified the KPMG colleagues who had developed experience with FLIP. He also encouraged the tax leaders to rely on a few tax partners—Gregg Ritchie in the L.A. office and Gary Powell in the Denver office—who had proven especially talented at identifying target markets and gaining entry.

Going forward, Pfaff emphasized, he "strongly desire[d] a close relationship with KPMG." Although a formal alliance would be "subject to scrutiny," presumably because the two firms would not be able to maintain a facade of independence if the government investigated, Pfaff was eager to enter into an arrangement under which Presidio gave KPMG a right of first refusal on products it had in development in exchange for preferred provider status at KPMG. Pfaff was tempted to recommend that KPMG sever its tie with Quadra in light of the latter's "open and notorious relationship" with Coopers & Lybrand, but thought the more prudent course was to continue to work with them since Quadra's cooperation would be needed to complete transactions already in the works and to maintain a united front in the event of an IRS investigation. In any ongoing relationship, however, KPMG had to obtain assurances that its "intellectual capital" was not "pipelined directly to C & L." Pfaff made clear too that Presidio would be loyal to KPMG in exchange for favored treatment. Special treatment would also be extended to Deutsche Bank, with whom Pfaff had begun to forge relations in the previous months. Pfaff's hope was to eliminate involvement by UBS and Quadra, the latter of which had brought the former to the table.[43] Shortly after Pfaff distributed his memo, the Tax Advantaged Transactions group started to rely on Presidio and Deutsche Bank to implement FLIP. DeLap, and the DPP review committee, which had also received Pfaff's memo proposing a special relationship, had no objection.[44]

A "Goldman-Sachs"-Type Practice

Upon their departure, Pfaff and Larson encouraged Lanning to put Gregg Ritchie in charge of the FLIP strategy.[45] Ritchie, a line partner in KPMG's Los Angeles office, saw great revenue potential among the technology entrepreneurs who were striking it rich in California's dot-com boom. Ritchie had sold the first few FLIP deals in early 1997 and was enthusiastic about the strategy. Ritchie was also a bulldog who was going to fight to make sure that FLIP and any successor strategies would survive the approval process and get to market. In Ritchie's own words, he was "more aggressive than most people in the firm about defending my positions and trying to become an advocate for interesting and creative ideas."[46] Not surprisingly, he was very successful at sales. Ritchie's go-getter attitude and his considerable marketing skills had been well rewarded and led to his quick rise in the firm.[47] Ritchie thought FLIP was "brilliant" and took on the assignment of overseeing its distribution with gusto.[48]

In the fall, Ritchie launched a new group inside the Personal Financial Planning (PFP) practice, Capital Transaction Strategies or "CaTS" whose assignment was to sell FLIP around the country.[49] He enlisted the participation of various PFP members around the country, including Randy Bickham, an income tax specialist in the Palo Alto office, who soon became an eager collaborator on developing and marketing strategies. Doug Ammerman, the partner in charge of the PFP services had set a $4 million revenue goal for the CaTS group for fiscal year 1998. With FLIP just beginning to generate revenue and delays with obtaining approval for another product in the group's inventory, Ritchie was concerned that it would be a "significant stretch" to achieve this revenue target.[50]

Ritchie also set about formalizing relations with Presidio and Quadra. He controlled the sales process to ensure that only CaTS members had access to the strategies his group sold. During preliminary planning meanings, he instructed his sales team to present only on a white board and never leave documents with clients. In addition, he insisted that clients should be strongly discouraged from consulting with their legal advisors when they were deciding to purchase FLIP. Ritchie was concerned that the strategy would get into the wrong hands—the hands of someone inside KPMG who would not "understand" the strategy or of someone outside the firm, such as a competitor or perhaps the government.[51]

Prior to leaving KPMG in the summer of 1997, Larson had planned to finish all of the outstanding opinion letters on FLIP, but some number remained unfinished. The task of finalizing them fell principally to Bob Simon, a new partner in the International Services group in the Denver office who had joined KPMG from a corporate law firm. Pfaff, who had also been in the Denver office, apparently recruited Simon to the firm, and Simon inherited Pfaff's reputation for technical know-how.

When Simon first saw the draft opinion for FLIP, he raised questions about the letter itself and about how the strategy was being executed. Many of his concerns focused on whether the transaction had sufficient economic substance. In particular, he was concerned about whether the Cayman entity was more than a "paper company." He also believed that the taxpayer's property interest in that entity was not adequate to justify the basis shift and that the foreign bank should bear some economic risk in the transaction.[52]

Ritchie, for his part, was not especially concerned about the legal weaknesses of the strategy in particular—the fact that its purpose as a tax loss generator was barely disguised. He did not see a meaningful difference between the Dupont-Seagram transaction and FLIP, and wanted to make sure that the strategy had sufficient window dressing so as not to be detected by the IRS on audit.[53] As far as Ritchie was concerned, if the firm could conclude that a taxpayer had "50.00001%" likelihood of prevailing in court, that was enough to issue a more-likely-than-not opinion and market the strategy.[54]

While not worried about the legal merits, Ritchie was annoyed at Simon's meddling. To Ritchie, who was trying to keep sales going at a brisk pace, Simon's suggestions were obstructionist. To make matters worse, Larry DeLap, the head of the Department of Professional Practice, took Simon's views seriously.

The conflict came to a head around whether FLIP needed to be registered with the IRS. The 1997 Taxpayer Relief Act had strengthened legislation, dating back to 1986, that required transactions that met certain characteristics to be registered with the IRS so that the agency could examine them to determine whether or not they were abusive transactions.

Promoters who failed to register transactions meeting the legislative definition of a shelter were subject to penalties. Simon first raised the issue of whether FLIP had to be registered at a meeting during the fall. Until Simon asked about the registration requirements, no one had thought to look at them. Simon's question threw the FLIP team for a loop. Ritchie was clear that registering the strategy would not be in the "clients' best interest."[55]

As of fall 1997, the Treasury had not issued regulations dealing with the new registration requirements under its authority pursuant to the Taxpayer Relief Act. Simon nevertheless had substantial concerns that FLIP met the definition of a shelter for purposes of the registration requirement that had been in effect since the late 1980s.[56] After some back and forth, DeLap concluded that KPMG was not required to register FLIP. But in mid-November, he instructed the CaTS team to cease marketing FLIP immediately. Ritchie was none too pleased that the "new kid on the block," as he called Simon, had persuaded DeLap to halt FLIP.[57] All told, KPMG sold FLIP to eighty clients, earning approximately $17 million in fees.[58] FLIP generated $1.9 billion in tax losses.[59]

The CaTS team's experience with FLIP demonstrated a significant demand for tax elimination strategies. Through their energetic sales efforts, the team had pitched the strategy to a number of clients who were eager to go forward. With the sudden discontinuation of the strategy, Ritchie and his team became concerned that they would not be able to satisfy client interest and would lose out to firms selling similar products. Randy Bickham, an active member of CaTS in the Palo Alto office who worked closely with Ritchie, emphasized:

The existing Foreign Leveraged Investment Strategy product currently has high market demand and we have a backlog of deals. Should we fail to deliver the existing product or a suitable substitute, the CaTs practice will lose the initial market position that has been created with high-wealth individuals to the competition and our commitment to participating in the tax product market will be subject to question by the market and our strategic partners.

If Ritchie and the CaTS team were to aspire to a "Goldman-Sachs"-type practice, Bickham emphasized, "to which high wealth individuals and their advisors [would] immediately look to when liquidating significant portfolio positions," then the group could not be "out-of-stock" when high-wealth customers came calling.[60] Earlier in the fall, a team consisting of Ritchie, Simon, Bickham, Ruble of Brown & Wood, and Larson and Pfaff of Presidio had already begun to brainstorm a new strategy. When DeLap pulled

FLIP off the shelves, "[t]hese discussions took on an air of urgency," Stein, who had been following the process closely, later noted.[61]

Ritchie and the CaTS members thought a new strategy could be developed by altering some of the features of FLIP. Simon, the technical leader of the development team, was skeptical and argued that a number of FLIP's weaknesses recurred in the new strategy under development. Simon believed he could develop a strategy that, based on other rules, was less vulnerable to IRS challenge.

As Simon continued to argue for his own approach, Ritchie became increasingly exasperated that the process was dragging. He also questioned Simon's motivations in bringing up objections and pushing his own strategy. Ritchie suspected that Simon was trying to develop a product that would compete with his. He also believed that Simon wanted a hand in the strategy so that Simon's group, the International Services practice, would get a share of the revenue credits that would come from marketing the new deal—credits that all should go to Ritchie's own group, PFP services. In late fall, he decided that the easiest course of action was to cut Simon out of the process altogether. By December, the development group began to participate in conference calls and meetings without including Simon, and soon developed a prototype for the Offshore Portfolio Investment Strategy (OPIS).[62]

In February 1998, Simon finally got to see OPIS. As he wrote to Ritchie, he thought the strategy failed on both conditions DeLap had set for it: to support a more-likely-than-not level of confidence and be sufficiently different from FLIP that "that we could justify registering the current product (but not FLIP)." Among the nine problems he flagged were that the foreign bank did not incur any economic risk, the deal looked "prewired" from the clients' perspective, and the Internal Revenue Service would use its antiabuse authority to disallow the loss. Simply put, OPIS was "Son of FLIP."

Ritchie would have none of it. As he wrote, "I disagree on your conclusion. We believe we can write a more-likely-than-not and expect DPP to agree." With regard to Simon's argument that the IRS was bound to step in, Ritchie remarked: "As we discussed in our conference call, there is simply nothing else to say on this topic. . . . This . . . is one element of why the strategy is only 'more likely than not.'"[63]

Ritchie was correct in one regard. Even before OPIS was approved for sale, a dispute had broken out as to how the revenue was going to be credited. Intent on making sure the International Services practice would get its fair share, Stein, the partner in charge, circulated several emails about Simon's role in developing the strategy. In one email, titled "Simon says," he listed the many weaknesses Simon had identified in the FLIP strategy. He explained, for example, that Simon was the first to point out that the client had purchased a warrant in the Cayman structure for a "ridiculously high amount of money" and that the warrant "stood out more like a sore thumb since no one in his right mind would pay such an exorbitant price for such a warrant." According to Stein, "[i]n kicking the tires on FLIP (perhaps too hard for the likes of certain people),"[64] Simon had discovered that the redemption of shares by the foreign bank from the Cayman company did not occur at the same time as the purchase of the same number of options in the foreign bank by the client. This put the putative tax benefits from the deal in doubt.

Needling Ritchie, Stein pointed out that he had made "an admission against interest" when he earlier had written Simon that OPIS was developed "in response to your and DPP's concerns over the FLIP strategy." Stein concluded by emphasizing that development of OPIS had been a team effort. "What I thought we are trying to do here was bringing the best minds we had in this Firm together to design the best product to go to market with." If the record was examined carefully, Stein claimed, then International Services was responsible for 80 percent of the OPIS product. For the sake of teamwork and collegiality, Stein was willing to stick with 50/50 and "forget about the Ides of March."[65]

Ritchie was not going to take Stein's email lying down. "The bottom line," he wrote to Stein, Ammerman, and other tax leaders, "is, had we allowed Simon to continue to try to develop the OPIS product, we would not have one. Period." In his opinion, "Jeff's comments in this message are not in line with the facts, are inflammatory, and I hope are not discoverable by the IRS."[66] Ritchie believed that Simon's proposed strategy had simply lost out. As he insisted, "Larry [DeLap] bounced this effort. Clearly Simon was not creative enough." Ritchie went on to try to discount every argument Stein made in his memo, concluding, "the facts are that without the PFP practice, the IS practice would still be moaning about not having a product."[67] By the time OPIS was approved for sale, the two practices had settled their disagreement and decided to share the revenue credits.[68]

Apart from his annoyance at Simon's involvement, Ritchie was frustrated that the process of obtaining approval for OPIS was taking months longer than he had anticipated. One wrinkle was that the banking partner on OPIS, brought in through Larson's contacts, was Deutsche Bank, an audit client of KPMG. Given the rules on auditor independence, DeLap thought it was important to include the Department of Professional Practice Assurance at KPMG to determine how to deal with potential conflicts of interest. KPMG was supposed to be independent of Deutsche Bank, and ethics accounting rules required that the two firms refrain from engaging in certain business relationships. Ritchie was aggravated that DPP Assurance took its time in deciding how to handle potential issues arising out of the relationship with Deutsche Bank and then imposed new rules on the marketing of OPIS. The head of DPP Assurance, for his part, was dismayed with Ritchie's aggressiveness, about which, he underscored, he had "nothing to say."[69]

In late spring, the question of whether OPIS had to be registered with the IRS arose. All along DeLap had assumed that this strategy would be registered. As OPIS was finally nearing approval in May 1998, Ritchie sent Jeffrey Zysik, a manager working under him, to investigate how much attention the IRS would give the strategy if it was registered. Zysik came back with good news. He had checked in with Phil Brand and Richard Smith, two partners who had left high-level positions at the IRS the previous year. They, in turn, had contacted IRS officials to find out whether there was a lot of activity following up on shelter registration. The short answer was "no." Smith had helpfully added that even if the IRS was interested in focusing on registered shelters, it did not have the capacity to match registration forms with partnership returns. There was little downside to registering the shelter.[70]

Despite the signs that the agency would likely not take notice, Ritchie continued strongly to believe that registering OPIS was a bad idea. Putting aside their earlier differences over revenue credits, Ritchie took his case directly to Jeff Stein. Stein, who would soon be promoted to vice chair of Tax Services, would most likely be sympathetic to Ritchie's point of view and knew how to apply appropriate pressure effectively. In a memo, Ritchie set forth the strongest business reasons he could marshal that the firm should not register OPIS, even if it fell within the registration requirements.[71]

As Ritchie explained, his view was based on the "immediate negative impact on the Firm's strategic initiative to develop a sustainable tax products practice and the long-term implications of establishing . . . a precedent in registering such a product." More specifically, Ritchie wrote, "the financial exposure to the Firm" from not registering OPIS was "minimal" since any penalties from noncompliance were much smaller than potential profits. At most, they would represent 14 percent of fees earned. Other promoters were not registering their products, so registering the product would put KPMG at a "severe competitive disadvantage" given "industry norms." In addition, there had been "a lack of enthusiasm on the part of the Service to enforce" the registration provisions. Lastly, Ritchie noted, there was a lack of guidance as to how the registration requirements should be interpreted. All told, he concluded, "the rewards of a successful marketing far exceed the financial exposure to penalties that may arise."[72]

When he read Ritchie's memo, DeLap erupted. In an irate phone call, he explained in no uncertain terms that the firm was not going to decide whether to register OPIS based on economic considerations. Ignoring the registration requirements on this basis could subject individuals or the firm not only to professional sanctions from the IRS but even to criminal liability for engaging in a willful violation of the Treasury's reporting requirements. One did not decide to disobey rules that reflected professional obligations and imposed penalties for intentional noncompliance based on financial considerations. Citing the relevant statute and regulation, DeLap urged Ritchie to look them up. Even after reading them, Ritchie still did not understand DeLap's point. Puzzled, he wrote DeLap that he did not see how the registration requirements implicated the ethics rules or criminal code. Since the registration requirements did not make explicit reference to either, how, he wondered, could failing to register subject someone to ethics or criminal sanctions? DeLap, for his part, recommended that OPIS be registered with the IRS, but was overruled by higher-ups in the tax practice.[73]

In early June 1998, DDP gave its preliminary approval for OPIS to be marketed.[74] When Ritchie announced the decision to the CaTS team, he reminded members that they were not to leave marketing materials with clients because "it will DESTROY any chance [that] the client may have to avoid the step transaction doctrine."[75] As the materials made clear, the purported investment "decisions" were really just prearranged steps with all risk sufficiently hedged and all parties prepared to act as prescribed. On hearing that the strategy was finally approved, Randy Bickham, who had worked closely with Ritchie to obtain approval, was very excited and congratulated him for successfully managing the KPMG organization to get the product to market.[76] Ritchie, for his part, was less sanguine about the firm's prospect for becoming a "Goldman-Sachs"-type practice. The firm, he concluded, was too big, too inflexible, and too set in its ways.[77]

In August 1998, Ritchie left KPMG to work as Chief Financial Officer at Pacific Capital Group, a private equity group founded by Gary Winnick. Along with Ken Lay and Bernie Ebbers, Winnick later emerged as one of the poster children for the accounting ploys that that helped drive the bull market in the late 1990s. Winnick created Global Crossing, a company dedicated to creating a global state-of-the-art fiber optic network and a darling of the stock market during the Internet boon. In 2001, the company went bankrupt amid allegations that it had manipulated its financial results, but not before Winnick salvaged $735 million from his investment. Class actions brought by investors against Winnick and his legal advisors settled for a total of several hundred million dollars, and Winnick narrowly avoided being sanctioned by the SEC.

After Ritchie's departure in August 1998, Jeffrey Eischeid took over direction of the CaTS team. OPIS was marketed through Presidio and Quadra, with Ruble, who had been involved in designing the strategy, providing purportedly "independent" opinion letters. In early December, DeLap sent around an email instructing PFP practice members to discontinue selling OPIS.[78] A threshold number of sales had been met and DeLap was concerned that if a court discovered that so many clients had done the identical transaction, it would find that the steps of the transaction were prewired and disallow its tax benefits.

Despite DeLap's instruction that marketing cease, members of the firm continued to market OPIS through 2000. The momentum behind such a lucrative product was impossible to stop. All told, KPMG sold the strategy to at least 170 wealthy individuals, generating approximately $2.3 billion in claimed tax losses and earning more than $28 million from OPIS.[79]

A Shelter for the Little Guy

In 1998, while it was in the middle of launching OPIS, KPMG became involved in another tax shelter known as Short Options Strategy or SOS. The strategy had come to KPMG's attention via an investment boutique known as Diversified Group Inc. (DGI), which was run by James Haber. At the turn of the century, versions of this strategy were being marketed by Arthur Andersen, Ernst & Young, BDO Seidman, and various law firms and investment advisory boutiques. SOS was one of a family of shelters that later became known as "Son of BOSS" or contingent liability shelters. (Although BOSS, a shelter marketed by PricewaterhouseCoopers, was itself not a contingent liability shelter, and Son of BOSS shelters actually predated BOSS, they acquired this moniker because they came to light after BOSS became public.)

Son of BOSS shelters derived from a shelter that media mogul Ted Turner used to avoid paying taxes when his company went through a reorganization. Although the rules on which Turner relied had subsequently been changed, shelter promoters began to devise strategies based on analogous techniques. Paul Daugerdas was among the first shelter promoters to market these strategies to individuals in 1994 when he was at Arthur Andersen. Emile Pesiri, then a lawyer at Jackson Tufte Cole & Black and a repeat player in the shelter market, provided the opinion letters on Daugerdas's earliest strategies.

Son of BOSS shelters, which became increasingly popular in the late 1990s, were designed around partnerships or other pass-through entities. Under the Internal Revenue Code, the amount and type of a partnership's income is calculated using the partnership entity as the relevant unit but the income is taxed to the individual partners. The partners pay taxes on their share of the taxable income of the partnership even if no funds have been distributed to them by the partnership. In the same vein, the partners can deduct a share of their losses incurred by the partnership against any capital gains they earn. These gains do not have to be related to partnership activities.

Generally, the tax code allows a taxpayer to subtract certain costs of acquiring an asset in determining whether a taxpayer has incurred taxable gains on its disposition. These adjusted costs are the asset's basis. On the one hand, if the sale price of an asset exceeds its basis, the difference between the two is treated as a taxable gain. If, on the other hand, basis exceeds sale price, the taxpayer has a loss that can be deducted against other capital gains. The Son of BOSS shelters all involved transactions designed to increase a taxpayer's basis in an asset, while avoiding rules that otherwise would operate to reduce the basis. The effect was to generate a loss for tax purposes when the taxpayer sold an asset for less than the amount of the basis—even though the taxpayer suffered no economic loss anywhere near the loss that she claimed for tax purposes.

These shelters created a tax loss without an equivalent economic loss by relying on how different liabilities are treated under the partnership rules. In the case of debt, the partnership rules are straightforward. When a partnership assumes a liability, each partner's basis—adjusted costs—is increased proportionate to his (or her) share. Suppose that a three-person partnership, in which each member has an equal share, takes out a loan for $30,000. This is treated as if each partner has contributed $10,000 in cash to the partnership. (The transaction is equivalent to each partner borrowing $10,000 and contributing it to the partnership.)[80] Each partner's basis therefore goes up $10,000.[81] So if the partnership shows a gain, each partner can subtract the amount of basis from his share of the profit in computing his taxable gain. (Remember, partners are taxed on the gain even if there has been no distribution to the partners.) If the partnership shows no gain, each partner can deduct the amount of his basis from his other capital gains. This approach is consistent with the pass-through treatment of partnerships.

A difficulty arises, however, about how to treat liabilities that are not certain—like debt—but instead are contingent on the occurrence of an event. Consider the following scenario: A partnership has sold an option to purchase land to a bank. Under the option contract, the bank is entitled to buy the property at a specified price through a certain date. The bank, however, is not required to buy the property. Under the tax code, the bank's payment for the option is considered a decrease in the partnership's basis, which, under pass-through principles, is ultimately taxable to the partners. If the partnership received $10,000 for the option, each partner's basis (that is, adjusted costs) would be lowered by a percentage of the $10,000 equivalent to each one's share of the partnership.

But how should the bank's right to buy the property under the option contract be treated? Should that right—whose value is reflected in the option payments by the bank—be considered a liability? The Internal Revenue Code's partnership taxation provisions are silent as to the definition of liability in general and contingent liability in particular. The issue arose in a 1975 case involving a couple named Helmer, who were partners in a cattle business. The Helmers argued that the bank's right under the option contract should be considered a liability and therefore the price of the option should be reflected in their basis—that is, their adjusted costs—in the partnership. (If the price of the option were included in their basis, they would end up with lower taxable gains.) The Tax Court sided with the IRS, emphasizing that the land options agreement did not require the Helmers to repay any amount if the option was not exercised, nor did it create any other liabilities. There was a possibility that the option would expire and the Helmers would not be obligated to transfer the property to the bank or owe any money.

Through the 1990s, the IRS and courts followed this approach to options sold by partnerships.[82] Short options, as they are known, created contingent liabilities, which did not increase a partner's liability interest in a partnership. In contrast, if a partner bought an option—called a long option—and contributed it to the partnership, the cost of the option would be included in the partnership's basis. Had the Helmers purchased an option to buy land, the payments for the option would have been included in the partnership's costs and passed through to them individually. The different treatment of long options and short option liabilities in this context makes intuitive sense. On the one hand, when the partnership has bought an option, the partnership is out the payment for the option. Even if the partnership decides not to exercise the option, the price of the option will not be repaid. On the other hand, when the partnership has sold an option, it will incur a cost only if the option is exercised.

The Son of BOSS shelters of the 1990s were designed to exploit this asymmetric treatment of sales and purchases of call options. Consider a simplified example: The taxpayer sells an option to buy securities or foreign currency to a bank (the "short" option). At the same time, the taxpayer buys an offsetting long option from the bank. The price of the long option is slighter higher than that of the short option.[83] Because the two transactions offset each other, the taxpayer is not taking an economic position in the transaction. The taxpayer then contributes the long option and the liability incurred under the short option to a partnership and receives a partnership interest in return. After the partnership engages in some pro forma—if highly complex—securities or options trading to give it a facade of economic activity, the taxpayer terminates her interest in the partnership. When the partnership is dissolved, the cost of the contributed long option, now worth nothing, is treated as a loss of the partnership. Under pass-through principles, the taxpayer is entitled to claim this loss against capital gains. (Ideally, the amount offsets most or all of the taxable capital gains the taxpayer would otherwise have to show.)

Meanwhile, the extinguishment of the liability created when the short option expires is ignored for tax purposes. Were this a debt owed by the partnership or some other certain liability, its cancellation would be treated as a decrease of the partnership liabilities and therefore the partner's share of the liabilities. (In other words, it would be the equivalent of a gain.) But because the obligation under the short option was not treated as a liability when it was transferred to the partnership, the expiration of the option, which fulfilled the obligation, does not decrease the partnership's liabilities, nor under pass-through principles, a partner's share of those liabilities. So it would not be subtracted from the loss claimed by the partner—equivalent to the value of the long option going from its purchase price to nothing when the partnership dissolved. The result of this transaction is that the taxpayer can claim losses for tax purposes without having incurred comparable economic losses.

Despite significant contrary authority, including IRS rulings, the partnership anti-abuse rules, and the economic substance doctrine, developers of these shelters took the position that *Helmer* stood for the proposition that any liability that is contingent—that is, that may not arise or whose amount cannot be calculated at the time it is incurred—should not be included in the calculation of a taxpayer's basis. In *Helmer*, tax law precluded using a putative liability to increase a taxpayer's basis; Son of BOSS promoters claimed that it also precluded using a putative liability to reduce a taxpayer's basis.

In each instance, of course, the taxpayer is attempting to maximize the amount of her basis. In *Helmer*, the taxpayers sought to do so by claiming that a noneconomic liability should be counted for tax purposes. In the example involving the short and long options, the taxpayers are attempting to do so by claiming that an economic liability should not be counted for tax purposes. Both efforts represent attempts to claim tax treatment at odds with economic reality. Reading *Helmer* in light of the Tax Court's focus on underlying purpose should lead to including the call option obligation in the taxpayer's basis and then subtracting it from that basis when the option is contributed to the partnership. Promoters of Son of BOSS shelters claimed, however, that the literal terms of the court's holding in *Helmer*, not its rationale, should govern.

The SOS shelter KPMG was offering had been developed by R. J. Ruble and Orrin Tilevitz, DGI's general counsel, who first came up with the idea when he was at Price Waterhouse.[84] In the DGI version, the taxpayer held the options during a sixty-day period. Because the investment was of such short duration, partners in KPMG's Washington National Tax office had not been able to conclude that the strategy had a more-likely-than-not probability of being upheld if challenged by the IRS.[85] Nevertheless, the firm was involved in marketing and implementing the shelter and prepared tax returns for clients who had purchased it.[86] Because the fees from SOS were comparatively modest compared to those from OPIS, KPMG had been treating SOS as something of a backup shelter. Partners offered the transaction to clients who were not able to meet the capital requirements for its high-end strategies, which required a client who wanted to generate a minimum $20 million tax loss.

When OPIS sales were discontinued, KPMG's tax shelter team continued to offer SOS. Tax leaders were eager, though, to find a replacement strategy aimed at high-wealth individuals that would prove just as lucrative. A new strategy with potential to generate substantial fees soon emerged.

5

Watson's Choice

As sales of the Offshore Portfolio Investment Strategy (OPIS) were winding down in 1998, leaders of KPMG's Personal Financial Planning (PFP) group were eager to find another product with similar revenue potential. Bond-Linked Issue Premium Structure, known under the acronym BLIPS, looked very promising. Two California lawyers, Emil Pesiri (who had been involved earlier with Son of BOSS shelters) and George Theofel, had thought up the idea for BLIPS and licensed it to Presidio, John Larson and Robert Pfaff's investment firm. BLIPS, like the earlier shelters Pesiri had done with Daugerdas in the mid-1990s, was a type of Son of BOSS shelter. BLIPS represented an important opportunity for Presidio, and solidified its position with KPMG. Larson and Pfaff had proprietary rights in BLIPS instead of having to compete with Quadra, as they had with OPIS, to be the financial advisor implementing the strategy. Through the fall, Larson and Pfaff worked closely with a multi-firm team consisting of Jeffrey Eischeid at KPMG, R. J. Ruble at Brown & Wood, and representatives of Deutsche Bank to design the shelter.

Watson's Rise

The technical expert put in charge of shepherding BLIPS through the approval process inside KPMG was a young tax partner and rising star named Mark Watson. Watson, an accountant by training, joined KPMG's PFP practice in 1992, after receiving a master's in tax from Texas A&M University. Soft-spoken, thoughtful, and quietly brilliant, Watson had contemplated following in the steps of his father, a physicist, and going into academics. After two years in KPMG's Houston office, Watson grew bored with tax compliance work. Looking for a change, he convinced his boss to allow him to do a rotation in the firm's

Washington National Tax (WNT) office, the firm's tax think tank. The firm offered postings at WNT to the young tax professionals who had promising futures in the organization. The fact that Watson did not have a law degree was not an impediment: by the early 1990s tax professionals with backgrounds in law and accounting played nearly interchangeable roles at major firms.

Watson flourished in D.C. The WNT environment—focused on sophisticated tax research and the intellectual give-and-take among the two dozen tax experts with training in law and accounting—came close to his ideal of an academic setting. He quickly earned a reputation as a talented, hard-working gift and estate tax specialist. Watson hoped to continue his career at WNT, but firm leaders asked him to move to KPMG's Dallas office to revive its moribund PFP practice. In return, the firm agreed to make him partner within the following year. Typically, it took entry-level tax professionals twelve years to work their way up to partnership; with the Dallas move, Watson would be made a partner in less than six. It was a difficult offer to resist.

In the Dallas office, Watson had his first experience with KPMG's growing tax shelter practice. When Gregg Ritchie was put in charge of developing and marketing tax shelters targeted at high-wealth individuals, he invited Watson to work on developing strategies based on gift and estate tax. Watson, who was knowledgeable about legitimate strategies in his field, was not initially averse to assisting with this project.

While working with Ritchie's group, Watson became familiar with OPIS—the aggressive strategy aimed at eliminating capital gains that succeeded FLIP. Watson was not completely persuaded that a court would uphold the transaction if challenged by the Internal Revenue Service. At one point in 1998, Ritchie asked Watson to make a sales call to a Dallas client who might be interested in buying OPIS. Watson was not enthusiastic, but recognized the importance of being a team player and agreed to visit the prospective buyer. When Watson finished his pitch, the client asked him directly whether Watson would purchase OPIS. Relieved that the client asked, Watson bluntly answered "no." After a second equally unsuccessful sales call, Watson was certain that he had little taste for product sales or the firm's expanding tax shelter practice.

After a few years, Watson grew tired of running the Dallas PFP practice and had become uncomfortable with its increased focus on shelters. He decided that the time had come to leave KPMG and pursue a teaching career. The firm's tax leaders, recognizing that KPMG was about to lose a highly talented tax expert, offered him a position back at WNT. Watson was delighted to accept. Back in D.C., he would be able to revisit the intellectual excitement he experienced during his first rotation. He would also be insulated from having to make sales calls. He assumed, moreover, that he would have a say in which products were approved for sale. When Watson returned to WNT in August 1998, he was put in charge of a growing staff charged with providing technical support to the PFP practice. In his new position, he was also responsible for overseeing the approval process for shelters to be promoted to high-wealth individuals through the group.

Soon after his arrival, Watson began to question whether his position at WNT would give him the authority to prevent conduct he considered questionable. The issue was how purchasers of the OPIS tax strategy could report their gains and losses on their tax returns. To Watson's dismay, a member of his group circulated a memo to Ritchie and his team arguing that shelter purchasers could use a grantor trust to "net" their gains and losses, a strategy intended to avoid detection of the shelter by the IRS.[1] In essence, the trust was supposed to function as a black box so that clients could avoid separately identifying their gains for the year and the loss they claimed from the shelter. This technique was directly contrary to federal income reporting requirements. Because a grantor trust does not change the ownership status of a property for income tax purposes, income tax laws did not recognize it as an appropriate form of reporting.[2]

When Watson discovered that a member of his group had recommended this strategy, he made clear his view that the technique bordered on criminal conduct. In September 1998, he wrote: "When you put the OPIS transaction with this 'stealth' reporting approach, the whole thing stinks."[3] Realizing several months later that partners were still recommending this reporting technique to clients, Watson followed up with a detailed analysis of why it was not permitted. He concluded: "I believe that we are filing misleading, and perhaps false, returns by taking this reporting position."[4] As the lead expert on trusts and estates practice, Watson assumed that once he had stated his opinion, grantor trust netting would cease. He subsequently discovered that, despite his strongly worded warning, partners were still advising clients into 2000 that they could use grantor trust netting as a reporting technique to hide their participation in tax shelters. (In the summer of 2000, the IRS issued a notice stating that this reporting technique could constitute a criminal offense.)[5]

When he returned to WNT in the summer of 1998, Watson reconnected with Steven Rosenthal, a well-respected partner with expertise in the taxation of financial products and services, whose office was down the hall. Watson had gotten to know Rosenthal during his earlier rotation at WNT and both had been named partners the same year. Of similar intellectual temperament and professional outlook, Watson and Rosenthal, whose offices were near each other, would drop in on each other often to talk about substantive tax law issues.

A 1985 graduate of the University of California at Berkeley Law School, Rosenthal had substantial experience in private and government practice, particularly in the area of taxation of financial services. The field held special appeal for Rosenthal. He had majored in mathematics in college and earned a graduate degree in public policy, focusing on finance, at Harvard. After practicing at the highly respected law firm Wilmer Cutler, Rosenthal went to work for Congress's Joint Committee on Taxation, specializing in financial institutions and products policy. When Republicans running on an antitax platform gained control of Congress in 1994, Rosenthal left the Joint Committee and joined KPMG as its National Director for Financial Services in the Financial Institutions and Products Group.

Recognizing Watson's intelligence and enthusiasm, Rosenthal took on an informal mentoring role, acting as a sounding board and helping him think through substantive tax problems and workplace dynamics. Watson, for his part, appreciated Rosenthal's sophisticated analysis and good judgment and looked to him for guidance on problems outside his area of expertise.

One frequent topic of discussion was the distinction under income tax law between legitimate business strategies, which might also confer substantial tax benefits, and abusive tax shelters, that is, transactions whose primary purpose was tax-motivated. Because the doctrine rarely arose in Watson's field of gift and estate tax, he found Rosenthal's detailed and nuanced explanations very helpful. As Rosenthal emphasized time and again, if a transaction lacked core economic characteristics, such as economic risk and reasonable opportunity for profit, he would not opine that it would "more likely than not" survive IRS challenge. This was the required standard for providing an opinion letter to a client that would avoid penalties if the tax benefits from a transaction were disallowed. As KPMG's emphasis on product development intensified, Rosenthal and Watson would often share their worries about the direction of the firm.

In recent years, Rosenthal had blocked some of the more questionable shelters under consideration. In 1997, David Smith, who had been involved in the creation of FLIP, joined Quadra, the Seattle-based firm that had functioned as an investment advisor for that transaction. At Quadra, Smith developed a shelter known as Contingent Deferred Swaps (CDS), which was offered to KPMG. Asked to review the shelter, Rosenthal, with Watson's support, quietly killed it. After KPMG turned it down, Smith brought the shelter first to Ernst & Young, which sold it to more than 132 clients,[6] and later to PricewaterhouseCoopers (PwC), which sold approximately twenty-six transactions.[7] After OPIS sales were officially discontinued at KPMG in late 1998, pressure at the firm mounted to find a strategy aimed at high-wealth individuals who were looking to shelter significant income or gains.

BLIPS

Mark Watson first saw BLIPS in early February 1999, in the form of a draft opinion letter Eischeid sent to him. Soon after Eischeid took over Ritchie's role in running the PFP products group, he and Watson were named co-leaders of a group called the Innovative Strategies group, the successor of CaTS. Eischeid was in charge of developing and implementing products aimed at high-wealth individuals. Watson's responsibility was to make sure that these products complied with applicable tax law.

BLIPS was developed in KPMG's PFP practice because line partners, whose clients were high-wealth individuals, were the obvious nationwide distribution channels for the product. Throughout the fall, Pfaff and Larson at Presidio, Ruble at Brown & Wood, representatives of Deutsche Bank, and Eischeid and Bickham at KPMG had worked together to flesh out the details of BLIPS. In early 1999, the multi-firm team had a prototype to present to WNT. As technical reviewer for products in the PFP practice, Watson was charged with shepherding BLIPS through the development and approval process.

Like the Son of BOSS shelters, BLIPS was a so-called contingent liability shelter, which sought to take advantage of how the partnership taxation rules treat different liabilities. The basic idea in broad outline was to create an artificial basis, or purported investment, in a partnership.[8] The taxpayer would borrow the money necessary to buy a financial asset, which represented a cost that could be used to reduce taxable income by increasing the basis. Later cancellation of part of that cost of indebtedness, it was claimed, would not reduce the basis.

Like the Short Options Strategy shelter described in chapter 4, BLIPS sought to take advantage of a purported asymmetry in the partnership rules, based on the *Helmer* case, which held that in certain situations the extinction of a contingent liability—one whose occurrence is not certain—is not deducted from the basis (or investment). In BLIPS, this was supposed to work by having a premium loan, that is, an above-market-interest loan, and a corresponding penalty for early repayment of the loan. Because the interest rate on the loan was above market, the bank would agree to advance the client an amount in excess of the face value of the loan.

The taxpayer would then transfer the loan proceeds to a partnership. When the taxpayer exited the transaction and dissolved the partnership, she would "repay" the face amount of the loan and the penalty, so she would not have made or lost money. Because the penalty only applied if the loan were repaid early, the argument was that it was "contingent" and should not be deducted from the basis in the partnership, which was equal to the amount of the premium. Under this rationale, eliminating liability for the interest on the loan would not be used to reduce the basis in the partnership. After the partnership was dissolved, its value would be equivalent to a nominal amount. (The net of the loan proceeds and premium advanced and the repayment with the penalty was zero.) But, the argument went, the taxpayer would still be able to claim the amount of the partnership's basis, equivalent to the amount of the original premium, as a loss and deduct it against her personal income under the partnership tax "pass-through" rules.

The lynchpin of the strategy was the above-market loan, whose premium was equivalent to the amount of tax loss to be generated. To eliminate any economic risk for the client, who would otherwise be deterred from entering the transaction, the loan was made non-recourse, meaning the client was not personally liable for repayment. To make the strategy look legitimate, the promoters structured a series of complex steps that were to be executed over a seven-year period. The expectation, however, was that the client would get out after the first stage—sixty days long—and realize the loss. In this first stage, the required investment was the fee for the transaction, set at 7 percent of the anticipated tax loss. With each stage over the following seven years, the amount that a client was required to invest increased. In addition, the seven-year period made it possible to set the loan interest at a plausible rate. During the period of the transaction, some amount of the money that the client had put in was used to trade on foreign currency options to make the transaction look as if it involved actual investment activity.

The moment BLIPS landed on Watson's desk in early February 1999, firm leaders began to exert pressure to approve it as soon as possible. To make sure Watson got the message, that same afternoon Eischeid emailed Doug Ammerman, the head of the PFP practice and Watson's direct report, and John Lanning, the firm's vice chair of Tax Services, to assure them that approval was expected within the month.[9] Lanning immediately wrote back exhorting Watson to approve BLIPS in a "dramatically accelerate[d] time frame."[10] Lanning may not have known much about whether the shelter would pass muster, but he apparently trusted Pfaff's judgment that the shelter worked—or perhaps it didn't matter. Under pressure to generate revenue for the tax practice, Lanning had his sights on the strategy's profitability. In the spirit of first to market, he emphasized, a month was "much too long," given "the market potential" of the product.[11]

Watson studied the eighty-page opinion and a PowerPoint presentation of graphs that illustrated the steps of the transaction.[12] BLIPS did not touch on gift and estate tax, Watson's area of expertise, but drew instead on partnership tax, income tax, the taxation of financial products, and international tax, among other specialized fields. Recognizing he was out of his depth, Watson began to identify the technical issues that arose in the transaction and enlist the participation of the various WNT experts needed to be involved in the approval process.[13] The team he assembled included Rosenthal, who would address the taxation issues around the bank loan; Richard Smith, the partnership tax expert who had recently come from the IRS and was a rising tax leader at the firm, and who would look at the applicable partnership tax rules; and Jim Sams,[14] who would research the tax rules connected with the foreign currency trading that was the ostensible investment piece of the transaction. Within a few days of making his initial assignments, Watson requested an update, explaining that Ammerman and Lanning were expecting a prompt progress report. "I don't like this pressure anymore than you do," he apologized in a postscript to his email.[15]

BLIPS presented several technical tax questions, but the hot potato that no one wanted to handle was whether the transaction had economic substance. To issue an opinion that the shelter would more likely than not be upheld in court if challenged by the IRS, the firm had to rely on representations from the investor that he or she had entered the transaction for the purpose of making a profit. Under the standards that applied to tax practice, the firm was not permitted to take the investor's representations at face value; its reliance on the investor's representations had to be reasonable. This meant that the transaction had to have the indicia of a legitimate investment. Someone at WNT would have to take responsibility for concluding that, given all he knew about the transaction, he could still envision an investor entering into it to make a profit. Because the transaction had been designed around the client's taking a tax loss without incurring any financial risk, reaching this conclusion in good faith was a challenge.

Because the doctrine of economic substance infrequently applied in gift and estate tax, Watson did not believe he was in a position to make this judgment. Watson first delegated the question of economic substance to Larry DeLap, head of KPMG's Department of Professional Practice and the partner responsible for risk management throughout the tax practice. Apparently seeking to avoid responsibility for making this critical call, DeLap soon punted the question to Philip Wiesner, the head of WNT.

After some preliminary work on their assignments, the BLIPS review and development team met in mid-February at Rosenthal's suggestion to discuss the various substantive issues and formally divide up responsibility for each one. During the brainstorming session, the group identified so many significant weaknesses and analytic flaws in the opinion letter that several participants left the meeting assuming that the product was not viable. Many of the questions went to whether tax regulations permitted the tax treatment sought and whether the opinion letter adequately discussed the applicable legal rules. The toughest issue, however—and the one about which the participants had the greatest doubts—was economic substance. Watson and Rosenthal, who had shared their many reservations privately, were relieved that BLIPS seemed to be dying a natural death, without their active intervention.

To their chagrin, BLIPS was resuscitated just two weeks later by Richard Smith. Smith and Wiesner had assumed joint responsibility for economic substance and, inexplicably, concluded that the transaction did indeed work. With the other outstanding technical issues also apparently resolved, BLIPS was back on track for quick approval.

But the problem of economic substance reared its head again. In mid-March 1999, Smith or someone else had begun to wonder what plausible business reason might lead an investor to borrow at an above-market rate. Since the loan was the heart of the shelter, an investor had to have a non-tax-based explanation for why the transaction was structured around it. Smith asked Rosenthal, an expert in taxation of financial instruments, to look into the premium loan to confirm that it was consistent with industry practices. Rosenthal had assumed his limited role in BLIPS was over, but agreed to follow up with Amir Makov, a financial markets quant recently hired at Presidio to implement the investment piece of the transaction.[16] During their conversation, Makov tried to produce a plausible explanation, but Rosenthal was skeptical. Following up in an email to Smith, Rosenthal neutrally noted that he continued to question the rationale for the loan premium.[17]

Apparently eager to launch BLIPS, PFP leaders misconstrued Rosenthal's email. Within a few days, Ammerman, the head of the group, announced that BLIPS was approaching final approval by DeLap, who was supposed to provide the last sign-off. According to Ammerman, Rosenthal had engaged in "extensive discussions" with Presidio and arrived at a "positive" assessment about the economic substance of the premium loan.[18] When he saw Ammerman's email, Rosenthal made clear that his assessment was not positive and that it had been based on a single conversation with Makov. In addition, Rosenthal underscored that he had not been asked to assess the business purpose or economic substance of the BLIPS investment program or the transaction generally, about which he continued to harbor doubts.[19] Meanwhile, word quickly got back to Presidio that Rosenthal wasn't predisposed to help BLIPS get approved and Larson instructed Makov to avoid any further interactions with him.[20] Larson also directed Makov to engage in immediate damage control and draft a memo explaining the business reason for the premium loan. Presidio did its best to prevent the memo from getting into Rosenthal's hands, sending it instead to Randy Bickham and BLIPS's other proponents within KPMG.[21]

A few weeks later, as part of the review process, Jeffrey Zysik, the head of the Tax Innovation Center (TIC) assisting Watson, sent

DeLap a revised opinion letter, the BLIPS PowerPoint presentation, and a draft engagement letter for final approval.[22] That evening, DeLap sent a lengthy email back identifying nearly thirty issues that still needed to be resolved and forwarded it to Stein to keep him updated. Behind the scenes, Stein was presumably checking with Pfaff, who would have been describing BLIPS's progress and the obstacles it was encountering. Stein was clear that he wanted the process wrapped up quickly. Writing back to DeLap, Stein sarcastically noted his "penetrating" analysis and made clear that he expected by this point that there would only need to be "perfunctory review and approval."[23] Addressing the remaining questions, he noted, could require "at least" two more weeks. Stein instructed DeLap to get together with "whoever was driving the process at PFP" and "resolve the issues as quickly as possible."[24]

It is not clear what DeLap thought. His first reaction to Stein's email was to point out that his role was more than a "rubber stamp."[25] The remaining issues were not just a matter of massaging the language of the draft opinion but raised substantive tax law questions that needed to be addressed by experts at WNT. But the very next day, in an unexplained about face, DeLap wrote Stein to reassure him that most of the issues had been worked out. Nonetheless, he still had doubts about economic substance: Could the firm reasonably rely on investors' representations that they intended to remain in the seven-year investment program when all "indications suggested that the intent was to bail out after 60 days?"[26]

DeLap's thinking is difficult to fathom, but he apparently was involved in a complicated defensive maneuver. Unwilling to risk the wrath of Lanning and Stein, who could make his life unpleasant if they chose, DeLap presumably did not want to take responsibility for vetoing BLIPS on his own despite his serious reservations about the product. Having made sure earlier that he was not responsible for resolving the issue of economic substance, he could repeatedly express his doubts in the hope that someone else would decide to pull the plug. In addition, putting his concerns in writing would allow him to distance himself down the road if, after the product was approved and marketed despite his concerns, BLIPS's lack of economic substance came back to haunt the firm.

In the following weeks, Bickham and DeLap worked on a final round of edits on the opinion letter.[27] Watson, meanwhile, confirmed that the technical issues were resolved, while carefully avoiding the question of economic substance.[28] Based on his conversations with Rosenthal, Watson continued to have serious misgivings. He did not believe, however, that he had sufficient authority to stop the transaction when Wiesner, a well-respected lawyer with significant expertise in the area and his immediate superior, had made the judgment that the transaction worked. By the end of April, BLIPS looked good to go.

Around this time, Watson began quietly to make inquiries about positions at the national tax offices of the other four accounting firms. He soon discovered that most of the firms were not about to offer him a partnership-level position given his relative inexperience. One firm expressed interest, but its hiring and recruitment process dragged on through the summer and into the following year without closure. Watson realized that he would not be able to make a gracious exit to an equivalent job at another firm. If he left, he would have to sacrifice his enviable position at the center of the firm's sophisticated tax practice, which he had worked very hard to obtain.

"Pie in the Sky"

With BLIPS poised for final approval by DeLap in April 1999, Doug Ammerman, the head of the PFP practice, assembled a BLIPS task force to begin the roll-out. A quick launch was imperative as there needed to be a several-month period to identify prospective investors, persuade them to sign up, and close the transaction—with enough time left for them to exit the transaction and realize the loss before year's end. During the last weekend in April, Ammerman summoned a dozen PFP client service partners, representing several regions of the United States, to a meeting at the Dallas/Fort Worth Airport to discuss implementation with the leaders of the BLIPS development team, representatives of Presidio, and Watson, who was available to discuss any technical questions that came up. Watson, for his part, secretly hoped that he would find out information about the transaction that would allow him to derail BLIPS.[29]

At the meeting, Eischeid and Bickham described what they called the "rules of engagement." For an investor to be eligible to participate, he had to seek to shelter a minimum of $20 million in gains or income. In addition, leaders of the Department of Professional Practice had capped BLIPS sales at fifty transactions. As Eischeid and

Bickham explained, the high participation threshold and the limit on the number of transactions were intended to lower the risk that the transaction would be detected in a random IRS audit and that the agency would notice that several taxpayers had engaged in nearly identical transactions with the same preorchestrated steps. Each investor would be required to pay a 7 percent fee, 1.25 percent of which represented KPMG's share, with the rest shared among the other promoters and facilitators. Credit for revenue generation would go exclusively to the PFP practice group, with other partners receiving cross-selling credit.[30] Eischeid and Bickham also explained that because the loan was non-recourse, the bank was putting strict limits on the use of the proceeds, effectively requiring the investor to keep all the funds in a money market account at the bank. The bank also required repayment by year's end. Watson now understood why the bank would agree to a non-recourse "loan"—an issue that had been puzzling him and Rosenthal. The bank wasn't actually going to allow the funds to leave the bank.

Eischeid and Bickham warned the audience members to be especially careful not to leave the draft opinion letter or PowerPoint presentation explaining the steps of the transaction that generated the tax loss with prospective clients. Were the IRS to get its hands on these documents during the course of an audit, they explained, investors would no longer be able to claim that they had entered the transaction for the purpose of making a profit, since the necessary steps to exit the transaction early and take a tax loss had been spelled out from the beginning.[31]

Toward the end of the session, Eischeid introduced Makov, the investment expert at Presidio, to explain the trading activity involved. The strategy involved shorting foreign currencies pegged to U.S. dollars in anticipation that the currencies would devalue during the investment period. Makov had been instructed not to be transparent about this lottery-like approach, and to describe, instead, the macroeconomic conditions in a developing economy that would lead to a sudden devaluation. As Makov spoke, a murmur of excitement rippled through his audience. Several listeners seemed to believe that investors in BLIPS stood to make a 300 percent return in a sixty-day period. Anxious to dispel this misimpression, Makov pointed out that this scenario was "pie in the sky" and that the possibility of making a profit from the transaction was "remote."[32]

As Makov described the slight prospect of profit, an arm grabbed him and pulled him back into his seat. Within minutes, Eischeid and Larson were hustling him out of the meeting, explaining that he and Larson had a plane to catch.

On hearing Makov's words, Watson thought he finally had ammunition to derail BLIPS—the investment advisors themselves had acknowledged that the transaction had no business purpose, and the loan that drove the transaction was not a real loan. He had serious concerns, however, about the consequences of using this information. On his way home from Dallas, he visited another KPMG partner who was a friend. After Watson described his dilemma, the friend reluctantly encouraged him "to do what he had to do." Watson recognized that if he tried to stop BLIPS at this stage, his career at KPMG, and certainly his enviable position at WNT, would be in jeopardy. Weighing his options, he decided to follow his instinct and his friend's advice. Back in the office early Tuesday morning, Watson sent an email to DeLap informing him that he (Watson) was not comfortable issuing a more-likely-than-not opinion and acknowledging that he would "catch hell" for the email.[33] The following day, he sent a similar email, recommending that the product not be released, to his other colleagues working on BLIPS.[34]

Meanwhile, Bickham was still struggling in the opinion letter to address yet another question that DeLap had raised back in February and that had not been satisfactorily resolved: who, for tax law purposes, was the borrower in the transaction? If the bank knew from the beginning that the investor would immediately donate the loan proceeds and the liability to the partnership, then a plausible argument could be made that it was the partnership and not the investor who was the borrower, and the investor was not entitled to the tax benefits from the deal. In late April, Rosenthal was enlisted to help Bickham address the issue. Around the same time, DeLap circled back to Rosenthal on the justification for the premium loan, sending along the memorandum that Makov had prepared after their phone conversation.

Rosenthal was not impressed with Makov's analysis. Making his skepticism clear, he noted that the memorandum was filled with "mumbo-jumbo that [was] not particularly useful." The argument for the premium loan relied on a concept that was "irrelevant" to the transaction and was "suspect."[35] After researching the separate question of who is the borrower under tax law, Rosenthal also concluded that the tax benefits from the transaction would not be available to the investor, which he communicated to DeLap.

Having heard Watson's renewed doubts about profit motive and the status of the bank loan and Rosenthal's legal analysis of the identity of the borrower, DeLap and the BLIPS team passed along these concerns to KPMG's tax leadership. Laying responsibility squarely on Watson, DeLap observed that he (DeLap) did not believe that the product should move forward "when the top PFP technical partner in WNT believes it should not be approved."[36]

On the afternoon of May 7, 1999, Smith and Wiesner hastily convened a meeting with Watson and Rosenthal to determine whether the problems Watson flagged could be addressed. Watson went into the meeting hoping that Wiesner and Smith would recognize the significance of the new information and reevaluate the decision to go forward with BLIPS. Over the course of the meeting, however, Smith and Wiesner concluded that appropriately drafted representations signed by Presidio, the investment firm, which stated that the transaction had a reasonable probability of making a profit, would cure the problem of the investor's motive. They also decided that the problem of whether there was a bona fide loan could be resolved with appropriate representations from Deutsche Bank. In essence, the bank had to state that it would treat and record the loan in the same manner as other loans.[37]

Although Watson was unsure that the representations from Presidio would suffice, he became persuaded that it was not up to the WNT to vet the investment aspects of the transaction. Amir Makov, who had supposedly been brought on because of his investment expertise, was the best judge of the transaction's profitability. As to the proposed representations by the bank, Watson had doubts that Deutsche Bank would sign on. But if the bank did agree, Watson would have some assurance that the transaction was legitimate. Watson reasoned that Deutsche Bank, a global financial institution, and its lawyers, the renowned corporate firm Shearman & Sterling, would not risk their reputations on an abusive tax shelter. What Watson didn't know is that Makov had been hired to give the transaction a fig leaf of legitimacy and knew from the outset that the investment arm of the transaction was a sham.[38] Watson also didn't know that officials at Deutsche Bank, who had vetted the transaction internally and carefully weighed the reputational risks of being associated with a tax shelter, were in on the ruse.[39] At the close of the meeting, Watson was tasked with drafting the specific representations required from the investment advisory firm and the bank.

The proposed representations might well solve some problems, but the question of the borrower's identity persisted. As Rosenthal explained to Wiesner and the other senior partners involved, "Actual indebtedness only occurs where there is an economically significant change in the tax-payer's wealth," which did not occur here where the investor is merely "serving as an intermediary" and the "partnership [could have] borrowed the proceeds directly."[40] Unwilling to accept the implications of Rosenthal's analysis, Smith wrote back: "Based on your analysis below, do you conclude that the tax results sought by the investor are 'NOT more likely than not' to be realized?" "Yes" Rosenthal answered tersely.[41]

In the meantime, Watson's earlier email describing his concerns was making the rounds. When Ammerman and Lanning read it, they were furious. Ammerman called from the West Coast to berate Watson. Lanning sent an incensed email to the group:

> I must say that I am amazed that at this late date (must now be six months into this process) our chief WNT PFP technical expert has reached this conclusion. I would have thought that Mark would have been involved in the ground floor of this process, especially on an issue as critical as profit motive. What gives? This appears to be the antithesis of "speed to market." Is there any chance of ever getting this product off the launching pad, or should we simply give up???[42]

Watson assumed that he would be fired. His back against the wall, he tried to explain that the problem was not due to an error or oversight on his part. His earlier analysis had been based on the only documentation that had been made available to him, the draft opinion and slide presentation sent by the BLIPS development team. It was only when he had met Presidio representatives on May 1, he explained, that he learned significant new information about the lack of profit potential and absence of a bona fide loan.

On Monday morning, May 10, 1999, Wiesner emailed his views to the tax leadership and the BLIPS development team. A 1971 graduate of Columbia Law School, Wiesner had joined KPMG in 1979 after a stint in the U.S. Department of the Treasury. He was a highly regarded tax attorney among KPMG partners and in the larger Washington tax community, with a reputation for careful and sophisticated analysis.[43] With the firm's growing emphasis on tax products, however, Wiesner may have sensed that his lack of enthusiasm for shelters had rendered him vulnerable. Rumors were circulating at WNT that if he was not more gung-ho, he would soon be replaced as head of the national office.

Wiesner's first instinct was to try to put the rabbit back in the hat or at least pretend that the rabbit was not in plain sight. In an email to the WNT review team, he noted that he "was under the impression that everyone had signed off on their respective technical issue(s)" and that he "had signed off on the overall more likely than not opinion." He was "troubled that at this late date the issue is being revisited, and . . . a prior decision being changed on a technical issue?!" Having apparently concluded that the transaction had economic substance as long as clients signed appropriate representations about their profit motive, Wiesner's impulse was to close his eyes to evidence that the transaction would not yield a profit—evidence that cast serious doubt on the reasonableness of the firm's reliance on the client's representation.[44]

In a second email to the tax leadership and the WNT reviewers, Wiesner was determined to show that he could—and would—pull the trigger. Several months earlier, he noted, he had concluded that he could reach a more-likely-than-not decision based on the information and the proposed representations provided at the time. He continued to stand by that original opinion, even in the face of the new information from Presidio. What an investor had in mind in entering into the transaction was at this stage hypothetical. As Wiesner noted: "The real 'rubber meets the road,' will happen when the transaction is sold to investors, what the investors' actual motive is for investing [in] the transaction, and how the transaction actually unfolds."[45] In other words, the issue of whether a client truthfully believed that the transaction could reasonably yield a profit and the reasonableness of the firm's reliance on that representation could be deferred to implementation.

According to Wiesner, the business considerations turned on whether the firm had sufficiently protected itself from liability in the language of the engagement letter the client would be required to sign. Wiesner also wanted to be sure that the firm was being "paid a lot of money for its opinion" because the IRS would consider BLIPS a very aggressive transaction, which clearly fell within the "tax shelter orbit." Ultimately it came down to a "business matter." Wiesner's opinion was that the moment had come for the firm to make a decision. His vote was to go forward with BLIPS. "The time has come to shit and get off the pot," he concluded.[46]

Soon Stein weighed in: "It's shit OR get off the pot. I vote shit."[47]

Ammerman, the head of the PFP practice, agreed. The team he had assembled in Dallas, he wrote to the group, was ready to start working with PFP line partners to identify prospects and begin marketing.[48] Watson's concerns were being addressed by Presidio and Deutsche Bank and should not, he assured the group, delay the roll-out. In conclusion, he "concur[red]" with Stein.[49]

Later, on May 10, Wiesner and Smith met again with Watson and Rosenthal to discuss the problem of whether the borrower was the partnership or the taxpayer for purposes of taking the loss. Wiesner and Smith argued that under applicable legal principles, the taxpayer could be treated as the borrower, and concluded that the firm was ready to issue a more-likely-than-not opinion for BLIPS. Watson, who was out of his depth, refrained from expressing a view. Rosenthal was still not persuaded. Carefully noting his disagreement, he observed, "though reasonable people could reach an opposite result," he could not reach a more-likely-than-not opinion on the issue of who was the borrower.[50]

After the meeting, Wiesner announced that the group, over Rosenthal's dissent, had decided to move forward with the product. DeLap, apparently still hoping that someone else would stop BLIPS—so long as it was not he—asked Watson in an email where he stood. "The essential question is whether *you* are comfortable with a more-likely-than-not opinion on this product," he insisted.[51]

Watson was astounded. In his experience, DeLap had always taken a forceful leadership role on professional practice issues, but now he was refusing to take a stance, looking instead to a junior partner to pull the plug. Watson was being thrown to the wolves, but was powerless to confront DeLap, a senior partner with much more experience, whose office was, in any case, three time zones away in California.

At this point, Watson believed that he had done all he could to stop BLIPS. The final decision was in the hands of his superiors, Wiesner and Smith. DeLap had declined to get involved. In a moment of self-doubt, Watson decided—despite deep misgivings—that it was acceptable to defer to their judgment. They had much greater expertise in the area, after all, and dissenting, when it was clear that the tax leaders were set on moving ahead, would only bring him grief. There was no point in holding out. He wrote to DeLap: "Larry, I don't like this product and would prefer not to be associated with it. However, if the additional representations I sent to Randy on May 9 and 10 are in fact made, based on Phil Wiesner's and Richard Smith's input, I can reluctantly live with a more-likely-than-not opinion being issued for the product."[52]

DeLap passed on Watson's lukewarm endorsement to the other tax leaders. Stein's answer was concise: "Yikes!"[53] Neither he nor the other tax leaders paused to reconsider the wisdom of going forward with BLIPS.

"Get Out of Jail Card"

During a meeting of the managing partners of the PFP in Colorado Springs later in the spring of 1999, Watson tried once again to prevent BLIPS from being marketed. Ammerman, the head of the group, invited Randy Bickham to the meeting to discuss the product's design, implementation, and revenue potential. After the presentation, Watson began to question Bickham about the reasonableness of relying on investors' representations about their profit motive. When the argument between Watson and Bickham escalated into a shouting match, Ammerman loudly instructed Watson to sit down and be quiet. Throughout the heated discussion, the other senior partners in the group sat by silently, none willing to follow Watson's lead and question the propriety of KPMG's being involved in a transaction like BLIPS. Watson was ready to throw in the towel again.

But another opportunity to stop BLIPS arose in the summer. Watson and Rosenthal were put in charge of reviewing the loan documents prepared by Deutsche Bank's lawyer, Gerald Rokoff, and the team of tax and corporate finance lawyers he had assembled at Shearman & Sterling.[54] If Watson and Rosenthal continued to harbor some lingering hope that the loan was legitimate, any doubt was dispelled in mid-July when they saw the documents, which made crystal clear that the proceeds and control over their use would remain with the bank. The loan was a loan in name only.

Meanwhile, a new player had arrived on the scene. Despite Phil Wiesner's support for BLIPS, he had been sidelined as partner in charge of WNT to make room for David Brockway, an important senior hire.

Brockway, a former chief of staff of Congress's Joint Committee on Taxation, had left the prestigious law firm of Dewey Ballantine, after nearly two decades of tax practice, to join KPMG. A brilliant tax lawyer, Brockway was credited with designing the ground-breaking tax reform package that eliminated the first round of tax shelters in 1986 when he served as director of the Joint Committee on Taxation.[55] He had a reputation as an independent thinker, and Watson and Rosenthal were hopeful that he would put an end to the BLIPS shenanigans once he became aware of them.

His optimism rekindled, Watson sent an email in late July 1999 to the senior tax leadership, including Brockway and DeLap, describing the problems he and Rosenthal had found with the loan documents. "[O]ur primary concern," he wrote,

is that these documents do not give the client ("the Borrower") meaningful use or control of the loan proceeds (i.e., the bank ("DB") will not allow the borrower access to the proceeds nor allow the Borrower effectively to determine how the proceeds will be invested)[.] As a result, we are concerned that (i) a bona fide loan may not exist, [and] (2) if a loan does exist, that the Borrower may not be considered the true borrower. . . .

Further, because DB effectively controls how the loan proceeds will be invested and because it seems to have no economic incentive to allow such proceeds to be invested in anything other than very safe investments (e.g., money market accounts), we are concerned as to whether there could be a reasonable expectation of making a profit on the loan transaction given that the cost of borrowing may far exceed the expected rate of return generated by the investments purchased with the loan proceeds. Perhaps Presidio can provide us with an economic analysis that will alleviate our fears on this matter. Such an analysis will also be important if a BLIPS transaction is ever challenged by the IRS.[56]

To Watson and Rosenthal's astonishment, the email was met with silence. Watson tried to schedule a meeting with Wiesner, to no avail. Rosenthal attempted to meet with Brockway but was unsuccessful.

Watson and Rosenthal were perplexed by Brockway's failure to respond. In retrospect, there are plausible explanations for his inaction. Having just come on board to oversee a busy office, he was likely disinclined to revisit decisions—however questionable—that had been made prior to his tenure. BLIPS was one of several transactions in the process of implementation that had been vetted and approved in previous years. To reconsider those that appeared problematic would have required a substantial investment of time and energy that Brockway might not have wanted to divert from ongoing projects. Brockway may have also feared that reviewing BLIPS would open the door to reconsidering a number of other transactions, putting at substantial risk fees that the firm had already banked on. In addition, Brockway might not have realized that BLIPS presented a level of risk to the firm an order of magnitude greater than other transactions being implemented when he arrived. Another possible reason was that he did not want to second-guess Wiesner, since, like other members of the tax bar, he likely would have held Wiesner's professional judgment in high regard. Wiesner's continued presence at the firm—after having been displaced as the head of WNT—put Brockway in an awkward position. Management prerogatives and intraoffice sensitivities, in other words, may have countered any inclination he had to consider BLIPS on its merits.[57]

After several days of waiting to hear from Brockway, Rosenthal persuaded Watson to give it one last try. In an email on August 4, 1999, Watson wrote: "I feel it is important to again note that I and several other WNT partners remain skeptical that the tax results purportedly generated by a BLIPS transaction would actually be sustained by a court if challenged by the IRS. We are particularly concerned about the economic substance of the BLIPS transaction, and our review of the BLIPS loan documents has increased our level of concern."[58] To underscore that Watson and he had not been asked to opine on economic substance, Rosenthal followed up a few minutes later, emphasizing that even though he also continued to be "seriously troubled by these issues," they were not assessing the economic substance of the transaction, but deferring to Wiesner and Smith on these issues.[59]

This time the response was swift. Shortly after the email went out, Smith marched into Watson's office and showed him a draft email by Wiesner, in which he stated his opinion that more likely than not a court would hold that the transaction had economic substance. That afternoon, Watson sent an email to the group stating that the review of the loan documents was complete and they were "ready to proceed."[60]

Bickham forwarded the email to R. J. Ruble, the lawyer at Brown & Wood who was to provide a second "independent" opinion on BLIPS. "We have received our 'get out of jail card' from WNT," he wrote.[61]

In the meantime, Deutsche Bank, which had provided most of the funding, failed to sign on to the representations requested by the BLIPS team. Watson and the tax leaders had requested the bank to represent that the above-premium loan complied with industry standards. The bank refused, agreeing only to affirm that the loan approval and documentation process was consistent with Deutsche's own internal procedures. By the time the issue came to a head it was already March 2000, and the firm was finalizing opinion letters for the clients who had bought BLIPS. Although Watson and Rosenthal argued that the bank's representation was insufficient, Richard Smith overruled them, and concluded that the representation, with some vague phrases thrown in, would have to suffice at this late a stage.[62]

Over the next six months, Watson provided technical assistance to the marketing teams and oversaw the process of issuing KPMG opinion letters. After that task was completed, he was transferred to KPMG's Amsterdam office where he was assigned the responsibility of coordinating the firm's various European tax practices. When he returned a year later, he discovered that the firm was still actively involved in promoting tax shelters. He resigned shortly afterward.

A few years later, Mark Watson—along with Wiesner, Stein, Smith, DeLap, Eischeid, and Bickham—was indicted for tax fraud in connection with his participation in the BLIPS approval process. Rosenthal was not.

The Push to Market BLIPS

After the roll-out meeting in the Dallas/Fort Worth Airport on April 30, tax leaders had to restrain PFP partners who were champing at the bit to line up clients for BLIPS. When the transaction was finally green-lighted in early August, marketing efforts went into high gear.[63] DeLap had initially only approved a total of fifty BLIPS transactions, and each region was anxious to get its share. Moreover, for BLIPS to achieve its desired tax benefits in 1999, team members had to sell and complete deals in a very brief period. To create a semblance of legitimate investment, clients were required to stay in the first stage of the transaction a minimum of sixty days. The loan with Deutsche Bank consequently had to close by mid-October so that trading on the account could begin on October 22 and clients could elect to exit the transaction by December 21. This left the tiniest of wiggle room for Presidio to unwind the transaction by year's end. By mid-September, KPMG had more than fifty active transactions, and Larson, Presidio's principal, recommended that sales efforts cease since a huge backlog of unfinished deals had developed.[64]

The crush of deals put logistical strains on Deutsche Bank, which suddenly had an enormous amount of paperwork to handle. Principals at Presidio, KPMG, and the bank discussed placing KPMG staff on site to help. Higher-ups at the bank nixed the idea when they realized that having KPMG employees in its offices would undermine the fiction that Deutsche Bank was acting independently and not as a facilitator of the transactions.[65] Although officials at the bank, including Deutsche Bank Americas' CEO John Ross, had reviewed the transaction carefully and understood that it was assisting in the implementation of a tax shelter transaction,[66] the bank needed to maintain a plausible degree of deniability. The deals could not look rigged. Instead, it had to appear that each investor, working with Presidio, had shown up individually to borrow money from the bank to do a transaction. Presidio also had problems handling the substantial paperwork generated by the number of transactions. KPMG devised an arrangement under which a number of its employees would assist in closing the deals, billing Presidio three-quarters of a million dollars for their efforts.[67]

A bigger problem with Deutsche Bank soon arose. By late summer, the bank had made nearly $3 billion in BLIPS loans and was quickly approaching the total capacity it had established internally for the transaction.[68] Many clients, however, still remained on the waiting list. Presidio had to find a new bank that could quickly get up to speed on the transaction in time to approve and close loans by mid-October—an impossible challenge given the hundreds of documents that would need to be reviewed. Larson and Pfaff at Presidio hit on the idea of looking for other banks that already had a relationship with KPMG and were represented by Rokoff's team of lawyers at Shearman & Sterling which was familiar with the documentation and could finalize the loans quickly.[69]

Presidio approached HVB, a Germany-based bank involved in earlier KPMG tax shelters, about financing the loans. Like Deutsche Bank, HVB stood to make 1 1/4 percent based on the interest charged on the loan, which corresponded to the desired tax loss. The gain represented an infinite return on investment since the funds stayed at the bank and no moneys had to be dedicated to the loan. Officials at HVB were aware that they were facilitating tax shelter deals but the easy money proved impossible to resist.[70] The bank agreed to a $400 million credit limit, which it later extended by an additional $500 million.[71] But even with so much money available, the funds were running out. And the last, biggest BLIPS deal of the year was still to come.

In the summer of 1999, Allan Abrams and his siblings had decided to sell their company Arrow Fastener, a global manufacturer of staplers and other construction fasteners. Morris Abrams, their father, had started the company in 1929, manufacturing tools in his home shop by day and selling them in his Brooklyn neighborhood at night. By the early 1990s, Arrow Fastener had grown into one of the largest and best-known manufacturer of industrial fasteners, with manufacturing and sales operations around the world. To deal with its accounting needs, the company hired KPMG, which also provided tax return and planning services. Over the years, the Abrams developed a close working relationship with several partners at the firm. With the sale of their family business on the horizon, they turned to the firm to prepare the financial data that needed to be reported to the buyer.

As a result of the sale, the Abrams family was going to realize more than $400 million in capital gains, which would be subject to a 20 percent tax.[72] During the spring and summer, the family's tax advisors at KPMG met with family members several times to persuade them to engage in a BLIPS transaction. During the meetings, the partners at KPMG insisted that the transaction complied with IRS rules and regulations. They also told the Abrams that they would find a way to report the transaction on their tax returns so as to not raise any red flags. KPMG's tax professionals assured the Abrams that even if the IRS detected the transaction they would only be liable for 50 percent of the tax due.

The Abrams were initially hesitant to engage in the transaction. By the fall, however, their advisors at KPMG had convinced them that there was no downside to going forward. The problem was that insufficient time remained before the end of the year for the Abrams to stay in the first stage of the transaction the minimum sixty-day "investment" period. Although the principals at Presidio were doubtful, Jeff Stein, KPMG's vice chair of Tax Services, made clear that the transaction was of great importance to the firm and assured the participants that KPMG would issue an opinion for the transaction. After another bank was brought in to provide a "loan" in the hundreds of millions, the Abrams entered into and unwound the transaction in a forty-seven-day period, subsequently claiming losses totaling $330 million on their tax returns.[73]

By the time Wiesner officially released BLIPS for marketing in early August 1999, the firm's tax leaders were no longer standing firm on their original limit of fifty transactions, presumably because significantly more than fifty client engagements were already in the pipeline. By late September, however, tax leaders had decided that BLIPS marketing had to cease.[74] In 1999, KPMG engaged in sixty-six BLIPS transactions. The following year it engaged in another handful, which were treated as "grand-fathered" in under the original sales initiative because they had already been marketed to clients who wanted to use the strategy to shelter gains anticipated in 2000. All told, BLIPS generated more than $53 million in fees and turned out to be one of the firm's most successful shelters.[75]

In early 2000, KPMG's Innovative Strategies team began to develop a replacement strategy for BLIPS that they called BLIPS 2000. After Steve Rosenthal wrote a long email to David Brockway describing significant problems with the strategy, Brockway decided to veto the transaction. Inside the group, the search was on for another strategy marketed to high-wealth individuals that would replace BLIPS.

"SELL! SELL! SELL!"

In early 2000, Wiesner sent an email to the partners in the WNT practice exhorting them to "temporarily defer non-revenue producing activities" and concentrate on meeting WNT's revenue goals for the fiscal year. Wiesner designated the "hot products" with "significant revenue potential" that the members of the office should focus on. "Thanks for help in this critically important matter," he added. "As Jeff [Stein] said 'We are dealing with ruthless execution—hand to hand combat—blocking and tackling.' Whatever the mixed metaphor, let's just do it."[76]

While the Innovative Strategies group had not hit on a blockbuster to succeed BLIPS, another group at KPMG, known as Stratecon, was busy developing a strategy with significant revenue potential. Stratecon, devoted to designing and selling tax shelters to businesses, was headed by Walter Duer, a partner in the firm's WNT office. In early 2000, the group was promoting a strategy under the acronym SC2 to S corporations, business entities that, like partnerships, are taxed as pass-through entities.

SC2 was created in late 1999 by Larry Manth, Robert Huber, Douglas Duncan, and Andrew Atkin, many of whom had come over from Deloitte to KPMG earlier that year. At Deloitte, they were familiar with a similar strategy that had been disallowed by the IRS.[77] In SC2, an S corporation donated a substantial portion of its nonvoting stock to a tax-exempt entity and then redeemed the stock for a small amount after two or three years. During the period that the tax-exempt entity owned the stock, the S corporation's income was allocated to the tax-exempt entity but no distributions of earnings were made. After the stock was redeemed, the S corporation could resume making distributions. Under the applicable tax code provisions, the strategy resulted in the benefit of a charitable deduction at the time the stock was donated. It also resulted in the deferral of income during the period that the tax-exempt entity held the stock, as well as the ultimate conversion of the S corporation's earnings from ordinary income to capital gains.

SC2's developers had already sold two SC2s before they obtained approval of the strategy by WNT.[78] As with BLIPS, participants in the review process raised serious concerns about whether SC2 would pass muster in court. Early on, Mark Watson noted that the strategy would be difficult to distinguish from the one the IRS had earlier shut down, and that clients might not be able to obtain the tax benefits promised. He also worried that the IRS would seek to impose penalties on KPMG for aiding and abetting the understatement of taxes with SC2. William Kelliher, another partner in WNT, also initially doubted that a more-likely-than-not opinion could be issued on the version he first saw, noting his concern that the IRS "could re-characterize the overall transaction . . . as a sham."[79]

Despite early qualms, the developers of SC2, with the assistance of Mark Springer, head of the TIC, continued to work toward obtaining approval of the strategy. The firm's economic incentives were strong. As Galbreath, a member of the TIC, emphasized during the review process, SC2 was receiving "very high level (Stein/[Richard] Rosenthal) attention."[80] Indeed, even before the strategy had been approved by the head of the Department for Professional Practice, Richard Rosenthal, the area managing partner for the Western Region, sent around an email to the SC2 team urging them to "SELL, SELL, SELL!!"[81]

The risk of detection by the IRS was not supposed to be a factor in deciding whether the firm would issue an opinion for the strategy; indeed, taking it into consideration was explicitly forbidden. Some reviewers nonetheless took into account the fact that the strategy would only be marketed to a small number of S corporations. Looking back a year later, Kelliher, who was involved in approving the final version, noted: "Going back to February, when SC2 first raised its head, my recollection is that SC2 was intended to be limited to a relatively small number of S Corps. That plan made sense because there was and is a strong risk of a successful IRS attack on SC2 if the IRS gets wind of it."[82]

By late March, Richard Bailine, a tax partner and expert in S corporation taxation, had also reviewed and approved a version of the strategy, and Larry DeLap had signed off. Before releasing the strategy, DeLap was emphatic that the engagement letter make clear the potential risks to clients. The risks that were to be highlighted to the client included that the IRS could reallocate the income allocated to the tax-exempt organization to the other shareholders; the IRS might disallow the charitable deduction contribution sought; the corporation could lose its subchapter S status and be subject to corporate tax; and the IRS might attempt to assess penalties against the shareholders of the business for understating their taxes.[83]

As the sales toolkit for the strategy was being finalized, the SC2 "champions" began an intensive firm-wide effort to find suitable clients. They combed through internal, commercial, and public databases and contacted professionals within the firm, including audit colleagues, clients, and other referral sources in the hope of identifying prospects. The firm also used the Indiana telemarketing firm it had hired to cold call S corporations that qualified for the strategy.

To facilitate sales, SC2 champions distributed a "Sticking Points" memo containing advice about dealing with recalcitrant clients. If a buyer thought the strategy was too good to be true, the KPMG representative was to remind the buyer that the strategy had been vetted in an extensive review by firm specialists, including some who were former IRS employees. In addition, the buyer was to be told that a number of sophisticated clients had already bought the strategy, and at least one outside law firm was available to provide an opinion. If a client needed to think about it, the memo suggested three approaches: the *"get even" approach*, which involved contacting the client again right around the time a large estimated payment is due, when she or he is likely to be "extremely irritated"; the *"Beanie Baby" approach*—named for the popular stuffed toy whose limited availability caused sales crazes in the late 1990s—which involved informing the client the firm has established a cap on the product that is quickly filling up; and the *"break-up" approach*, which involved informing the client that because the cap has been reached, he or she should no longer consider purchasing the product.[84] (For obvious reasons, this last one was risky and could only be used in the limited number of cases when the client could be expected to fall for the ruse.) The memo also offered strategies to do end runs around "stubborn outside counsel" who had advised against purchasing SC2.[85] As part of the sales process, the firm also offered to arrange insurance on the strategy to cover losses in the event the IRS challenged it and prevailed. Almost half a dozen SC2 purchasers took the firm up on the offer and purchased insurance.[86]

The firm's efforts to market SC2 were so extensive that in December 2001, Kelliher, who earlier had approved it, complained that KPMG seemed "intent on marketing the SC2 strategy to virtually every S corporation with a pulse."[87] With all this activity, he worried, the IRS would find out about the product. "Call me paranoid," he added, but the "widespread marketing is likely to bring KPMG and SC2 unwelcome attention from the IRS. . . . I realize the fees are attractive, but does the firm's tax leadership think that this is an appropriate strategy to mass market?"[88] To reassure Kelliher, DeLap explained that Richard Rosenthal and other tax leaders had already agreed, some nine months earlier, that SC2 would no longer be mass marketed.

The firm finally discontinued marketing SC2 when it received a subpoena from the IRS requesting documents relating to the transaction in the spring of 2002.[89] During the more than two years it was on the market, SC2 was sold to more than fifty subchapter S corporations, generating $26 million in revenue.[90] In 2004, the IRS prohibited SC2 as a "listed transaction."[91]

SC2 was only one of several shelters developed by Stratecon members and sold to businesses. The most lucrative strategy that has come to light was marketed under the name Contingent Liability Acceleration Strategy or CLAS. CLAS was purchased by twenty-nine companies, including Delta Airlines, Whirlpool, Clear Channel, WorldCom, Tenet Healthcare, and the U.S. units of the global biopharmaceutical AstraZeneca. The brainchild of Carol Conjura, a former IRS official and WNT partner who specialized in tax accounting, CLAS permitted a company to accelerate the timing of deductions for settlements of lawsuits and other claims.

Under the strategy, a corporation created a contingent liability trust with itself as beneficiary and then donated noncash assets, for example an intracompany note, whose value was equal to the amount of the anticipated settlements. A company could then take deductions for the anticipated settlement amounts years before the claims were settled and the amounts had to be paid.

Under the fee agreement for CLAS, KPMG charged 0.4 percent of the accelerated deduction, with a minimum fee of $500,000. Target clients were required to have a minimum of $150 million in pending claims against them. KPMG focused its sales efforts on companies that had implemented aggressive strategies in the past, targeting their CFO or vice president for tax. The firm's sales pitch emphasized "the true beauty" of the strategy: "What is not required—cash!" CLAS, which earned the firm approximately $20 million, resulted in $1.7 billion in lost tax revenues to the Treasury, more than any other single shelter that has come to light.[92] In 2003, the IRS listed CLAS as an abusive strategy.

While Stratecon was rolling out SC2, CLAS, and other corporate tax shelters, the Innovative Strategies group in the PFP was trying to replicate its success of previous years. In 2000, the group was pursuing two approaches that together would deliver, Eischeid hoped, $38 million in sales. One was a version of the Short Options Strategy, described in chapter 4, that the team planned to market without a more-likely-than-not opinion letter from the firm under a special finder's arrangement. The second involved more customized solutions targeted at the upper end of the market. This approach would focus on deals exceeding $100 million in which KPMG's fees were expected to surpass $1 million per deal.

The group was well on its way to implementing these plans when the IRS issued Notice 2000-44 in August 2000, listing Son of BOSS shelters as strategies it considered abusive and whose claimed tax benefits it would challenge in court. As the Innovative Strategies leaders acknowledged, the notice "specifically described both the retired BLIPS strategy and the then current SOS strategy."[93] They concluded the time had come to lie low. "Business decisions" were made "to stop the implementation of 'sold' SOS transactions and to stay off the 'loss generator' business for an appropriate period of time.'"[94]

But not for very long. By May 2001, the Innovative Strategies practice was anticipating generating $27 million for the coming fiscal year. Among the strategies it was promoting was one it called Partnership Option Portfolio Securities or POPS which, if approved, was expected to produce $12 million in fees.

By 2002, the tax leaders who had spearheaded KPMG's focus on developing and promoting abusive tax shelters had risen to the highest positions at the firm. In April, Jeff Stein, who had succeeded Lanning as vice chair of Tax Services when the latter retired in 2000, was named KPMG's deputy chair, the second in command of the firm. Smith, the partnership tax expert who had helped the firm arrive at a more-likely-than-not opinion on BLIPS, had been named area managing partner for the Western Region at the beginning of the year. He was then promoted to vice chair of Tax Services when Stein became deputy chair that spring. Richard Rosenthal, who had helped propel Stratecon's corporate tax strategies, was named vice chair of Tax Operations directly under Stein in the summer of 2000. Two years later, he was promoted to CFO of KPMG.[95] Eischeid, who had headed the Innovative Strategies practice, was named partner in charge of the firm's Personal Financial Planning practice.[96]

At the turn of the century, tax shelters were the driving force behind the enormous profits produced by KPMG's tax services. As we describe in chapter 12, the firm's tax shelter activities were eventually stopped, but not before they generated more than $100 million in fees and billions of dollars in fake tax losses.[97]

6

Accounting for Fraud

KPMG was not the only firm among the then Big Six to play a major role in the tax shelter industry. Ernst & Young (E&Y) was eager to participate too. PricewaterhouseCoopers (PwC) was involved but withdrew after it was publicly embarrassed during Congressional hearings. Arthur Andersen was active, but its demise in the wake of the Enron debacle limited the amount of information about its shelter activities that came to light. Only Deloitte Touche remained unscathed. Although that firm was described in Janet Novack and Laura Sanders's 1998 article in *Forbes* as a tax shelter promoter, no official account of wrongdoing at the firm has emerged.[1]

Ernst & Young: The VIPER Strikes

Getting in the Game
As 1998 began, Arthur Andersen, KPMG, and PwC were all involved in developing and marketing generic shelters aimed at high-wealth individuals, and E&Y decided it needed to play catch-up. The firm had offices in 120 countries and 70,000 employees worldwide; like the other Big Six firms, it was feeling significant market pressure. Tax shelters were viewed as a potentially major new source of revenue.[2] A natural location for such work was the firm's Personal Financial Consulting (PFC) unit, headed by Robert Garner, which offered tax advice and planning to individuals. In early 1998, Garner got approval from Richard Bobrow, then the partner in charge of the firm's National Tax Department,[3] to form a group devoted to pursuing high-fee strategies for high-wealth individuals.

Emphasizing E&Y's new aggressiveness, the group was called VIPER: "Value Ideas Produce Extraordinary Results." Inside the firm, the acronym sometimes stood for "Value Ideas Produce Extraordinary Revenues."[4] VIPER's mission was to work with financial institutions, investment companies, law firms, and tax shelter promoters to design and market tax strategies. To lead the group, Garner tapped tax lawyer Robert Coplan, a former branch chief of the IRS Estate and Gift Tax Regulations Division, who was in the PFC group within E&Y's National Tax Department and had been named partner four years earlier. Garner also recruited Martin Nissenbaum, a lawyer and accountant who was a specialist in income tax and executive compensation in the PFC unit. In addition, while he didn't formally join VIPER until 2000, Richard Shapiro, a lawyer who focused on the taxation of financial instruments, worked closely with the group from its inception. Shapiro had joined E&Y as a partner in 1995 after working at both law and accounting firms.

E&Y management decided to establish a sales team dedicated to marketing the strategies developed by the VIPER group, and recruited Brian Vaughn to lead the new team. Hailing from Louisiana, a certified public accountant and financial planner with experience marketing tax shelters for Deloitte Touche, Vaughn was a brilliant salesman who exuded charm and self-confidence. E&Y first heard of him when several of the firm's clients told E&Y that Vaughn had been offering them a tax shelter known as a flexible gain deferral strategy, which Vaughn had brought to Deloitte from KPMG, where he had earlier been employed. At Deloitte Vaughn worked with Belle Six, who was also a CPA and financial planner. Although both Vaughn and Six were married to others, they had developed a romantic relationship at Deloitte.[5] Vaughn told E&Y that he and Six were a package deal. Vaughn also insisted that their positions be in the National Tax Department so that they would have a central role in designing and marketing tax shelters. Vaughn's further requirements were that E&Y give them a percentage of sales on top of their salaries, relief from needing to keep detailed billing and expense records, and carte blanche with regard to travel expenses.

The firm balked at first but eventually agreed, and the two CPA/financial planners joined Ernst & Young in late January 1998 as the VIPER sales force. Vaughn and Six were excited that E&Y was committed to providing significant resources to developing a shelter practice aimed at high-wealth individuals, especially since Deloitte did not seem interested in doing so.[6] They also knew that they were going to have to deliver serious sales results to justify the employment packages they had obtained. Six months after they had come on board, Vaughn circulated a presentation to VIPER members in which he anticipated revenues of $3.5 million for 1998, increasing to $15 million in 1999, and $25 million in 2000.[7] The pressure to produce was on.

The VIPER team spent most of its time brainstorming on possible high-value tax strategies. Team members believed that it was unlikely they would get authorization to offer shelters that completely eliminated taxes. Ernst & Young had been more cautious than other firms in entering the personal shelter market, and a tax elimination strategy might draw unwelcome IRS attention. VIPER therefore focused its efforts on strategies designed to convert ordinary income to capital gains and to defer taxation until a later time. By late 1998, however, the group had produced little in the way of marketable products. Vaughn and Six became concerned that their jobs might be in jeopardy. The other VIPER team members had other responsibilities at the firm, but the two-person sales team was dedicated solely to marketing VIPER strategies.

At a VIPER meeting at the end of 1998, Richard Shapiro mentioned a tax shelter that the group had discussed before and had rejected as too complicated. The idea had originated with David Smith, the former KPMG tax manager who had moved to Quadra and then formed Private Capital Management Group (PCMG), a purported "investment" firm. Vaughn assured the group that if someone could explain the shelter to him, he would be able to explain it to potential clients. He and Six were told to meet with Smith and learn more about it.

Vaughn, Six, and Smith met at the Mansion on Turtle Creek hotel complex in Dallas for the better part of a day in December 1998. Smith explained something known as a "contingent deferred swap" (CDS).[8] The objective of the transaction was first to defer taxation for one year. The shelter then converted ordinary income into long-term capital gains. This would cut the tax rate in half for a client from about 40 percent to 20 percent. This combination of deferral and conversion seemed a good fit for E&Y, given the firm's wariness toward shelters that intended to eliminate tax liability completely.

As with other tax shelters, the transaction was organized around forming a partnership that would show losses that taxpayers could claim on their individual tax returns. For CDS to work, this partnership needed to be characterized for tax purposes as a "trade or business," to generate "business deductions" that clients could use to offset their taxable income. To make it appear that the "trading partnership" was engaged in trading for profit, funds contributed by the taxpayer were placed in a trading account that engaged in a high volume of short-term trades. The partnership would also engage in a swap with a bank, which had the effect of creating a loss in the first year equivalent to the amount of income the client wanted sheltered. Because the partnership purported to be in the business of trading, IRS rules allowed it to deduct this loss from the ordinary income earned by the taxpayer in the same year.[9]

In the second year, the partnership took steps designed to convert the taxpayer's ordinary income to capital gains, which were taxed at about half the rate. The most important step was terminating the swap contract before it matured. Early termination triggered a payment to the partnership from the financial institution that was the counterparty to the swap. Under the applicable tax provisions, the payment would be treated as a capital gain rather than ordinary income because it had been earned from an early termination rather than from a payment at the maturity date of the swap. Conceived as a tax strategy, CDS permitted a taxpayer with a large amount of ordinary income to defer paying taxes on it for one year and then convert it into capital gains. In economic terms, taxpayers ended up in virtually the same condition they were before the transaction—but with a significantly lower tax liability.

As with other shelters, for CDS to have any plausibility, it had to have economic substance. The taxpayer, therefore, had to have some funds at risk in the transaction. The trading activity of the partnership, however, was explicitly designed to result in little or no change in the economic position of the taxpayer, belying the claim that the partnership was involved in actual trading. Equally important, the early termination of the swap had to purport to represent a business decision by one of the partners in the transaction, not a planned step in a preorchestrated process.

After meeting with Smith, Vaughn and Six reported back to the other VIPER members. Over the next several months, the team engaged in further research to develop the strategy, consulting regularly with David Smith and Brent Clifton, a partner at Locke, Liddell & Sapp, the law firm that had agreed to provide the opinion letter for the strategy. During the same period, Smith had persuaded PwC to design and market CDS,[10] a fact that may have been a factor in Ernst & Young's decision to jump in.

Locke Liddell would receive at least $50,000 for each opinion concluding that the transaction more likely than not would be upheld if challenged by the IRS. E&Y and PCMG would receive 1.25 percent of the amount of the desired tax loss, or a quarter of a million dollars on a $20 million transaction. As the shelter neared implementation, UBS was recruited to serve as the bank that would engage in a swap with the partnership. Andrew Krieger, a principal at Deerhurst Management, was enlisted to do the trades, which were overseen by Bolton Capital Trading, one of the investment companies in a group owned by Memphis-based Charles Bolton. At one time Krieger was a highly regarded derivatives trader who pioneered currency options trading at Banker's Trust when the bank moved aggressively into proprietary trading in the mid-1980s. At some point, Krieger had met Smith and Michael Schwartz of KPMG and then PwC. Schwartz got Krieger involved in executing the trading for a number of other tax shelters.[11]

In late summer 1999, E&Y began to move forward with its first CDS transactions. Although one partner at the firm's National Tax Department had expressed concerns about the shelter, the firm did not have a formal process of review. One outside lawyer who had been shown CDS by a client wrote to the firm characterizing the strategy as a "classic 'sham' tax shelter" that would be successfully challenged on audit by the IRS.[12] No one in the VIPER group paid any mind. The group was intent on pressing forward. As sales of CDS surged during 2000, the team became more and more ambitious. At the beginning of 2000, the team set its goal as a total of $1 billion of CDS losses. In a CDS update in late April, Brian Vaughn crowed that the team was "well on our way" to meeting this goal.

As part of its firm-wide efforts, the VIPER group had developed an internal "Action Plan" that set forth fifty-four steps to implement a transaction. One was to have the client sign an engagement letter with a fixed dollar amount as the fee, rather than to refer to tax losses as the basis. "**DO NOT** reference tax losses in the engagement letter," directed the Action Plan.[13] Step 45 in the draft plan dealt with another sensitive issue: "At the appropriate time within the swap period, G[eneral] P[artner] will terminate the swaps with the bank."[14] At least one member of the team was concerned that putting this so starkly in writing would be a red flag for the IRS. As Richard Shapiro observed,

One of the problems with tax advantaged transactions when they are reviewed is that they are perceived—correctly, I might add—as too scripted. While having a plan is important, should we have in writing "before the fact" such things as the fact that our swap will be terminated early? Clearly that is necessary for the flow of the transaction. But should there be a document in existence (such as this) that has all chapters and verses laid out? I question that seriously. The fact that no materials are to be left behind at a sales call is not enough, in my opinion. Before anything is in stone here, we should consider what our record should look like.[15]

In response, the reference to early termination was removed. Going forward, the VIPER team was careful to eliminate references in CDS documents suggesting that taxpayers had planned on terminating the swap early from the time they entered the transaction. Team members were also very careful to refer to the CDS as an "investment" and not a "tax" strategy.[16]

The team went to great lengths to create material for the files so that clients who purchased CDS would be able to document ostensibly nontax business purposes for electing to terminate the swaps early. A convenient excuse arose with the terrorist attacks in September 2001. Three days after the attacks, Coplan sent a letter to clients suggesting that they use 9/11 as the reason for exiting the transactions. Coplan proposed to clients that they write: "Based on the recent terrorist attacks and the possible economic repercussions resulting from such attacks I have decided to re-evaluate my investment activities and market exposure." The client, "after carefully considering the effects of the recent events," should express the intention to begin closing down positions in the trading account.[17]

By late 2000, CDS began to attract attention from the IRS. Despite inquiries from the agency, Brian Vaughn's enthusiasm for the transaction did not wane. Vaughn emphasized to Coplan that Vaughn would buy the transaction knowing full well that the IRS was investigating it. "As I told you," Vaughn wrote,

I am a fighter. I don't enjoy giving up before I get my chance to fight. Remember our opinion on CDS is a should. Let them bring their guns!!!! I believe they will turn their tales [sic] and run the other direction. CDS has economic substance and has the best promoter in the business associated with the trade. I think we owe it to Belle [who by then had gone to work for David Smith implementing CDS] and ourselves not to give up and stop the sales process at this point. Let the clients decide.[18]

Ernst & Young continued to promote CDS aggressively into 2001. All told, it sold seventy transactions involving 132 taxpayers, obtaining nearly $28 million in fees. The IRS listed the transaction as a potentially abusive shelter in May 2002.[19]

From VIPER to COBRA

Belle Six had left E&Y to work at PCMG with David Smith in August 1999. Six was struggling to extricate herself from her affair with Vaughn, which had become very tumultuous. She hoped that a different workplace would make it easier.[20] The financial benefits of the move were also substantial. At PCMG, Six was going to earn 40 percent of the company's fees, which were 1.5 percent of the losses claimed by a client. In her new position, she continued to work on CDS transactions as a liaison to E&Y.

The next month, Vaughn sent an email to more than two dozen people at E&Y. "Based on meetings today with Brent Clifton at Locke, Liddell, David Smith and Belle Six of PCMG," he wrote, "we believe we will have a permanent capital loss/ordinary loss strategy by September 15th."[21] Despite E&Y's earlier reluctance at offering tax elimination strategies, Vaughn and the remainder of the VIPER team were preparing to move into this market, where KPMG, PwC, and Arthur Andersen were already active. As Vaughn explained, "The strategy . . . involves the use of foreign currency contracts, 'contingent liabilities,' trading partnership, and NO bank loans. . . . The new strategy will create a 1999 permanent capital or ordinary loss. We anticipate a $1 billion worth of loss for 1999. A great start to the new fiscal year. . . . Let's have fun with this new strategy and kick some KPMG, PWC and AA. . . . No more BLIPS and BOSS."[22]

The shelter that E&Y was developing was the short option strategy that it eventually marketed as Currency Options Bring Reward Alternatives (COBRA), a version of the Son of BOSS shelter described in chapters 4 and 5. This shelter sought to increase taxpayers' basis in a partnership by the amount they paid to buy an option, while ignoring a reduction in basis that should have been triggered by the partnership assuming the taxpayers' liability to deliver shares under an option they sold.

Rather than working with Locke Liddell, E&Y sought to jump-start the shelter by collaborating with Paul Daugerdas at Jenkens & Gilchrist, whose experience designing and promoting contingent liability shelters dated back to his days at Arthur Andersen during the mid-1990s. The E&Y version of the option strategy that Daugerdas was offering provided for a slightly greater chance of a profit, although the likelihood was still miniscule. In addition to issuing an opinion letter, Jenkens prepared most of the transaction documents and arranged for Deutsche Bank to execute the trades. Jenkens would receive a fee of about 3 percent of the tax loss generated by the transaction, while E&Y would get 1.5 percent. R. J. Ruble of Brown & Wood would also receive a fee for issuing a second legal opinion.

After reviewing the shelter, the VIPER partners—Coplan, Nissenbaum, and Shapiro—concluded that it would more likely than not be upheld if challenged by the IRS. The sole dissenter was David Garlock, a partner in E&Y's National Tax Department, who did not believe the transaction had merit. By October, the VIPER team was ready to roll out the strategy—"I smell fees" Vaughn chortled.[23] Because of the strategy's riskiness, the VIPER leaders had decided to limit sales of COBRA to a small number of eligible clients. The "quick strike" team, as the sales group called itself, had to sell and implement the strategy by year's end so that clients could take advantage of the losses generated to shelter 1999 income.

A month or so later, sales efforts came to halt, at least temporarily. In December 1999, COBRA came to the attention of Michael Kelley, the partner in charge of overseeing E&Y's geographic area practices and the number two person in the firm's tax practice. At about the same time, the IRS issued Notice 99-59, which targeted the BOSS shelter that PwC had been marketing. Concerned about the propriety of marketing a loss elimination strategy, Kelley asked several members of the firm's Strategic Business Solutions group (SBS) who were experts in partnership taxation to review the transaction. Although E&Y had been selling COBRA aggressively to high-wealth individuals through the Personal Financial Counseling group, apparently no one with specific knowledge of partnership tax had actually reviewed the strategy before it had been approved.[24] By this time, the firm had already completed sixteen transactions, earning $13 million in the month the strategy became available.[25] When Coplan heard from Kelley, he reluctantly put a hold on COBRA deals in the works pending a decision.

As part of the SBS's belated review, Jerred Blanchard, a partner in that group, was asked to analyze the transaction. Blanchard was highly critical. In his review, Blanchard noted that the argument for excluding the partnership's assumption of the taxpayer's short option obligation from the calculation of basis was unpersuasive, and that the mere paper loss that the taxpayer incurred was unlikely to be recognized by the government.[26] As Blanchard further emphasized, "The transaction does not seem to be one that a reasonable investor would entertain in the absence of the anticipated generation of a $20 million federal income tax benefit."[27] The expected value of the loss exceeded the expected value of the potential gain, he noted, by $570,000. In other words, from a business perspective, the deal was almost certainly a loser. When Coplan saw Blanchard's analysis, he dubbed it a "hatchet job."[28]

In early January, Kelley convened a meeting in the Washington office with several members of SBS; Coplan; Ron Friedman, the head of the firm's National Tax Quality and Standards group; Robert Carney, a partner in Tax Controversy Matters; and Michael Frank, in-house counsel, to discuss whether E&Y should continue to sell COBRA.[29] After discussion, Kelley directed the group to stop marketing COBRA, a decision subsequently supported by William Lipton, the vice chair of tax.[30] Kelley proposed that, going forward, new strategies should require sign-off from two tax partners with subject matter expertise before a product was approved for marketing. Kelley also advised the tax strategy group to stop using clever reptilian acronyms, which, he noted, could be given an "inflammatory characterization by critics."[31] In response, Coplan agreed to "defang" the names the group was using.[32] In February, VIPER was changed to the "less sinister sounding acronym"[33] SISG, which stood for Strategic Individual Solutions Group.

At around this time, tensions were surfacing between Coplan and Vaughn. Vaughn was miffed that he had not been included in the review meeting and was feeling left out when it came to team decisions. "I cannot afford to be excluded from this process," Vaughn complained to Coplan. "Many people in the field view me as the leader of the VIPER team and in charge of the sales process. By excluding me from these calls and meetings I am not able to fulfill this role and help the local offices."[34] For his part, Coplan was annoyed that Vaughn was a little careless with regard to communications with the team. Over time, he and Shapiro also noted a tendency of Vaughn's to go around the team to deal with higher-ups in the National Tax Department.[35] Hired to market the group's product and out of his league when it came to substantive tax expertise, Vaughn nevertheless considered himself an important participant in substantive decisions about the strategies.

Despite Kelley's decision that E&Y cease marketing COBRA, he apparently made an exception for one last, lucrative transaction. In early 2000, Coplan asked him for permission for one more deal, emphasizing that the clients, who had signed an engagement letter in late 1999, were still very eager to go forward and understood the attendant risks. The

Murphy family were highly successful hog farmers in North Carolina who were planning to sell their operations in early 2000 for about $200 million, with an expected profit of nearly $100 million. Kelley gave Coplan the green light, but insisted that the family sign a "hold harmless" agreement, under which they agreed that they would not bring any claims against the accounting firm if it turned out that the tax benefits of the strategy were disallowed. After the Murphys were informed that the strategy was very risky and the firm was seemingly shielded from potential lawsuits, Coplan got the go-ahead to sell the Murphys COBRA.

By the end of 1999, the VIPER group had decided to stop using Jenkens & Gilchrist to provide legal opinions for COBRA. Members of the group had become concerned, somewhat belatedly, that since Jenkens had been involved in developing the strategy, the law firm would not be viewed as independent for purposes of providing an opinion that protected a taxpayer against penalties. In addition, members of the VIPER group were displeased at the huge fee Jenkens was charging, a whopping 3 percent of the losses claimed in COBRA transactions. For the Murphy family, or "Murfam" COBRA, Coplan brought in Ira Akselrad, of the New York law firm Proskauer Rose, who was willing to provide the necessary legal opinions for about $400,000 each. Ernst & Young declined to pass on the full savings to the Murphys, instead increasing its fee from 1.5 percent to 2 percent. The firm ended up earning $2 million from the transaction.

Despite the substantial fees, the firm's implementation of several COBRA transactions hit some bumps along the way. In the Murphys' case, several important documents were finalized months after they should have been. As a result, the Proskauer law firm had the Murphys execute backdated documents. With a number of earlier COBRA transactions, E&Y missed a deadline for IRS filing extensions. When Coplan became aware of this "COBRA screw-up," in June 2000, he got nervous. "If this leads to an audit," he worried in an email, "we are dead meat."[36]

After the COBRA review in early 2000, Kelley and members of the SBS team decided to take a look at CDS.[37] Kelley concluded that sales of CDS shelters could continue as long as clients fit the appropriate risk profile. A celebratory Coplan titled the subject of an email reporting this news "CDS lives!"[38] As he underscored to the SISG team, "One point Mike Kelley stressed is that we should be very certain that the individuals we approach with this transaction are sophisticated investors who fully understand the economic and tax risks of the transaction, and would not likely seek compensation from us if the anticipated tax benefits are not ultimately realized."[39]

Coplan closed his email to the SISG team with a promise to find a new strategy that would produce sufficient revenues to replace those lost when COBRA was discontinued. "Finally let me congratulate you on a phenomenal first quarter," he wrote. "The next quarter will pose challenges without COBRA, but we will strive to bring you new solutions and complete those in the pipeline to restock your quivers."[40]

In the meantime, some SISG leaders continued to get negative feedback from lawyers in the tax bar who were repelled by the transactions E&Y was promoting. In May 2000 Shapiro, who practiced in the firm's New York office, complained to Coplan: "I got one of those 'unpleasant' calls I now get from time to time from dan shapiro [sic], senior tax partner at schulte roth [sic], who used to think highly of me he severely questioned COBRA; now I think he is about to question CDS."[41]

Restocking the Quiver

The search for new shelters was rewarded a few months later. In early May 2000 Vaughn met with Six, who had moved with David Smith to work at Bolton, and other staff at E&Y to discuss a new strategy for clients who participated in the CDS shelter. The basic idea was to graft a COBRA-like tax eliminator onto the CDS shelter so that taxpayers would be able to defer taxation, turn it into capital gains, and then postpone any tax indefinitely. After the taxpayer died, the gains would not be subject to income tax.[42]

Excited about this new strategy, Vaughn contacted Coplan: "If we could integrate CDS and the foreign currency trading program with the short option transaction, we could have a great transaction," he enthused.[43] Coplan forwarded Vaughn's message to Nissenbaum and Shapiro. Vaughn urged the firm to move ahead, saying, "I am only trying to seize the moment. If not us, another firm will."[44] Coplan tried to encourage Vaughn, but emphasized: "It will not be easy to turn our folks around on a COBRA-like strategy" in light of the earlier directive to discontinue the COBRA shelter.[45] He and others in SISG knew that they had to provide a credible business purpose for the add-on feature to get it approved within E&Y. The story that Coplan and others concocted was that the idea to consolidate the partnerships and their trading activity had come from a manager handling CDS trades who believed that this consolidation would make trading "exotic" options with nonstandard features on behalf of the partnerships more efficient. Coplan and his colleagues represented that the trader already had planned to take these steps before they had learned of it and that whatever tax benefits might result were simply an incidental advantage. To get what they dubbed CDS Add-On past the firm's SBS group, Coplan used the ruse to obtain the assistance of Dale Hortenstine, a member of the group and a partnership tax specialist. After the COBRA review, Hortenstine had explained to others in the firm that the reason this earlier strategy had been shut down by his group was that "we perceived there to be a lack of meaningful potential for economic profit or other business purpose to justify the transaction under an ACM analysis."[46] The fabricated story about CDS Add-On persuaded Hortenstine to assist SISG, and the strategy was approved.

Brent Clifton's opinion letter for CDS Add-On on behalf of Locke Liddell described the ostensible business purpose for the steps necessary to effectuate the transaction for a given partnership. The letter stated that the general manager of the partnership had enlisted the services of Andrew Krieger of Deerhurst Management based on his sterling track record. Krieger had expressed his wish "to consolidate his trading strategy in one partnership rather than among the several partnerships" because a single, consolidated account would enable him to "obtain accounting efficiencies, a greater pool of capital, and risk diversification." In addition, such consolidation would enable Deerhurst to engage in exotic option trades through Bear Stearns, which had indicated that it would not execute such trades on behalf of individual partnerships because of administrative burdens. On the basis of these discussions and conversations with investors in the partnerships, the letter explained, Bolton had formed the limited liability company (LLC).[47]

As investor experience indicated, these considerations were in fact irrelevant to the creation of the LLC involved in the CDS Add-On shelter. Joel Leonard, for instance, was a partner in a proprietary options trading company in Chicago known as Cornerstone Partners. In mid-2000, Leonard's accountant suggested that he contact Jeff Brodsky at Ernst & Young about some transactions in which Leonard might be interested. Brodsky and other E&Y personnel then came to Leonard's office and arranged for Brian Vaughn to participate in the meeting by phone. The first question they asked Leonard was whether Cornerstone would be earning at least $20 million that year. When Leonard indicated that the firm would come close to that, Brodsky told him that E&Y had a shelter that would defer taxes on that income indefinitely. During the meeting, SISG members tried to explain the steps of the transaction, but Leonard, despite his financial acumen, could not make heads or tails of the presentation. As he later recalled, his most important question was, "Can I go to jail for this?" After being reassured that it was legal, Leonard decided to do the transaction.[48]

As with the earlier tax strategies, the SISG team was sensitive to the need to establish a record that the CDS Add-On transaction had a nontax business purpose. Whereas documents inside SISG were explicit about the tax purpose of the strategy, materials the group was to provide to clients had to underscore the purported business purpose of the transaction and could not refer to any facts suggesting that the purpose of the transaction was to obtain tax benefits. As with earlier techniques, the steps of the strategy had to appear to be the product of the taxpayer's independent decisions over the period of the transaction. Coplan instructed: "There should be no materials in the clients' hands or even in their memory that describes CDS as a single strategy that includes the Add On feature."[49]

In August 2000 the IRS issued Notice 2000-44, which was clearly directed at contingent liability shelters like COBRA. The SISG team never doubted that this strategy was encompassed within the IRS's notice.[50] Rather than revisit the transactions and perhaps unwind them, as the team knew PwC had done with BOSS a year earlier, the E&Y team resisted the IRS's position. The notice "only represented the Service's views, which we knew would not be favorable as to the transaction," Coplan remarked.[51] Assuming that the notice had no retroactive implications, Coplan believed that since the transactions had already closed, the law firms engaged to provide opinions could analyze the facts as they existed before the issuance of the notice and still conclude that a court would more likely than not uphold the transaction.[52] Soon after the notice came out, E&Y instructed offices that had sold COBRAs to set aside reserves to cover client audits, which it now believed were likely.[53] Around the same time, the *Wall Street Journal* published an article that singled out PwC's tax shelter activities. Tax practice leaders were relieved that E&Y had been overlooked in the article.[54] PwC had been "too greedy" remarked Michael Kelley, the partner in charge of geographic tax practice areas who had approved the Murfam shelter.[55]

Into the fall of 2000, Coplan felt it was necessary to continue to paper client files to substantiate business reasons for engaging in transactions.

In the case of CDS Add-On, Coplan emailed Belle Six seeking a brochure describing Deerhurst's trading record prior to the date of the consolidation of a client's partnership into the LLC. "It would be useful to have such a statement in the client's files," Coplan observed, "showing the hopefully impressive performance of Deerhurst prior to the client's decision to . . . transfer a portion of their trading account to the LLC."[56] The problem was that by the time Coplan requested the brochure, clients had already made their decisions to engage in the strategy.[57]

In 2000, E&Y had also begun to market another shelter that proved to be quite lucrative. The objective of this strategy, sold under the name of Personal Investment Corporation (PICO) was to defer taxation and convert ordinary income into capital gains. The strategy involved the creation of an S corporation jointly owned by the client and an investment advisor. An S corporation, like a partnership, does not pay taxes. Instead, gains or losses from its investment activities are reported directly by its shareholders. In this tax shelter strategy, after the S corporation engaged in some options trading that would produce nearly equivalent gains and losses, the taxpayer and investment advisor terminated the transaction through a series of steps that allowed the gains to be allocated to the investment advisor, while the losses could be claimed on the taxpayer's return. As usual, the taxpayer would depict the transaction as profit-seeking investment activity. There would be no meaningful change in economic position, however, and the client would simply follow a prescribed series set of steps that produced an economic loss on paper.

To develop the PICO transaction, E&Y worked with Andrew Beer of an investment company called Bricolage. Beer had dreamed up the transaction in the "wee hours" of the night.[58] To find out if the transaction "worked," Beer turned to Peter Cinquegrani, a tax specialist at Arnold & Porter and former lawyer in the IRS's Chief Counsel Office. Beer had previously worked on tax strategies with Cinquegrani, including two shelters, COYNS and POPS, marketed by Arthur Andersen. After reviewing the PICO documentation in early 2000, Cinquegrani concluded that the transaction was a viable shelter. After Cinquegrani gave the transaction a thumbs up, Beer put him in touch with Richard Shapiro on the SISG team, the lead contact at E&Y during the development process.[59]

For the PICO transaction to have any hope of passing IRS scrutiny, there had to be a plausible nontax reason why someone would create an S corporation in collaboration with an investment company and then buy that party out after only sixty or ninety days. The story that E&Y fabricated was that the client formed the S corporation for asset protection and estate planning purposes. The taxpayer included the investment advisor because she wanted to try out Bricolage's trading strategy for a limited period to determine whether it was sound. At the end of that period, if she was satisfied with the results she would buy out the other members of the corporation and enter into a two-year asset management contract with the advisor or one of its affiliates.

Following a now familiar modus operandi, the SISG team had to make sure that no client materials suggested that PICO was anything other than a business strategy. One aspect of the PICO shelter that created a risk of unfavorable documentation was the E&Y fee. The firm's fee was about 2 percent of the loss that the client wanted to generate, an amount that was quite large compared to the size of the initial investment. The size of the fee made it difficult to argue that the taxpayer expected any economic gain from the transaction. Coplan directed that a fee of only $50,000 be listed in the client's engagement letter with E&Y for the PICO transaction. E&Y then arranged for the remainder of its fee to be paid by the client to a Bricolage entity, and for that company to pay this amount to E&Y. To support this payment, E&Y fabricated a contract under which E&Y supposedly provided consulting services to one of Bricolage's affiliates. These contracts often were created after the fees had already been passed on to E&Y and so had to be backdated to avoid any discrepancies.

All told, E&Y marketed the CDS Add-On shelter to sixty-one individuals in 2000. CDS Add-On generated more than $24 million in revenues for the firm. The firm sold ninety-six PICO transactions to 150 individuals, generating more than $56 million in fees.[60]

Dead Meat

Coplan's concern that the files be papered to deflect IRS attention was not far-fetched. In December 2000 the IRS had begun to make inquiries of Bolton about a number of CDS shelters that E&Y had registered. In response to a letter from the IRS, Bolton insisted that "[a]t no time did [Bolton Capital] present to any investor or potential investor any other analysis or opinion related to the intended tax benefits of such a transaction." Bolton claimed that the partnership's investment objective was "capital appreciation for the investment through a variety of financial instruments." In fact, the actual goal of the trading was "capital preservation," which would leave the client's financial position essentially unchanged. Bolton also maintained that "[t]he partnership incurred recourse debt in order to pursue trading activities, as well as make investments in swap transactions with large notional amounts."[61] In fact, debt was incurred only for the swap, not for trading activity. In addition, Bolton represented that "[a] portion of the assets of each partnership was invested to seek profits through short-term trading strategies." In reality, trading activity was aimed at establishing the partnership as a trading business only for tax purposes. Bolton's description also declared, "If the general partner based on market fluctuations terminates contracts early, capital gain would arise on such termination."[62] In fact, the plan from the outset in all cases was to terminate early; termination had nothing to do with market movements.

When the IRS began to audit David Smith's Private Capital Management Group (PCMP) and sought information on the CDS transactions, Coplan sent an email in June 2001 to Belle Six about how the CDS Add-On shelters were numbered. "It may be too late," he said, "but would you please reconsider your rejection of my suggestion that the different partnerships be named individually by the limited [partners] instead of being named numbers in sequence. We are obviously making it too easy for the IRS to simply find one transaction and then look for all other partnerships with a similar name filed in the same service center. The fact that they are going in sequence has me reasonably convinced they are mowing through all the PCMG returns."[63]

During the same period the IRS was looking into CDS, Coplan received worrisome news about COBRA. The IRS had started to investigate one of the partnerships that had used that strategy. In mid-March 2001, the partnership had received a notice from the IRS seeking information and documents. Over the next few weeks, Shapiro, Coplan, Thomas Dougherty, who had sold the strategy, and Dennis Conlon, a lead partner in E&Y's Tax Controversy group, brainstormed about plausible business purposes that might have led the taxpayers to form the partnership and invest in foreign currency options. In May, Dougherty, Conlon, and Shapiro—the team assembled to deal with the IRS audit—appeared for an IRS interview on behalf of their clients. The team suggested to the IRS agent that in their preliminary discussions with the clients, E&Y had discussed the financial implications of entering into the transaction and that this was the basis for their clients' decision. The E&Y audit team also claimed that the fee paid to the firm was for "financial planning and investment advisory services."[64] When asked by the IRS agent whether the clients had received promotional materials, team members prevaricated.[65] At the close of the meeting, the team was handed an Information Document Request asking for additional documents. Request No. 9 sought marketing documents and all other documents relating to the financial or tax consequences of participating in the transaction.[66]

Over the next few months, team members struggled to figure out how to answer Request No. 9 to avoid handing over COBRA marketing materials. Following Coplan's instructions when COBRA was first rolled out, Dougherty had not left any materials explaining the tax benefits of the transaction when he pitched it to the clients, so they had no promotional documents in their possession. The problem was that Dougherty had documents in his files that he had shown clients. Over the next two months, the audit team went back and forth about how to answer the request truthfully but still avoid handing over COBRA promotional material. They did not want to suggest that they had anything in response to the request. At the same time, they did not want to indicate misleadingly that they had nothing. In early July, Dougherty had come up with a draft response that stated that the clients did not believe they had promotional documents in their files and that the request as worded was seeking information covered by the attorney-client, work product, and statutory accountant privileges.[67] Coplan continued to be dissatisfied with this response, which apparently raised too many red flags. On July 17, the E&Y group assembled to deal with the IRS audit and Coplan held another phone conversation during which they tried to come up with more satisfactory language.[68]

At this point—perhaps believing that no matter how the team answered Request No. 9 the IRS would insist on obtaining COBRA documents in the firm's files—Coplan must have panicked. That same afternoon, he sent out a blast email to the SISG team and other E&Y personnel involved in selling COBRA, instructing them to destroy all documents discussing the tax implications of the strategy. In an email with the subject line "Important—Purge of all key COBRA documents," he wrote:

In an effort to eliminate unnecessary material from files—both paper and electronic—you are hereby instructed to immediately delete and dispose of any and all materials in your drawers and on your computers related to the COBRA transaction other than 1) documents related to the currency trades made by the client and research done to assist in deciding on those trades, 2) documents supporting the economic purpose and bona fide nature of the investment in the transaction, and 3) your copies of the opinion letters issued to the client.[69]

Coplan's purge order must have come to the attention of someone in E&Y's general counsel's office. The following day, Coplan sent out a follow-up email with the subject heading "CANCEL PURGE REQUESTS OF COBRA DOCS." "Based on some information I just received from general counsel's office," he explained, "I must ask you all NOT to purge ANY COBRA documents to the extent you have not done so already." By then, E&Y personnel had already destroyed COBRA promotional materials.[70]

As audits of clients who participated in CDS, COBRA, and CDS Add-On increased over the next two years, tax professionals at E&Y continued their pattern of trying to mislead the IRS about the nature of the transactions. Clients were coached to tell the IRS they had engaged in the transactions for business reasons. Dennis Conlon, for example, emphasized to Leonard (the options trader who had not been able to understand the basic mechanics of CDS Add-On) that Leonard needed to say that he participated in the transaction "for the chance to make a lot of money."[71] Conlon used a spreadsheet to show Leonard the range of outcomes from the digital trading that went on as part of the transaction—trading of which Leonard had been wholly unaware. As he went over the figures with Leonard, he would say things like, "As you know, Joel," and "So you remember, Joel, that the reason you did this trade was because . . ."[72] Pointing to the "sweet spot" that represented the lottery payout, Conlon said, "See, you had a chance if you did this trade, that you could have made . . . almost $38 million, remember? That's why you did this trade. See? That's why you did this trade, right? It had that sweet spot where you could have made that money, as you know."[73]

In coaching clients, E&Y tax professionals seemed more intent on protecting the firm than looking out for the interests of their clients, who might have suffered fewer repercussions by coming clean to the IRS. In any event, it would only be a matter of time before the government trained its sights directly on E&Y.

Arthur Andersen

Arthur Andersen appears to have participated extensively in the market for tax shelters, and in particular in the promotion of Son of BOSS contingent liability shelters like those described in chapter 5. Because the firm went under in the wake of the Enron scandal, however, only piecemeal evidence of its involvement has come to light.

The public documents available suggest that Arthur Andersen was involved in promoting shelters as early as the mid-1990s when Paul Daugerdas, then a partner at Andersen, developed his first versions of contingent liability shelters using Treasury bills.[74] By 2000, the firm was marketing a slew of tax elimination shelters, under names and acronyms such as Short Sales, COINS, POPS, and Leveraged Options Strategy. Many of these transactions were designed and implemented with the help of Deutsche Bank and the financial boutique Bricolage. The transactions involved legal opinions obtained from Peter Cinquegrani, the Arnold & Porter tax lawyer who had provided opinions to E&Y clients on PICO, and William Bricker, a tax lawyer at Curtis, Mallet-Prevost.[75] What documents have emerged also suggest that tax leadership at Arthur Andersen drove its shelter activities. By the early 2000s, the firm had a team dedicated to developing and selling shelters. A formal "opinion committee" consisting of tax partners in the Office of Federal Tax Services, the firm's Washington office, reviewed and approved shelters before they were marketed.[76]

Arthur Andersen got in the game early and stayed in late. In 1999, Ken Mandel, the partner responsible for designing, selling, and implementing "leading-edge tax solutions" in the firm's Western U.S. area, had developed, with the approval of firm leaders, a variation of Son of BOSS, known internally as a "call-option spread." In 2000, the firm had about twenty of these transactions in the works, which ended up generating almost $15 million in fees. After IRS Notice 2000-44 was announced, which targeted so-called contingent liability or Son of BOSS shelters, Mandel and tax leaders at the firm persuaded themselves that it did not apply to the call-option spread and continued to promote it through at least the end of 2001.

That fall James Thomas and Edward Fox, two highly successful real estate investors and developers—and, among other things, owners of the Sacramento Kings basketball franchise—purchased the call-option spread in an ultimately unsuccessful attempt to shelter approximately $45 million in income. The ubiquitous R. J. Ruble, now a partner at the recently merged Sidley Austin Brown & Wood, provided opinion letters for the strategy. The multinational insurance company AIG, which routinely paid Arthur Andersen a finder's fee to participate in the spread strategy, assisted in its execution.[77] After the IRS disallowed the claimed tax deductions, Thomas and Fox challenged the determination in court. In 2009, a district court upheld the IRS's decision, concluding that the transaction lacked economic substance. It also found that the taxpayers were liable for penalties because they had failed to show that they acted in good faith in claiming tax benefits from the strategy.[78]

Since that ruling, the government has presumably gone after individual taxpayers for tax benefits claimed in connection with Arthur Andersen's shelters. It has not, however, pursued actions against the firm or the professionals involved. After its indictment in connection with its conduct in Enron, Arthur Andersen lost its audit license, and effectively ceased operations. The government had little to gain from bringing charges against the defunct accounting firm. Former clients with potential claims against the firm settled quickly to make sure they obtained some recovery. As a consequence, no detailed chronology of the firm's tax shelter involvement has emerged.

PricewaterhouseCoopers

PwC sold about fifty FLIP transactions to clients in 1997 and 1998, twenty-six contingent deferred swap (CDS) transactions in 1998 and 1999, and around 120 BOSS transactions in 1999. FLIP was brought to PwC by Michael Schwartz, who in 1997 had come to Coopers & Lybrand, one of PwC's predecessor firms, by way of KPMG. Schwartz had left KPMG because he was unhappy with the compensation he received for his involvement in designing and marketing FLIP.[79] After the merger between Coopers & Lybrand and Price Waterhouse, Schwartz worked in the firm's Finance and Treasury Group. He introduced FLIP to various partners and presented the product to potential clients. By 1998, the Personal Financial Services group within the firm had assumed primary responsibility for marketing and implementing the shelter. In 1997 and 1998, Coopers & Lybrand participated in twelve FLIP transactions and PwC was involved in thirty-eight, for a total of fifty altogether.

At PwC, Schwartz recreated the type of arrangement for marketing and implementing FLIP that KPMG had used. Under the arrangement, First Union National Bank, which was later acquired by Wachovia, referred its customers to PwC for a FLIP presentation. PwC also used the investment firm Quadra, later renamed Quellos, to implement the transactions involved in the shelter. Schwartz worked with David Smith, with whom he had collaborated in designing FLIP when both were at KPMG. Implementing the shelter involved helping to set up offshore partnerships and working with various banks to arrange millions of dollars in financing. PwC did not register FLIP with the IRS but advised Quellos to do so, which it did in 1998 and 1999. PwC issued opinion letters to clients who purchased FLIP stating that the shelter more likely than not would be upheld in court if it was challenged by the IRS.

Schwartz was also involved in the marketing and sale of BOSS, which was brought to him by Smith. In the BOSS strategy, the client made a payment of 8.5 percent of the desired tax loss or sheltered income, about half of which went to PwC, the investment firm, and Refco Bank, which provided financing. As with FLIP, PwC relied on First Union for referrals, and the bank sent twenty-five investors to the firm for presentations on the BOSS shelter. BOSS had originally been reviewed and rejected by partners in KPMG's Washington National Tax office, including Steve Rosenthal, the expert in taxation of financial instruments who, with Mark Watson, had unsuccessfully tried to derail BLIPS (as described in chapter 5). PwC decided to promote the shelter. It first used PCMG and then Bolton Asset Management, where Smith later moved his projects, to implement the transactions. Smith also brought PwC the CDS strategy that he had created.

One reason why Schwartz was so successful in marketing shelter ideas within PwC was the weakness of the firm's internal review process. Each individual business unit within PwC created its own ad hoc review committee, which usually comprised senior tax members chosen by the tax partners advocating a new idea. The committee then analyzed whether the proposed product complied with the technical requirements of federal tax law, but did not take into account the economic substance doctrine or reputational or ethical considerations. Each committee was supposed to reach a consensus on whether the proposed transaction more likely than not would be upheld in court if subject to challenge. Individual committee members, however, were not personally required to reach this conclusion. Instead, the standard was whether a member could reasonably believe that others could come to such a conclusion based on the technical characteristics of the transaction. Once a committee approved a new product, the business unit was then free to market it without obtaining approval from anyone else at the firm. As the U.S. Senate committee investigating tax shelters later noted, "this process lacked independence from the business unit which stood to profit if the product was approved."[80]

PwC also developed and marketed at least one individualized contingent liability strategy in 2000 aimed at eliminating taxes. In the late 1990s, infighting among the heirs of the founder of the *San Francisco Chronicle* and owners of Chronicle Publishing Company, the media conglomerate that owned the paper, prompted the family to sell the company. In the summer of 2000, family members turned to PwC, which designed a complex transaction that allowed the family to shelter the gains from the sale using the section 752 technique on which the Son of BOSS shelters relied (described in chapter 4). Ruble, predictably, wrote the opinion letters for the transaction. After the IRS disallowed the claimed tax benefits, the family members challenged its decision in court and lost. Not only did the district court conclude that the transaction had no economic substance, it also upheld the imposition of penalties, concluding that the family did not have good cause for understating its income and had not relied in good faith on Ruble's professional advice. The fact that the transaction was executed after the IRS issued Notice 2000-44, which made clear that it viewed Son of BOSS transactions as abusive, was not lost on the court.[81]

Purveyors of the tax shelters of the 1970s and 1980s for the most part had been institutions on the margins of professional respectability. In the tax shelter boom at the turn of the twenty-first century, in contrast, global accounting firms considered to be the epitome of professionalism played major roles in generating fraudulent tax losses of billions of dollars. As chapter 7 describes, the financial success of first-tier accounting firms from tax shelter work inspired at least one second-tier accounting firm to launch an aggressive effort to join the tax shelter game.

7

Dances with Wolves

In March 1999, the accounting firm BDO Seidman was struggling. Founded as Seidman and Seidman in New York in 1910, the firm expanded a few years later to Grand Rapids, Michigan, to serve the furniture industry, for which it developed the first furniture plan costing system. The firm developed a strong presence in the Midwest and opened additional offices on the East Coast. Former managing partner L. William Seidman had served as chair of the Federal Deposit Insurance Corporation from 1985 to 1991 and had played a lead role in liquidating hundreds of failed savings and loan associations that had gone into federal receivership during the collapse of the industry in the 1980s. BDO, which moved its headquarters from New York to Chicago in 1997, occupied the second tier of accounting firms below the Big Five. The firm didn't have the extensive sales network of global or even national offices that the Big Five had. Instead, it relied on programs like its Alliance Distribution Channel, which involved relationships with smaller accounting firms across the country. BDO provided these firms with tax expertise in return for a fee and access to their customer bases.

On March 17, 1999, the BDO board passed a resolution declaring "serious negative variances" in "operations and trends at the end of January 1999."[1] In other words, the firm's financial situation was dire. Especially troubling was the prospect that the firm would be in violation of its debt covenants establishing the minimum amount of cash that it had to have on hand.[2] According to the board, its financial oversight committee and national tax director Denis Field would work with BDO's executive committee to "analyze financial statements and [would] take actions at the appropriate offices."[3] Ultimately, several partners were terminated. Chief executive and board chair Dan Pavelich resigned and was succeeded by

Richard Roedel. In attempting to address the firm's financial troubles, Roedel relied on an inner circle of partners. Among them was Denis Field, who had led the firm's charge into the shelter market.

"Tax ell!"

Field's star was on the rise at BDO. He had come to the firm after earning a master's degree in tax law at New York University. Highly regarded for his technical expertise, he worked in international tax before becoming the national tax leader of the firm in 1996. In that position he had begun to boost BDO's revenues from various products designed to minimize clients' taxes. He called together key tax partners in New York in May 1996 to brainstorm about how to make tax practice more profitable. Like tax leaders at other accounting firms, Field wanted to move away from a focus on tax returns toward an emphasis on "value-added" consulting services. BDO had first done such a transaction when it approached an investment bank about handling a tax transaction for a BDO client. The bank had charged the client based on a percentage of the tax savings from the transaction and then paid BDO a fee from that.[4] Terry Kelly, a partner in the Grand Rapid office, suggested at the May 1996 meeting that the group call itself the "Wolf Pack," and soon Wolf Pack teams were visiting local BDO offices to help strategize about how to become more profitable.[5]

Field also encouraged firm members to develop and capitalize on networks such as the Alliance Distribution Channel to market the firm's products. He created a fund to pay bonuses to partners and employees who sold value-added transactions, some of which were tax shelters. Field had unilateral authority to determine who would receive bonuses from this fund before any other distributions were made to partners.

In 1998 an informal BDO tax products leader group was formed consisting of Field, Charles Bee, Adrian Dicker, Michael Kerekes, and Lorin Luchs. Members informed the national sales executive group which tax products were available, and the latter group worked to find clients who would be interested in these products. BDO also sought out tax shelter providers and put them in touch with BDO clients. Clients who bought the shelters would pay the providers a fee, who in turn paid BDO for the referrals. The firm formed a tax opinion committee as part of the tax leader group. This group was charged with reviewing potential products and determining which ones the firm would market. The committee also determined which products would generate bonuses for those who sold them and assumed responsibility for allocating these bonuses among sales force members.

In June 1999—in the midst of the firm's financial crisis—Adrian Dicker, after extensive discussion with Field and other key partners, sent a memo to Richard Roedel suggesting the establishment of the tax product program as a separate business line. The new business would be formed as a limited liability company (LLC), which meant that BDO would not be responsible for its liabilities. Dicker proposed that he, Field, and Bee would receive compensation based on the profitability of this business. This represented a shift from the traditional compensation system in accounting firms, which allocated units to partners that represented entitlement to a portion of the overall earnings of the firm. Roedel approved Dicker's proposal, and in October 1999 the tax leader group and the national sales executive group were merged into what was called the Tax Solutions Group. Field, Bee, and Dicker would each receive 10 percent of the net profits generated by its activities.

In early fall, Field announced the formation of the group to BDO partners. As he explained, the group's sales model provided that any BDO partner who had a client expecting a large gain from the sale of stock, a company, or other assets would notify a member of the Tax Solutions Group, who would then pitch the shelter to the client. The referring partner would receive a bonus for his or her referral. Field informed firm partners that members of the group would be in close communication with them in whatever way was most effective. "This may be via conference calls or meetings," his memo noted, but "is unlikely to be via pieces of paper setting out the transactions."[6] As at other firms, the absence of a paper record minimized the likelihood of competitors' learning the details of BDO's shelters and was a precaution to prevent information from getting into the hands of the IRS.

In the new group, Dicker focused on administrative matters such as accounting of money for bonuses, Bee on technical tax issues, and Field on motivating partners to find clients to do transactions. The tax opinion committee, which reviewed and approved tax products, was comprised of Field, Bee, Dicker, and Robert Greisman, who had been recruited a year earlier to BDO by Field's assurance that tax partners at the firm would routinely make $1 million a year. For the committee to approve a transaction, a unanimous decision was required.[7] Michael Kerekes, a partner in Los Angeles, was responsible for reading new cases and notices and apprising everyone of their implications.[8] Tax Solutions Group members, who numbered around twenty, covered different parts of the country. The general tax partner referring a client to the group would tell the client that BDO had a Tax Solutions Group that had ideas to reduce or eliminate taxes. The partner would outline to the appropriate group member the client's gain, how it arose, and when it was expected. The group member then scheduled a phone call or a meeting to discuss the shelter with the client.[9]

Field was a tireless cheerleader for tax shelters within the firm, with an aggressive style that "pushed people."[10] The slogan "Tax ell" was plastered on coffee mugs, documents, screen savers, and mouse pads throughout the firm. More than a slogan, Field declared, "Tax ell" was a "vision for the future," a strategy for "selling products, increasing fees, and increasing profitability." Finally, Field said, and "[m]ost importantly,'Tax ell' is a change in the culture of all our people and our attitude to tax services."[11] Field seized on the idea that the group was a wolf pack. He was without question "the alpha wolf,"[12] and led Wolf Pack members in howling like wolves at sales meetings.[13]

Field did a presentation to tax partners in the fall of 1999 that exemplified his approach to selling tax products. His presentation, which discussed the tax services business line, was entitled: "Wolves—Always Friendly But Never Tame."[14] One slide proclaimed:

We can turn the grayest sky to green
June 30, 1998 $2.2 Million Actual Profit.
We can make it rain whenever we want it to!
June 30, 1999 $14.8 Million Actual Profit.
We can turn a raging fire into a green river.
June 30, 2000 $75+ Million Profit Goal
With all the *power we possess* we can change BDO into a green ocean.[15]

A few slides later came the proclamation: "One word sums up the strategy of the Tax Business Line. MONEY! All of us in the Firm need to focus on money. Think Green. Green is good! There's nothing wrong with trying to make more money."[16] In case anyone wondered, "Where is the real money? SHOW ME THE MONEY," the answer was: "It's right in front of our faces. Our clients have the money. And we have the services they'll pay for."[17] Those services included tax consulting, financial planning and financial services, and "the super product category: Tax Solutions."[18] Field underscored the bonuses paid to the Tax Solutions Group the previous year, which totaled $4.6 million. In 2000, the goal was to pay $7.3 million. "You can all get in on this sea of green at BDO," Field's presentation concluded. "With the power, talent, and knowledge we possess in our Wolf Pack, we can turn BDO into a green, green ocean."[19]

With the Tax Solutions Group booming, Field ran a successful campaign in late 1999 to be named to the BDO board by its nominating committee. Bee also became a board member then, giving tax solutions even more clout. Field continued his meteoric rise when not long afterward a majority of the board decided to name him to replace Roedel as CEO and chair of the firm. Field assumed office at the beginning of 2000. At forty-one, he was the youngest partner ever to hold these positions. He would also continue as a member of the Tax Solutions Group. After taking over as CEO, he named each Tax Solutions Group leader a vice chairman to distinguish them from other partners. This resulted in a substantial increase in compensation for all members of the group. For Bee and Adrian Dicker, who joined the board shortly afterward, compensation jumped from $250,000 to $750,000 a year. "Tax $ells!" had effectively been Field's campaign platform, and the alpha wolf was now clearly in charge.

The Daugerdas Connection

A year earlier, Robert Greisman had had a meeting that would catapult him to a rarefied level in the BDO pecking order. A corporate lawyer at the Chicago law firm of Altheimer & Gray, whom Greisman knew from his prior work at Grant Thornton, introduced him to Paul Daugerdas. Greisman and Daugerdas met for dinner at Trattoria No. 10 in Chicago. The two discussed Daugerdas's work with an accounting firm that referred clients to him for transactions that would reduce or eliminate their tax liability. Daugerdas went on to describe a transaction called Basis Enhanced Security Transaction (BEST), which involved selling a two-year Treasury note short, purchasing another note, contributing both to a partnership, and taking advantage of partnership tax rules to increase the taxpayer's basis. When the partnership was liquidated through the transfer of its assets to a subchapter S corporation, taxpayers used the increased basis to claim a loss sufficient to offset whatever income they wanted to shelter.

As Daugerdas explained, he created the partnership and the S corporation, arranged with Deutsche Bank to execute the purchase and sale of options, and provided a legal opinion that stated that the tax treatment more likely than not would be upheld if challenged by the IRS.[20] He charged a fee equal to 3 percent of the capital gains tax savings and 4 percent or more for tax savings on ordinary income, which was taxed at a higher rate. Daugerdas offered to share a portion of his fee in return for BDO's referral of clients to him.

Greisman reported back to Field about his dinner with Daugerdas. His interest piqued, Field asked Greisman to set up a conference call to follow up. Greisman did so after signing a confidentiality agreement on behalf of BDO that had been prepared by Daugerdas. Although no one in the group had worked with Daugerdas, Bee had overlapped briefly with him at Arthur Andersen. According to Bee, Daugerdas had a reputation as a tax whiz. Field, Dicker, Bee, Kerekes, and a few other BDO partners participated in the call, quizzing Daugerdas about various aspects of the shelter he was selling.

The tax opinion committee then considered the proposed arrangement. Despite the appetite at BDO for value-added transactions, there was some concern about a fee structured as a percentage of what could be huge tax savings. Greisman mentioned that he had never seen a fee for a tax opinion letter that was based on a percentage of the tax savings. The fear was that the IRS might recharacterize the fee as a transaction cost that offset any potential for profit from the trading. This would eliminate any economic substance to the transaction—since it eliminated the reasonable possibility of making a profit—and make reliance on the tax opinion unreasonable. Another firm, for instance, charged a flat $100,000 fee and did no other legal work on the transaction. As an internal BDO memo suggested, "The fee paid for [this] tax opinion is not a cost of the transaction, and at the level of $100,000, where the law firm provides no additional services, is presumed to not be in danger of a recharacterization as a transaction cost."[21] By contrast, Jenkens & Gilchrist performed work forming and dissolving various entities and managing the short-sale process. Daugerdas nonetheless took the position that his fee was for a tax opinion and should not be considered a cost of the transaction because the economic analysis of that transaction did not include consideration of its tax impact.

During the committee's discussion, Bee questioned whether there was any meaningful potential to profit from a short sale of such brief duration. He was worried that Daugerdas's role in designing and promoting the shelter eliminated the possibility of treating his legal opinion as independent. He and Dicker also apparently believed that one or more IRS Revenue Rulings had indicated that tax losses from a transaction like the short sale would not be recognized by the agency.[22] The opinion committee discussed these and other concerns in deciding whether to establish a referral relationship with Daugerdas. Field eventually persuaded the committee to approve the arrangement, arguing that even if the IRS disallowed the tax treatment for the transactions and assessed interest and penalties on the taxpayer, the worst that would happen to BDO would be that it would be sued by a client for the fees that the client had paid. In November 1998, BDO began to market the Treasury short sale with Daugerdas.

Under the arrangement, BDO made the sales pitch to clients and secured the business before introducing them to Altheimer & Gray and, when Daugerdas and his colleagues moved firms, to Jenkens & Gilchrist. The lawyers took care of the logistics, provided a legal opinion, and arranged for David Parse of the investment bank Alex. Brown & Sons to execute the trades. Very few clients actually met with Daugerdas, but one who did asked why everyone wasn't using the shelter if it worked so well. "Everybody doesn't know me," Daugerdas replied.[23] Greisman originally worked with Daugerdas on the transactions, but eventually came to work more with Donna Guerin as his main contact at the firm. The parties agreed that BDO would get 20 percent of the fee that the law firm received.

BDO's arrangement with Daugerdas proved profitable from the beginning. A January 12, 1999, letter from Greisman to Daugerdas listed fees due to BDO. BDO's involvement in the shelter had begun only in November of 1998; by January, the total came to almost $2.2 million.[24] A large portion of the fees was generated by Paul Shambron of BDO's Detroit office. Denis Field had asked Greisman to keep him closely apprised of the fees BDO was earning from the relationship with Daugerdas because the report was that this arrangement was going to be a big moneymaker.

In October 1999 Greisman learned from Daugerdas, who by then had moved to Jenkens & Gilchrist, that Jenkens would be changing the shelter transaction to substitute trading in currency options for Treasury bill short sales. The new arrangement provided some flexibility to fine-tune losses. If clients wanted a capital loss, they would trade stocks or bonds;

if the desire was for a loss to offset ordinary income, the trading would be in foreign currencies.[25] The product essentially would be the same, but Daugerdas was concerned that legislation might be passed that would explicitly close the loophole in the treatment of Treasury short sales under partnership provisions of the tax code.[26] Trader David Parse at Deutsche Bank would continue to arrange for the trades to effectuate the shelter transactions.

The BDO tax opinion committee reviewed the revised shelter to decide if the firm should participate. BDO was familiar with a short option strategy involving options on foreign currency because it had been recommending such shelters to clients. There were still, however, some concerns about the new Daugerdas transaction. Bee feared that there was little meaningful profit potential when the two trades were analyzed together and suggested to Daugerdas that a 4 percent fee was quite large in comparison to this potential. Daugerdas continued to insist that his fee would not be counted as a transaction cost related to the investment and claimed that if an IRS investigation occurred, description of that fee on the bill would be protected from disclosure by the attorney-client privilege.[27] By the end of the meeting, Bee's misgivings were outweighed by the substantial fees that BDO would earn on the shelters. He gave the transaction a green light.[28] Eventually, BDO informed Jenkens that it was arranging for the client to add some additional cash to the partnership and to engage in some additional trading to make it appear that there was more profit potential. The detailed instruction sheet Greisman prepared for the Tax Solutions Group members to use in executing the transactions, however, made clear that every step was scripted and that concerns about investment returns were irrelevant.[29] BDO personnel referred to the change in the transaction that ostensibly provided a reasonable opportunity for a meaningful profit as the "lottery" feature.[30]

The Tax Products Group took pains to create a record to support a claim that the transaction had economic substance in case the taxpayer was audited by the IRS. Kerekes in particular was sensitive to the need for an appropriate paper trail. In an email to other group members, he noted with alarm that Jenkens had sent clients certain forms with simply a blank for the dollar amount. "The clients had no clue what to fill in," Kerekes said. "Are the clients supposed to sign and send back blank forms? Talk about a bad fact for business purposes."[31]

In late 1999, Tax Solutions Group members discussed the need to put material into clients' files that gave the impression of serious consideration of the transactions' investment potential. Kerekes eventually prepared a handout for the group with examples of how to create a record to support an argument that the client had a business purpose for entering into a transaction that had economic substance.[32] One template of a memo to the client, for instance, opened with the sentence: "As we have previously discussed, this memorandum addresses some of my preliminary thoughts regarding the investment program you are considering entering."[33] It also said, "As I understand it, you are planning to pursue a series of investments in various derivative securities, particularly securities that are sensitive to interest rates."[34] The memo went on to say, "The partnership is scheduled to end after 30 years. The partners will have the option of extending it should they choose to do so."[35]

In fact, of course, all the partnerships were scheduled to end before the end of the taxable year in which the transaction started. Kerekes's form memo ultimately concluded, "Over the long term, your potential profits appear essentially unlimited." Similarly, one letter sent to clients said, "Just a short note to confirm that I thought about the business and tax issues we've been discussing and concluded that you should contribute the investment to the partnership."[36] Another said, "For your information, below are some web sites that I came across that may be of interest to you in light of your recent interest in foreign exchange investing," and listed four websites.[37] Still another purported to "[confirm] our recent discussion regarding your plans relative to the hedging, currency, and related derivative investment strategies you are pursuing."[38] Communications like these were sent to various clients notwithstanding that none reflected any discussions that had actually occurred.

Some BDO personnel also suggested that clients take certain steps that would make it more difficult for the IRS to determine that they were engaging in tax shelter activity. Apparently taking their cue from similar advice provided by tax partners at KPMG, BDO's tax products group advised their clients to report the results of their trading activities through a grantor trust. (KPMG's use of grantor trusts was described in chapter 5.) This mechanism permitted clients to net their gains and losses from multiple transactions, which hid the large losses at the heart of their shelters from the IRS.[39] BDO also advised clients not to deduct their fees for the transactions because the size of those fees might attract attention from the IRS.

In early 1999, BDO revised its fee arrangement with Jenkens so that BDO directly billed the client for fees. The size of the Jenkens & Gilchrist fee had still been a concern because of its potential to undercut any claim that the client was entering into trading activity to pursue a profit. Greisman proposed two alternatives to the tax opinion committee to address the size of the fee. The first option was that the firm continue to execute the short sale transaction but retain the law firm of Ryan & Sudan to issue a tax opinion identical to the Jenkens one, for which that firm would charge $100,000. Greisman was apparently floating the possibility that BDO might part ways with Daugerdas, since he suggested that this first option would involve retaining appropriate legal counsel for the basic corporate work involved in the transaction. Greisman maintained that the size of the legal fee under this alternative would pose no danger of being recharacterized as a transaction cost that would offset any profit potential of the transaction. While he did not discuss it, Greisman also probably had in mind a negative implication of switching to a different law firm. It would incur the wrath of Daugerdas, who might well pursue legal action against BDO for using his shelter without compensating him for it.[40]

The second alternative was the one that BDO eventually chose. BDO restructured the fee arrangement with Jenkens & Gilchrist so that it billed the client directly for its fee and paid the law firm its fee, rather than receiving a portion of the amount paid to the law firm. The fees to the accounting firm and the law firm would ostensibly remain the same, as would the total fee paid by the client. Restructuring the fee reduced the risk that a client's shelter would be challenged based on economic substance because the client did not have a reasonable prospect of making a profit once the total fees for the transaction were factored in. To accomplish this, BDO would enter into a "consulting" agreement with the taxpayer under which it ostensibly provided financial planning and investment advice. Since the agreement did not refer specifically to the shelter transaction, the hope was that "the IRS would think that the fee was for something else other than the transaction."[41]

Another important advantage of billing the client directly was that BDO did not have to wait until the Jenkens & Gilchrist opinion was provided near the end of the transaction to receive its fee; nor was its fee limited to a percentage of the Jenkens fee. Eventually, BDO charged the client 7 percent of the amount of capital losses and 10 percent of ordinary income losses. It then distributed 2.4 percent of the 7 percent and 3.2

percent of the 10 percent to Jenkens & Gilchrist, which effectively provided the law firm with the same fees that it had been receiving under the prior arrangement.[42] BDO never told Jenkens, however, that it was now earning a larger fee than Jenkens for simply referring clients to the law firm that had developed the shelter.[43]

The arrangement proved very lucrative for the accounting firm. As of mid-December 1999, the transactions being executed with Jenkens & Gilchrist were generating fees of almost $18.7 million for BDO. For the last six months of the 1999 calendar year, revenues for BDO were over $185 million, and the projection for the next six months was almost $215 million. If these numbers held for fiscal year 2000, the firm would earn almost $100 million more in revenue than it had in fiscal year 1999. Perhaps more salient for the Tax Solutions Group, the revenues for 2000 would represent more than a $150 million increase—almost 62 percent—over fiscal year 1998, the year before BDO began its initiative with Daugerdas. Even after he became CEO and chair, Field continued to monitor sales and exhort Tax Solutions Group members to push themselves. In a firm-wide email in July 2000, for example, Field celebrated Shanbrom's success in closing a very substantial deal: "Congratulations to Paul Shanbrom of the Detroit office, who closed a tax solution transaction, resulting in GROSS REVENUES OF $1,900,000 TO THE FIRM!!! TAX ELL!!!"[44]

Warning Signs

In 2000, the IRS issued Notice 2000-44, entitled "Tax Avoidance Using Artificially High Basis." The notice contained some worrisome pronouncements for BDO. First, it described transactions identical to the Short Options Strategy that BDO was promoting with Jenkens and explicitly stated that "[t]he purported losses from these transactions . . . are not allowable as deductions for federal income tax purposes."[45] Second, the notice indicated that transactions the same as or substantially similar to BDO's strategy were "listed transactions."[46] This meant they had to be registered with the IRS and promoters had to maintain a list of investors to turn over to the agency upon its request. Finally, the notice directly targeted the practice of grantor trust netting: "In addition to other penalties, any person who willfully conceals the amount of capital gains and losses in this manner, or who willfully counsels or advises such concealment, may be guilty of a criminal offense."[47]

Notice 2000-44 triggered a profound shock in Adrian Dicker, who apparently had not fathomed the implications of promoting abusive tax shelters and had not appreciated that members of the Tax Solutions Group were recommending reporting techniques that amounted to criminal conduct. "I couldn't sleep," he later recalled. "I was crying. I lost concentration. I was tingling. I was just physically and mentally shot."[48] Dicker's ongoing reservations about the short sale shelter had led him to suggest at least twice that BDO end its association with Jenkens & Gilchrist. Most recently, he had expressed his view to Denis Field that another provider had a shelter that could be defended more strongly than the one that Jenkens was providing. Field, however, insisted that the Jenkens transactions were suitable for smaller amounts of loss that could be used by many more BDO clients, which gave the partners more opportunity to find clients, generate revenues for the firm, and earn bonuses.[49]

When Notice 2000-44 came out, Dicker told Field that he wanted to resign not only from the Tax Solutions Group but from the firm altogether. Field suggested that he take a week off to consider. Dicker took Field's advice and never returned. He resigned from the partnership effective at the end of October. A month later, Field invited Dicker to join the BDO board, which would allow Dicker to continue his health insurance benefits, a concern of great importance to him.

BDO partners tried to take stock of where things stood after the IRS issued Notice 2000-44. Kerekes prepared a memo for the tax opinion committee the day the notice came out discussing its implications at length. He noted that the combination of the notice and Treasury regulations effectively expanded the list maintenance requirement beyond corporations to include individual investors in listed transactions, those lacking economic substance, and other tax-structured transactions.[50] Before Notice 2000-44, Kerekes contended, while BDO transactions may have been structured for tax avoidance they had been used only by individuals, so BDO had not been subject to the list-keeping requirement. Now Kerekes observed: "It seems clear that our transactions are listed transactions under Notice 2000-44. In addition, it seems very probably that our transactions lack economic substance and/or are tax-structured."

The question, Kerekes suggested, was to which transactions the new list requirement should apply. His provisional conclusion was that the requirement applied only to clients who signed their engagement letters after August 11, 2000. Kerekes suggested that BDO confirm his analysis with Lawrence Hill, a tax partner at White & Case with whom the group consulted. Hill was not due to be in the office for about ten days, but Kerekes urged the firm to formulate a position immediately: "I don't think BDO can be without a policy during the coming week." The group had also begun to investigate how many clients had been advised to engage in grantor trust netting.

BDO decided that it would proceed with the short option shelter in any transaction for which an engagement letter had been received before August 11, which it regarded as the effective date of Notice 2000-44. As Bee noted, the firm "would sign returns and we would go ahead with those tax returns as if the notice hadn't been issued."[51] BDO did give clients whose transactions were in progress the option of canceling. The firm lost about $15 million in fees as a result of taxpayers who walked away. The overall effect of Notice 2000-44 was to trigger a wind-down of the Jenkens short option shelter because of both the notice and more general concern that tax shelters were now a high-priority concern of the IRS. BDO nonetheless continued to market shelters covered by Notice 2000-44 for at least another two years by collaborating with other promoters.

Dicker was not the only one who had concerns about BDO's tax activity. BDO general counsel Scott Univer believed that some features of the Tax Solutions Group's activities might warrant closer review. The fact that the group charged fees based on a percentage of tax savings instead of hourly rates was unusual for the industry, as were the size of the bonuses paid to partners in the group. In early summer of 2000, Univer ran into a law school classmate at a reunion who was at Skadden, Arps, Slate, Meagher & Flom and discussed the possibility of the firm conducting a review of the Tax Solutions Group. The general counsel was able to convince Denis Field that such a review would be useful. In May 2000, Bee signed an engagement letter with Fred Goldberg, a former IRS Commissioner and Assistant Secretary of the Treasury for Tax Policy and a partner at the firm. Univer apparently asked Skadden to review the substance of some of the BDO transactions. Goldberg responded that the law firm did not issue opinions on transactions designed to minimize taxes and did not want to delve into the ones that BDO was offering. Skadden would confine itself to reviewing and providing advice on the procedures that BDO followed in connection with the transactions on which Tax Solutions Group members worked.

Skadden's lawyers interviewed people in BDO's Tax Solutions Group and partners outside the group who worked on tax matters or otherwise were involved in tax transactions and reviewed documents and files that had been created in the provision of services. On September 6, 2000, Skadden provided an oral report to selected BDO partners, with some partners participating by conference call. The gist of the report was that Skadden believed that it had identified problems that "created significant institutional risk for BDO both with respect to its clients and with respect to the government."[52] After the meeting, Field cautioned Bee not to make any statements at an upcoming board meeting about the concerns that Skadden had expressed. As a result, Bee told the board that "there was no problem related to the Skadden report."[53]

Given the nature of the report's conclusions, Goldberg decided to put them in writing to avoid confusion or uncertainty. On November 6, Goldberg and Albert Turkus of Skadden faxed a nine-page memo to Univer.[54] The memo summarized observations and recommendations based on interviews with key individuals and described "a possible course of action the IRS could take if it were to focus upon the Tax Solutions Group's activity."[55] Skadden's objective in conducting the investigation, the memo indicated, was to gather information about the "processes and procedures" of the Tax Solution Group to see what "could be improved to promote compliance with best practices and minimize the possibility of unfavorable tax consequences to BDO, the Tax Solutions Group, or its clients."[56] While the memo made clear that it did not purport to analyze the proper tax treatment of the transactions in question, it noted that "[t]hat substantive issue is, of course, an important threshold question that directly affects the relevance of certain matters covered here."[57]

The memo described several "consistency issues" that existed because of "significant variations in certain aspects of the interaction between Tax Solutions Group members and clients." Members of the group did not provide clients with the same material or information, or inform them of the same risks. In addition, there was variation in the extent to which the clients' outside advisors conducted a separate analysis or had any meaningful discussions with BDO. With respect to "process issues," the memo stated that the compensation incentive plan "sends powerful signals throughout BDO (facilitated by the 'Tax ell' broadcast emails and similar announcements) about which activities are valued by the firm."[58] The memo noted that the client fees and commissions paid to the Tax

Solutions Group members were linked to the size of the tax benefits. As the memo emphasized, the group members were "incentivized to implement the largest possible transactions, without regard to the size of transaction that would best meet a particular client's needs."[59]

In addition, the memo questioned whether the IRS would regard the legal opinions for transactions as independent. It suggested that BDO might want to consider alternative arrangements, such as requiring each client to obtain an opinion from "an independent advisor having no pre-existing relationship with BDO or other parties" connected to the transaction. The memo also noted the fact that some members of the tax opinion committee received compensation for every group transaction sold to a client and that management was present on the committee "may create the appearance that it is difficult for committee members to review new transactions with impartiality."[60]

Finally, a pointed section of the memo headed "Possible IRS Reaction" began with the statement, "Based on the information we learned, the activities of the Tax Solutions Group could be characterized in a very negative light."[61] A number of practices, the memo suggested, might "be seen as signaling a lack of confidence in the merits of the transactions sold to clients, or as attempts to conceal those transactions from the IRS."[62] These practices included: the suggestion by some group members that clients not challenge any adjustments proposed by the IRS and that they invest their tax savings until the applicable statutes of limitations had run; various forms of advice, such as grantor trust netting, on "how to report transactions in a manner that will make detection by the IRS less likely"; the formation of the Tax Solutions Group as a limited liability company, which "could be viewed as evidence that BDO is not confident about the merits of the transactions"[63] offered by the group; and the refusal to accept clients who wished to claim a refund for the tax benefit provided by a transaction because this was more likely to trigger IRS scrutiny. The last portion of this section contained an ominous observation:

There are a number of partners in BDO who expressed to us some discomfort with the merits of the transactions presently being offered by the Tax Solutions Group. In some cases, this discomfort extends to pessimism. Members of the Tax Solutions Group have been advised not to spend their compensation bonuses pending the clarification of tax law relating to their transactions. If BDO were to become the subject of a broad IRS inquiry, these sentiments, and perhaps stronger ones, could surface.[64]

The memo concluded that Skadden's analysis raised "serious issues"[65] concerning a number of aspects of the Tax Solutions Group's activities. It recommended in particular that BDO examine the incentives created by the existing compensation system, require that clients obtain legal opinions from their own independent advisors, modify the structure and operations of the tax opinion committee, and eliminate any behavior "that suggests an attempt to conceal the transaction from the IRS."[66]

Univer passed the Skadden memo along to Field, Bee, and Pamela Packard, director of the National Tax practice. The word came back that BDO wanted to revise the memo, mostly through deletions. Most significantly, Univer was instructed to inform Fred Goldberg that BDO wanted to eliminate the final section on possible IRS reactions. Univer sent a February 16, 2001, message to Goldberg with a revised version of the document that contained this and other changes. The most noteworthy additional revisions were to eliminate the sentence that stated that the substantive merit of the transactions "is, of course, an important threshold question that directly affects the relevance of certain matters covered here," and a reference to the "'Tax ell' broadcast emails and similar announcements."[67] The final Skadden draft contained BDO's revisions.[68] With respect to deleting the final section on the possible IRS reaction, Goldberg said that the firm had not been hired to discuss that issue and that it had been included in the original draft simply to ensure that BDO took the memo's recommendations seriously.

Ultimately it didn't matter what was in the Skadden memo because it was never provided to the BDO board or the Tax Solutions Group. Univer was instructed to draft a memo to the board summarizing the memo's recommendations for the group, but his draft was never circulated. Indeed, in December 2000, before the final version of the memo was done, Bee had told a Tax Solutions Group meeting that Skadden had given BDO "a clean bill of health."[69] Similarly, Field told a meeting of BDO managers that Skadden had reviewed the Tax Solutions Group practices and had said they were fine. Univer then clarified to the group that Skadden's review was limited to the group's procedures, not the substance of the transactions.[70] No one beyond a small group of top managers knew that Skadden had serious concerns about how the Tax Solutions Group activities were being conducted.

Univer continued to press for more oversight over the group. He and Field were on the risk management committee, which examined possible sources of liability for BDO. The committee also was charged with deciding whether to take on a client, instead of the partner directly involved making that decision. In an exchange of emails with Univer in May 2001, national tax director Packard argued that the Tax Solutions Group activity should not be reviewed by the committee because it was a separate LLC; what it was doing therefore posed no risk to BDO as a whole. Univer strenuously disagreed. Field was copied on these emails. Eventually he resolved the issue by abolishing the risk management committee.[71]

Feeling Some Pressure

On September 26, 2000, shortly after Notice 2000-44 was issued, the IRS Office of Tax Shelter Analysis received an anonymous letter accompanied by several documents. Addressed "To Whom It May Concern," it said that BDO Seidman "has been offering tax shelters to hundreds of individuals and some corporations through out [sic] the United States."[72] When the "'tax product'" program first started, the letter said, "very little information was made available to BDO's partners and staff since there was [sic] some concerns about the IRS picking up on what they were doing and putting a stop to it."[73] The letter explained that BDO had decided not to work with corporate taxpayers "since the tax return would require an M-1 item listed on the reconciliation of book income to taxable income and that would be a red flag to the IRS."[74] The author went on to say that "it was explained to me that any interest penalty would be offset by the earnings the taxpayer may have benefited from by having the tax dollars not paid to the IRS available to the person to earn on until payment had to be made."[75]

"BDO and some legal firms have made a tremendous amount of money off of these products," continued the letter, "at a great expense to the American taxpayer and federal government. . . . These tax products are worse than Al Capone in the amount of tax dollars literally not reported and paid due to the abusive tax shelters being utilized. We are talking about millions of tax dollars lost or deferred." The letter concluded, "I wish to remain anonymous at this point until I learn about any legal protection that may be available to me since I am sure BDO would pursue my demise. However, I would be willing to be a witness if adequate protection and compensation could be offered me."[76] The author said that he would call the IRS hotline periodically and would use a code to identify himself when he did.

The IRS swung into action. On December 5, 2000, it sent a letter to the BDO Chicago office that said, "We believe that your organization was involved in the promotion of transactions substantially similar to those described in Notice 2000-44. . . . Such transactions may be tax shelters [under] the Internal Revenue Code." If so, the letter said, the transactions should have been registered and BDO would have "an obligation to maintain a list of investors and to make that list available for our inspection." The letter then requested within ten days "(1) a detailed description of the transaction, including a description of its structure and the intended tax benefits, (2) a copy of any written materials that were presented to potential or actual participants in connection with the offering of sales of interests in the transaction, including any analyses or opinions relating to the intended tax benefits of the transaction, and (3) the list of investors in the transaction."[77]

Greisman received a call about the letter as he was heading to a previously scheduled meeting of the tax opinion committee at the O'Hare Hilton. Field, Bee, Kerekes, Shanbrom, and BDO partner Larry Cohen were in attendance. When Greisman arrived, he told the group about the letter, which they then read. Field was incensed. He noted that the bottom of the letter indicated that a copy was sent to two persons, one named "Chris Leisner." Christopher Leisner was a BDO partner in the Chicago office who had been a vocal critic of Field, who now suspected that Leisner might have turned whistleblower. Field instructed Greisman to contact Leisner and tell him to come immediately to the meeting at the hotel. When Leisner arrived, Field grilled him relentlessly. Leisner never admitted that he was the source of the leak.

Tellingly, Univer was never informed by BDO management about the IRS letter. He only learned of it from Larry Hill at White & Case, who was retained by the Tax Solutions Group. Univer then sent an email to Field asking whether he thought that as general counsel of the firm Univer ought to be aware of communications such as the IRS letter. Field's email response was terse: "No."[78]

BDO's response to the IRS letter was to claim that none of its transactions were identical or substantially similar to those covered by Notice 2000-44. The firm refused to register any shelters or to turn over any list of clients to the IRS. "In effect," Bee later observed, "we hardballed them."[79] BDO also decided not to inform any of its clients about the IRS's inquiry. "It was in BDO's interest that the clients not be aware of the letter," Greisman explained.[80] Otherwise, they "would have been perhaps suing or concerned or asking for fees back."[81] When some clients began receiving audit notices from the IRS, BDO's strategy was to be closely involved with the client's counsel and to keep the process going as long as possible in the hope that ultimately there would be a global settlement on lenient terms.[82] The firm would "rehearse the client to say, 'I had an investment motive.'"[83] Greisman prepared a spreadsheet that helped the firm keep track of the audits in progress. BDO also decided not to offer the IRS any legal opinions connected with the shelter transactions at the beginning of any audit for fear that these opinions would provide a detailed roadmap of the transactions that would be useful to the IRS. Instead, BDO withheld the opinions on the ground that they were protected by the attorney-client privilege.

BDO played a substantial role in assisting clients in dealing with the IRS audit process. For example, it helped prepare responses to IRS information document requests (IDRs) for its clients Larry and Nancy Moore and their partnership Ellsworth Partners.[84] The first IDR asked for a description of how the taxpayer became involved in the formation of the partnership, the decision to engage in foreign currency option transactions, and the decision to transfer the partnership interest to LHM Ellsworth Investors, Inc., a subchapter S corporation. The response to the request stated that Mr. Moore had become "familiar with currency issues and ways to make money with currencies" in the course of founding and running a company that had numerous overseas operations and engaged in transactions in different currencies. He and his wife, the response said, "began investing in the stock, currency and bond markets subsequent to the sale of his company in 2000." They then "decided to purchase foreign currency options to diversify their portfolio, and to earn a profit." Finally, "[a]t some point, a decision was made to transfer the investing and profit-seeking activity to an S corporation, thus LHM Ellsworth Investors, Inc. was formed."

The IRS evidently found these responses inadequate and followed up about four months later with another IDR that asked the Moores to discuss "the reasons for engaging in the foreign currency transactions" and "why the partnership interest was transferred to LHM Ellsworth Investors, Inc." With respect to the first request, the Moores directed the agency to the description in its earlier response. With respect to the second, the Moores provided a more detailed explanation. Because of the substantial risks involved in the partnership's highly speculative investments in technology stocks and foreign currencies by the partnership, they said, Mr. Moore "determined that it was best to liquidate Ellsworth Partners into LHM Ellsworth Investors, Inc. This transfer also had the effect of giving Mr. Moore increased limited liability protection under state law." A last IDR about three months later asked the Moores to "[e]xplain how the amount of the fees paid to Jenkens & Gilchrist and BDO Seidman were determined." In response, the Moores stated, "The fee of $230,400 paid to Jenkens & Gilchrist for the legal opinion was established by Jenkens & Gilchrist. The fee of $514,000 paid to BDO Seidman for various consulting services was established by BDO Seidman." BDO's fee, of course, had been simply for referring the Moores to Jenkens.

The IRS inquiry was troubling, but BDO may have felt that it could emerge unscathed if it maintained an aggressive posture toward the government. Denis Field had been the driving force behind a transformation at BDO that moved it beyond traditional audit and tax preparation services. During his tenure as CEO, the firm's revenues had increased by 60 percent and average partner revenue more than doubled.[85] Tax services accounted for nearly half of BDO Seidman's $420 million in U.S. revenues in 2002, up from 28 percent in 1998.[86] An observer of the accounting industry had once remarked, "Denis Field is such a significant person at [BDO that] he's the equivalent of Bill Gates at Microsoft."[87] Could the same hard-charging approach that had transformed the firm enable it successfully to fend off a sustained government inquiry into how the firm had come so far so fast?

Some of the major accounting firms in the world moved aggressively into the tax shelter business in the 1990s and early 2000s. These firms drew on their audit and attest relationships with clients, marketing networks, and talented tax practitioners to earn substantial profits from this activity. Accountants were not the only professionals involved in the shelter industry, however. Lawyers at respectable law firms lent their services to transactions generating billions of dollars in fraudulent tax losses.

Part III

Law Firms

8

The Texas Juggernaut

In January 1998 the *National Law Journal* ran a front page article celebrating the rapid ascent of the Dallas-based law firm Jenkens & Gilchrist. Under the leadership of its chief executive David Laney, the firm had grown over the preceding three years from 160 to 340 lawyers. The article identified Jenkens as the fastest-growing law firm in the United States and described it as a "juggernaut."[1] The article noted the firm's addition of practice groups from other firms as the basis for its growth, saying that Laney "inspired these lawyers to dream Texas-size dreams."[2] It suggested that "being rewarded for rain appears to be what lured many newcomers,"[3] quoting one lateral hire's dissatisfaction with other firms that compensated lawyers based on seniority. Another attraction of the firm was that branch offices set their own budgets, decided in which areas to specialize, and made associate hiring decisions independent of Dallas.

For many at the firm, the next challenge was to "develop a national presence."[4] Jenkens & Gilchrist's board of directors was investigating the possibility of entering the New York market and the head of the intellectual property practice said that the firm almost certainly would be moving into the Silicon Valley. "He has expectations of us being the largest technology 'boutique' in the country," the lawyer said of Laney. "David Laney doesn't stop at being No. 10."[5] At the beginning of 1998, Jenkens & Gilchrist epitomized the law firm of the twenty-first century: restless, entrepreneurial, and focused on constant growth as the core of its competitive strategy.

Later that same year, the firm continued its aggressive strategy by hiring Paul Daugerdas as a lateral partner to open its Chicago office. Daugerdas, who brought with him a handful of colleagues from Altheimer & Gray, had a lucrative practice built around designing and selling tax shelters. After vigorous internal debate about whether Daugerdas's aggressive tax practice was a good fit for the firm, Jenkens decided to hire him. The move paid off handsomely. From 1999 through 2002, Jenkens & Gilchrist received well over $200 million in fees from tax shelter work done by Daugerdas and his Chicago colleagues.

A major national firm like Jenkens almost certainly would not have entertained the idea of hiring someone like Daugerdas a decade earlier. The elite tax bar considered lawyers who worked on tax shelters to be suspect, not worthy of being considered true professionals. With intensified competitive pressures, the consensus about the norms that governed tax practice had begun to disintegrate, and a divide had arisen in the tax bar about where the line between an aggressive tax strategy and an abusive tax shelter was located. With the acquisition of Daugerdas, Jenkens became the most prominent law firm to push the boundary in the new tax shelter industry.

Jenkens & Gilchrist: Rise, Fall, and Rise

Jenkens & Gilchrist was founded in 1951 by Holman Jenkens and William H. Bowen. Jenkens had served since 1946 as the personal lawyer of Clint Murchison, Jr. The Murchison family was active in the oil business and other ventures, and Clint Murchison was an influential member of Dallas society. The firm's stable long-term relationship with the Murchison family was a typical feature of law firm practice in the mid-twentieth century.

Although it expanded as the Texas economy grew, Jenkens & Gilchrist was a small high-end firm that expected to stay relatively small. By 1985, the firm had grown to 125 lawyers, but 20 to 30 percent of its business still came from the Murchisons. The firm was known as collegial and friendly. It typically did not cut the compensation of lawyers whose billable hours fell temporarily due to marital or health problems. In this respect, the firm was similar to others during the period whose stable client base and insulation from stiff competition allowed them to avoid relying on financial considerations as the driving force of their decisions.

Jenkens & Gilchrist's halcyon existence was destroyed in the mid-1980s with a sharp decline in the Texas economy provoked by failures in the energy, real estate, banking, and savings and loan sectors. The firm also faced litigation by the Federal Savings & Loan Insurance Corporation (FSLIC) over its representation of two savings and loans that had failed. In addition, it was a defendant in a lawsuit by twenty-six investors who had lost money from participation in a failed oil project that the firm had assisted in making a private stock offering in 1981. The firm settled with the FSLIC for $18 million in 1989 and was found liable for just under $6 million in damages in the investor lawsuit.

The combination of the business downturn and legal troubles left Jenkens in a precarious position. The firm had cultivated a client base of influential companies and wealthy individuals in Dallas. To a large degree, its practice was organized around clients at least as much as around practice areas. The firm provided a wide range of services for these clients. This client-oriented organization and the firm's relative insulation from significant competition meant that Jenkens's leaders likely spent little time thinking of the firm's market position.

By the end of the 1980s, however, this business model was no longer viable. The firm could no longer focus its work on a single geographic market or in a limited number of industries. Nor could it count on long-term relationships with clients any more, since corporations had begun to sever exclusive relationships with firms to foster competition for their legal work. Jenkens was also handicapped in moving forward because authority was dispersed within a large executive committee. As a result, many in the firm were uncertain whether it could survive.

Faced with the possible demise of Jenkens & Gilchrist, a group of young partners sought to develop a strategy that addressed the firm's predicament. The first priority was revising the governance structure. The firm became a professional corporation, its partners the shareholders.[6] This limited the financial liability of the firm's principals for its obligations. Jenkens adopted a three-person executive committee (later expanded to five) and a strong-president model. The executive committee would be advised by an electoral committee consisting of the heads of major practice groups.

At the end of 1989, forty-one-year-old David Laney became president of Jenkens & Gilchrist. Laney was from a prominent Dallas family. His father for many years was head of the major Dallas law firm now known as Locke, Liddell & Sapp and his mother was the granddaughter of the founder of the *Dallas Morning News*. Laney was deeply involved in folk music and sports growing up and counted as one of his high school classmates the actor Tommy Lee Jones. He graduated from Stanford University, where he played football his first two years, enrolled in the doctoral program in American Studies at Brown University, but then decided instead to attend law school at Southern Methodist University.

On assuming the firm's leadership, Laney began to chart a course he believed would enable Jenkens & Gilchrist to succeed in the new legal services market. One objective was to diversify both geographically and in practice areas. Another was to identify and expand those practices that were likely to be most lucrative. Under Laney, the firm undertook to revise its compensation to compete more effectively with the large Houston firms. The last goal was a challenge because Dallas for the most part had a "mid-market" client base. Companies generally were not as large, diverse, and prosperous as those in Houston. This meant that Dallas firms were often unable to bill at rates as high as Houston firms' because their clients simply could not afford this. In turn this constrained Jenkens & Gilchrist in compensating its lawyers.

The next step in remaking the firm was to let go one-fourth of its lawyers—reducing the total from 225 to 165. Laney later reflected, "It was a low point, one of the lowest in my life, but for the firm, it was a galvanizing point, and in retrospect, inescapable."[7] The firm started to recruit lawyers from other firms who practiced in intellectual property, construction and government contracts, franchise law, health law, government relations, and tort litigation, all areas in which the firm anticipated significant growth. The intellectual property practice area was especially profitable and represented a movement into at least a high niche in the mid-tier market. By 1998, the firm had increased the number of lawyers in this field to seventy, compared with just five in 1994.

Through much of the 1990s, Jenkens & Gilchrist acquired practice groups of various sizes, expanding beyond Dallas and then beyond Texas. In 1992, Jenkens opened a Washington, D.C. office and in 1997 it opened one in Los Angeles. In 1996, Jenkens moved into the *American Lawyer*'s Am Law 100 in gross revenue and profits per partner, ranking 98 and 64 in these categories. By 1998, the firm moved to 68 in the *National Law Journal* ranking of the largest 250 firms in the country, up from 166 in 1994. In its prominent front page article, the publication noted the firm's rapid growth, aggressive lateral recruiting, and big ambitions.

When the *National Law Journal* profile of the firm appeared in 1998, Jenkens was a regional firm with national aspirations. Like most regional firms, most of its work was for medium-size corporate clients at rates lower than those in major legal centers like New York and Washington. At the same time, some of its intellectual property litigation conceivably could involve higher-end work. The desire to diversify had led the firm to feature a total of thirteen practice groups by 1998. Some of those likely were not as profitable as intellectual property, but they generated revenues and were a hedge against falling victim to reliance on too narrow a practice base. Jenkens thus pursued a strategy of strengthening and diversifying its existing practices, while looking to add lawyers in practice areas and locations that might give it access to more complex work at higher rates.

The legal services market in Dallas was especially robust at this time, but there was strong competition from peer firms in the city that were following a similar business strategy. The belief was that firms had to grow quickly to survive. This meant that acquiring laterals, rather than growing from within, was the best way to diversify and expand the firm's economic base. The firm made itself attractive to laterals by insisting on merit-based compensation that rewarded business generation. Because of intense competition in the regional market, expansion beyond Texas and the Southwest was important.

Crucial to success in the lateral market were the firm's profits per partner (PPP). If Jenkens were to become a national firm, this figure had to keep increasing. Recruits automatically asked the firm about its balance sheet and profits when considering an offer to relocate to Jenkens. If the firm hoped to crack the New York market, keeping PPP up would be especially important, given the profitability of firms in that market.

The most recent figures from the *American Lawyer* at that time indicated that the firm ranked 84 in the Am Law 100 in gross revenues in 1997, posting a 30.6 percent increase over the previous year. This was the third-highest gain among Am Law 100 firms. But the firm's PPP was less reassuring. By the end of 1998, when Jenkens & Gilchrist leadership was considering whether to extend an offer to Daugerdas, the firm was about to close the books on a year in which it would drop from 75 to 79 in the Am Law 100 with profits per partner of $390,000. This figure was only 0.3 percent larger than in 1997. More troubling, the gap between the Am Law 100 average firm's PPP and Jenkens's had increased during the year from $212,000 to $232,000.

In its description of the 1998 Texas legal services market, the *American Lawyer* noted that increasing competition was coming from out-of-state firms. "The past few years have been a period of consolidation," said the publication, "as firms look to beef up their ranks in order to compete."[8]

During the year, Locke Purnell Rain Harrell of Dallas and Liddell, Sapp, Zivley, Hill & LaBoon of Houston had merged to create the fifth largest firm in the state. Its combined revenue would have ranked it in the Am Law 100 for 1998. Boosting profits at Jenkens & Gilchrist thus was critical in order to fund the continued growth that was seen as necessary for survival in a consolidating market.

At this point, Jenkens & Gilchrist was a very successful firm by many standards. It was one of only two Dallas-based firms in the Am Law 100. It had weathered the crisis of the late 1980s and embarked on a path of substantial growth in size and revenues. For Jenkens to compete on a national stage, however, this was not enough. It had to figure out a way to boost profits per partner so that it could compete for laterals with other Am Law 100 firms, as well as defend itself from firms seeking to raid its own partners.

Offering Shelter

Paul Daugerdas had come from Arthur Andersen to the law firm of Altheimer & Gray in 1994 at the age of forty-seven with a salary of $350,000 and a goal to transform the firm's tax practice into a major source of revenue from tax shelter products. By 1998, he had succeeded. The stocky lawyer and CPA with a blonde mustache earned $1 million that year and generated considerably more than that in revenues. He did not feel that he was adequately compensated for his work, however. He had understood when he came to Altheimer that he had an agreement with the firm's steering committee that he would receive 50 percent of all "premium" billing based on a percentage of the taxes that each shelter saved a client. By his calculations, the steering committee had not honored that promise. In fact, the firm had some concerns about the magnitude of the revenues he was generating and conducted an inquiry into whether they posed an unacceptable risk for the firm. Daugerdas was not shy about voicing his displeasure about his compensation and the firm's concerns about his practice. When he concluded that the firm was unlikely to be responsive to his dissatisfaction, Daugerdas began to seek opportunities elsewhere.

The practices of two Altheimer partners were closely tied to Daugerdas. Tax partner Donna Guerin, petite, dark-haired, and somewhat retiring, was also both a lawyer and a certified public accountant. She performed much of the technical work for the clients Daugerdas brought to the firm. This involved activities such as creating various business entities and preparing opinions that addressed the likelihood that a client's tax treatment of a shelter transaction would prevail. Erwin Mayer had been in the estate planning group at Altheimer. The boyish-looking partner sometimes commuted to work with Guerin, and they often had lunch together. Mayer became intrigued by Guerin's description of the tax shelter work she was doing and in 1995 began introducing some of his clients to Daugerdas. He learned the mechanics of the transactions and their necessary documentation. By 1998, unlike Guerin, he had become a major source of clients in his own right. When Mayer learned that Daugerdas was considering leaving Altheimer, he assumed that Guerin would go with him. He made clear to Daugerdas that he would like to do the same.

Daugerdas approached the firm through an intermediary, a former colleague at Altheimer who had read the *National Law Journal* article on Jenkens and hoped that the firm would be interested in both Daugerdas's tax practice and his own international law practice. He called Laney and told him Daugeredas helped high-net-worth individuals shelter their income through cutting-edge tax strategies. This was the kind of sophisticated high-end practice that could be a boon to Jenkens.

Laney received calls like this all the time because of the firm's growing profile. This call had particular appeal for several reasons. First, Chicago was an attractive market in which to expand because it had a lot of mid-market clients and firms with rate structures comparable to Jenkens's. The firm had not made much headway in Washington, D.C., because it did not have a niche regulatory practice. It had moved into Los Angeles but talks with firms in San Francisco had not yielded anything. The firm had considered Atlanta but found that market oriented mainly to the East Coast corridor from Boston to Washington. It had considered London and was looking at New York but needed higher profits per partner to compete in those high-end markets. Chicago, in other words, could be a good fit.

Daugerdas's practice could be valuable to Jenkens for another reason. Its focus on high-wealth clients could provide the boost in prestige and profits per partner that could attract other laterals who brought high-value work with higher margins than the firm usually enjoyed. This could help enable the firm to enter New York, a step that would validate its claim to be a national law firm. Ideally, it also would enable Jenkens to be less reliant on mid-market clients who were sensitive to billing rates. The firm's leaders were convinced that expanding its geographic and practice scope was necessary to respond to increasing competition from both law and accounting firms.

Finally, bringing Daugerdas into the firm would help further the aim of doing more high-end work for which cost containment was not the predominant concern. Not many firms could find such opportunities, especially regional firms whose work was subject to a fair amount of price competition. Daugerdas's practice, with fees based on a percentage of tax savings, effectively provided Jenkens with work based on a version of value billing. It had an appealing combination of features.

First, fees were based on a percentage of the value of a matter rather than hourly rates. For this work, the firm therefore could escape the constraints of the billable hour and reap a share of the financial benefits that it made available to clients. In this respect, tax shelter billing represented a version of what elite firms like Wachtell Lipton did when they charged a fee based on the value of a merger or acquisition.

Second, after a tax shelter opinion was created, it could be recycled for the same type of transaction sold to other taxpayers. The cost of producing the opinion for future transactions was negligible, while the fee as a percentage of tax savings could be substantial. In this respect, the firm would be able to use value billing on transactions that had become routine commodities. The firm would enjoy the benefits that came from high-end practice. At the same time, it did not have to incur the cost of designing customized solutions for every client, as did elite firms engaged in work at the top of the value pyramid.

A third feature of tax shelter opinions was designed to insulate them from the competitive pressures of the legal services life cycle that push toward the commoditization of legal work. While higher-end work is subject to the least amount of pressure to minimize costs, firms still find it difficult to avoid the legal services life cycle altogether. A firm that develops a cutting-edge strategy for a transaction, for instance, can't keep that work confidential. It discloses the details of its innovation when it distributes documents to the other parties involved in the deal. As the information becomes more widely known, competitors look for ways to provide the same service more cheaply or to develop superior innovations. The result is that the original firm may enjoy only a brief period when it reaps the lion's share of benefits from its creativity.

Daugerdas's tax shelter arrangements sought to avoid this dynamic by restricting information about the terms of the shelters. Clients were prohibited from sharing information about the shelter on the grounds that it was a trade secret and were forbidden to consult any lawyer other than the one recommended by the tax shelter designers. As a result, potential competitors were deprived of the information they needed to compete on the basis of cost-efficiency and price. Indeed, there was some talk of trying to patent the transactions. In any event, treating them as trade secrets prevented what was essentially a commodity service from being priced as one.

Daugerdas therefore had particular allure for Jenkens as a profitable lateral who could provide the firm some respite from the fee reduction pressures to which mid-tier firms are subject. His tax shelter practice, in other words, offered Jenkens a possible path across the great market divide.

Laney asked board member William Durbin to follow up the lead about Daugerdas. Durbin had come to the firm from St. Louis as a young associate and worked in a bank lending practice that had been steady but not especially robust. Durbin shared the vision of Jenkens as a major player in the law firm world. He devoted considerable attention to the firm's revenues and had a poster of the American Lawyer Top 100 law firms on the wall near his desk. As one former partner recalls, Durbin "would say that a law firm's stock price is its profits per partner."[9] Durbin has acknowledged, "I had a reputation for being bottom line oriented."[10] Part of his job was to locate and help recruit promising lateral lawyers and practice groups to the firm.

Durbin also had his sights on Laney's job. He had been on the board's executive committee in the mid-1990s and continued to be involved in management once he left. He was trying to build a power base within the firm to launch a challenge to Laney and hoped to rely on lateral partners as a source of support. Although Laney was aware of Durbin's aspirations, he did not realize how actively Durbin was building a constituency within the firm. There was no love lost between the two, and Laney may have put Durbin in charge of the Daugerdas project so that he would be held responsible if the venture failed. What Laney may not have anticipated was how much Daugerdas's practice would boost Durbin's stature when it became substantially more profitable than anyone had imagined.

While the firm had a strong tax practice, it had lost some lawyers so a new tax partner might strengthen that group. Laney suggested to Durbin that he consult with tax partners about Daugerdas's practice. He felt that they would not hesitate to ask any necessary unpleasant questions about what Daugerdas was doing.

Laney was right on that score. Durbin set up a meeting among Daugerdas, a key tax partner, and himself. The partner found Daugerdas overbearing and arrogant, quick to promote his own talents and belittle those of others. Daugerdas said that he wanted to join the firm as a professional corporation, a move that, as it later turned out, was a vehicle for using tax shelters to wipe out tax liability for his income from the firm. Mitchell told him that the firm's articles required that partners be individuals rather than organizations. Daugerdas responded that the firm had to change its articles to accommodate him. By the end of the conversation, the Jenkens tax lawyer still needed to do more analysis of Daugerdas's practice but he had definite doubts about his suitability as a colleague.

The process for hiring laterals at Jenkens provided a role for both the board and the electoral committee. The committee at the time was composed of a little over twenty partners elected by their respective practice groups. The board would make the ultimate decision but the electoral committee offered advice. The latter was influential enough that the board generally was disinclined to move ahead without endorsement of a decision by the committee.

Daugerdas made his pitch to the board and committee. He described Currency Options Bring Reward Alternatives (COBRA), the tax shelter described in chapter 6 that was subsequently marketed with E&Y. He estimated that he would be able to generate $6 to 8 million in annual revenues by charging wealthy clients a percentage of the taxes they saved. This form of premium billing was a rarity at Jenkens, where hourly billing produced the overwhelming share of income. Considering the amount of work required to market the shelter and document the transactions comprising it, the profit margin on this activity was well above any other practice area at the firm. The economics of this practice and the opportunity it offered to expand to Chicago made Daugerdas and his colleagues an attractive practice group for Jenkens to acquire.

Daugerdas's presentation nonetheless raised concerns among several partners, especially those on the electoral committee. Some were concerned that his business model simply seemed too good to be true. For a minimal amount of work, a given matter could generate tens or even hundreds of thousands of dollars. If this practice was so profitable, why weren't more firms doing it—and why was Altheimer willing to let Daugerdas walk away? The two partners in charge of risk management for the firm suggested that even if the shelters technically were defensible under the letter of the tax law, they could be highly risky. The work had the potential to create tensions either with clients or with the government if questions were raised about the legality of the shelters and the firm's advice in support of them. Publicity from such challenges could damage the firm's reputation, lessen its credibility with the government, and perhaps even lead to aiding and abetting liability.

Some partners had reservations because they believed that Daugerdas was not really enhancing the firm's ability to provide legal services. It was clear that he was not selling himself on the basis of his tax expertise but on the fact that he had a "product" to market. His work would not expand the scope of the firm's tax practice. Instead, it was a world unto itself that happened to touch upon the tax law. As one former partner recalled, "It had nothing to do in my mind with practicing law." Yes, the margins were impressive, but he noted: "My concern was, well, the margins on Slurpees are pretty good too; are we going to start selling Slurpees?"

The reaction among tax lawyers to Daugerdas's practice was mixed. Some noted that respectable accounting firms were designing and selling similar shelters, that COBRA appeared to conform to the letter of the tax code, and that in any event the line between a valid and invalid shelter had always been ambiguous. While a taxpayer could not plausibly claim a profit motive from entering into the transactions if legal costs were taken into account, it was not entirely clear whether such fees should enter into the calculation. At the time, there were no IRS interpretations or court decisions that clearly precluded the tax consequences that taxpayers claimed as a result of the shelter. The firm therefore had a plausible defense of its position if its work were ever challenged.

Other tax partners, however, were highly critical of Daugerdas and his shelter practice. The work was novel, unprecedented, and very technical. Evaluating the legitimacy of a shelter required immersion in complex sections of the tax law that typically were not analyzed together in ordinary tax practice. The firm had no one who had done work in this area who could provide meaningful review. In addition, assessing the validity of a shelter required intimate familiarity with a particular taxpayer's financial situation and the suitability of a given set of transactions to accomplish a client's business objectives. Was the firm prepared to allow Daugerdas to make those calls on his own? If not, who would be able to spare the time to conduct the kind of monitoring that would be necessary—and would Daugerdas be cooperative with any such effort? The last question raised a more fundamental one: would Daugerdas be a genuine colleague or effectively a solo practitioner?

One tax partner had especially strong feelings about these concerns and took the lead in articulating them in a presentation to the board and electoral committee. He knew how time-consuming reviewing a tax shelter could be since he had analyzed one in response to a client's request. Although he was an accomplished tax lawyer, the process still took more than fifty hours. Even then, although there was technical support for each step in the transaction, he couldn't confidently tell the client whether an opinion was likely to be effective in avoiding penalties. Advising clients on whether engaging in the transaction made sense required an extensive conversation about what the clients wanted to achieve and the risks they were prepared to take in connection with that. This experience left him skeptical that Daugerdas was providing any genuine tax counseling to clients as opposed to selling them standard-form transactions designed simply to reduce or eliminate taxes. The firm had no one who could devote several hours to analyzing each shelter that Daugerdas sold to determine if there were a plausible business purpose or economic substance associated with it.

The partner suggested to the board and electoral committee that the firm was taking the risk of selling its good name. Daugerdas's practice, he said, was completely independent of the firm. If it was so successful, why did he need the firm to sell his shelters and opinions except to draw on Jenkens & Gilchrist's reputation? If his shelters were legitimate, why were clients willing to pay such exorbitant fees when they probably could get a top-tier Wall Street firm for less on an hourly basis? Furthermore, Daugerdas was a lone wolf who was not suitable to serve as the manager of a branch office. In effect, the tax partner was saying, "We can't effectively monitor Daugerdas's practice so we have to depend on his judgment and integrity. Are we really prepared to do that?" The firm had not been able to discuss Daugerdas with anyone at Altheimer because Daugerdas didn't want his old firm to know he was leaving. Jenkens & Gilchrist had heard from other sources, however, that Daugerdas was brilliant, that his practice was aggressive, and that a firm needed a good supervisory system in place to ensure that he stayed between the lines.

Another complication of the negotiations with Daugerdas was his demands about compensation. It's not clear how widely known this issue was outside of a handful of lawyers in management. Like most firms, Jenkens paid its partners a share of the firm's overall profits. Daugerdas wanted his compensation to consist of a percentage of the revenue that he generated, at a percentage higher than the typical partner share of profits. His revenue therefore would be tracked separately from that of the firm as a whole. He also wanted his compensation to be paid to a subchapter S corporation, which is a separate entity whose income is passed through to the partner. This would require that Jenkens amend its articles to eliminate the requirement that a partner in the firm must be a licensed individual lawyer.

Daugerdas's compensation demand was "really traumatic for the firm, a totally new idea."[11] Jenkens had made special compensation deals with other laterals, with compensation based to varying degrees on business origination, revenues generated by hourly billing, collection of billings, the distinctiveness of a practice, and involvement in management. The deals were disclosed to the electoral committee that made recommendations on laterals, although the amount of some bonuses were not. Compensation and performance metrics generally were available for inspection in the firm's "blue book." Laney had built up something of a cadre of supporters among the laterals with whom the firm had made such arrangements. But the firm had never entered into the kind of agreement that Daugerdas was proposing.

Daugerdas insisted that he wanted a fixed percentage of revenues so that he would not have to rely on the discretion of the compensation committee. He argued that the firm's costs for the shelter transactions would be quite low and therefore recovered by the firm from revenues fairly quickly. Anything above that would be a premium, of which he should receive a significant share. It was true that this type of compensation arrangement was unprecedented at Jenkens, but the firm had never had a high-end niche practice before. This was the cost of acquiring one, Daugerdas argued.

Durbin eventually assumed the role of Daugerdas's champion within the firm and worked hard to convince other partners that his acquisition made sense. He discounted the concerns of Daugerdas's main critic as based on a combination of personal dislike and a sense of being threatened by the prospect of another prominent tax lawyer joining the firm. Indeed, Daugerdas had made clear that he wanted to be the co-head of the tax practice, if not the sole head. The sense among most of the partners was that Laney was cautiously supportive of Daugerdas. At a minimum, they believed, he would have been able to stop the candidacy if he hadn't wanted him in the firm.

The electoral committee eventually took a straw vote on Daugerdas, which indicated that a narrow majority of members were opposed to him. The firm's board of directors was concerned enough about this sentiment that it delayed making any formal proposal to the committee. Some of the committee members were relieved and believed that the idea had been abandoned. Durbin and other supporters, however, continued their efforts to convince a majority of the partners that the firm on balance would gain significant benefits from bringing Daugerdas on board.

Over the next few months, Durbin and the board crafted an arrangement intended to address concern about the risks posed by Daugerdas's practice. This involved having Michael Cook, a well-respected tax partner and certified public accountant in the Austin office, review and sign off on all tax opinions rendered by the Chicago office. If there were reservations about Daugerdas's character, there were none about Cook's. He was someone whom, as one former Jenkens lawyer put it, "everyone loved and respected," and he had a reputation as straightforward and conservative tax lawyer. The board decided to move ahead with a recommendation to the partners that Daugerdas, Mayer, Guerin, and two other lawyers from Altheimer's Chicago office be hired on this basis. Although the debate continued, by this point enough members were convinced that Daugerdas's practice would be a profitable acquisition and that the firm could contain whatever risks it posed. A majority of partners voted to accept the board's recommendation, although there was still a respectable number of dissidents.

The agreement with Daugerdas provided that he would be equity shareholder, manager of the firm's Chicago office, and co-chairman and joint practice group leader of the firm's Tax Practice Group along with Michael Cook.[12] The firm was required to operate as a general partnership under Illinois rules, so a professional services agreement stated that Jenkens & Gilchrist Texas was engaging Jenkens & Gilchrist Illinois to assist it in rendering services to clients of the Texas firm that it believed could be serviced by the Illinois firm.[13] The agreement also provided that Michael Cook would "be retained as a consultant on all federal tax opinions rendered by" the Illinois firm.[14] Daugerdas's compensation would be paid to "Paul M. Daugerdas, Chartered," a corporation that he formed to become a partner in Jenkens.[15] His annual compensation for the 1998, 1999, and 2000 fiscal years would be $600,000, comprised of $480,000 in salary and $120,000 in a bonus based on certain conditions.[16] In addition, "Excess Collections Compensation" would be 50 percent of the premium billings up to $5 million, and 70 percent of anything from $5 million and above.[17]

Mayer had sought to negotiate a deal like the one given Daugerdas, under which he would receive a percentage of the client revenues that he generated. The firm refused. Mayer therefore decided to join the firm as an income partner for the first few years because he didn't want his bonus to be limited by the constraints on the equity partner bonus pool, which was calculated based on the revenues of the firm. He hoped, in other words, to generate revenues that would warrant a bonus that at least began to approach the kind of deal that Daugerdas had received for excess collections. Mayer's base salary for the remainder of 1998 and in 1999 would be $250,000 and he was eligible for an annual bonus. In addition, he was to receive $25,000 on December 31, 1998, and an additional $25,000 on July 1, 1998.[18] Guerin joined the firm as an equity partner at a salary of $200,000, and was also eligible for an annual bonus.[19]

The agreement between Jenkens & Gilchrist and the former Altheimer lawyers became effective on December 29, 1998. Two other lawyers from Altheimer involved in corporate merger and acquisition work also joined Jenkens along with Daugerdas, Mayer, and Guerin. They, along with support staff, formed the Chicago office of Jenkens & Gilchrist a few blocks away from Altheimer & Gray's office.

The debate within Jenkens over Daugerdas illustrated the subtle shift in norms that was occurring within the legal profession in general and among tax lawyers in particular. Tax shelter work had traditionally carried a stigma within the tax bar because it was seen as inconsistent with the way that a genuine professional should approach tax practice. Seen in this light, shelter work raised issues of honor and professional reputation. Many tax lawyers expressed this perspective when they suggested that

Jenkens would be selling its good name if it admitted Daugerdas into the firm. By contrast, other lawyers—including at least some tax partners—framed their concern in less normative terms. For them, Daugerdas's practice posed the risk that one or more of his shelters would be held invalid and that a client would have to pay taxes he thought he had avoided. The client might then sue the firm for malpractice, claiming that its lawyers should have known that the shelter would not withstand a challenge.

For these lawyers, the relevant questions therefore were how much the firm could reduce this risk through due diligence and whether it had enough insurance to pay for any claims that were brought against it. The firm assured its insurance carrier that it could minimize its risk and received assurance in turn that the firm would be covered for whatever amount remained. The likelihood of a malpractice action stemming from Daugerdas's work was seen as similar to the type of risk that any other practice area posed, which the firm felt that it could handle with appropriate diligence. Jenkens had enjoyed success in bringing in a substantial number of laterals over the past several years. This gave management confidence that it could smoothly manage the arrival of Daugerdas with the arrangement it had devised. For supporters of Daugerdas, the decision whether to hire him required a sophisticated cost-benefit analysis, not deliberation about professional values. Their sense apparently was that things had changed enough within tax practice that any reputational fallout from hiring Daugerdas would be minimal.

A Bump in the Road

Shortly after Daugerdas began at Jenkens, the firm found itself in the middle of a controversy between Daugerdas and Altheimer. On the day he left Altheimer in late 1998, Daugerdas approached a senior partner of the firm and proposed that Daugerdas and the firm execute mutual releases of claims in connection with his departure. When the partner expressed puzzlement about what claims Daugerdas might have against the firm, the latter falsely said that he had a religious discrimination claim that he would be willing to drop.

The partner refused to provide the release and ordered an investigation into the outstanding client fees that Daugerdas was attempting to take from Altheimer to Jenkens. This led to the discovery in early 1999 that Daugerdas, Mayer, and Guerin stood to collect over $30 million in tax shelter fees for work they had conducted for Altheimer clients in 1998. Daugerdas would receive considerably more under his compensation agreement with Jenkens than his agreement with his former firm. Altheimer pressed Jenkens for the return of these fees. Daugerdas maintained that the opinions for these transactions were not prepared until after he came to Jenkens, and insisted that Altheimer had no claim to them. Eventually, however, Jenkens paid $8 million to settle the claim. The controversy was not regarded as a red flag at the time, since it was not uncommon for there to be disputes over the allocation of fees involving lawyers who went from one firm to another.

One aspect of the incident was more unsettling. Daugerdas had known of the outstanding $30 million in fees when he approached Jenkens. He had nevertheless estimated to the firm that he would generate annual revenues of only six to eight million dollars. Had Jenkens been apprised of the larger figure at the time Daugerdas approached it, the firm might have wondered how aggressive the practice needed to be to generate such enormous fees. If the shelters were legitimate, Daugerdas presumably would have encountered competition from other firms and would have had to charge lower fees. It's conceivable that Jenkens may then have scrutinized Daugerdas's practice more closely. At a minimum, the firm might not have accepted a compensation arrangement with Daugerdas under which he would be entitled to 70 percent of all revenues he generated over $5 million. Admitting someone who generated that much in revenues would surely shift the balance of power within the firm, and tie its fortunes closer to a single partner than the firm might want.

The firm could have revisited its earlier decision in light of this new information from the Altheimer & Gray claim about the magnitude of the revenues that Daugerdas was likely to generate. At a minimum, it could have reevaluated how well it was organized to manage the risks of Daugerdas's practice with just one lawyer in Austin providing a second opinion. The volume of opinion letters was likely to be much larger than the firm had originally anticipated, which meant that it could be a challenge simply to keep up with them, much less give them close scrutiny. Reconsidering such issues, however, would have been uncomfortable and potentially disruptive. It was also now clear that the cost of turning Daugerdas away, or even constraining his activities, could run into the tens of millions. The easiest course was simply to move along as planned and let Daugerdas work his magic.

The Shelter Factory

From the start, Daugerdas's tax shelter work was the focus of the Chicago office. As one former associate remarked, the office was built "on his visions, his ideas."[20] Daugerdas and his colleagues had built up an extensive network of people in organizations such as accounting and financial advisory firms who referred clients to them seeking to reduce or eliminate taxes on income they expected to receive from the sale of a business or from other sources. One important source of referrals was the accounting firm BDO Seidman, based on the relationship that Daugerdas had developed with Robert Greisman of BDO shortly before Daugerdas left Altheimer & Gray. This led in late 1998 to the beginning of collaboration with BDO's Tax Solutions Group in selling shelters to BDO clients, described in chapter 7. Jenkens generally charged the clients a fee of 3 percent of tax losses that could be used to offset capital gains and 4 percent of the desired tax loss for ordinary income. The firm paid their referral sources anywhere from 20 to 50 percent of the fees they received. When they made such referral payments, Jenkens typically increased the fee to the taxpayer to 4 percent of capital losses and 5 percent of the ordinary losses.

What exactly was Daugerdas selling? The shelters on which he and his colleagues worked were mainly variations on the Son of BOSS shelters described in chapter 4. The shelters designed by Daugerdas involved, at their core, selling and purchasing offsetting options. As with the other Son of BOSS shelters, the tax benefits were based on the claim that selling an option should be treated differently under the tax code from the cost incurred to purchase one. The options that Daugerdas used initially were options to purchase Treasury notes as part of a shelter that he had developed at Arthur Andersen and had been selling at Altheimer. He discontinued this shelter in October 1999, however, when it looked like Congress would clarify the law to eliminate the tax advantage that it supposedly provided.

At that point, Daugerdas switched to the Short Options Strategy (SOS), which involved the use of options based on movements in currency exchange rates. SOS generated the largest amount of tax losses during the time Daugerdas was at Jenkens & Gilchrist. In 1999 and 2000, it was sold to about 550 clients, who claimed to avoid a total of $3.9 billion in taxes. In addition, a shelter known as the Swaps shelter was sold to at least fifty-five individuals and generated more than $420 million in supposed tax losses, while a Hedge Option Monetization of Economic Remainder (HOMER) shelter was sold to at least thirty-six individuals, generating more than $400 million in ostensible tax losses. Precise figures are not available on Daugerdas's Treasury shorts shelter sales while at Jenkens, but his indictment indicated that the shelter was sold from 1994 to 1999 to at least 290 taxpayers who claimed $2.6 billion in losses for tax purposes. Finally, the Jenkens Chicago office sold the COBRA version of SOS that Daugerdas had first pitched when in talks about joining the firm. Some idea of the losses that COBRA generated is reflected in the fact that the firm settled a class action brought by purchasers of the shelter for around $81.5 million in January 2005.

The Treasury short sales, along with SOS and its COBRA variation, involved transactions designed to increase a taxpayer's basis in an asset while avoiding rules that otherwise would operate to reduce the basis. The effect was to generate a loss for tax purposes when the taxpayer sold an asset for less than the amount of the basis—even though the taxpayer suffered an economic loss nowhere near the loss that she claimed for tax purposes.

To illustrate this, suppose that a taxpayer sells a call option, which means that she agrees to sell to a party the option to purchase from the taxpayer, say, 100,000 euros for $150,000. That is, taxpayer agrees to sell 100,000 euros at an exchange rate of $1.50 to the euro. Assume that the option remains available for two weeks. The buyer of the option believes that the value of the euro will go up during this period, which would enable her buy the euros for $150,000 and sell them for more. The buyer is willing to pay $2 million for the call option. If the value of the euro instead falls below $1.50 over that period, the buyer will not be interested in buying euros at $1.50 each and will simply let the option expire. In any event, the taxpayer who sold the option keeps the $2 million profit on the transaction.

There is a possibility, however, that the price of the euro may rise within two weeks so the taxpayer must have 100,000 euros available to sell to the buyer of the call option. She therefore buys a call option for herself to purchase 100,000 euros at a rate of $1.50 per euro, which expires in thirteen days. She pays $2,001,000 for this option, which ensures that she will have the euros necessary to meet her obligation to the buyer of the first call option on the next day if the need arises. She pays $2,001,000 for this, which is $1,000 more than she received when she sold the first call option. She therefore has suffered a net economic loss of $1,000 in the two transactions.

The next step in the transaction involves using a partnership to claim a loss considerably higher than the $1,000 actually lost. The taxpayer forms a partnership with a friend and contributes to it both the call option she bought and the one that she sold. The one she bought is an asset valued at its $2,001,000 purchase price, so the amount of this contribution becomes her basis in the partnership. The one she sold represents her obligation to sell 100,000 euros at $1.50 per euro if the buyer makes this demand. This is a liability for which she is responsible, which is valued at its $2 million purchase price. Partnership rules say that when a person transfers a liability to a partnership, as the taxpayer did here in transferring the call option that she sold, this relieves the individual of the liability. This benefit is treated for tax purposes as a distribution of money by the partnership to the partner. Such a distribution in turn reduces the partner's basis in the partnership by that amount. In this example, the taxpayer's $2,001,000 basis representing the call option that she purchased and then contributed to the partnership should be reduced by $2 million, which is the value of the call option she sold for which she has liability, which she contributed to the partnership. The result is that the taxpayer's basis in the partnership after her contributions is $1,000.

Most of the shelters on which Daugerdas and his colleagues worked, however, were predicated on the claim that the liability in this example was contingent—it might never arise. They argued that for tax purposes this contingent liability should not be treated as a definite liability that reduces the taxpayer's basis in the partnership. This means that the taxpayer claims a basis of $2,001,000. The partnership then makes a payment to terminate its call obligation and accepts a payment to terminate its option to buy shares, which results in net proceeds of $1,000. The partners next liquidate the partnership and share the proceeds between them. Assume that the taxpayer's share of the proceeds is $500. Subtracting this amount from the basis that she claims in the partnership, the taxpayer then claims a loss for tax purposes of $2,000,500. She uses this to reduce her overall taxable income by this amount—even though her actual economic loss from these transactions is $500. This represents her $1,000 loss from the sale and purchase of the options, minus the $500 she received when the partnership was liquidated.

Promoters of the shelter claimed, and Daugerdas and his colleagues opined, that this tax treatment of the transaction likely would be upheld if challenged. The rationale for this assertion was that the treatment of the liability as contingent was consistent with tax law as declared in *Helmer v. Commissioner*,[21] a 1975 U.S. Tax Court case described in chapter 4. To reiterate the basic facts of that case, a partnership received periodic payments to keep open an option to buy partnership property. In the event that the party with the option elected to exercise it, these payments would be deducted from the purchase price. Taxation of the payments to the partners was deferred until either the option expired, in which case they would be taxed as ordinary income, or the option was exercised, in which case they would be taxed as part of any capital gain that the partners enjoyed from the sales price that they received. The partners claimed that granting the option created a partnership liability that should be included in their basis in the partnership, which in turn reduced their tax obligation. The Tax Court disagreed, observing that no obligations accompanied receipt of the option payments. The payments did not have to be returned if the option terminated and would be applied against the purchase price if the option were exercised. Recognition of the payments as income was deferred only to determine whether they would be taxed as ordinary income or capital gains, not because the payments created any obligation to repay the funds or to perform any future services in order to keep them.

Daugerdas and his colleagues took the position that *Helmer* stood for the proposition that any liability that is "contingent"—that is, that may not arise or whose amount cannot be calculated at the time it is incurred—should not be included in the calculation of a taxpayer's basis. In the preceding example involving euros, it is possible that the taxpayer's obligation under the call option that she sold might never arise, since the purchaser would let the option expire if the price of the euro went down. It is thus inappropriate to reduce the taxpayer's basis by her obligation to sell the euros to the option purchaser for $1.50 per euro, the value of which is represented by the $2 million the purchaser paid her for the option. In *Helmer*, tax law precluded using a putative liability to increase a taxpayer's basis; Daugerdas claimed that it also precluded using a putative liability to reduce a taxpayer's basis.

In each instance, of course, the taxpayer is attempting to maximize the amount of her basis. In *Helmer*, the taxpayers sought to do so by claiming that a noneconomic liability should be counted for tax purposes. In the example involving euros, the taxpayers are attempting to do so by claiming that an economic liability should not be counted for tax purposes. Both efforts represent attempts to claim tax treatment at odds with economic reality. Reading *Helmer* in light of the court's underlying purpose should lead to including the call option obligation in the taxpayer's basis and then subtracting it from the basis when the option is contributed to the partnership. Daugerdas claimed, however, that the literal terms of the court's holding in *Helmer*, not its rationale, should govern. Jenkens & Gilchrist issued a lengthy opinion concluding that the tax treatment of the options transaction more likely than not would be upheld if challenged by the IRS.

The risk always exists, of course, that the tax consequences of a transaction that complies with the letter of the law will not be honored because the taxpayer had no nontax business purpose for entering the transaction or the transaction had negligible economic substance. In the euro example, the simultaneous purchase and sale of virtually offsetting options has the net effect of costing the taxpayer $1,000. If the price of the euro goes above $1.50, she is entitled to buy the euros at $1.50 each to meet her obligation to sell them at the same price to the party to whom she sold the option. If the price of the euro goes below $1.50, the option buyer will have no interest in purchasing them at that price, nor will the taxpayer. Both options will expire. It is hard to imagine any nontax business purpose an investor would have for entering into two transactions that ultimately have such negligible economic substance.

COBRA Unveiled

The COBRA variation of the SOS that Daugerdas designed and marketed at Jenkens & Gilchrist in collaboration with Ernst & Young (E&Y), discussed in chapter 6, was designed to provide an ostensibly more plausible argument that the purchase of offsetting options had a nontax business purpose and possessed economic substance. E&Y needed a legal opinion, however, that the shelter more likely than not would be upheld if challenged. E&Y was aware of the shelter work going on at Jenkens & Gilchrist and asked Grady Dickens at the Dallas law firm of Scheef & Stone for an introduction to the firm. Dickens knew Patrick O'Daniel, who worked with Michael Cook at Jenkens; Dickens put O'Daniel in touch with Robert Coplan and other E&Y partners. O'Daniel in turn got Daugerdas involved. Scheef and Jenkens then entered into a fee agreement under which Scheef would receive 20 percent of the fees that Jenkens received on each E&Y shelter, as compensation for "provid[ing] legal services" to Jenkens in connection with Jenkens's preparation of legal opinions.[22]

Jenkens and E&Y worked together to refine COBRA, and Daugerdas suggested that they use Deutsche Bank to perform the currency trades necessary to produce the tax loss from the shelter. The shelters were marketed out of the Jenkens & Gilchrist Chicago office. In all but one of the COBRA transactions involving E&Y, Jenkens created the necessary entities and wrote the legal opinion. Because E&Y was concerned that the Jenkens opinion might not be regarded as sufficiently independent in light of the firm's role in designing the shelter, they arranged for an additional opinion from R. J. Ruble of Brown & Wood. Each opinion letter was virtually identical. E&Y insisted that each taxpayer sign a confidentiality agreement not to disclose the marketing material to any outside parties, including any attorneys. In these agreements, Jenkens expressly disclaimed any fiduciary responsibility to the taxpayers.

The COBRA shelter was a digital option. It involved not simply a bet that the price of a currency would go up or down, but that it would be at a specific value by a certain date. A COBRA sold to one investor, whom we'll call John Smith, illustrates the shelter's basic features. Smith was advised to enter into a transaction that involved purchasing options based on the exchange rate of the euro to the English pound. When Smith entered into the transaction, the rate was $1.6024 to the pound. He paid $10 million for a put option at a strike price of $1.6024 to the pound. If the euro were at this or a lower price, Smith would be entitled to a payment of $20 million from Deutsche Bank. At the same time, Smith sold a call option to the bank for $9.5 million with a strike price of $1.6022 to the pound. If the euro were at this or a lower price on the same date, he was obligated to pay Deutsche Bank $18.5 million. Thus, on the expiration date of the options, if the pound traded at less than $1.6022, Smith would have the right to receive $20 million from Deutsche Bank while owing it $18.5 million, which would result in a gain of $1.5 million. Of course, to obtain this he had to have purchased one option for $10 million and sold another for $9.5 million and pay a fee that was about 4.5 percent of the $10 million he purchased, or $450,000. He thus would have paid a net total of $950,000 to gain $1.25 million, which would put him $75,000 ahead. Estimates were that the likelihood of this occurring was about 30 percent.

If the pound were trading above $1.6024 on the expiration date of the options, Smith would have no interest in selling the pound at $1.6024 to the pound and Deutsche Bank would have no interest in selling the pound to Smith at an exchange rate of $1.6022. Thus, neither party would be entitled to any payment from the other. Smith then would simply have incurred his net payment of $950,000. Estimates were that there was a 65 to 70 percent chance that this would occur. Whichever way the exchange rate moved, it would be hard to argue that Smith had a nontax reason for entering into this complex series of transactions.

Jenkens & Gilchrist and E&Y nevertheless maintained that Smith stood to gain $20 million from his investment if the exchange rate dropped below $1.6024 but above $1.6022. If this were to happen, Deutsche Bank's obligation to pay Smith $20 million would be triggered but Smith's obligation to pay the bank $18.5 million would not. There was as much as a 5 percent chance, they argued, that this could occur. This was referred to as the "lottery feature" of the shelter. A taxpayer, in other words, was taking a gamble that she might get lucky and reap a $20 million windfall for her $950,000 investment.

Even if we assume the most optimistic odds of 5 percent that this could occur, a straightforward expected value analysis would indicate that paying $950,000 for this chance is not a good idea. There was a 30 percent chance that the exchange rate would drop below $1.6022 and the taxpayer would net $75,000, for an expected value of $22,500. There was a 65 percent chance that the rate would rise above $1.6024 and the taxpayer would lose $950,000, for an expected value of $617,500. Finally, there was a 5 percent chance that the rate would fall between $1.6024 and $1.6022 and the taxpayer would receive $20 million, for an expected value of $1 million. All together, the three expected values come to $607,000. This obviously is less than the $950,000 the taxpayer would have to pay to enter this lottery in the first place. Keep in mind that this figure reflects the most optimistic assessment of the chance of winning the lottery; the odds in most transactions were virtually negligible. Indeed, the likelihood was so remote that the Deutsche Bank foreign currency desk didn't even bother hedging its supposed $20 million exposure on any transaction.

There was another even more fundamental reason that the lottery feature didn't infuse the COBRA with economic substance—Deutsche Bank would not allow it to be triggered. There is never a single foreign currency rate throughout the world. Rather, different institutions offer similar but slightly different rates at any given time. As a complaint filed by investors later described, for instance, there were twelve spot rates listed as of 8:21 a.m. on May 8, 2003, ranging from $1.1463 to the euro to $1.1468 to the euro. Deutsche Bank was authorized to decide which exchange rate would be used at the precise time specified in the contracts. This enabled it to ensure that the exchange rate never hit the narrow "sweet spot" that would trigger a large payout to the taxpayer.

The reason for entering into the COBRA transactions, of course, was to reduce or eliminate taxes. Before the options expired, Smith contributed both his put option and his call obligation to a partnership. The put option was valued at its $10 million purchase price and became Smith's basis in the partnership. The call obligation, however, was treated as a contingent liability so that transferring it to the partnership was not treated as relief from a liability and the $9.5 million that Smith received for it was not subtracted from his basis. Smith then contributed a small amount of cash to the partnership. When the options expired, the partnership bought a small amount of currency. To reduce it to essentials, the currency was sold at a price far less than Smith's $10 million basis in the partnership. The difference of close to $10 million was recorded as a loss for tax purposes, even though Smith actually had incurred a loss of only the $500,000 difference between the $10 million he paid to buy his put option and the $9.5 million he received for selling the call option.

IRS Notice 2000-44, issued in August 2000, described a transaction in which a taxpayer buys and sells options and then contributes them to a partnership: "Under the position advanced by the promoters of this arrangement, "the taxpayer claims that the basis in the taxpayer's partnership interest is increased by the cost of the purchased call options but is not reduced . . . as a result of the partnership's assumption of the taxpayer's obligation with respect to the written call options." This, of course, described COBRA and other similar shelters. The notice continued, "The purported losses resulting from the transactions described above do not represent bona fide losses reflecting actual economic consequences. . . . The purported losses from these transactions (and from any similar arrangements designed to produce noneconomic tax losses by artificially overstating basis in partnership interests) are not allowable as deductions for federal income tax purposes."[23]

Jenkens lawyers discussed this notice but ultimately told previous purchasers of shelters that it was legally inapplicable to them and did not affect the propriety of their COBRA transactions. As one letter to an investor said, "One of the described transactions in Notice 2000-44 bears similarities to the transactions described in our enclosed opinion. While 2000-44 sets forth the IRS position on these transactions, the Notice does not change the existing law which is relied upon in our enclosed opinion and does not change our conclusions as stated in such opinion."[24]

Standard Operating Procedure

Any claims of business purpose or economic substance to the shelters that Jenkens sold were belied by the uniform steps in the transactions, the virtually identical legal opinions that the firm issued for all the taxpayers, and the absence in most cases of any contact between the firm and the taxpayer. The experience of investor Henry Camferdam was typical of the people who purchased COBRA from Ernst & Young. Camferdam and three colleagues were founders of an Indiana company known as Support Net, which distributed mainframe computer systems and peripheral devices. Ernst & Young provided accounting, auditing, and consulting services to the company and two of the individuals through its Indianapolis office. When the owners sought to sell the business, they retained E&Y to help market and sell it.

The business was sold in 1997 and the founders were scheduled to receive a final payment in August 1999 that represented a combined capital gain of $70 million for the four of them. In late October, Wayne Hoenig, senior manager of the E&Y Indianapolis office, called Camferdam about a strategy that could wipe out his portion of the capital gains from the sale of the business. Camferdam suggested that he and his three colleagues meet to hear a presentation of the strategy. Hoenig told him that they needed to start the transaction within the next week to ten days because it took about six to eight weeks to complete and needed to be done before the end of the year. Before receiving any more details about the shelter, the four businessmen had to pay E&Y a nonrefundable fee of $1.056 million and sign a nondisclosure agreement. They then formally retained E&Y as accountants and tax advisors for COBRA transactions.

In early November, the four men met with Hoenig and two of his colleagues at the E&Y office in Indianapolis. They were told in the course of a PowerPoint presentation that E&Y and Jenkens & Gilchrist had developed a tax strategy for a select group of individuals who had sold large businesses or enjoyed large capital gains. The strategy, the E&Y representatives said, took advantage of a "loophole" in the tax law that served to shelter most or all of their gains from any tax liability.[25] They said that the E&Y regional office had already implemented five of these transactions, which were being offered only to taxpayers with gains in excess of $50 million. The four men then were given a form to fill out indicating how much of a loss they wanted to create.

E&Y then showed the men an opinion letter from Jenkens & Gilchrist that E&Y said would provide "insurance" in case of an audit.[26] Camferdam and his colleagues were not told that Jenkens had helped design the shelter. They were told, however, that they should obtain a second legal opinion "just to make sure," and that the firm of Brown & Wood could provide one.[27] Hoenig told the four men that they needed to have a "business purpose" for entering into the transactions. The men didn't understand the transaction and asked Hoenig to figure out a business purpose, which he agreed to do.[28]

A few days later, Hoenig and other E&Y representatives met with the four men on a golf course before three of the latter were about to start a round of golf. Hoenig had told the men that getting the transactions underway was urgent and asked to squeeze in the meeting just before tee time. Hoenig had picked the loss that the parties needed to generate and needed them to sign all the necessary paperwork, including transaction documents. The meeting lasted no more than half an hour. The taxpayers received no copies of the documents but were told that the paperwork would be mailed to them. During the meeting one of the men asked Hoenig, "What is the strategy?" Hoenig replied, "It['s] already done; don't worry about it."[29] The fee for the shelter would be 4.5 percent of the capital loss created, or $3.15 million. E&Y would receive $1.05 million, with Jenkens earning $2.1 million.

Camferdam and his colleagues were then instructed by Deutsche Bank which currencies to choose for purposes of entering into the purchase and sale of options. The bank advised Camferdam to choose the euro and the other three men to choose the Japanese yen. They were then told the exact amounts of each option and the amount of the premiums that they would pay and receive for each. Camferdam, for instance, was told to purchase an option on November 16, 1999, that pegged the value of the euro at $1.0187. If the price was at or below that amount one month later, at 10:00 am New York time on December 16, the bank would pay Camferdam $100 million. Camferdam paid a $50 million premium for this option. He was instructed simultaneously to sell an option to the bank that pegged the value of the euro at $1.0186. If the euro were trading at or below that price at 10:00 am New York time on December 16, Camferdam would pay Deutsche Bank $93.75 million. He received $47.5 million as payment for this option, leaving him with a net premium cost of $2.5 million. Camferdam thus would be entitled to $100 million from Deutsche Bank without having any obligation to it if the euro was worth between $1.0187 and $1.0186 at the appointed time. The bank's ability to select the exchange rate used to determine the parties' obligations ensured that this would never happen.

Camferdam's colleagues were instructed to enter into similar purchases and sales of options with respect to the yen. The four then contributed their buy and sell contracts to a partnership. They counted as their respective bases the amounts they had paid for their options, but treated their liabilities on the options they had sold as contingent. These liabilities therefore were not taken into account in determining the taxpayers' bases. The taxpayers next contributed cash to the partnership to purchase a small amount of stocks or currencies. They then transferred their partnership interests to an S corporation, which for tax purposes was treated as a partnership. This terminated the partnership and the corporation then sold the stock or currencies for an amount substantially lower than the taxpayers' basis. The businessmen claimed losses for tax purposes of $50 million, $12 million, $7 million, and $1.4 million, respectively. Not surprisingly, this roughly equaled the amount of the capital gains that they had enjoyed from the sale of the business.

All of this may have seemed too good to be true, but Camferdam and his business partners had used Ernst & Young for years and trusted the firm. E&Y had been their company's main source of financial guidance and business advice, working closely with Support Net across all its operations. As the outside auditor for the company, E&Y attested that its financial statements presented a fair and accurate picture of its condition. Furthermore, the firm advised the businessmen on the sale of their company and helped effectuate it. When Ernst & Young told Camferdam and partners that they could avoid taxes by entering into these transactions, they had no reason to doubt it. The firm, in other words, exploited the relationship that it had built over the years as a trusted advisor.

The transaction with Camferdam and his colleagues made apparent that investment deals constructed around COBRA and other shelters were driven solely by the desire to reduce or eliminate tax liability. Working backward from the loss that the taxpayer wanted to create, the price of the premium payment generally reflected the desired loss, the price that the taxpayer simultaneously received for selling a second option was only slightly less, and the options that were bought and sold were virtually offsetting. In other words, the transaction was designed to generate a large tax loss while producing a minimal genuine economic impact.

The fact that the transactions were solely tax-driven rather than the result of the particular investment strategies of individual taxpayers meant that the process of executing the transactions followed a template that could be easily replicated for hundreds of taxpayers. Paralegals and administrative assistants filled in names on a standard set of documents used to create the necessary partnerships and other corporations, obtained taxpayer identification numbers for the entities, created a brokerage account for the taxpayer in each transaction to conduct the necessary trades, and monitored the flow of paperwork through the routine steps of the transactions. The streamlined sequence of routine steps is what made possible the mass marketing of the shelters.

Similarly, Jenkens & Gilchrist issued virtually identical opinion letters with broad declarations about the motivation to enter into the shelters that were ostensibly applicable to every purchaser. The opinion provided to the taxpayer typically made the representation: "You entered into the purchase and sale of the Options for substantial nontax business reasons, including (i) to produce overall economic profits because of your belief that [currency exchange rates] would change; and (ii) your belief that the most direct way, with the most leverage, to realize gain from expected changes in currency prices was the purchase and Partnership for substantial nontax business reasons, including, but not limited to, potential diversification of the risks of certain investments, the desire to coinvest as partners with the other co-partners and for your convenience."[30] The opinion represented that "[t]o the best of your knowledge, you have provided to us all the facts and circumstances necessary for us to form our opinion and the facts stated herein are accurate."[31] In fact, Jenkens lawyers never received any representations from purchasers about their particular circumstances or their purpose in engaging in the transactions. No client, for instance, ever asked to use a partnership as the vehicle for engaging in investments. Indeed, sometimes the firm had no contact with the client at all.

Reducing the Audit Profile

Jenkens and the other entities involved in the shelters engaged in several activities as part of a process known as "reducing the audit profile."[32] One of these was "cosmetic trading," which consisted of executing numerous option trades on behalf of shelter purchasers to create the impression that the purchasers were actively involved in trading as an investment strategy.[33] Another activity was to identify "dog tech stocks," which were high-tech companies that had a highly successful initial public offering (IPO) but whose stock then fell precipitously because of financial problems.[34] After the taxpayers contributed their option contracts to the partnership, they were instructed to invest in the stock of these companies to create the impression that the losses that the shelter purchasers incurred were based on market conditions rather than on a tax loss strategy.

Although the use of an S corporation in the shelter transactions was not a necessary step, according to Daugerdas "it was generally better to report the losses on separate tax returns, then have them flow through the S corporation. The S corporation was not essential, it was just less likely to be audited."[35] When the shelters would result in a tax loss so large that the government owed the taxpayer a refund, clients were advised to adjust their W-4 forms to reduce the amount of the refund to minimize the likelihood of an audit.

Similarly, the fees to participate in the shelters typically were deductible, but some clients didn't deduct them because they were so large that they might trigger an audit. Engagement letters also generally did not refer to the fees because of concern that their amount would be taken into account if an issue ever arose about whether the transactions had a business purpose or economic substance. For the COBRA transactions, Jenkens & Gilchrist's legal fees were not itemized as deductions on investors' tax returns. Rather, they were capitalized into the basis of the partnership interest, which was then included in the basis of the S corporation out of which payments ultimately were made. The ostensible rationale was that key Jenkens services were not the provision of a legal opinion, but the structuring of the partnership, document preparation, and the formation of entities. As an email from Ernst & Young stated, "The significance of this is that the returns will not force the individuals to show the large payment to J&G as a miscellaneous itemized deduction, which could be a red flag on the 1040."[36]

Daugerdas and Mayer also debated whether it was safer to eliminate all tax liability for a given year. Mayer thought that it might be better not to do so because the taxpayer was less likely to be audited if the returns were relatively consistent from year to year. Daugerdas, however, believed it was better to show a loss rather than report any income, on the theory that this made the IRS less likely to conduct an audit because there appeared to be little prospect of recovering revenue. Participants in implementing the shelters were "always refining" their efforts to reduce the audit profile of the shelter purchasers.

Lawyers at the firm also found it necessary sometimes to backdate documents so that investors would receive the tax losses they sought. One wealthy taxpayer who owned car dealerships engaged in a Treasury short sale to shelter $20 million from the sale of stock. The Jenkens & Gilchrist lawyers discovered that certain documents were dated one day too late, which resulted in the taxpayer having unintended taxable income. They agreed to backdate the documents so that the client received the tax benefit he was seeking. Similarly, another client failed to sell enough stocks in 1999 to trigger the desired tax loss. Mayer approached the taxpayer's broker at Deutsche Bank in the spring of 2000 and asked him to sell stock to the taxpayer but to record the sale as occurring in 1999. This was done, and the opinion letter for the transaction didn't mention the discrepancy.

On another occasion, a group of tax shelter clients sought to shelter substantial income that they expected from the sale of stock. The value of the stock dropped unexpectedly, however, so that the short sales in which they engaged resulted in gains rather than in the intended losses. To obtain the loss that the taxpayers wanted, Mayer agreed to alter the date on the document assigning the options to a partnership. He whited out the November 5, 1999 date and inserted November 15, 1999 in its place. Mayer discussed this with Daugerdas and Guerin, and all agreed on the change to keep the clients happy.

The Texas Connection

Under the arrangement within Jenkens & Gilchrist, Michael Cook in Austin had the final sign-off on the opinion letters generated by the Chicago office. Cook delegated the task of traveling to Chicago to review the client files to Bryan Lee, a partner in the Austin office. Lee periodically commented on the opinion letters and Cook relied on his assessment in providing the final signature. Lee also occasionally made presentations to prospective clients about shelter products. One email from Cook to a partner in Dallas inquiring about a shelter for a client preparing to sell a business stated, "Bryan Lee is as good as any of the three Chicago attorneys when it comes to presenting the short option strategy."[37] Cook mentioned that neither he nor Lee received any business development credits for any shelter sales, but that the Dallas partner and Daugerdas would each get half of the development credit for the sale of a shelter to the partner's client.

Daugerdas, of course, had vastly underestimated when he claimed that he expected to generate $6 million in annual revenues. In 1999, his practice produced about $28 million in income or almost five times the amount that the firm anticipated. This figure was more than 13 percent of the firm's total revenues. In 2000, he generated almost $91 million in revenues or almost a third of Jenkens's revenues. Over a thousand taxpayers participated in these transactions, which would have created a challenge for Cook and Lee even if they had been experienced tax shelter lawyers. Ideally, they would have had to verify every taxpayer's motivation for entering into the transaction to ensure that it was based on the prospect of economic benefits apart from tax consequences. In addition, they would have needed to be intimately familiar with the economic substance and business purpose doctrines as applied in numerous cases to determine whether the lottery feature in each transaction constituted enough of a profit opportunity that a court likely would uphold the shelter. This was a daunting prospect under the best of circumstances, but the fact that Cook and Lee were traditional tax lawyers with no experience in tax shelters virtually doomed the oversight process from the start. Despite the weaknesses in the process, there is no indication that either Cook or Lee asked for additional resources or declined to participate in signing off on the shelter opinions.

Exacerbating the problem, Daugerdas repeatedly locked horns with Cook over whether the tax shelter work accorded with the latest court rulings and IRS pronouncements. "I would regularly get a read that it was increasingly unpleasant dealing with Daugerdas," recalled Laney. "It was a very difficult interaction, and it grew increasingly difficult. Mike would say, 'No, you can't do it this way.' Paul didn't like to have his opinions tinkered with." Roger Hayse, former chief operations officer of the firm, observed of Daugerdas, "His attitude was that his view was the definitive one, and if you didn't agree with him, it was because you simply didn't understand him."[38]

The huge volume of transactions also made it daunting to complete them in time for taxpayers to claim tax benefits before the year ended. Jenkens lawyers from Texas periodically were sent to Chicago to reduce the backlog of opinions the Chicago office faced because of the volume of shelter activity. One email from Guerin to Jenkens lawyer Patrick O'Daniel in Austin, for instance, refers to an "opinion preparation training session" for eight Jenkens lawyers who would be arriving at the Chicago office.[39] Guerin explained the steps in the transactions and how certain entities were used to minimize the likelihood of an audit. What the Texas reinforcements mainly did, however, was fill in information on the standard transaction documents and opinions about each of the taxpayers and the transactions in which they participated.

The Money Flows In

With the infusion of profits from Daugerdas's practice, Jenkens & Gilchrist ended 1998 with gross revenue of $140 million and profits per partner of $390,000. Those figures jumped dramatically in 1999, when gross revenue increased by 43 percent to $200 million, and the firm moved from 77 to 57 for this metric in the Am Law 100 ranking. Even more important, profits per partner increased in 1999 by 36 percent to $530,000. This moved the firm up 17 places in the Am Law 100, from 79 to 62. It also placed comfortable distance between Jenkens and its main Dallas-based rival, Locke Liddell & Sapp, which vaulted into the Am Law 100 for the first time in 1999. Daugerdas had dramatically boosted Jenkens's odds of realizing its ambition to become a major national—and possibly international—law firm. Indeed, in late 2000 the firm entered the New York market by merging with the firm of Parker Chapin.

From 1999 through 2002, Jenkens & Gilchrist received $230 million in fees from Treasury short sales, SOS, and other shelters.

Other entities affiliated with the shelters earned an additional $148.2 million. Of the Jenkens amount, Daugerdas received $95.7 million, Mayer $28.7 million, and Guerin $17.5 million. That left $88.1 million for the firm. This amount appears not to include revenues from the COBRA shelter, which the IRS estimated had been sold to 600 individuals. The Jenkens board of directors memo to partners at the end of 1999 described the year as "spectacular,"[40] and said, "With special recognition and thanks to the extraordinary contribution from our Chicago office, congratulations to all of you."[41] The board sent a similar memo to members of the firm at the end of 2000 congratulating them on Jenkens & Gilchrist's strong financial performance for the year.[42] The memo named Daugerdas and Mayer as the top business generators, and Guerin, Lee, and Cook as providing support for them.

Daugerdas had agreed with Mayer and Guerin that he would pay them bonuses out of his own pocket if he felt that Jenkens was not compensating them as they deserved. When the lawyers moved to Jenkens from Altheimer, Mayer didn't have a track record of generating business and wasn't going to be compensated on that basis. He therefore had an agreement with Daugerdas that the latter would get credit for 50 percent of Mayer's deals, which funded the payment that Daugerdas would make to him. Mayer eventually received $875,000 in such payments from Daugerdas. Daugerdas also agreed to make payments to Guerin, who received over 80 percent of her income from such bonuses. In 2000, for instance, Guerin's compensation was $11.5 million, of which almost $9 million came from Daugerdas. The following year Daugerdas made a payment to Guerin of around $4 million. Guerin served as more of a service partner to Daugerdas than did Mayer, who tended to have his own clients and assistants separate from what Guerin was doing. The firm's management was very distressed when it learned of Daugerdas's payments to his colleagues, since this upset the compensation balance at the firm. From that point on, the firm asked Daugerdas each year if he was compensating anyone else; it's not clear how he responded.

Daugerdas persistently lobbied management for more compensation for himself, Mayer, and Guerin. "Mr. Daugerdas believed our compensation system didn't adequately compensate the people in Chicago who assisted him with opinions," observed Hayse. If Mr. Daugerdas felt that he was getting short-changed, added Laney, "it was like the wrath of

Khan."[43] A May 28, 2001, memo from Daugerdas to the Jenkens board of directors provides an example of Daugerdas's dissatisfaction. The memo stated that, with respect to approximately $19.6 million earned in 1999 and 2000 on Ernst & Young transactions:

> I disagree with the fact that almost $9.8M in development credit that was given to Associate Attorney Patrick O'Daniel, whose sole contribution was to introduce me to Scheef & Stone, who, after entering into an agreement to be compensated by the Firm, introduced me to Ernst & Young (who, after lengthy negotiations regarding structure, referred me to prospective clients). This allocation was contrary to the written policy of the Firm, the facts of the situation, and my agreement with Mr. O'Daniel. Under my agreement with the Firm, I should have received 70% of the $19.6M in financial products from the Ernst & Young transactions.[44]

Daugerdas's efforts to create tax losses were not confined to paying customers. The reason he wanted his compensation at Jenkens paid to a corporation was so he could use it to generate losses to offset his own tax liability. Each year from 1999 through 2002, he generated tax losses from shelter activity that resulted in a net loss on his tax return. In 1999, PMD Chartered received about $19.3 million in income but used Treasury short sales and SOS to produce a net loss for tax purposes of $1.02 million. In 2000, he earned a whopping $50.3 million. His corporation paid Guerin almost $9 million and he used SOS to generate a $1.3 million net loss, ending up with no tax liability. He did not pay taxes in 2001 or 2002. In 2001 he earned $19.9 million, paid Guerin $4 million, and then used SOS to create a net $1.7 million loss on his return. In 2002, as shelter work declined, his compensation was $2.8 million. He used SOS to produce a $1.5 million net loss and applied for a refund of almost $968,000. From 1999 through 2000 he created a total of $82.6 million in ostensible losses resulting from shelters he created for himself. Mayer was less ambitious but used SOS to generate almost $4 million in tax losses in 1999 and over $22 million in 2000. Mayer approached Guerin about using shelters to reduce her taxable income as well, but she replied that she "did not have the risk appetite" to do that.[45]

Increasing Tension

Concern about Daugerdas within Jenkens & Gilchrist heightened when he was sued in 2000 by James Haber, president of a business engaged in designing tax shelters known as Diversified Group, Inc. (DGI).[46] Daugerdas and Haber had first met in 1992 and over the next several years Haber had asked the lawyer for his assessment of various shelters that DGI had developed. Daugerdas was entitled to market the shelters to clients and split the fees with DGI. Haber claimed that in 1998 DGI had developed a shelter known as the Option Partnership Strategy (OPS) that involved trading digital options and transferring them to a partnership to create a substantial basis in the partnership interest.[47] This shelter was identical in all material respects to COBRA. Haber alleged that he had provided information on OPS later that year to Daugerdas to help evaluate and develop the shelter. Haber maintained that their understanding was that Daugerdas would be able to market the shelter to investors as long as he obtained DGI's consent to do so and shared the fees with the company.[48]

Daugerdas was marketing the Treasury short sale shelter to taxpayers. When he discontinued doing so in the fall of 1999 because of concern about pending legislation, he shifted to using OPS instead. Haber alleged that from October 1 to December 31, 1999, Daugerdas had sold OPS to twenty-five clients and had not shared the fees from these matters with Haber.[49] Haber's lawsuit sought $10 million in damages. Jenkens found to its annoyance, however, that Daugerdas would not cooperate with them in the litigation or any of the settlement discussions. In late March 2001, the trial court granted summary judgment motions by Daugerdas and Jenkens on two of DGI's claims, but denied them with respect to a third.[50]

DGI then sought from Jenkens production of information about the firm's revenues from Daugerdas's practice. The parties reached settlement only hours before a scheduled hearing on DGI's motion to compel production of the information. Jenkens's insurance carrier paid $10 million, and Daugerdas's compensation was reduced by the amount of the settlement.

Shortly afterward, in an agreement dated November 2, 2001, Jenkens and Daugerdas entered into mutual releases from any obligations or claims relating to the DGI matter. "In consideration of the foregoing," the agreement stated, the Jenkens Texas firm agreed to indemnify Daugerdas "in any action in which Daugerdas is a named defendant (or where a claim has been made against him) from any and all liability," as well as counsel's fees, related to any work on the Option Partnership Strategy, including legal opinions, "on and after January 1, 1999."[51] Considering that the IRS later estimated that Daugerdas sold at least 600 COBRA shelters, many of which were after January 1999, the firm was assuming a potentially substantial financial risk by agreeing to provide such indemnification.

The most disturbing aspect of the DGI litigation for Jenkens was not the dispute with DGI but information that had come out during the lawsuit that Daugerdas had hidden fees from the firm. When Daugerdas came to Jenkens, he continued work for a shelter promoter for whom he had done projects while working at Altheimer. He did a transaction in 1999 for the promoter that involved issuance of a Jenkens & Gilchrist opinion letter, resulting in fees to the firm. Under his compensation agreement, Daugerdas was entitled to a portion of those fees. Unbeknownst to Jenkens, however, Daugerdas arranged to have an additional fee of $2,270,000 for the same transaction paid by the promoter to an entity controlled by him known as Treasurex. In addition to creating tax losses to offset his compensation from Jenkens, Daugerdas generated losses that offset his Treasurex income as well. Daugerdas had testified that "Treasurex acted as an intermediary and arranged a buyer and seller to come together and was compensated for that. As part of the same transaction, one law firm I was associated with did corporate work on behalf of the purchaser, and another firm I was associated with rendered a tax opinion to the purchaser."[52]

Daugerdas's disclosure of the fees paid to Treasurex, his ongoing complaints about compensation, and his sometimes contentious dealings with Michael Cook deepened concern in some quarters within Jenkens. One former partner describes a lot of "anger and frustration" within the firm about what people regarded as Daugerdas's breach of his fiduciary duty to his partners. On November 7, 2001, five days after the indemnity agreement was signed, David Laney dictated a confidential memo to the board.[53] "Now that we have settled the DGI litigation," it said, "and with his current calendar budget utility coming to a close, I propose that we now begin seriously considering and planning the termination of Paul Daugerdas's employment with the firm, so that the Board will be positioned to deliver the message in January 2002." The memo continued, "Paul is not qualified to continue as Office Managing Partner of the Chicago office, but more importantly, Paul is unfit to be a partner in the firm.

He represents by far the highest risk practice exposure to the firm. And he represents a continuing degradation of the firm's integrity, character, and culture." The memo went on to say:

Without question, Paul has proven valuable to the firm from an economic standpoint, but he has also proven extremely costly from an economical standpoint—the DGI litigation was the costliest litigation from the standpoint of the firm's settlement contribution in the history of the firm—as well as from the firm's image and reputation in the legal and insurance industries. Fortunately, the level of his financial performance this year, and probably in future years, will not be so great as to blind us as effectively as it did in 1999 and 2000 to the character we have seen exhibited since his arrival, and particularly since the inception of the DGI litigation.

The memo concluded, "Whether Mayer and Guerin choose to stay or go should not affect the decision regarding Paul, although I presume they will move together."

Laney asked for two straw votes from the board about Daugerdas's future with the firm. In each case, five of the six board members favored asking Daugerdas to leave. There was some reluctance, however, to follow through at that point. One reason, Laney later said, was that it was the fourth quarter of the year and the firm was concerned about collecting on clients' unpaid bills. The board feared that firing Daugerdas might disrupt his collection efforts and distract the entire firm. Laney stated, "We wanted to wrap up the year in good shape," then take action the following year. The firm also consulted with its litigation counsel in the DGI matter. That led to the conclusion that it might be better to have Daugerdas inside the tent than outside. People were not sure what else Daugerdas might have done without the firm's knowledge. As one lawyer put it, the firm decided that it "wanted to keep him close to us to make sure that he didn't have any claims against us or throw us under the bus saying, 'Jenkens told me to do all this.'" One final complication was that Daugerdas's fate was becoming intertwined with a political coup within the firm. David Laney didn't know it yet but his tenure as chair of the firm was about to end.

Durbin's Triumph

William Durbin had been campaigning for some time to take Laney's job. Laney had been somewhat less active in running the firm in 2000 and 2001. He had been involved in George W. Bush's campaign for president in 2000 and had been serving as chair of the Texas Department of Transportation. He was hoping in 2001 for an appointment in the new Bush administration that drew on his expertise in transportation issues. Durbin had taken advantage of Laney's greater focus on outside matters to begin building support within the firm.

Durbin had been courting support in particular from the Jenkens offices in New York and Chicago, as well as among more recently arrived lateral partners. The New York office had opened in early 2001 with about a hundred lawyers from Parker Chapin, but had never been fully integrated into the firm. It faced additional difficulties after the terrorist attacks of September 11, 2001, and was being kept afloat in large part because of the revenues that the Chicago office was generating. The Chicago office, of course, was dominated by Daugerdas's practice. Durbin had continued to support Daugerdas after he joined the firm. He periodically intervened on Daugerdas's behalf with Laney on various issues, suggesting that the firm should be sensitive to the Chicago lawyer's concerns.

Durbin openly announced his candidacy in November 2001, the first time a challenger to Laney had arisen since Laney had assumed the presidency in 1989. One issue on which Durbin focused was Laney's concerns about Daugerdas. Many partners had come to rely on the significant boost in compensation that the Chicago office had made possible. Daugerdas's departure would threaten this income and the resulting reduction in profits per partner could also make the firm vulnerable to losing partners to more profitable firms. While the revelations concerning Treasurex had engendered some suspicion of Daugerdas, a number of partners still believed that the benefits of having him with the firm outweighed the risks. In addition, some partners felt that Laney had accomplished much of what he had set out to do, and it was simply time for new leadership.

Durbin approached Laney later in November and said that he had enough votes to be elected as the new president. Laney informally consulted with several partners and came to the same conclusion. At that point, he had to decide whether to wage an active campaign against Durbin to hold on to his seat. Conversations with Henry Gilchrist and other key partners led him to decide that taking such a step could generate conflict that would hurt the firm. As a result, Durbin was elected and became the new president of the firm at the beginning of 2002.

In February Laney sent a memo to the board following up on his earlier message about Daugerdas. "During the last quarter of 2001," he wrote, "on several occasions a clear majority of the Board concluded, without taking formal action, that Daugerdas would be/should be terminated for his perceived ethical shortcomings, subject to our first awaiting the year-end arrival of his collections. . . . I see now that Daugerdas has once again been named O[ffice] M[anaging] S[hareholder] for Chicago, and as such, an E[xecutive] C[ommittee] member. Would one of you let me know what's going on with respect to Daugerdas' employment status."[54] By then, the firm had decided that the best thing to do was to keep Daugerdas close rather than oust him and create a potential adversary as the government began to ramp up its enforcement against abusive tax shelters. The board took no action in response to Laney's memo.

Jenkens & Gilchrist's willingness to hitch its star to aggressive tax shelter work had substantially boosted its profitability, providing resources that could be used to realize its national ambitions. At the same time, the firm's involvement with Daugerdas eventually spelled its demise. Jenkens was hardly the only firm, however, to earn outsized profits by participating in the tax shelter industry.

9

Lowering the Bar

The tax shelter crisis almost certainly generated the largest number of criminal prosecutions against lawyers in connection with any set of events in United States history. At least twenty-nine lawyers were charged in an indictment or criminal information for their work on abusive tax shelters. Some were involved in private practice, while others worked in accounting or financial services firms. Eight were convicted, eleven pled guilty, two were acquitted, two had their convictions reversed on appeal, one is a fugitive from justice, and five had their indictments dismissed when KPMG terminated payment of their attorneys' fees at the behest of the government.[1] Other lawyers who were not prosecuted were publically criticized because of their work on abusive shelters.

Although prosecutions have mainly focused on the activities of individual lawyers, their tax shelter activities were very much a product of the organizations in which they worked. Accounting firms, as previous chapters underscore, created organizational structures and incentives that rewarded shelter participation. In law firms, different organizational influences tended to operate. Jenkens & Gilchrist took on Paul Daugerdas and his tax shelter practice as a part of a strategy to get ahead in the increasingly competitive market for legal services. Firm leaders failed to appreciate the significant risks of the shelter work. What risks they did recognize they wrongly believed they could manage successfully.

At other firms, tax shelter activity was often seen and characterized as "rogue" behavior—the behavior of individual lawyers who had become involved in the market without the firm's permission and knowledge. It was rogue behavior, however, that was facilitated by the loose oversight structure characteristic of law firms. In addition, it was behavior that inured to firms' financial benefit. Designing tax shelters and writing shelter opinions brought in substantial fees that not only enriched firm partners but also enhanced firms' profiles in the never-ending challenge to stay competitive. Under these circumstances it was not difficult for firm leaders to turn a blind eye to shelter activity.

Brown & Wood: "Opinions R Us"

Founded in 1914, New York-based Brown & Wood was a prestigious law firm well known for its representation of issuers and underwriters in securities offerings. From 1993 through the end of 1996, Brown & Wood ranked first among all law firms in the number of public debt and equity securities issues in which it had been involved. It ranked second in terms of the total dollar amount of securities issued in such transactions. The firm had an especially strong reputation for its technical expertise in structuring transactions involving complex financial securities, and was one of only four firms ranked in the top ten in six or more categories of capital markets work.

The lawyer who spearheaded shelter activity at Brown & Wood was the peripatetic R. J. Ruble, who had joined the firm as a partner in 1993. Between 1996 and 2003, Ruble issued more than seven hundred opinions on at least thirteen transactions that were listed as abusive by the IRS.

Ruble issued the vast majority of his opinions before Brown & Wood merged with Sidley & Austin in 2001. Ruble also wrote opinions after the merger, despite that fact that he had represented to the firm that he would cease doing so. The impact on tax revenues of the shelters in which Ruble participated was substantial. The government claimed that FLIP generated at least $1.9 billion in fraudulent tax losses, OPIS produced at least $2.3 million in such losses, and BLIPS generated a whopping $5.1 billion in fraudulent losses. Another shelter, SOS, resulted in bogus losses of at least $1.9 billion. In some circles, Ruble and Brown & Wood were known as "Opinions R Us." As one shelter promoter observed, the firm would provide tax opinions "pretty much for any product. Any time anybody needed a tax opinion, it [would] be hard to find one that Brown & Wood didn't participate in."[2]

There is substantial evidence that Ruble operated as a classic rogue partner, concealing his most culpable activities from the firm and on occasion engaging in actual misrepresentation. He was able to do this because

Brown & Wood did not have robust institutional mechanisms in place to prevent and detect such misbehavior, and whatever review of his work did occur was not especially thorough. Ruble did not act completely on his own. At least one other Brown & Wood partner was named as a defendant in a lawsuit by a taxpayer whose losses from a shelter were disallowed by the IRS.[3] The firm profited handsomely from the shelter activity. For just three shelters, FLIP, OPIS, and BLIPS, the firm estimated that Ruble had issued 314 opinions and generated revenues of $23.1 million.

In 1996, Ruble was a partner in the firm's New York office. He had earned an LLM in taxation from New York University Law School and had worked for several years at Rogers & Wells in New York advising corporations on international tax issues. Shortly after he joined Brown & Wood, he began devoting more of his time to work involving tax shelters for wealthy individuals. Ruble soon built up an expansive network of contacts who played various roles in shelter transactions. One group included tax shelter boutiques that specialized in designing "tax-advantaged" transactions. Another consisted of accounting firms that had both expertise and large client bases that could be mined for potential shelter customers. Still another group was comprised of banks and other financial institutions that could execute trades and provide funds that ostensibly financed investment activity. Ruble developed shelters with KPMG, Ernst & Young; Diversified Group, Inc. (DGI), PricewaterhouseCoopers, Bricolage/ICA, Arthur Andersen, BDO Seidman, Multi-National Strategies, Chenery Advisors, Presidio, Deutsche Bank, and Grant Thornton, among others.[4] As Ruble himself put it, "I do work for a number of people who have potentially complementary tax advantaged products. In addition, each of them has a relationship with one or more financial institutions who provide credit, derivative trades, etc. necessary to execute the product."[5] He added, "I'm beginning to feel like a dating service."[6]

Ruble's most lucrative connection was most likely the one that he formed with KPMG. The accounting firm was an attractive partner because of the scope of its activities and its organizational push to develop and market shelters. Ruble was valuable to KPMG because of his network of relationships, his ability to provide help in both designing shelters and issuing opinions for them, and Brown & Wood's preeminent reputation in capital markets work. The result was a strong desire by both parties to establish a mutually beneficial partnership.

Ruble was involved with KPMG's shelters from the firm's first foray into the shelter market with FLIP. As an internal KPMG email noted in the fall of 1997, "OUR DEAL WITH BROWN & WOOD IS THAT IF THEIR NAME IS USED IN SELLING THE STRATEGY THEY WILL GET A FEE. WE HAVE DECIDED AS A FIRM THAT B&W OPINION SHOULD BE GIVEN IN ALL DEALS."[7] To assist KPMG's shelter efforts, Ruble sought to put the firm in touch with his network of contacts. "I am not trying to push any of these on KPMG," he wrote, "but it might be useful if you are trying to get a repitoire [sic] of products jump started to talk to some or all of them."[8] Most of them, he indicated, knew one another and some used the others' strategies for deals they could not do themselves. If KPMG was interested, Ruble could "give you direct exposure to people I have seen closing deals."[9]

In order to embed himself in the accounting firm's expanding shelter activities, Ruble made efforts to formalize the relationship. As KPMG was experiencing its early success with FLIP, Ruble wrote to Randy Bickham: "This morning my managing partner, Tom Smith, approved Brown & Wood LP working with the newly conformed tax products group at KPMG on a joint basis in which we would jointly develop and market tax products and jointly share in the fees, as you and I have discussed."[10] (Smith later testified that no such conversation occurred; nor is there other evidence suggesting that it did.) When Bickham received Ruble's email, he forwarded it to Gregg Ritchie at KPMG with the note,

The B&W initiatives is [sic] moving ahead as you can see from the attached. I asked RJ about ABA constraints, etc. on joint ventures/fee splitting. His thought was that the only situation where a problem arises is when an opinion is involved, but he is following up with their person who specializes in the area on specifics. Today I will summarize my thought on the [sic] how the B&W relationship would be structured and the associated benefits.[11]

Bickham followed up with a message entitled "Business Model—Brown & Wood Strategic Alliance."[12] The message began, "The cornerstone of our business model is the development of strategic alliances to develop and market products for both high-wealth individuals and publicly-traded corporations." Potential partners in such alliances included "'Wall Street' law firms that specialize in corporate finance (e.g., Brown & Wood)." Bickham noted, "we need to negotiate a formal alliance with Brown & Wood. Brown & Wood is unique in that it can make significant contributions to the product development process and would allow immediate brand recognition." The firm could provide "market perception of technical excellence in the development of complex financial securities (from a branding perspective) and participation in the IPO market to enhance our distribution network." The latter referred to contact with founders of high-tech start-ups who might be interested in sheltering the gains they received as a result of issuing stock to the public. While the firm had not done significant work to date in the IPO sector, "they are making a significant strategic investment by building up their San Francisco-based practice."

Bickham continued, "The primary objective of the alliance between KPMG and Brown & Wood should be to build a mutually successful business based upon the products that are jointly developed." KPMG needed to "identify an initial product that can be the focal point for negotiating a strategic alliance with Brown & Wood. The most promising candidate was the "LLC product currently under development," which was OPIS. The goal would be to work with the law firm to get the new product out to customers by mid-January 1998, targeted at "large capital gain transactions where a co-branded product could potentially give us a competitive advantage."

In late 1997, when Bickham sent his email, Ruble was already part of a joint working group with KPMG and Presidio that was developing a new shelter ostensibly designed to address the weaknesses in FLIP. This shelter would turn out to be OPIS.[13] Ruble's integral role in creating the shelter emerged as Bob Simon, who had raised many of the concerns that led to FLIP's retirement argued with Ritchie about whether Simon was being sidelined during the successor shelter's development. Noting an important meeting to which he hadn't been invited at which Ritchie, Bickham, Larson, and Ruble had revised certain features of the shelter, Simon complained that he had not been kept in the loop on developments with OPIS.[14] In response, Ritchie explained that "[a]s product owner of the OPIS product, I elicited input from a variety of sources, including Brown & Wood, Presidio, Rick Solway, Richard Smith, and others."[15] He emphasized that OPIS was not yet being marketed, and that he was not aware of anyone "outside of a very small group of people . . . who know anything about the product."[16]

Ruble continued to participate as a member of the OPIS working group to design the shelter, assist in preparing documents necessary to implement it,[17] engage in discussions about whether to register the shelter,[18]and eventually issue opinions to taxpayers intended to protect them from the imposition of penalties in case the IRS disallowed tax losses resulting from the shelter. Handwritten notes of a March 4, 1998, meeting between KPMG and Ruble on OPIS also suggested that "B&W [could] play a big role in providing protection" for shelter materials under a claim of privilege.[19]

Even as Ruble worked closely with KPMG and Presidio on OPIS, the accounting firm sought further to "institutionalize the KPMG/B&W relationship."[20] A March 2, 1998, email from Bickham to Ritchie focused on "the key profit drivers for our joint practice."[21] For KPMG, these included its customer list and financial commitment to invest in developing shelters. For Brown & Wood, these included "[i]nstitutional relationships within the investment banking community," its name and goodwill, and "[m]ore panache in closing larger deals where the buyer brings in his Wall Street/D.C. tax advisor."[22] Bickham noted that in transactions in which Brown & Wood acted as a "co-venturer," the law firm would not be able to write a concurring opinion.

In the same vein, an August 30, 1998, KPMG email reported, "We have used the existing OPIS product as the mechanism for establishing close strategic relationships with Deutsche Bank and with Brown & Wood at both an institutional level and with key individuals within the organizations."[23] The strategy was to "co-develop products with Deutsche Bank and Brown & Wood and sell into the $1 million to $5 million market segment on a joint basis. . . . The respective participants from each institution ha[ve] agreed to commit the resources to participate in our internal product development group as well as to become active participants in the marketing process."[24] The same memo referred to Brown & Wood's role as an "R&D function."[25]

Ruble continued to play this role as KPMG moved from OPIS to developing the shelter that became BLIPS. In a December 3, 1998, memo to KPMG recipients, Ruble discussed a technical issue that he had identified as a result of "looking at the bond premium rules in another context (i.e., a legitimate deal)."[26] He questioned whether a particular Treasury regulation could override another provision that he had been assuming would govern one step in the BLIPS transaction. Ruble provided this comment some three months before KPMG began its formal internal review and approval process for BLIPS. An email that same day from

Randy Bickham to Ruble and several KPMG recipients noted that Bickham had spoken to Ruble about a "tax-focused meeting" the following week.[27] Bickham explained that he and Ruble had concluded that "we should first draft the base of an opinion letter in an outline format which will be circulated for comment before getting everyone together for an 'all-hands' meeting."[28] He indicated that they planned to circulate a draft the following week.

Bickham's email illustrates that Ruble's legal opinions for KPMG shelter transactions were not independent in any sense of the word. This meant that the IRS would not regard his opinion as protecting any taxpayer from liability for a penalty if the agency disallowed losses resulting from a shelter. Aside from the fact that someone who helps design a shelter cannot provide a disinterested analysis of its legal merits, the evidence makes clear that KPMG and Ruble closely collaborated in preparing opinions that were almost identical. A December 1998 email from KPMG to a FLIP investor says that "[t]he Brown and Wood opinion is generally being issued based on (and subsequent to) the KPMG opinion."[29] Another internal KPMG email a day later about the same transaction asked, "Can B&W be the sole issuer of a FLIP opinion? I have not heard of a situation where we did not write the opinion first."[30] Similarly, Ruble was on the routing list for review of the opinion that KPMG would be delivering on the BLIPS shelter in February 1999.[31]

In September of that year, Ruble sent to Bickham a preliminary draft of the Brown & Wood opinion for BLIPS. Ruble noted, "It is also our policy to work with KPMG to develop a common factual statement, which has yet to be done. You'll notice our approach in laying out the opinions is different from KPMG's but that everything is there."[32] A Ruble email three weeks later to Bickham and Jeff Eischeid underscored the virtual identity of the two organizations' opinions:

Here's our opinion. In going through it I noticed some minor changes that need to be made to both. I have put in an assumption about functional currency, I don't think yours has it and we probably both want it as a rep. There are a number of investor reps in the text that aren't in the Reps section. I think that they should go in there. I also think that we should figure out whether we want more in the way of representations from the Investor's single owner. We both need to get our aggregation opinions ready. Lastly, we probably both need a set of fresh eyes to go over the opinions one last time. At this point I'm not sure I have anyone. Do you and if so could I prevail on him/her to look at mine as well? A side-by-side is also a good idea to make sure we each cover everything the other has.[33]

In the same vein, a May 2000 email within KPMG commenting on a draft Brown & Wood BLIPS opinion letter said, "As we discussed, the B&W opinion touches all the necessary bases. The fact and representation sections are almost identical to the ones in our Opinion and many analysis sections are exact copies of our Opinion."[34]

The average fee that Brown & Wood received for KPMG transactions was approximately $75,000.[35] On one occasion, a group of taxpayers insisted on participating in FLIP transactions even though KPMG had discontinued the shelter and would not issue an opinion. Ruble wrote the sole opinion for the transactions and was paid $100,000 per opinion, or double his usual rate. From December 10 through December 31, 1999, alone, Ruble issued sixty-five BLIPS opinions for fees totaling more than $9.2 million.[36] This was an average of almost three a day, at a fee of $142,000 per opinion. The firm estimated that Ruble spent about 2,500 hours preparing opinions for KPMG shelters. With about $23 million in fees from such work, this came to an hourly rate of more than $9,000 per hour.[37] At the same time, Ruble was issuing opinions for Ernst & Young's COBRA shelter, which was sold to roughly fifty taxpayers in the last few months of 1999.

In addition to fees for opinions, Ruble periodically earned profits from participation in certain Presidio transactions that Pfaff and Larson made available to him.[38] Ruble had expressed an interest in joining Presidio so that he could enjoy the kind of income available from participation in a tax shelter boutique. Pfaff and Larson discouraged this idea. Ruble was more valuable to them at Brown & Wood than he would be at Presidio because of his ability to provide ostensibly independent legal opinions for Presidio shelters. The additional payments to Ruble were intended to encourage him to remain there. Pfaff emphasized to Presidio's accountant that such payments were not to appear on Presidio's tax returns, which could be accomplished by recording them as loans.[39] These "side payments" to Ruble came to about $500,000.[40]

Ruble received additional fees through an arrangement with shelter promoter Chenery Associates in San Francisco to market a shelter that Ruble had developed known as Custom Adjustable Rate Debt Structure (CARDS). CARDS purported to provide a taxpayer with a line of credit from a foreign bank denominated in foreign currency that could be used to make investments. It was designed, however, simply to create paper losses to offset capital gains for tax purposes. In May 1998, Ruble, on behalf of an entity known as the Family Investment Statutory Trust, entered into an agreement with Chenery to license CARDS as a "proprietary technology that potentially yields users who purchase assets [to obtain] certain tax, financial accounting, or other commercial benefits."[41] Under the agreement, Chenery agreed to pay the Trust 20 percent of the gross fees earned from use of the shelter. An investor in one lawsuit against the CARDS promoters, International Air Leasing, indicated that it paid Chenery a fee of $14.75 million and that Chenery used part of this fee to pay Brown & Wood $500,000 for its opinion in the transaction. Under the licensing agreement, Ruble's trust presumably would be entitled to as much as $2.95 million in addition to this.[42] An investor in another lawsuit claimed that Brown & Wood received $250,000 for its opinion letter, and that Chenery received $1.5 million in fees. If 20 percent of the latter went to Ruble's trust, that would amount to $300,000.[43]

On Friday, December 11, 1998, Thomas Humphreys, the head of Brown & Wood's tax practice group, came by Ruble's office to discuss a concern. The firm had recently recorded the receipt of two separate fees of $900,000 and $650,000 from KPMG for work by Ruble. Fees of that size for tax work raised the question whether Ruble might be issuing opinions for transactions that could expose the firm to liability. The conversation was brief since Ruble was in the midst of attempting to close some transactions and preparing for a trip to London. He told Humphreys that he had issued no such opinions and handed him a memo that he had prepared that analyzed one of the KPMG shelters.

Upon reflection, Ruble felt the need to explain himself more fully. The following Tuesday morning, he sent an email to Humphreys, copying Thomas Smith, the firm's managing partner. "When you came in to ask about the KPMG fees on Friday," Ruble said, "I was fairly stressed" because of the closings and his travel preparations.[44] "When you pointed out the magnitude of the fees and asked whether I had issued any opinions for which we could get sued, I took your question as a criticism that I would knowingly expose the firm to risk, and I answered no." Ruble said that he now wanted to "clarify what you could fairly interpret as a misstatement." He said that he had answered based on his view that he had not issued any opinions for which the firm could successfully be sued. "There have been opinions, however," Ruble said, and he wanted to provide some background for what he had done.

Ruble then described his history of working with KPMG on shelter transactions. In 1996, he said, a team from KPMG was marketing a "capital loss product" (which would have been FLIP) to its clients that was encountering some resistance from clients' advisors. KPMG asked him if he would speak with the advisors about the product as "someone unrelated to KPMG." Ruble said that he reviewed the product and KPMG's legal opinion, and "conducted my own research." He concluded that it was more likely than not that the shelter would withstand legal challenge, although it could be improved. Ruble said that he then "agreed to act as a sounding board for their clients' advisors and we got paid by KPMG for rendering that advice on a fixed fee basis that was a premium to time." He also agreed to help KPMG modify FLIP for its 1997 sales campaign and "worked with their products people and their national office tax partners to make some changes and improvements" (which would culminate in OPIS). He also agreed to play the "sounding board" role as he had in the previous year.

As KPMG sought to close transactions in the fall of 1997, Ruble said several clients asked for "a concurring opinion which confirmed the conversations I had with their advisors." He explained:

Given that I had worked the development through very closely with KPMG, given my knowledge and understanding of the opinion process, and that based on my independent research believed their conclusion was correct on a more likely than not basis, I agreed to do so, but only if KPMG first issued their opinion on the deal. On that basis, KPMG agreed to pay us $50,000 per deal in which we were involved.[45]

Ruble said that in 1998 he worked with KPMG, Presidio, and Deutsche Bank to develop a new shelter for 1998 (this would have been BLIPS). He also agreed to provide an opinion but requested that the fee be based on deal size.

Ruble then explained the unusually large payments of $900,000 and $650,000 the firm had received from KPMG. He said that in November he had asked KPMG if they could accelerate payment of all or a portion of fees so that the law firm could get the cash before the end of the year. KPMG agreed and identified each transaction for which Brown & Wood was due payment. The law firm's accounting department "treated as one item all the KPMG bills issued on the same day, so that it appeared that there was a single $900,000 and a single $650,000 bill, when in fact these are the . . . aggregate sums of a few smaller deals."

Smith later stated that when the revenues from Ruble's practice "increased materially" in 1998, he asked Humphreys about it.[46] Humphreys followed up by asking Ruble about his work, which prompted the explanatory email by Ruble. Smith said that he asked four or five tax partners to review Ruble's opinions, and that they said that "they were valid opinions under the then law." According to Smith, when he and other members of management inquired into the firm's role in providing opinions, Ruble told them that it was to "provide concurring opinions to taxpayers, and a lot of times to their financial advisors." The understanding was that Ruble was not involved "in the design of these products, but that KPMG would approach him with a product and ask if he could render an opinion." Smith conceded that if Ruble had seen a way to improve the product, he might have passed that information on to KPMG, but that his role essentially was to opine on what KPMG had created.

Ruble's email is interesting for several reasons. First, it suggests that, contrary to Ruble's December 1997 representation to KPMG, Smith had not authorized the firm to enter into an agreement with KPMG to jointly develop and market tax products. If he had, Ruble likely would not have felt the need to explain in detail how he had become involved with KPMG and the work that he had done in connection with its shelters. Second, Ruble's email misrepresents the role he was playing. Shelter investors generally had to sign confidentiality agreements that prevented them from discussing the shelter with third parties such as independent advisors. It is unlikely that Ruble had many, if any, conversations with such advisors, so his opinions were not simply a reiteration of the points he had made in discussion with them. In addition, characterizing his role as that of a sounding board suggests that he was providing his assessment of products that KPMG first had developed and then brought to him. In fact, of course, Ruble was intimately involved from the outset in designing the shelters that KPMG marketed. To the extent that Brown & Wood based its understanding of Ruble's work on this characterization, it therefore would have been misled.

At the same time, Ruble provided enough details about his involvement in the shelter development process to raise the question whether Brown

& Wood was a shelter promoter and therefore had obligations to register the shelters and to maintain lists of investors in them. He describes working with KPMG to "make some changes and improvements" in its 1997 product, and with KPMG, Presidio, and Deutsche Bank to "come up with a new variant" for 1998. Indeed, after the IRS issued Notice 2000-44 in August of 2000, Brown & Wood, presumably through Ruble, entered into an October 31, 2000, agreement with several parties, including Diversified Group, that the agreement described as "involved in activities as organizers and/or sellers of investments that may be considered to be tax shelters by the Internal Revenue Service."[47] The purpose of the agreement was to take advantage of an IRS regulation that provided that multiple organizers or sellers or both may designate one party to maintain a list of investors and to designate Diversified Group as that party. Ruble's email, however, apparently did not prompt anyone at Brown & Wood to inquire into whether the firm might be considered a shelter promoter. At a minimum, Ruble's involvement in the shelter design process should have raised a serious question about whether any investor could reasonably rely on his opinion to avoid a penalty.

With respect to the review of Ruble's opinions by Brown & Wood tax partners, nothing on the face of the opinions necessarily would have alerted anyone to a problem. The transactions were all described as investment programs that relied on leverage in the pursuit of capital appreciation, selected by clients who had "reviewed the economics underlying the investment strategy and believed [they] had a reasonable opportunity to earn a reasonable profit from each of the transactions" beyond any fees and costs and without regard to any tax benefits.[48] The opinions also contained representations that each investor would make an individual decision about how long to continue participating in the various transactions. These portions of the opinion letters were all false, but someone reading them generally would have had to delve deeper into the facts of the transactions to discover this. An experienced tax lawyer presumably would know that the factual representations were critical to whether the opinion was defensible. It's not clear, however, how deeply the Brown & Wood tax partners who reviewed the opinions probed these representations in the course of arriving at their conclusions. It's also not clear how much motivation they had to do so, given the fees that Ruble was generating.

In any event, later updates from Ruble to Smith and Humphreys suggested that there were risks involved in Ruble's practice. An email of June

1, 2000, to both men said that KPMG was trying to distance itself as a tax promoter because of the adverse publicity that PwC had received in connection with the BOSS shelter.[49] The accounting firm was planning to work with tax shelter boutiques to create products and to refer its clients to these firms so that they could decide which shelter they wanted to use. KPMG would be providing clients with a list of law firms from which to choose in seeking opinions. It would receive a fee for reviewing the deals and opinions, on the theory that this role "gives it better optics." Ruble suggested that because there was market resistance to the fees that traditionally had been charged, pressure on fees likely would result in only about 25 percent of what Brown & Wood historically had collected. There might also be fewer deals altogether, Ruble said, because "there is a risk that the IRS will begin to focus on individual transaction[s] in the same way that it has on corporate shelters."

On August 10, Ruble wrote to Humphreys and Smith to inform them that the IRS would be issuing Notice 2000-44. The subject line of the email said: "IRS to Issue Notice on Friday 8/11 to Shut Down KPMG, E&Y, and AA etc. deals."[50] The notice, Ruble said, would be declaring that transactions "that were the core of these firms' tax products for the past 2 years don't work and are abusive." Brown & Wood had given opinions in these transactions that accounted for a "substantial part of the revenues from these firms." Ruble expressed his belief that the opinions were well reasoned and their bases well documented, "but there is going to be a certain amount of questioning, I'm sure." He concluded by saying that he was "at meetings at KPMG" for most of the day "to come up with some new ideas"—a statement that clearly indicates his close involvement with KPMG in the development of tax shelters.

As a merger between Brown & Wood and Sidley & Austin approached in the spring of 2001, both firms agreed that the combined firm would no longer provide tax shelter opinions like the ones Ruble had been issuing. The managing partner of the merged firm later said that the decision "did not and does not reflect on the quality of the work performed earlier,"[51] but it is not hard to imagine that firm leaders saw Ruble's shelter practice as simply too risky. In any event, the firm later learned that Ruble had continued to issue opinions for some time after the merger, which he defended by claiming that he had premerger commitments to deliver them to investors. That work ultimately would be the basis for a criminal investigation of Sidley Austin Brown & Wood.

Law Firms Collaborating with E&Y

When several Ernst and Young (E&Y) partners were charged in 2007 in connection with promoting tax shelters, the indictment described the activities of four law firms, identified as Firms A through D, that had assisted in the shelter activities.[52] Firm A was later revealed to be Locke Liddell & Sapp (later Locke Lord Bissell & Liddell). Firm B was Sidley Austin Brown & Wood. Firm C was Arnold & Porter and Firm D was Proskauer Rose.[53]

As the indictment charged, Locke Liddell had written opinion letters for the Contingent Deferred Swap (CDS) and CDS Add-On Shelters and had "assisted the defendants in structuring, marketing, and implementing the CDS transaction."[54] The firm's fee for the CDS opinions, which stated that the client "should" prevail in case the transaction was challenged by the IRS, was $50,000 per opinion. The fee for the CDS Add-On opinions, which said that the client more likely than not would prevail, was $75,000 for each opinion. The opinion for each shelter falsely stated that the client was entering the transaction to achieve certain business objectives and that there was no predetermined outcome for the transaction. In the case of the CDS shelter, the opinion failed to disclose that it was being issued by an attorney who had participated in devising the transaction.

Brent Clifton was the attorney at Locke Liddell who spearheaded the firm's involvement with the CDS and CDS Add-On shelters. The CDS was developed by David Smith in concert with Graham Taylor, who kept his involvement a secret from Pillsbury, Madison & Sutro, the firm at which he worked. After Pillsbury learned about the transaction, it declined to issue an opinion for it. Grady Dickens, a friend of E&Y's Brian Vaughn at the law firm of Scheef & Stone in Dallas, suggested that Vaughn get in touch with Clifton.[55] Clifton wrote to another partner that he had been contacted about providing opinion letters for an "aggressive tax shelter proposal" being sold by Ernst & Young to "extremely high net worth corporate officers."[56] Clifton indicated that the firm "will be asked to provide a 'should opinion'" that would conclude that the taxpayer had a 70 percent to 80 percent likelihood of success if litigated."[57] Clifton explained that he had been contacted "because Locke Liddell & Sapp was recognized as a large firm with reputable tax expertise."

According to one attorney who had been asked to review a Locke Liddell opinion by a client, "the transaction appears to be a classic 'sham' tax shelter that would be successfully challenged on audit by IRS. The transaction apparently has little, or any, economic significance outside the tremendous tax breaks promised to the investors and is apparently highly tax motivated."[58] As his analysis continued, "The opinion provided to me did not discuss the relevant facts, as I understand them. There was little discussion of the hedging within the transaction that will protect the investors against risk of loss or the high level of tax motivation behind the concept. The analysis of the downside to the transaction was weak and often irrelevant."[59]

The biggest problem with both the transaction and the opinion, the attorney noted, was that the partnership would not be engaged in business as a trader, "which is critical to claim the deductions discussed in the opinion." The opinion "wrongly states that the Fund Manager's activities will be attributed to the partnership," and relies on a "50 year old case that has nothing to do with trader vs. investor status." It also "fails to address the relevant case law," particularly a U.S. Tax Court decision explicitly holding that the trading activities of others are not attributed to the taxpayer. That decision "unequivocally states that the taxpayer must personally ma[ke] the trading decisions and cannot delegate this task to others." This analysis underscored the multiple deficiencies in the CDS shelter that negated any plausible claim that it had any economic substance.

As it turned out, the involvement of Locke Liddell in tax shelter work proved to be an embarrassment for the Bush administration when the President nominated White House Counsel Harriet Miers, a former Locke Liddell managing partner, for the Supreme Court in October 2005. A report earlier that year by the Senate Permanent Subcommittee on Investigations had mentioned the firm as among those that provided opinion letters for potentially abusive shelters. Upon Miers's nomination, Senator Norm Coleman of Minnesota, chair of the Committee, said, "I have a high standard for the ethics of a Supreme Court justice. These were very questionable transactions, and the volume of work done on this was substantial—in the millions of dollars."[60] Senator Max Baucus, the ranking Democrat on the Finance Committee, sent the firm a five page letter requesting detailed explanations about Locke Liddell's work on the CDS shelter.

Locke Liddell partner John McElhaney confirmed that the firm had issued 132 opinions on the CDS shelter for revenues of about $5.4 million. Just over half of the transactions were done while Miers was still at the firm. McElhaney conceded that it was a "fair assumption" that Miers was aware of the activity in light of the amount of income that it generated. He stated, however, that no court had ever ruled that the transaction was unlawful and maintained, "Just because there's been an opinion by the IRS doesn't mean it's illegal."[61] Among the lawsuits by investors that the firm eventually settled was one by several Cisco Systems executives who claimed that they paid the IRS more than $20 million in back taxes, penalties, and interest. The White House eventually withdrew Miers's nomination in light of criticism that she had insufficient experience to serve on the Court.

The fourth law firm identified in the indictment of the former Ernst & Young employees was Proskauer Rose. Investors in E&Y's Personal Investment Corporation (PICO) shelter in 2000 and 2001 were given a choice of obtaining an opinion either from Proskauer or Arnold & Porter, with fees for the opinions ranging from $50,000 to $100,000 depending on the size of the transaction. The opinions falsely stated that the taxpayer had formed an S corporation to engage in investment activity and to protect its assets in connection with estate planning, and that the trading was not designed to result in a predetermined outcome.

Lawyers from Proskauer also helped eleven E&Y partners generate tax losses to offset income from the accounting firm's sale of its global consulting business in 2000 to Cap Gemini. The firm helped partners form an entity known as Tradehill Investments to carry out a short option strategy similar to COBRA. Ira Akselrad, a member of the firm's executive committee, worked from December 2000 through mid-April 2001 with Martin Nissenbaum, one of the E&Y partners using the shelter, to prepare a legal opinion that the partners could use to protect themselves from a penalty if the government refused to recognize the tax losses from the transaction. In connection with this, Nissenbaum helped prepare a "Certificate of Facts" that stated that the partners engaged in the purchase and sale of options to pursue investment returns and that their decision to withdraw from the trading entity was based on several factors, including their assessment of likely future market conditions.

In April 2001, Proskauer issued a backdated opinion letter that incorporated the Certificate of Facts and said that all relevant facts regarding the transaction had been disclosed in the opinion. The eleven partners then filed their returns in 2001 using the losses generated by Tradehill to eliminate most of their tax liability for the income they received from the sale to Cap Gemini.

In May 2003, the IRS notified the partners that their returns were being audited and sent information document requests (IDRs) to each of them. Akselrad worked with Nissenbaum to draft responses to the IDRs on behalf of each partner. Those responses stated that the Tradehill transactions were motivated by the desire to pursue investment returns and to hedge investments, and that there was no expectation or referral of any future business to Proskauer.

Ernst & Young was not the only tax shelter promoter with whom Proskauer worked. The firm also provided opinion letters to KPMG in connection with the sale of Son of BOSS shelters and, in some cases, helped design the shelter. A lawsuit brought by Richard Egan, former ambassador to Ireland and "one of the most successful businessmen in the history of the United States,"[62] provides insight into the firm's role in these transactions. Egan used a shelter devised by shelter boutiques Helios and Diversified Group International (DGI) to claim almost $160 million in ordinary losses in 2001, and $1.7 million in ordinary losses and $167.1 million in capital losses in 2002. Proskauer and Sidley Austin provided legal opinions in connection with the transactions. When the IRS disallowed his losses, Egan challenged the government's position. In a 357-page opinion upholding the IRS, Judge Saylor of the Court of Claims declared that "[n]one of the participants in these complex transactions believed that they were real business transactions, with any purpose other than tax avoidance." Indeed, Judge Saylor suggested, "It is highly doubtful that any participants believed, even for a minute, that the transactions would withstand legal scrutiny if discovered." Rather, the participants "were simply following a script—a script that had little or no connection to any underlying business or economic reality."

The legal opinions "were just additional acts of stagecraft. The lawyers were not in the slightest rendering independent advice; the promoters of the tax shelters had arranged favorable opinions from those firms well in advance, and as part of their marketing strategy." The opinions also were not independent because Akselrad and R. J. Ruble had actively assisted DGI and Helios in designing, marketing, and implementing the shelter, while the two shelter boutiques "played a substantial role in the drafting and the delivery" of the opinions. The opinions "were themselves fraudulent; they were premised on purported 'facts' that Egan and the law firms knew were false, and reached conclusions that everyone involved knew could not possibly be correct." Proskauer provided at least twenty-eight opinions, as well as legal advice to DGI and Helios, and Akselrad himself participated in a DGI shelter transaction in 2000.

Judge Saylor noted that the Proskauer opinion letter assumed that the transaction to which it referred would be upheld if the taxpayer subjectively was motivated by a nontax business purpose, even if the transaction had no economic substance. The opinion letter then accepted as dispositive the taxpayers' representations that this was their motive. "No reasonable tax attorney," said the court, "would assume that a transaction of that nature would be recognized and upheld by the courts simply because the taxpayer made a self-serving statement about his or her supposed business purpose." The opinion contained "virtually no analysis of the actual facts of the transaction."

Serving Shelters

The participation of several other lawyers at various law firms in designing, marketing, or issuing opinion letters for tax shelters has also come to light. Graham Taylor was a tax lawyer who practiced in San Francisco with Pillsbury, Madison & Sutro from 1981 to 1999; with LeBouef, Lamb, Greene & MacRae from 1999 until 2003; and then with Altheimer & Gray and Seyfarth Shaw. Over the course of his career Taylor wrote almost two hundred opinions for eight different types of shelters, for fees totaling between $9 million and $10 million.[63] He began in 1994 by working with David Lippman (Smith), then with Quadra, on a "redemption trade" shelter.[64] Taylor issued between thirty and forty "more likely than not" opinions, at a price of $50,000 per opinion,[65] without the knowledge of anyone in the firm that the transactions were designed principally to reduce or eliminate taxes.

In 1998, when he was at Pillsbury, Taylor began discussing a contingent deferred swap (CDS) shelter with Smith that would be marketed by Ernst & Young. He traded several drafts of an opinion with Smith but told no one in the firm that he was working on the project. In early summer 1999, someone from E&Y called Pillsbury to discuss the CDS shelter when Taylor was out of the office. Tax partner Julie Divola took the call instead. This prompted a vigorous debate inside the firm about whether it should be involved in issuing opinions in connection with tax shelters.[66] Eventually, the answer was no. As a result, Smith and E&Y turned to Dallas-based

Locke Liddell to provide opinions on the CDS shelter. In the fall, Taylor left Pillsbury to join the San Francisco office of LeBoeuf Lamb, a firm based in New York, where he remained until 2003.

Over the next several years, Taylor also issued about thirty opinions for the CARDS shelter at between $85,000 and $150,000 per opinion; thirty opinions for a distressed debt shelter at between $100,000 and $150,000 per opinion; and twenty opinions for another shelter known as ICA. In contrast to his time at Pillsbury, Taylor worked with other partners and associates on his opinions while at LeBoeuf Lamb but testified that he did not believe that any of his colleagues knew that the opinions contained any false statements or representations.[67] Nor is there any evidence that Taylor's colleagues at Altheimer & Gray or Seyfarth Shaw were aware of his work on abusive shelters.

Peter Cinquegrani, a partner at Arnold & Porter, collaborated in 2000 and 2001 with promoters at Ernst & Young and others to develop and write opinions for the shelter known as Personal Investment Corporation (PICO). Approximately 150 individuals participated in 96 PICO transactions during this period. Cinquegrani received fees of between $50,000 and $100,000 for each letter. He also prepared a phony consulting contract between E&Y and shelter promoter Bricolage that was intended to disguise the fact that the accounting firm's fees for the shelter were based on a percentage of the tax loss that the client wanted to generate.[68]

Jay Gordon, former head of the tax practice at Greenberg Traurig, issued legal opinions for abusive shelters between 2000 and 2003, charging between $10,000 and $30,000 for each opinion. These letters contained false representations that the taxpayers had entered into the shelter transactions with a reasonable expectation of realizing a significant pretax profit, as part of an overall investment strategy.

In addition, Gordon engaged in tax evasion in connection with referral fees he received for steering clients to tax shelter promoters. He received more than $400,000 in such fees in 1999 but did not disclose those to Greenberg Traurig or the IRS. In 2001, he received an additional $268,000 in referral fees. He did not disclose those to his firm but did so on his tax returns. He participated in an abusive tax shelter, however, that enabled him to evade taxes on this and other income. In addition, Gordon claimed over $10,000 in false deductions on his income tax returns for the period 1999 through 2002.

In November 2004, Gordon resigned from Greenberg Traurig when a prominent real estate developer client complained to the firm that the IRS had disallowed losses from a shelter Gordon recommended. The outside lawyer hired by the firm to investigate the matter learned that the shelter promoter had paid Gordon almost $300,000 to refer the client to it. The firm refunded fees that this and other clients had paid for shelters and referred the matter to the state bar disciplinary committee.[69] Two years later, Gordon resigned from the New York bar after admitting that he earned $1.3 million in referral fees between 1999 and 2002 in connection with tax shelters without informing his clients or firm.[70]

John Campbell was the managing partner of the Kalamazoo, Michigan, office of Miller, Canfield, Paddock & Stone. From 1999 through 2006, he worked closely with four tax shelter promoters and employees of an insurance company in the U.S. Virgin Islands to sell clients a tax shelter that involved the use of ostensible insurance premium payments. His client, Oskar Rene Poch, used the shelter to improperly deduct more than $3.9 million in premiums from 1999 through 2001, which resulted in fraudulent tax savings of over $1.63 million.

Matthew Krane, a Los Angeles lawyer, served as tax counsel for entertainment industry billionaire Haim Saban. In 2001, Saban had $1.5 billion in capital gains from the sale of his stake in the Fox Family Channel to Walt Disney. Krane steered him to the investment fund Quellos to participate in a shelter transaction known as Portfolio Optimized Investment Transaction (POINT). Krane, along with Jeffrey Greenstein and Charles Wilk of Quellos, drafted documents that made it appear that Saban was paying the fund $46 million to participate in the shelter. Unbeknownst to Saban, $36 million of that payment went to Krane for his referral of Saban to Quellos. That money was deposited by Greenstein and Wilk in an offshore account controlled by Krane.

The Long-Term Capital Tax Shelter

Two other law firms were the target of sharp criticism for their involvement in tax shelter work. On July 24, 2004, the federal district court in Connecticut upheld the IRS's disallowance of $106 million in tax losses claimed by partners in the Long-Term Capital hedge fund for the 1997 tax year.[71] The hedge fund, run by prominent economists, including Nobel

Prize winners Robert Merton and Myron Scholes,[72] had been the beneficiary of a bailout by banks arranged by the federal government when its prospective demise in 1997 prompted fears of a system-wide financial crisis.[73]

Scholes, who is the author of a widely adopted textbook on business taxes, had designed the tax strategy. At trial, Scholes initially denied that he was an expert in business tax. After the government showed him his own textbook in the field, he reluctantly acknowledged that he had expertise in the area. He also acknowledged that for the tax benefits of the transaction to be upheld it needed to have economic substance. During cross-examination, Scholes admitted that he had used the Black-Scholes formula he had developed for pricing options to ensure that other investors in the transaction were not at risk of losing money. Scholes eventually conceded that once the substantial payment he received for creating the transaction was taken into account in determining the costs of entering into the transaction, the possibility of making a profit disappeared. After trial, Judge Janet Bond Arterton held that any analysis of whether there were realistic expectations of profit from the transaction had to include the costs and fees incurred to participate in it. Because the costs of the transaction exceeded the prospective profit, Judge Arterton concluded that it lacked economic substance.

Judge Arterton further ruled that the hedge fund partners were liable for penalties because they could not establish that they reasonably relied in good faith on opinions provided by Shearman & Sterling and King & Spalding that different aspects of the transaction "should" serve to support the tax treatment that the taxpayers sought. Judge Arterton found that Long-Term Capital paid Shearman & Sterling $500,000 for five virtually identical opinions that "contain[ed] no legal reasoning or analysis."[74] When a separate memorandum was offered to show "part of the analysis" that the firm conducted for the opinions, the court observed: "Notably absent [was] any analysis of the step transaction doctrine, [of whether certain ostensibly independent companies] were alter egos, and sham transaction theories."[75]

The court was even more critical of King & Spalding's work. The court did not find credible the testimony of Mark Kuller—who had coauthored the King & Spalding opinion—that he had performed and discussed at length with Long-Term Capital's in-house tax counsel a calculation of the hedge fund's expected profits before taxes. (Kuller had written an opinion for the transaction that was struck down in ACM.) Emphasizing the absence of any contemporaneous records, Judge Arterton found that the tenor of Kuller's testimony "had the distinct quality of advocacy, not an effort to just accurately report recollection."[76] As to the written opinion, which the Long-Term Capital partners received after they had claimed the loss from the transaction, the court observed that it "contain[ed] no citation to any decisions of the Second Circuit Court of Appeals whose case law would apply to any appeal related to Long Term Capital's tax return."[77] As the court remarked acerbically, "With hourly billing totals exceeding $100,000 there could not have been research time constraints."

The court's overall assessment was harsh:

> In essence, the testimony and evidence offered by Long Term regarding the advice received from King & Spalding amounted to general superficial pronouncements asking the Court to "trust us; we looked into all pertinent facts; we were involved; we researched all applicable authorities; we made no unreasonable assumptions; Long Term gave us all information." The Court's role as fact finder is more searching and with specifics, analysis, and explanations in such short supply, the King & Spalding effort is insufficient to carry Long Term's burden.[78]

Judge Arterton's opinion made clear that highly respected law firms had been earning outsized fees providing legal opinions that gave questionable transactions a patina of legitimacy—and assumed they would be able to get away with it.

Lawyers who helped design and sell abusive tax shelters were a caricature of the fiduciaries they purported to be. They wrote opinion letters on behalf of "clients" they never met and with whom they never spoke, and used boilerplate language to describe the supposedly personal intentions of each "investor." They claimed to protect taxpayers from penalties in cases in which they knew that their opinions would be worthless for that purpose because they had helped design the shelter on which they were opining. Other lawyers who were not involved in designing shelters issued opinions containing elaborate and lengthy analysis that one court described as "incomplete, incorrect, and misleading in multiple respects," which failed to meet basic standards of professional competence.

Lawyers involved in abusive shelters eschewed any responsibility to promote respect for the tax system. They helped further activity that they knew would be successful only because it probably would never be detected, not because it conformed to the requirements of the law. They adopted a purely adversary stance toward the government in a setting in which the integrity of the law depends crucially on the integrity of taxpayers. In these ways, they helped undermine allegiance to the basic duties of citizenship.

For several years, it seemed as though nothing could stop the boom in abusive tax shelters. Little by little, however, government officials were beginning to take steps to combat the activities of promoters, professionals, and taxpayers who fueled the boom. As the next three chapters describe, these efforts gradually coalesced into an all-out assault on the abusive tax shelter industry.

Part IV

The Reckoning

10
Turning the Tide

The Challenge

At the close of Congressional hearings in 1998, the Internal Revenue Service was on the ropes. Its credibility was low, its employees' morale even lower, and there was skepticism that the agency could competently perform even its basic function of collecting taxes. Its difficulties ran even deeper: the IRS was a tax collection agency in an era in which there was acute hostility toward the very idea that the tax system had legitimacy. The blistering Congressional criticism of the IRS had left it chastened and cautious—just as trends were converging that would dramatically increase efforts to design and market tax shelters. One veteran observer of the agency described the Congressional hearings as akin to a "lynching."[1] The best course for IRS personnel seemed simply to avoid any activity that might incur the wrath of taxpayers or their elected representatives.

The IRS Reform and Restructuring Act, adopted in May 1998, directed the agency to reorganize its operations to become friendlier to taxpayers. The Act attempted to reinforce this mandate by granting taxpayers greater rights vis-à-vis the IRS, establishing a new oversight board to monitor its operations and imposing new reporting obligations on the agency. In addition, newly appointed IRS Commissioner Charles Rossotti announced that his priority would be to modernize the agency's basic tax collection functions and to improve its relationship with its taxpayer "customers." This created an environment in which any attempt to identify and challenge tax shelters would run into both resource constraints and concern about engaging in activity that could anger taxpayers and get the agency hauled before Congress once again.

Even in the best of times, attempting to combat tax shelters was a formidable challenge. The first difficulty was a basic one: how could the IRS know what shelters were out there and who was using them? There are millions of corporate and individual taxpayers in the United States engaged in innumerable business transactions. How could IRS revenue agents comb through all of the returns filed and find the deals that had no economic substance or business purpose? The difficulty was compounded by the format in which transactions are reported on returns. When reviewing tax forms, agents have to work with a series of abstracted categories and numbers; few red flags alert them that further investigation is needed. Losses reported on returns can signal legitimate economic losses as easily as abusive tax shelter activity. And tax shelter promoters made sure to add lots of window dressing so that shelters looked as much as possible like legitimate transactions. To make matters worse, at the time the IRS did not have a system in place to match individual income forms with partnership returns. As a result, agents were unable to cross-check information provided on different returns filed by the same taxpayer.

One way to catch shelters, of course, was to audit tax returns. Historically, however, the IRS has been able to audit only a miniscule portion of returns in any given year. Not surprisingly, in fiscal 1998 the audit rate for all classes of individual taxpayers was the lowest in modern history. The IRS audited less than 0.5 percent of such returns. By contrast, the rate in 1981 had been three times as high. The IRS 1998 audit rate for individuals earning over $100,000 was 1.13 percent, or less than half of what it was in 1992. In 1998 the IRS audited 37 percent of corporations with $250 million or more in assets, compared to 55 percent in 1992. Criminal prosecutions had declined in all but two of the preceding ten years, dropping from 1190 in 1989 to 766 in 1998. In addition, the IRS suffered a 900-person decrease in staffing from 1997 to 1998. Focusing on these figures, the well-respected publication *Tax Notes Today* asked: "Is this not a major shift away from law enforcement?"[2]

Catching an abusive transaction was only the first step. In the rare cases in which taxpayers were audited and the IRS agent disallowed the claimed tax benefits taxpayers might be liable at most for the amount of taxes that they owed. They could avoid any additional penalty payment by establishing that they had reasonably relied on a lawyer's opinion that the shelter more likely than not would be upheld if challenged. In addition, corporations and wealthy individuals had enough resources to impose significant costs and delay on the process so that the agent might be willing to settle for less than what the taxpayer supposedly owed. For those revenue agents who held firm, there was always the risk that their efforts would be undermined by an appeals unit within the IRS, which tended to be more lenient with taxpayers. Even more worrisome was the prospect that an agent might be charged by a taxpayer with harassment, a potentially career-ending blow under the new law.

If a tax dispute ended up in litigation, the agency had found that courts tended to be inconsistent allies. Common law anti-abuse doctrines were vague, and some courts were sympathetic to claims that the doctrines gave taxpayers insufficient guidance about what was and was not permitted. Even a court that regarded the common law as a legitimate dimension of tax law was faced with the difficult task of determining whether complex financial transactions had enough risk or possibility of profit that taxpayers should receive the tax benefits that they claimed. In addition, the stakes of litigation were large for the IRS because of the visibility of the dispute. A loss could embolden shelter promoters and taxpayers to engage in even more aggressive behavior. It also meant that the agency had to decide whether to fight the same or a substantially similar transaction in a different jurisdiction. The result was that the agency might be loath to litigate any case that it was not confident of winning.

In addition to a weakened and underfunded audit process, the IRS had a few other weapons in its arsenal. It had long had the authority to require taxpayers to disclose potentially abusive shelters on their tax returns. During the shelter episode of the 1980s, Congress had granted the IRS the authority to require promoters to register potentially abusive shelters with the agency and maintain lists of clients who bought those shelters.[3] Because these laws had been drafted with particular types of shelters in mind, their definition of potentially abusive shelters did not neatly fit the shelters that were coming into vogue in the late 1990s. The 1997 Taxpayer Relief Act expanded the definition of shelters subject to the registration and list maintenance requirements to include transactions entered into by corporate taxpayers that had as a significant purpose the avoidance of taxes, met a minimum fee threshold, and were sold under conditions of confidentiality. Those new requirements did not explicitly apply to shelters purchased by individual taxpayers. Moreover, they did not go into effect until the U.S. Treasury enacted specific regulations applying them. Reeling from the beating it had received at the hands of Congress, the Treasury did not get around to proposing new rules until 2000.

The IRS also had the power to list certain shelters it considered abusive. Listing a shelter put taxpayers on notice that the agency planned to challenge it in court. It also meant that if the IRS disallowed the shelter, taxpayers would not be able to claim that they reasonably relied on a legal opinion in claiming tax benefits from the transaction; they would also be subject to increased penalties for failing to disclose the shelter on tax returns. This required that the agency first learn of a shelter, of course, which might well be after its use had become widespread. Relying on the listing process to combat shelters was like trying to empty the ocean one teaspoon at a time. It might eliminate one shelter as an alternative, but promoters were likely to rush in with new ones that were just different enough to provide an argument that they were not on the list. The IRS was playing a perpetual game of catch up.

Listing a shelter was just a warning shot across the bow. It only meant that if the IRS found the shelter on audit, it would challenge it in court. The IRS still needed to persuade a court that the shelter was abusive. The more widespread a shelter became, the bigger the challenge to convince courts to disallow its benefits. Taxpayers who had bought the shelter transaction and firms promoting it were bound to put up a vigorous fight, requiring the IRS to expend significant resources to combat it.

Traditionally the IRS had been able to rely to some extent on the tax bar to compensate for information barriers and resource limitations. Tax practitioners in law and accounting firms were in a position to constrain their clients by informing them of the acceptable boundaries of aggressiveness and advising them not to venture too close to the line. Conversations in the lawyer's office thus could have as much or more impact as announcements by the IRS. Beginning in the early 1990s, however, the agency was hearing from knowledgeable tax practitioners that a new wave of tax shelters aimed at corporations was beginning to sweep through boardrooms and management suites. Some lawyers in a company's tax department or general counsel's office were being approached directly by a growing number of promoters offering transactions that could sharply reduce a company's tax liability. Other in-house lawyers were hearing of shelters from management, who wanted them to assess whether the promoters could make good on their promises. Lawyers in law firms were being asked the same questions by their corporate clients. Some of these lawyers were being offered the opportunity by promoters to earn substantial fees for writing a legal opinion saying that the tax treatment of a shelter more likely than not would be upheld in court if challenged by the IRS.

In short, the IRS could no longer be assured that tax practitioners were attempting to constrain aggressive behavior. Events were moving quickly enough that some distinguished tax lawyers in private practice began to urge government officials and members of Congress to address what they regarded as a spreading contagion. And even as the Treasury, Congress, and the public were becoming aware of how widespread corporate tax shelters had become, the contagion was spreading downstream, as accounting and law firms began to market similar shelters to high-wealth individuals.

In the fall of 1998, the IRS received some assistance from another, perhaps unexpected, quarter. Courts had only sporadically elaborated on the concepts of economic substance and business purpose that many saw as originating with the Supreme Court's 1935 decision in *Gregory v. Helvering*.[4] It was not clear whether *Helvering* had meant these concepts to be equivalent or distinct and, if distinct, whether the government could deny tax benefits if a transaction lacked just one of these characteristics or if it had to lack both. In addition, there was uncertainty about how significant the economic substance or business purpose connected with a transaction had to be to justify the tax treatment that a taxpayer desired. In the fall of 1998, the U.S. Court of Appeals for the Third Circuit provided some clarification on these issues when it largely upheld a 1997 decision by the U.S. Tax Court (mentioned in chapter 4) denying tax benefits resulting from a shelter in *ACM Partnership v. Commissioner*.[5]

At issue in *ACM* was a transaction engineered by Merrill Lynch that Colgate-Palmolive had used to offset a gain of $105 million resulting from the 1988 sale of a subsidiary. Colgate-Palmolive used a complicated structure involving a partnership with a foreign corporation that did not pay U.S. taxes and a purchase and installment sale of securities to create a $98 million loss. This loss did not correspond to any economic losses that the company incurred. Colgate-Palmolive claimed that it could use this loss against the gain it earned in the sale of its subsidiary. In March 1997, the tax court sided with the IRS and disallowed the loss. The Third Circuit affirmed this decision, providing substantial guidance on the scope and application of the economic substance doctrine.

The Third Circuit's decision in *ACM* made clear that the doctrine retained vitality as a basis to challenge abusive tax shelters that relied on complicated financial instruments and far more complex transactions than promoters had used in the 1970s and 1980s. The court clarified that whether a transaction had a business purpose and economic substance were not "discrete prongs of a 'rigid two-step analysis," but were factors that should inform an overall analysis of whether a transaction was created simply to generate tax benefits.[6] The court held that a nominal non-tax financial impact was not sufficient to justify the tax benefits resulting from a transaction and that the costs of participating in the arrangement should be taken into account in determining whether there was any reasonable expectation of profit. The opinion also brought to light the magnitude of the fees that promoters could earn in shelter transactions, which were far greater than many had realized. Merrill Lynch, for instance, had earned $1 million for finding someone to purchase the securities from the partnership shortly after it had acquired them. As the case wended its way through the courts, it also emerged that Colgate-Palmolive was not the only company that had purchased this type of shelter, nor was Merrill Lynch the only financial institution selling them.

The *ACM* decision signaled that courts were willing to be skeptical, even when it was a major U.S. corporation claiming tax benefits based on a transaction designed by a prestigious financial institution and blessed by a major accounting firm. Colgate-Palmolive tried to suggest outside of court that such deals were presumptively legitimate because they had been approved by some of the biggest names on Wall Street. In an interview with the *Wall Street Journal* before the court issued its decision, Fred Goldberg, a former IRS Commissioner and the lawyer representing Colgate-Palmolive, wondered if "the court would react to this case differently if the court knew that Goldman Sachs or Bankers Trust or Salomon Brothers had been involved in transactions of this sort . . . or if it knew that four different Big Six accounting firms had concluded that it was appropriate?"[7] The court was not swayed by the fact that a well-respected bank and accounting firm were involved in the transaction. Its decision demonstrated that it was willing to disallow losses resulting from abusive shelters, regardless of the pedigree of the organizations involved.

In the years following *ACM*, the IRS would achieve a mixed record of success in the courts. Nonetheless, the decision offered some hope to the agency that if it could muster the resources and the will to challenge corporate shelters, it might receive a sympathetic reception in at least some courtrooms.

Shining Light in Dark Corners

Two months after the *ACM* decision, a cover article in *Forbes* entitled "The Hustling of X-Rated Shelters" hit the newsstands. The issue came out during the Christmas holiday lull, but by early the next year it was creating a stir in business circles. In the article, Janet Novack and Laura Saunders described the sale of corporate tax shelters as "a thriving industry that has received scant public notice." This industry relied on the fact that "neither the tax code nor the IRS can keep up with the exotica of modern corporate finance." The result was that "respectable accounting firms, law offices and public corporations have lately succumbed to competitive pressures and joined the loophole frenzy." Tax shelters, in other words, had moved from the margins of economic life in the 1970s and 1980s to invade the mainstream by late in the twentieth century. Relying on "arcane quirks in the tax code," companies were costing the U.S. Treasury $10 billion a year according to a tentative estimate by Stanford tax law professor Joseph Bankman.[8] Their ability to do so, Novack and Saunders suggested, reflected reliance on derivatives that could split financial instruments into different cash flows, contingent returns, and tax benefits that were separate from the underlying economics of a deal.

Novack and Saunders described a market for shelters that brought together increasing corporate demand with the supply of sophisticated "products." For many companies, the tax department had become a separate profit center devoted to minimizing the corporation's effective tax rate.[9] Accounting firms, financial institutions, and shelter boutiques were responding by poring over the Internal Revenue Code to find anomalies that could be used to design transactions generating substantial tax losses without significant economic risk. Once they did so, they used extensive distribution networks to engage in mass marketing of the transactions to top executives and board members, "not unlike the armies of pitchmen who sold cattle and railcar tax shelters to individuals in the 1970s and 1980s." Rather than being paid by the hour, promoters' fees were based on a percentage of the tax savings that the shelter provided. The journalists pointed to two letters from Deloitte & Touche that offered a tax strategy for a fee of 30 percent of the tax savings, plus expenses. Deloitte promised to defend the strategy in an IRS audit and to refund part of the fee if the agency ultimately did not recognize the tax benefits that the firm promised.

An official from PricewaterhouseCoopers (PwC) was the only accounting firm partner in the article willing to talk on the record about these activities. He was surprisingly candid about the firm's shelter operations. Fernando Murias, the co-chair of the firm's Mid-Atlantic and Washington, D.C, Washington National Tax Services (WNTS), explained that PwC had two databases of about a thousand mass-market shelter ideas. Many of these were conventional strategies but others were more aggressive. According to Murias, the firm actively promoted about thirty mass-market products, using "product champions" to coordinate marketing efforts for each. PwC used more than forty recently hired sales personnel to pitch the products to companies that were not current clients. In addition, the firm sold what Murias called "black box" products that were "complex and unique strategies that we do not publicize broadly."[10] These strategies could save from tens to millions of dollars in taxes and were marketed only to a select group of companies. The firm took care not to "saturate the market" for fear that widespread use would trigger Congressional and IRS attention. "A whale can't get harpooned unless it surfaces for air," emphasized Murias.[11] PwC's contingency fees ranged from 8 percent to 30 percent of the customer's tax savings.

Novack and Saunders's article depicted a tax shelter industry on steroids. In contrast to the previous wave of shelters two decades earlier, large corporations, not doctors and dentists, were taking advantage of shelters to deprive the U.S. Treasury of hundreds of millions of dollars. These shelters were more complex and difficult to analyze than those that had preceded them. They used exotic financial instruments to create transactions that supposedly provided opportunities for economic gain, even as they hedged any risks associated with pursuing it. Not only promoters on the margins of respectability but also some of the country's largest accounting firms, law firms, and financial institutions were now intimately involved in propelling the industry. They were catering to a new corporate attitude toward tax obligations, which regarded minimizing taxes as a competitive advantage that a corporation's tax department was responsible for creating and sustaining.

A few months after the *Forbes* article, in 1999, a highly respected academic weighed in. Joseph Bankman, a tax professor at Stanford Law School, published an article, "The New Market in Corporate Tax Shelters," in *Tax Notes*, a publication widely read by tax practitioners, academics, and tax policy experts. Drawing on conversations with tax lawyers at firms, Bankman was able to describe the rise of new types of shelters that were being marketed to Fortune 500 companies and privately held companies controlled by wealthy individuals.[12] The new shelters, according to Bankman, relied on interpretations of the tax law more aggressive than those offered on behalf of the shelters of the 1970s and 1980s. Indeed, promoters tended to assume that the shelters likely would be shut down if the government discovered them. Despite being expensive to develop, these shelters that typically involved the use of financial instruments were highly lucrative because there was a low probability that the IRS would ever audit the taxpayer and learn about the shelter. Even if it did, the agency likely would invalidate the shelter only prospectively. Once these factors were taken into consideration, Bankman wrote, "the cost benefit analysis leans decidedly in favor of the new corporate tax shelter."[13]

Bankman described the competitive forces within the legal services market that made providing opinion letters attractive. "'You break your back for a firm, month after month,' one partner reports, 'and the next month the firm is going to ask 'What have you done for me lately?' Then a Merrill Lynch comes to you—maybe for the first time—to ask you for an opinion. You know that if you give the client what it wants, there is more work in the future. It's a real temptation.'"[14]

With "the elevation of the tax department to a profit center," aggressive tax planning had become a "new norm." Bankman noted that the corporate executive most responsible for Colgate-Palmolive entering into the installment sales shelter the *ACM* court struck down had been promoted despite the unfavorable legal result and bad publicity because, Bankman was told, "'management and shareholders thought it was pretty good that the company took such aggressive actions.'" The result was a vicious cycle in which investment banks shopped for firms willing to provide opinion letters, which led to more aggressive opinions, which made it possible to design shelters with even less economic substance, which expanded the development of tax shelter products, which led lawyers to think more positively of shelters and to consider developing their own tax products practice.[15] In the world depicted in Bankman's article, corporations could come close to selecting the amount of taxes they were willing to pay and respect for the tax system was a quaint anachronism.

On the heels of Bankman's article, the U.S. Treasury Department weighed in with its report *The Problem of Corporate Tax Shelters*.[16] The report, issued in July, was intended to elaborate on the Clinton administration's proposals to address tax shelters in the Fiscal Year 2000 budget, which had been announced in February. Recognizing that obtaining new legislation was an uphill battle, the administration issued a meticulously argued report marshaling all the evidence the IRS had amassed on abusive tax shelters and describing its well-grounded suspicions about as-yet-undiscovered abusive activity.

The report noted the "widespread agreement and concern among tax professionals that the corporate tax shelter problem is large and growing."[17] Corporate tax payments had lagged behind recent increases in corporate profits and the difference between book income and income for tax purposes had risen sharply in the last few years.[18] The report observed that the growth of sophisticated financial engineering had expanded the number of tax reduction strategies available and that technological advances had made them easier and less expensive to deploy. According to the report, taxpayers also had less reason to fear that their aggressive positions would be discovered because audit rates had been falling. Audit rates for corporations with assets over $100 million had fallen from 77 percent in 1980 to 35 percent in 1997. While this to some extent reflected the impact of real economic growth and inflation, the overall audit rate for corporate tax returns had declined from 2.9 percent in 1992 to 2 percent in 1998.

Finally, the U.S. Treasury report echoed Bankman's point about a change in corporate norms regarding tax obligations. "Corporations increasingly view their tax departments as profit centers," said the report, "rather than as general administrative support facilities. Effective tax rates may be viewed as a performance measure, separate from after tax profits. That has put pressure on corporate financial officers to generate tax savings through shelters."[19] More generally, the report noted, some observers argued that the growth in corporate shelters reflected "more accepting attitudes of tax advisors and corporate executives toward aggressive tax planning. Put another way, the psychic cost of participating in tax-engineered transactions to avoid tax appears to have decreased."[20]

Raising the Stakes

Treasury officials were also hearing disquieting rumors suggesting that the abusive shelter problem was on the rise. Tax practitioners, barred from disclosing the confidential information of their clients, would drop hints during informal chats. And every so often, an anonymous manila envelope arrived containing materials describing a shelter currently on the market. In 1999, a group of tax bar leaders, including John "Buck" Chapoton and Ron Pearlman, both former assistant secretaries at the U.S. Treasury, and Stefan Tucker, a highly respected member of the tax bar, began to discuss the problem among themselves. The group formed a subsection of the ABA Tax Section to draft proposals to impose more stringent obligations on lawyers writing opinion letters intended to protect clients from penalties. They also met with members of the Treasury and legislators on the Hill to urge them to take the tax shelter problem seriously and enact new regulation to combat it.

Officials at Treasury knew they had to convince a highly skeptical Congress. Only one year earlier, in 1998, Congress had been persuaded that the IRS was running amok and enacted a landmark bill to rein it in. Now Treasury needed to ask for more resources and new powers to address an enemy that remained largely hidden. The Clinton administration supported legislation that would increase the penalties for understating income, impose new penalties for failure to disclose reportable transactions, sharpen the definition of abusive transactions, and significantly increase the resources available to the IRS to fight tax shelters. As members of the administration began to prepare to leave office, Treasury officials still hoped that they could obtain enforcement tools that would allow them to slow the spread of shelters and leave a regulatory framework in place that would allow their successors to continue to pursue a systemic response.

In seeking stronger legislation, the Clinton administration was up against a formidable adversary. Ken Kies, a brilliant tax expert and forceful advocate, had been, until a year earlier, the chief of staff to the Joint Committee on Taxation and had driven its Republican-leaning agenda. Among his allies, Kies counted Bill Archer (R, Texas), the chair of the House of Representatives' powerful Ways and Means and Committee. In March 1999, Kies testified before the House Ways and Means Committee against the Clinton administration's proposals in his capacity as managing director of PricewaterhouseCoopers's WNTS. In fifty pages of written testimony to the Committee, he made no secret about his strong opposition to the proposals. According to Kies, the recommendations were "overreaching, unnecessary, and at odds with sound tax-policy principles."[21] There was no evidence, Kies maintained, that corporations were using tax shelters to erode the tax base. To the contrary, corporate tax revenues were on the rise. There was already a laundry list of statutes and regulations, Kies insisted, which gave the government more than enough tools to combat abusive transactions. In Kies's strongly voiced opinion, the Clinton administration's proposed definition of a tax avoidance transaction was excessively vague and would effectively grant broad power to the government that could inhibit the use of legitimate business transactions. Opposing the administration's proposal, Kies did not hesitate to play on concern about IRS overreaching. Only eight months earlier, Congress had passed broad legislation to curtail the IRS's power. Kies observed that, if enacted, Treasury's proposal "would represent one of the broadest grants of authority ever given to the Treasury Department in the promulgation of regulations and, even more troubling, to Service agents in their audits of corporate taxpayers."[22]

Toward the end of the hearing, Representative Lloyd Doggett (D, Texas) took Kies on. "If I understand your written and oral testimony correctly," he asked, "you oppose every single proposal that the administration has advanced relating to corporate tax shelters?" Kies replied, "That is precisely correct."[23] Doggett proceeded to grill Kies on the information disclosed in the *Forbes* article about PwC's tax shelter practice, most of which Kies denied was true. In response to a question about whether PwC charged contingent fees in connection with tax avoidance schemes, Kies replied, "Mr. Doggett, we don't advise people on tax avoidance schemes."[24] When Doggett persisted, Kies eventually acknowledged that while he did not know the exact amount, his firm charged contingent fees on tax shelters based on a percentage of the tax loss.[25]

Stefan Tucker, testifying that day on behalf of the ABA Section of Taxation, urged Congress to take action in the face of a grave threat. "We have witnessed with growing alarm the aggressive use by large corporate taxpayers of tax 'products' that have little or no purpose other than reduction of Federal income taxes," he declared.[26] Tucker expressed particular concern that the "lynchpin" of shelter transactions was the tax advisor's opinion about the likelihood that the tax treatment the taxpayer claimed would be upheld. The role of the advisor in these instances, he said, "often disintegrates into the job of designing or blessing a factual setting" necessary for the transaction to satisfy the requirements of the economic substance and business purpose doctrines."[27] Tucker concurred with the Treasury's proposal to expand disclosure, increase penalties, and provide additional resources to the IRS to fight shelters. Although recognizing that a broader definition of reportable shelters might give rise to uncertainty, Tucker insisted that "[t]axpayers and their advisors know that relative certainty can easily be achieved in legitimate business transactions by steering a safe course and staying in the middle of the road."[28] Acknowledging that many of the shelter enablers were tax lawyers, Tucker paraphrased the comic strip character Pogo. "We have met the enemy, and sometimes it's us."[29]

A month later, the Senate Finance Committee held hearings dedicated in part to the corporate tax shelter problem. Senator Roth, the committee chair who had spearheaded the hearings on IRS abuses a year earlier, was disinclined to support legislation to expand the power of the agency to combat shelters. Echoing the objections raised by opponents, Roth was concerned that new legislation would subject "legitimate business transactions to tax shelter penalties."[30]

If the battle for new legislation was at a standstill, the Treasury had other fronts on which to advance. Much of the shelter activity could be investigated and prosecuted criminally. Unlike other penalties, the threat of criminal sanctions could have meaningful deterrent effects. The IRS's Criminal Investigation Division (CID), however, had come under withering fire during the Roth hearings.[31] At the time of the hearings, Commissioner Rossotti had requested that former FBI Director William Webster head an independent investigation of the CID. In April 1999, Webster submitted his report, which broadly exonerated the CID. According to the report, "Generally, CI[D] employs sound methods of investigation and does not routinely violate the constitutional rights of the subjects of its investigations. While isolated and individual incidents of misconduct exist, no evidence was found of systemic abuses by CI[D]agents."[32]

The report did note that the CID had strayed from its core mission of investigating criminal violations of the tax code because it had been drafted by other agencies to help with projects investigating money laundering, narcotics violations, and other activities that called for the CID's financial expertise. As a result, the percentage of CID investigations based on referrals by the IRS Exam and Collection units had "dropped precipitously."[33] The report recommended that the Criminal Investigation Division be established as a separate operating division within the IRS, headed by someone who would report directly to the IRS Commissioner and his or her deputies.

In October 1999, Rossotti announced that the IRS would be launching an initiative "to identify—and where appropriate, to stop—transactions which have no real business purpose other than tax savings."[34] Rossotti provided few details beyond indicating that the agency would be bringing together IRS audit and technical resources within its Office of Chief Counsel to address those shelters. While the IRS was getting a late start, the sense was that the agency would finally be turning its attention in earnest to the growth in shelter activity that had occurred in the last several years.

Following up the report's recommendations, in early October 1999, Rossotti named Mark Matthews, a former assistant to Webster at both the FBI and the CIA, as the new assistant commissioner for Criminal Investigation.[35] Matthews, a partner in the Washington law firm of Crowell & Moring, had served as deputy assistant attorney general in the Justice Department's Tax Division and as deputy chief of the Criminal Division of the U.S. Attorney's Office in the Southern District of New York. He had won high marks both for his legal skills and his understanding of the dynamics of government agencies. As Matthews debated whether to take the position, it became clear to him that his extensive experience in different prosecutorial settings and his status as an IRS outsider would give credibility to the office. He agreed to come on board.

Matthews undertook several initiatives to reinvigorate CID, including giving agents greater say in the decision to bring criminal charges. He also recognized the importance of using the media to publicize the agency's renewed emphasis on criminal prosecutions to maximize deterrence. CID began to emphasize that individual cases were part of a larger story about national trends in tax evasion. The office began systematically to use its website, reach out to news outlets, and make special agents available to speak with reporters. When a judge sentenced a doctor to take out a full-page advertisement in a local newspaper, the CID sent a transcript of the sentencing hearing to reporters and the story appeared in *Wall Street Journal*.

A Manila Envelope and an Early Victory

In mid-fall 1999, an unmarked manila envelope appeared at the U.S. Treasury Department. The envelope contained a complex strategy, known by the acronym BOSS (Bond and Option Sales Strategy), which the accounting firm PwC was marketing to high-wealth individuals. Whoever had sent the envelope, a concerned tax lawyer perhaps, had given the Treasury a big break. The administration now had a detailed roadmap of one of the more abusive shelters on the market.

The timing could not have been better. In November, the House Ways and Means Committee was scheduled to resume its hearings on corporate tax shelters. The hearings had an inauspicious start when chairman Bill Archer opened the hearing by chastising the Treasury for dragging its feet and failing to issue new regulations pursuant to its powers under the 1997 statute. During the hearing, government officials again made the case that a systemic corporate shelter problem existed that needed to be addressed through new Congressional legislation.

Ken Kies was back, too. The PwC representative reprised the arguments he had made several months earlier. There was still no tax shelter problem, according to Kies. If Congress were to rely on the correct economic calculations, it would find that corporate tax revenue had, in fact, gone up since the early 1990s. And the estimate of $10 billion in lost tax revenue, which had been put forward by Bankman the Stanford tax professor, was just a guess from a "part-time" academic.[36]

Questioning Kies again, Representative Doggett determined what had happened to Fernando Murias, in 1998 the co-chair of PwC's Mid-Atlantic and WNTS, after he had given his forthright description of the firm's active tax shelter practice to two *Forbes* reporters. Although Murias remained a partner, Doggett ascertained that in the previous six months he had been reassigned to a different position at the firm.[37]

Doggett went on to ask whether the details Murias had provided—during casual cocktail party conversation according to Kies—were accurate. Was PwC promoting thirty mass-marketed shelters? Doggett also wanted to know whether the firm had designated special managers as "product champions" to coordinate sales, and had hired a professional sales force to pitch ideas. Kies insisted that these details were wrong. At most, he conceded, the firm might have a planning strategy that it might bring to more than one client.

Reaching over the table in front of him, Doggett grabbed a thick document. "Let me ask you, sir," he said, brandishing the document, whether "your company is still promoting the bond and option sales strategy that you call the BOSS plan, a way to circumvent what this Committee did [with a section of the tax code] in June."[38]

Kies responded that he was not "even familiar with that transaction" but was "happy to look at it and get back to [Doggett]." "I am sure you would," Doggett retorted. "It has got PricewaterhouseCoopers on the cover, so I am sure you can find out about it when you get back. Thank you for your responsiveness, Mr. Kies."[39]

Within a few weeks, *Tax Notes Today* had published PricewaterhouseCoopers's description of BOSS. Soon after, Kies sent a letter to the Ways and Means Committee distancing PwC from BOSS. After inquiring in the firm about the transaction, Kies had learned that "[f]irst, PricewaterhouseCoopers has not been engaged by any client to assist, advise, or otherwise consult on execution of the specific Bond & Option Sales Strategy transaction outlined in the draft opinion letter that Rep. Doggett provided." But he added: "Second, we did advise clients with respect to transactions similar to the ones describe in the draft. Third, it is the position of my firm that we will not issue an opinion on this transaction or such similar transactions."[40]

Shortly afterward, the IRS issued Notice 99-59 shutting down BOSS. According to the notice, the agency would not recognize a tax loss from a BOSS shelter or any similar transaction because in the shelter "[t]hrough a series of contrived steps, taxpayers claim tax losses for capital outlays that they have in fact recovered." Significantly, the notice made clear that the IRS would pursue the range of penalties available to it, including return preparer and promoter penalties. "There will be no Christmas bonus from the 'BOSS' this year," Representative Doggett, announced as he congratulated the Treasury for shutting down the shelter. But he cautioned, "We can't make a serious dent in tax abuse as long as Treasury and Congress act only on a case-by-case basis; we'll always be one step behind."[41]

Back at PwC, firm leaders took swift action, launching an internal investigation to determine the scope of its tax shelter activities. After the IRS published Notice 99-59 in December, PwC decided it could not issue any opinion letters for BOSS. As a consequence of its investigation, the firm decided to unwind the BOSS transactions, refunding clients approximately 85 percent of the cash that they had invested in BOSS transactions, including all fees paid to PwC in connection with the shelter. The firm also withdrew from seven FLIP transactions and refunded fees that had been paid for them.[42]

As Samuel A. DiPiazza, the chair of PwC's U.S. operations, explained, "The evolving state of the law and the changing environment surrounding tax shelter investments cause the firm to change its view . . . [as a result] the firm believed it would be irresponsible to encourage investors to proceed."[43] Looking back on the episode, PwC acknowledged "The BOSS transaction triggered widespread public attention and controversy in the fall of 1999. As a result, we decided that we had made a regrettable mistake being in this business. Our reputation was hurt; our clients and people were embarrassed."[44]

By April 2000, the firm had disbanded the group of approximately ten people who were responsible for developing and marketing shelter transactions. Michael Schwartz, who had brought BOSS to PwC from KPMG, left the firm. Schwartz, who apparently had an insatiable appetite for shelter work, soon launched his own firm, Coastal Trading LLC, which continued to participate in client referrals and shelter implementation.[45]

A few years later, when the IRS sought under its statutory authority to obtain the names of investors who had purchased shelters from PwC, the firm complied without a fight. Soon afterward, PwC resolved the IRS's claims against it arising out of its shelter activity, becoming the first major accounting firm to settle with the IRS. The firm's decision to get out of promoting shelters and the subsequent settlement showed that sufficient reputational pressures and legal threats could lead one of the Big Five accounting firms to desist from engaging in tax shelter activity, even as other firms were ratcheting up their involvement.

Two Steps Forward

By November 1999 the IRS had won five tax court cases involving corporate tax shelters, a string of victories that *Business Week* highlighted in an article entitled "Kiss That Tax Shelter Goodbye?"[46] According to the article, the rulings had left tax professionals "stunned." Within a few months, the agency would win another important case in the D.C. Circuit of Appeals involving a shelter very similar to the one used by

Colgate-Palmolive. While some observers predicted that this trend would lead people to be more careful, using judicial doctrines to attack specific transactions had significant limitations. As one former Treasury official described it, the process was like the game of "whack-a-mole," where new shelters endlessly arose even as others were knocked down. In this game, the promoter would always be ahead of the government.[47]

In February 2000, Treasury Secretary Lawrence Summers described the multipronged approach the department planned to pursue to go after corporate tax shelters, which he identified as "the most serious compliance issue facing the American tax system."[48] Under this approach, the Treasury was issuing new disclosure regulations pursuant to its authority under the Tax Relief Act of 1997. In the meantime, the IRS was being reorganized to focus its resources on identifying potentially abusive transactions. In addition, the Clinton administration would seek new legislation increasing the penalties for abusive shelters and codifying the economic substance doctrine. The Treasury would also focus on strengthening the regulatory standards governing tax practitioners.

The same day as Summers's speech, the Treasury Department issued temporary proposed regulations. Under the new regulations, corporate taxpayers were required to flag transactions that had multiple tax shelter characteristics on their tax returns so that the IRS could examine these transactions more closely.[49] The new regulations also required promoters to register with the IRS transactions that bore the indicia of potentially abusive transactions.[50] In addition, promoters were required to keep lists of investors who purchased such transactions so that the IRS could cross-check taxpayer disclosures against information it obtained from promoters.[51] The new shelter regulations provoked a lively discussion among tax professionals about whether they targeted the right transactions, were overly broad, and could be easily circumvented. Promoters, meanwhile, still took the view that the regulations did not apply to individual taxpayers. By enacting the new regulations, however, the Treasury had at least forestalled one argument made by Kies and other opponents of new legislation that the Treasury had failed to take full advantage of previously granted enforcement powers.

Seeking to use its resources as effectively as possible, the IRS also created a new Office of Tax Shelter Analysis, which would review all disclosures by taxpayers and promoters under the new regulations to identify potentially improper transactions.[52] It also would serve as a clearinghouse for all information on tax shelters that came to the agency and would help evaluate new transactions so that the IRS could provide guidance on them as early as possible.

Prospects for legislation expanding the enforcement power of the IRS, however, remained dim. But government officials supporting new legislation had won one important new convert. Senator Roth, the chair of the Finance Committee, who only a few years earlier had overseen the hearings that had generated such intense criticism of the IRS, now recognized that shelters posed a serious threat to the integrity of the tax system and was in favor of enacting legislation to address the problem. In the spring of 2000, a coalition of Democratic and Republican members of Congress had drafted a sweeping legislative proposal that sought to strengthen the government's hand. Representative Archer, the chair of the House's Ways and Means Committee, remained highly skeptical. Anyone reading the tea leaves knew that without his support, nothing would go forward in Congress.

In the meantime, indications that shelters were moving downstream to individual investors were growing. Evidence was also emerging that some promoters were going so far as to advise investors to report misleading information on their tax returns to hide their involvement in questionable transactions. In August 2000, the IRS announced that it was listing "Son-of-BOSS" shelters as abusive transactions, whose tax benefits it would disallow.[53] This type of transaction, of which BLIPS, SOS, and COBRA were examples, relied on the supposedly distinctive tax treatment of certain partnership liabilities. This treatment inflated a taxpayer's basis producing a tax loss despite the absence of any economic loss. The notice stated that such losses were not allowable as deductions and that any transactions that were the same or similar to these transactions had to be registered under the temporary regulations then in effect.

The notice also described the advice that some promoters were giving taxpayers that enabled them to conceal the amount of their capital losses by using a "grantor trust" to report only the net amount produced by offsetting gains and losses against one another. Tax partners at KPMG and BDO Seidman had given just such advice to clients who were filing their returns. The notice warned that any taxpayer who used this method or any advisor who recommended it was at risk of criminal prosecution. It is not clear how the IRS originally got wind of "Son-of-BOSS" shelters or the grantor trust technique. There was speculation among tax partners at KPMG, who were in the midst of marketing BLIPS and had advised some clients to use grantor trust netting on their tax returns, that someone inside the organization had alerted the IRS about the firm's tax shelter activities.[54]

The notice caused alarm bells to go off throughout the tax world. It was not just—or even principally—corporations that were engaging in tax shelter activity. As the abusive transaction described in the notice made clear, tax shelters had migrated on a very large scale to wealthy individual taxpayers. "Shelters are going retail," warned Lee Sheppard, a prolific contributing editor for *Tax Notes Today* and astute observer of the tax practice world.[55]

Policy experts and politicians have always been somewhat ambivalent about the wisdom of taxing corporations—some argued that it amounted to double taxation, once on the corporation and once on the shareholder who earned income from the corporation.[56] For a handful of policymakers and government officials, corporate shelters were not cause for serious concern. Shelters were just mechanisms for corporations to avoid the unfairness of a double tax. A growing industry of shelters that were mass marketed to wealthy individuals was an altogether different story. No one doubted that such a market could substantially undermine the legitimacy of the tax regime. The knowledge among average Americans that an increasing number of rich people were getting away with not paying taxes could throw the whole system into crisis, breeding tax evasion on an even larger scale. As Sheppard emphasized, "Retail tax shelters engender a loss of respect for the system, and the belief that the rich don't have to pay. Even in a system where most of the revenue is collected through wage withholding, those attitudes are unhealthy and dangerous."[57] Recognizing the danger from mass-marketed individual tax shelters, in August the Treasury amended its proposed tax shelter regulations so that the requirement to maintain a list of investors in a potentially abusive shelter applied not only to shelters sold to corporate taxpayers but also those sold to individuals.[58]

The fact that the shelter industry was breeding fraudulent tax reporting raised even more serious concerns. When it came to questionable transactions, some commentators believed the shelters were aggressive but not necessarily illegitimate, in that they appeared to comply with the technical requirements of the tax law. Almost everyone agreed, however, that using or recommending a reporting technique to net gains and losses with the intent of hiding the underlying tax shelter was criminal wrongdoing.

In early 2001, the Treasury made good on its earlier promise to strengthen the practice standards that governed tax practitioners, known as Circular 230.[59] Treasury officials proposed to add a due diligence requirement for more-likely-than-not opinions that were intended to be relied on by taxpayers to avoid penalties. Among other obligations, the opinion author had to "make inquiry as to all relevant facts." An opinion "could not be based, directly or indirectly, on any unreasonable factual assumptions," which included "a factual assumption that the practitioner knows or has reason to believe is incorrect, incomplete, inconsistent or implausible" or "a factual assumption that the transaction has a business reason, an assumption with respect to the potential profitability of the transaction apart from tax benefits, or an assumption with respect to a material valuation issue." Simply put, opinions intended to provide penalty protection could not rely on farfetched factual assumptions about the purpose and profitability of the transaction. More-likely-than-not opinions had to be comprehensive, addressing all of the relevant judicial doctrines and applying them to the relevant facts. Similar requirements applied to opinions being used by third parties to market shelters, which, because they were not obtained from an independent advisor, could not be relied on to avoid penalties.

Reflecting recognition of the importance of organizational structure and climate on tax practice, the regulations required that practitioners who are responsible for a firm's tax practice "take reasonable steps" to ensure that "the firm has adequate procedures in effect for purposes of ensuring compliance" with tax opinion regulations. The IRS Director of Practice would be authorized to take disciplinary action against any practitioner for failing to do so under certain circumstances when there was a "pattern or practice" in a firm of failing to comply with the regulations.

By January 2001 Some 2,500 transactions had been filed with the IRS as a result of the corporate disclosure regulations and the agency had issued nineteen "soft" letters to promoters requesting additional information. In March 2001, IRS Senior Counselor to the Commissioner Michael Shaheen announced that the number of attorneys in the Office of the Director of Practice would increase from nine to thirty and that the IRS would increase the number of administrative law judge cases that involved tax shelters.[60] The IRS was ramping up for what it expected to be a larger number of investigations and proceedings. It was also signaling that it was serious about scrutinizing the activities of tax professionals alleged to be involved in shelter activity.

A few months later, the IRS announced its settlement with Merrill Lynch in connection with the 1989 and 1990 installment sales transactions that the firm had failed to register. Courts had upheld the IRS's denial of tax benefits arising from these shelters in *ACM*, *ASA Investerings*, and other cases. Merrill agreed to make a "substantial payment" as part of the settlement, although a Merrill spokesperson said that it was not a "material" amount.[61] The firm agreed to review all of its investment products to ensure that they complied with federal law. The IRS's hand obviously had been strengthened by court decisions finding these shelters abusive. In light of the twelve years that had transpired between the sale of the shelters and the settlement, however, it was clear the agency couldn't afford to wait for such vindication before it moved against promoters.

Two Steps Back?

If 2000 had been a good year for the IRS in court, 2001 proved to be a bad one. The summer brought several defeats, as the Eleventh and then the Eighth Circuit Courts of Appeal reversed decisions in which the IRS had successfully argued that features of a tax-advantaged transaction were a sham.[62] In the fall, the agency lost a district court case involving an installment sales shelter sold by Merrill Lynch.[63] These defeats were capped with two more losses in December 2001, as the D.C. and Fifth Circuits reversed tax court decisions that had been favorable to the agency.[64] Commentators worried that these losses were blowing new winds into the sails of the tax shelter industry. PwC's Kenneth Kies urged the Treasury to change its policy with regard certain shelters, arguing that the appellate decisions, "cast significant doubt on the economic substance test" relied on by IRS.[65]

In mid-December 2001 the IRS's Office of Tax Shelter Analysis (OTSA) reported on the information it had received from taxpayer disclosures and promoter registrations since its creation in March of 2000.[66] OTSA had received fifty-one disclosure statements regarding reportable transactions from twenty-one taxpayers in 2000. The total claimed tax losses from these transactions was $3.7 billion. From the beginning of 2001 until November 30 of that year, OTSA received 272 disclosure statements from ninety-five taxpayers, representing claimed losses of $14.7 billion. OTSA also had received over 3,600 registrations from promoters since its inception. Based on this information, it had issued twenty-eight letters to twenty-two different promoters and was conducting investigations of twelve promoters for failure to file shelter registrations.

As an IRS official acknowledged, the numbers were deceptive. Closer analysis of the OTSA data indicated that about 100 of the 272 transactions disclosed in 2001 were "plain vanilla" leases that an IRS notice had earlier indicated were not abusive. Of the remaining transactions, seventy-two were listed and half of those were contingent liability shelters that the agency had already listed in February of 2001.[67] In other words, the IRS wasn't learning much from the disclosures about previously unknown shelters.

Just before Christmas 2001, the IRS announced an initiative that officials hoped would dramatically increase taxpayer disclosure of shelter transactions.[68] Announcement 2002-2 amounted to an amnesty program for taxpayers who disclosed their participation in any shelter for which they might be subject to an underpayment penalty. These taxpayers would not be subject to the penalty if they came forward by April 23, 2002, and satisfied certain conditions. To take advantage of this offer, a taxpayer was required to provide a description of the shelter and its tax treatment; information about anyone who promoted the shelter and had a financial interest in the taxpayer's decision to participate, as well as anyone who advised the promoter regarding the shelter; and, if requested, copies of all documents connected with the transaction, including legal opinions and memoranda. The IRS hoped to break the disclosure logjam on shelters by giving taxpayers an incentive to turn over information that the agency could use to pursue promoters, whom it regarded as the root of the problem.

The IRS publicized the initiative to tax practitioners and urged them to advise clients to take advantage of it. Larry Langdon, commissioner of the IRS Large and Mid-Size Business Division (LMSB), spoke to several groups. At a January 18, 2001, meeting of the ABA Section of

Taxation Financial Transactions Committee in New Orleans, Langdon
said that the disclosure initiative was designed to prompt taxpayers to
come forward while knowing that others in their situation were doing
the same.[69] He called it a "once in a lifetime opportunity" that provided
for expedited resolution of any issues. One member of the audience said
that he couldn't help but detect "an unmistakable air of revenge" on the
part of the IRS toward those who didn't come forward. Langdon didn't
soft-pedal his response. "That's why we're discussing it now," he said.
About a week later, speaking to the Federal Bar Association Tax Section
in Washington, D.C., Langdon remarked that the initiative gave taxpayers
a choice: "pay me now or pay me later."[70] He added, "But if you pay me
later, you'll pay penalties."

The tax bar expressed concern about the impact of disclosure on the
attorney-client privilege since taxpayers were being asked to disclose legal
opinions and memoranda as a condition of obtaining amnesty. Its fears
were confirmed when Langdon asserted, "We're in effect asking people to
waive appropriate attorney-client privilege."[71] In an effort to resolve the
issue, the IRS announced on February 19, 2002, that it had developed a
standard agreement between the agency and a taxpayer making a disclosure under the initiative that addressed the privilege issue. It stated: "This
agreement confirms that the Internal Revenue Service will not assert that
[Taxpayer's] production of the document listed below constitutes a subject matter waiver of the attorney-client privilege or the work product
doctrine with respect to other documents addressing the same subject
matters as those discussed in the listed documents."[72] The IRS reserved
the right to challenge the assertion of privilege on other grounds. Members of the tax bar were not impressed. Lawrence Hill at White & Case
scoffed that the IRS was giving people "ice in the winter."[73] He suggested
that the agency could still depose a tax advisor and ask questions about
all documents produced under the disclosure initiative. Furthermore, he
noted, a court, other agency, or third party was still free to claim, based
on traditional court doctrine, that there had been a broad subject matter
waiver.

Despite lingering concerns that taxpayers would be broadly waiving
the attorney-client privilege, some shelter participants began to disclose.
Slow at first, the response began to pick up momentum. In March 2002,
the IRS announced that by February, midway through the amnesty period,

more than seventy taxpayers had disclosed transactions involving claims of $1.5 billion in tax losses.[74] Even more striking, in February alone, some twenty-one taxpayers had disclosed more than $1 billion in claimed losses. The number of participating taxpayers had more than tripled in the previous two weeks, observed David Harris, the manager of OTSA. "The volume has been fairly steady," he emphasized, and more "keep rolling in every day."[75] Harris suggested that the $1.5 billion figure for the amount of losses and deductions at stake was "quite understated," because many disclosures informed the IRS of the transactions but did not specify a dollar amount.[76] Despite setbacks in the courts, the agency's tough talk was starting to yield results.

Expanding the Arsenal

Although the amnesty initiative was beginning to bear fruit, many corporate taxpayers and shelter promoters were still not complying with the Treasury's disclosure regulations. Some officials believed that the complexity of the existing disclosure rules invited creative interpretation, and the penalties for refusing to comply with them were inadequate. Moreover, given the growth of shelter activity among individual taxpayers, imposing a disclosure obligation only on corporate taxpayers was unduly narrow. In late March 2002, the Treasury proposed new regulations that required partnerships, S corporations, trusts, and individuals to disclose reportable transactions.[77] The new regulations also eliminated defenses to penalties for underpayment, such as relying on a legal opinion, for any reportable transaction that the taxpayer had not disclosed.[78]

Although the new regulations expanded the opportunity to identify potentially abusive transactions, the IRS still lacked the resources to enforce the rules aggressively. The previous spring, IRS Commissioner Rossotti testified before the Senate Finance Committee that the agency was "deeply concerned about the continued drop in audit and collection activity" over the last year.[79] As Rossotti pointed out, customer service had improved, but at the cost of enforcement. Audit and collection activity had fallen due to a long-term decline in staffing, coupled with a shift of agency personnel from compliance to customer service.

Much of the underenforcement, moreover, was occurring in connection with business filings. Trust and partnership filings had steadily increased since the mid-1990s, but the IRS still lacked the capacity to match these returns with the returns of individual or corporate taxpayers. According to Rossotti, up to 20 percent of income that passed through from entities to their owners was not reported. Unmatched partnership return forms represented approximately $500 billion in pass-through income. "These pass-throughs" Rossotti emphasized, "are not being identified by the IRS and therefore are not available for compliance reviews. Abusive tax shelters are taking advantage of IRS' inability to match, regulate or analyze this information."[80]

A year later, the situation had not improved. In testimony before the Senate's Finance Committee, Rossotti described identifying and combating tax shelters as the IRS's highest priority.[81] The agency's resources, however, were stretched to the limit. In testimony during hearings of the Joint Committee of Taxation review of the IRS, James R. White, the director of the independent General Accounting Office, identified "large and pervasive declines across the compliance and collection programs, except for returns processing, between the years 1996–2001." Among other areas of decreased enforcement and collection activity, White noted declines in audits of individual and corporate tax returns and an increase in deferred collection activity on delinquencies. The drop in overall enforcement activity created a disincentive for voluntary compliance. White observed, "Taxpayers' willingness to voluntarily comply with the tax laws depends in part on their confidence that their friends, neighbors, and business competitors are paying their share of taxes."[82]

These dire figures were replicated in the Joint Committee on Taxation's report. Levies, liens, and seizures had seen an uptick in 2000 but total enforcement actions were "a fraction of levels in fiscal years 1995 through 1998."[83] The audit rate in 2001 was slightly higher than in the previous year, but overall the audit rate had declined since 1997. Audits of corporations had steadily declined. When it came to pass-through entities, a favorite vehicle to hide tax shelter activity, the IRS only audited one out of 256 returns, a rate equivalent to 0.39 percent. Meanwhile, the IRS had identified the "misuse of trusts and pass-through entities to hide or improperly reduce income" and "the use of complex and abusive corporate tax shelters" as areas of "systemic non-compliance" on which it planned to concentrate its "limited" enforcement resources.[84] As his five-year term was winding down, Rossotti underscored in speech after speech the need for adequate funding to strengthen the agency's compliance functions.

For all Commissioner Rossotti's efforts, there was some skepticism about whether the Bush administration was seriously committed to addressing corporate tax shelters. A *Wall Street Journal* article portrayed the amnesty program announced in late 2001 as too generous to tax shelter participants and noted that the Bush Treasury, in contrast to the Clinton administration, was slow to shut down individual shelters.[85] In the previous two years, the Treasury had also been ambivalent about the need to pursue new legislation to address the problem.

The government's enforcement efforts might have continued to limp along but for the fact that a major corporate scandal was erupting in the news. In late 2001, Enron Corporation was forced into bankruptcy. Only a year earlier the company had been a darling of the business community, listed among the biggest twenty public companies in the world and a poster child for innovative business strategies and management style. On February 1, 2002, William Powers Jr., Dean of the University of Texas School of Law, issued a scathing report on behalf of a special committee of the Enron board, describing the mind-numbingly complex accounting maneuvers that the company had used to make its mounting losses disappear from its books.[86] As the disclosures emerged, the public was treated to a parade of indictments and guilty pleas, as one high-ranking Enron executive after another came under criminal investigation. It was soon clear that Enron was not the only company that had engaged in large-scale fraud. WorldCom, Tyco, and others joined a growing list of major corporations engaged in massive accounting scandals.

Powers's report demonstrated that the extent and depth of Enron's fraud would not have been possible without the complicity of a major accounting firm. The revelations about Arthur Andersen's role destroyed the accounting firm's reputation and put to rest the myth that such firms were committed to safeguarding the integrity of the securities market. In the period of a few months, the behavior of several partners at Andersen fell under public scrutiny and the partner in charge of the Enron engagement plead guilty. The firm itself was indicted for obstruction of justice in March 2002.

As the disclosures showed, Enron's wrongdoing went beyond accounting fraud. The company had also participated in abusive shelters to avoid paying taxes on the revenue it earned. In January 2002, Senator Charles Grassley (R, Iowa), ranking member of the Senate Finance Committee, emphasized that Enron's tax avoidance strategies underscored the need for new legislation.[87] In the spring, the Committee held a new round of hearings on abusive shelters. It did not escape notice that the IRS, which had been vilified only four years earlier, was now producing the star witnesses in the proceedings. Senator Grassley, a one-time critic of the IRS, was publicly cheering the agency's enforcement efforts.[88] Even as it considered new legislation, the Senate Finance Committee was aggressively negotiating to obtain Enron's tax records, which the company claimed were privileged under the statutory accounting privilege.[89]

In May 2002, the *Washington Post* ran a front-page story describing "Enron's Other Strategy."[90] According to Robert Hermann, Enron's former general tax counsel who was interviewed for the story, the company had been able to produce almost $1 billion in tax savings from engaging in tax avoidance transactions. In 2000, nearly a third of the profit reported by the company came from savings from these one-time transactions. According to Hermann, the tax unit was under intense pressure to produce reportable earnings. Enron's tax department created a "structured transactions" group, which grew to about twenty employees, who worked with the assistance of King & Spalding, Chase Manhattan Bank, and Bankers Trust to identify and implement transactions. These deals were expected to produce nearly $2 billion dollars in reported revenue by the mid-2000s.

Although Hermann insisted that the transactions were permissible tax avoidance mechanisms, further investigation revealed that many were abusive tax shelters. Lee Sheppard of *Tax Notes* observed that at least one Enron transaction involved a basis-shifting shelter similar to the shelters that had moved downstream to individual taxpayers.[91] Enron had also used tax havens to avoid paying taxes. Observers hypothesized a connection between Enron's participation in abusive shelter activities and its accounting fraud. As tax professor Alice Abreu noted, if line crossing in tax compliance led to pushing the envelope in other areas, then "corporate tax shelters would be like cancer—bad not just because it damages an organ but because it spreads."[92]

The widespread attention to tax abuses prompted by Enron's collapse lit a fire under the Senate. By summer, several senators had proposed separate bills to address the issue. In a surprise move, meanwhile, the Appropriations Committee gave the IRS $10 million more than the Bush administration had requested in its budget to fight tax shelters.[93]

Representative Doggett, for his part, sponsored a bill that would yield an estimated $16.5 billion in tax revenue, otherwise lost to corporate shelters, over ten years. Still the Republican-controlled House was not eager to move quickly to enact legislation to curb tax shelters and the use of tax havens to shield income. While the push for new legislation was stalled again, no one expected that this would be the last attempt to address abusive shelters through Congressional action.

By 2002, it was clear that the issue of abusive tax shelters had become an important topic of public debate. Publicity in the press about shelters, court decisions affirming the use of anti-abuse doctrines, and Congressional hearings had moved the Treasury Department to issue a report on corporate shelters and to stiffen regulations. The IRS had listed two major shelters as abusive and had enacted an initiative to encourage taxpayers who had used shelters to come forward. A new IRS Office of Tax Shelter Analysis was beginning to gather more information about questionable tax avoidance transactions. From this point forward, government efforts would gain momentum. Over time, these efforts slowly tightened the noose around the accounting firms and law firms that had helped perpetrate a major assault on the United States income tax system.

11

The Government Closes In

When the Internal Revenue Service announced in December 2001 that taxpayers who had engaged in questionable shelters could escape penalties if they disclosed their participation to the agency by the following April, Representative Lloyd Doggett (D, Texas) criticized the IRS action as "all carrot and no stick."[1] The stick was soon to come in the form of IRS enforcement actions against major accounting firms, law firms, and advisory boutiques to require them to disclose the identity of taxpayers who had participated in shelters, soon to be followed by Congressional hearings, criminal investigations, and prosecutions.

The Summons Weapon

By spring 2002, the IRS had summonses outstanding to accounting firms KPMG, Ernst & Young (E&Y), Arthur Andersen, PricewaterhouseCoopers (PwC), and BDO Seidman, as well as to several law firms and investment advisors. By law, the agency is authorized to issue a summons to obtain information relevant to ascertaining the accuracy of tax returns and determining the liability of any persons in connection with their obligation to file returns and pay federal taxes.[2] The IRS may also issue a summons for the purpose of "inquiring into any offense in connection with the administration or enforcement of the internal revenue laws."[3] The first firm to exit the shelter market, PwC, reached an agreement with the IRS in June 2002 to resolve the agency's investigation of the firm's tax shelter activities. Under the settlement PwC agreed to pay $10 million to the agency and to cease marketing abusive tax shelters.[4]

The summons directed at E&Y sought information about compliance with registration requirements in connection with COBRA transactions. After receiving the summons in April, the firm concluded that identities of taxpayers were not privileged because the information was disclosed in their tax returns, which reflected their claimed losses as a result of participating in the shelter transactions. The accounting firm notified its clients of its decision.

Among those clients were Henry Camferdam and three colleagues who had participated in the COBRA shelter described in chapter 6 to wipe out a tax liability of more than $70 million. When they received the notice, Camferdam and his colleagues informed E&Y that they objected to the disclosure of any information, including their names and documents. The next day, Jenkens & Gilchrist instructed the accounting firm, on behalf of clients who had participated in the COBRA transactions, not to disclose information or documents related to them.

When E&Y responded that, on advice of its law firm, it planned to identify clients who had engaged in the transactions, the former clients sued, seeking a temporary restraining order to prevent any disclosures. After the district court denied the request for a restraining order in early fall, E&Y disclosed the names of the investors to the IRS. After the firm complied with the IRS summonses, the agency began interviewing E&Y personnel about the firm's shelter activities.

That same spring, the IRS issued nineteen summonses to Arthur Andersen relating to potentially abusive tax shelter transactions involving at least forty-eight different investors.[5] The agency estimated that improper tax deductions in each transactions ranged from at least $10 million to as much as $1.6 billion. In response to the summons, Arthur Andersen initially played hardball. After the IRS petitioned a court to enforce the summonses,[6] the firm entered into an agreement to produce the information the agency was seeking and notified former clients that it would be handing over their names to the IRS. Like E&Y's former clients, the clients who purchased shelter transactions from Andersen tried to prevent disclosure, arguing that their identities were protected by the statutory tax practitioner-client privilege.[7]

The government also sought information from BDO Seidman. In April and May 2002, IRS Revenue Agent Michael Friedman met with the firm's counsel. In those meetings, BDO claimed that it had not promoted any potentially abusive tax shelters and therefore could not be subject to any penalties under the registration and list maintenance requirements. The firm also refused to acknowledge the existence of its Tax Solutions Group. On May 2, Friedman issued summonses to BDO

requesting documents relating to twenty potentially abusive shelter transactions. BDO responded by asserting that it had no responsive documents
and, even if it did, those documents were privileged under the statutory
tax accountant-client privilege.

In July, the Justice Department filed suit in federal district court in
Chicago to enforce the summonses against BDO. In support of its actions,
the Department made available hundreds of pages of documentation,
which provided detailed descriptions of how a previously well-respected
accounting firm had engaged in systematic efforts to design and market
tax shelters. Among other documents, the enforcement petition contained
a list of individual BDO offices' contributions to the generation of over
$100 million in Tax Solutions Group revenues for fiscal year 2000, end-
ing on June 30, 2000.[8]

Later in 2002, Camferdam and other COBRA purchasers were notified that the IRS would be auditing their tax returns for 1999 and that the
agency would not recognize losses resulting from COBRA transactions.
On December 20, 2002, Camferdam and fellow investors filed suit in
federal court in New York against several defendants, among them E&Y,
Jenkens & Gilchrist, and Paul Daugerdas, contending that the defendants
"knew or should have known" that COBRA was "an illegitimate tax
sham."[9] The suit sought more than $40 million in compensatory damages
and $1 billion in punitive damages. Eventually, it was consolidated with a
class action suit in which Thomas Denney, another tax shelter purchaser,
was the lead plaintiff. The consolidated action would come to include another group of investors and eventually encompass 1,100 class members
who had obtained opinions from the firm on COBRA, PICO, and other
shelters.

The IRS's enforcement actions gained momentum as more and more
reports were appearing in the news that wealthy individuals were using
tax shelters, purchased from major accounting firms, to avoid paying
taxes. In early 2003, telecommunications giant Sprint—beleaguered due
to its ties to scandal-ridden WorldCom—announced that it had terminated
its top two executives without severance pay when it discovered that they
had purchased tax shelters from E&Y, the company's auditor. The shelters allowed the executives to indefinitely defer taxes when they exercised
stock options, which resulted in excess of $300 million in profits. Accord-
ing to some estimates, had the executives not participated in the shelter,
they would have owed more than $123 million in taxes.[10]

Although Sprint did not explain its decision, the sale of risky tax strategies to the company's CEO and president compromised E&Y's capacity to function as an independent auditor. Sprint subsequently changed auditors—to KPMG—and adopted a policy that prohibited its auditing firm from offering tax advice to company executives. Soon other stories appeared describing how other executives at Sprint had participated in the same shelter and how executives at other companies, including Dennis Kozlowski, the disgraced CEO of Tyco, had purchased similar shelters from Arthur Andersen.

Outrage at the spread of tax shelters among the very wealthy soon spread beyond the business press. In a 2003 editorial, the *New York Times* denounced the "unbridled greed" that had led the executives to award themselves the options and then try to avoid the taxes after exercising them. The *Times* also faulted E&Y, declaring, "Auditors should be protecting shareholders, not peddling tax schemes to the companies they audit, or their officers." Tying the Sprint controversy to the Enron debacle, the editorial noted that the company had managed to avoid paying any taxes to the IRS between 1996 and 1999 on reported profits of $2 billion. The editorial linked these activities to a large tax shelter industry driven by major professional firms. "Enron may be gone," the *Times* said, "but many of those who were complicitous in its tax shenanigans—the prestigious law firms, investment banks and accounting firms—are still making big money instructing companies on how to beat the taxman."[11] As it happened, the lead developer of Enron's shelters was Bankers Trust, which was subsequently sold to Deutsche Bank, the most active financial institution in the individual shelter market.[12]

In late February after three years of comments, the Treasury Department issued final regulations governing taxpayer disclosure, promoter registration, and promoter list maintenance in connection with potentially abusive transactions. The regulations sought to identify straightforward categories of suspect strategies so they would easily come to the IRS's attention without deluging the agency with disclosures involving legitimate tax-favored transactions. Among the categories that the regulations identified were transactions offered under conditions of confidentiality, those that had been listed by the IRS, and those that generated significant losses and included losses claimed by individuals, S corporations, trusts, and partnerships involving individuals.[13]

The following month, IRS Chief Counsel B. John Williams reported on the agency's continuing pursuit of abusive shelter promoters. Based on an examination of seventy-eight entities such as law firms, accounting firms, and investment banks, Williams announced that there had been a "wholesale failure to comply with registration requirements."[14] Five cases involving seventy-six summonses had been referred to the Justice Department for enforcement, and he suggested that there would be more. Turning to the taxpayer settlement offers, Williams announced that although the response to the contingent liability shelter initiative was still not known, 92 percent of the 488 taxpayers known to have been involved in basis-shifting shelters had accepted the settlement terms. The IRS subsequently reported that about half of the 126 known participants in contingent liability shelters had applied for settlement.[15]

The enforcement actions against Arthur Andersen and BDO, however, had become mired in questions of privilege. Trial courts in those cases had recognized limited protection for client identities under the statutory taxpayer privilege and were attempting to sort out what standards applied. By the spring of 2003, the issue was pending in the Court of Appeals for the Seventh Circuit, which observers hoped would clarify whether—and, if so, under what circumstances—taxpayers could prevent accounting firms from disclosing their names to the IRS.

A New Team at the IRS

On May 1, 2003, the Senate confirmed Mark Everson to succeed Charles Rossotti as IRS Commissioner. Everson had served as the Deputy Director for Management at the Office of Management and Budget after working as a finance executive at two global companies. Earlier in his career, he had served in the Reagan administration as special assistant to Attorney General Edwin Meese and as deputy commissioner of the Immigration and Naturalization Service. During his confirmation hearings, Everson assured the Senate Finance Committee that "enforcement will be a principal responsibility of the IRS."[16] Soon after his confirmation, Everson reported at a House Appropriations panel hearing on IRS compliance efforts that the agency had 372 civil and 464 criminal promoter investigations ongoing.[17] In May, the IRS had also estimated that the disclosures under the initiative that ended on April 23, 2002, had provided information on shelters involving more than $30 billion in claimed tax losses or deductions.

Within a few months of Everson's confirmation, Mark Matthews returned to the agency as the new Deputy Commissioner for Services and Enforcement, a position Everson created as part of a realignment of the IRS's management structure.[18] Matthews, a former prosecutor, had been head of the IRS Criminal Investigation Division (CID) from 2000 until he left in May 2002 to serve as the global co-head of Deutsche Bank's anti-money-laundering compliance program.[19] A year later, he was back. By recruiting Matthews for a new high-level enforcement position, Everson underscored that bringing criminal actions for participation in abusive tax shelter promotion was a top priority. He reinforced the message that the IRS was committed to combating abusive shelters by hiring John Klotsche, a tax lawyer and former chair of Baker & McKenzie, as a senior advisor to coordinate the efforts against shelters and to oversee enforcement more generally.

By summer, the IRS's enforcement actions against accounting firms were gaining momentum. The IRS investigation of E&Y's failure to register its shelters eventually ended in a settlement between the agency and the firm in July 2003. Under the agreement, the firm would pay a $15 million penalty and agree to ongoing IRS review of its compliance policies. IRS Commissioner Everson was delighted: "We are pleased that Ernst & Young has cooperated fully with the IRS in resolving these matters. In particular, the ability of the IRS to review the firm's compliance on an ongoing basis will help to reduce the likelihood of future violations of the registration and list maintenance requirements. This represents a real breakthrough and is a good working model for agreements with practitioners."[20] All clients who had purchased CDS, COBRA, CDS-Add On, and PICO were ultimately audited, and many ended up paying back taxes, interest, and often penalties.

Later that summer, the Justice Department enjoyed another major victory. In a case involving summonses issued to BDO Seidman, the Seventh Circuit held that the IRS list maintenance requirements defeated any claim that taxpayers could reasonably expect that information about them would be kept confidential. The court further held that the tax accountant privilege did not encompass communications occurring for the purpose of preparing a tax return.[21] The court's ruling put to rest the issue of whether former clients who had purchased a shelter could prevent disclosure of their names to the IRS.[22] Based on the Seventh Circuit's decision, the court in the enforcement action against Arthur Andersen ruled that investors in shelters promoted by Andersen could not prevent disclosure of their identities to the government.[23] In the fall, the IRS forged ahead against another accounting firm, issuing summonses to Grant Thornton.[24]

Continuing to exert pressure on accounting firms that had participated in the shelter market, the IRS moved in late September 2003 to enforce nineteen summonses for documents that it had issued to Arthur Andersen.[25] The agency described a series of requests for information about shelter activity to which Andersen had been unresponsive dating back to December 2000. According to the IRS, at least forty-eight different investors had participated in potentially abusive shelter transactions promoted by Andersen, none of which the accounting firm had registered. The IRS estimated that "the amount of likely improper tax deductions in these transactions ranges from at least $10 million to as much as $1.6 billion." Former clients again moved to intervene, arguing that their identities were protected by privilege.

At BDO, meanwhile, government pressure was mounting, and the board decided to clean house. In fall 2003 it removed Denis Field as CEO and board chair and Charles Bee as vice chair, placing them on indefinite leave.

Around the same time, the IRS announced that it was examining the activities of thirty promoters. In addition, it reported that over 1,200 taxpayers had disclosed questionable transactions in response to the amnesty that had ended in late April. Using information obtained from the disclosure initiative to identify specific types of shelters, the IRS offered settlements to taxpayers who had engaged in "basis shifting" shelters, like FLIP and OPIS, and contingency liability shelters, like BLIPS and COBRA. The government's two-pronged approach—encouraging taxpayers to come forward while requiring promoters to disclose clients' identities—was beginning to bear fruit.

Summoning Sidley Austin

Under the IRS amnesty offer that concluded in April 2002, some eighty taxpayers had disclosed participation in shelters that the law firm Sidley Austin Brown & Wood had promoted, solicited, or recommended. The vast majority of these were executed at Brown & Wood before it merged with Sidley & Austin in April 2001. On the basis of this information, the IRS petitioned the federal district court in Chicago on October 14, 2003, for authority to issue a John Doe summons to the firm. A John Doe summons, which requires judicial approval, is a request to a third party for the names of taxpayers whose identities currently are unknown to the IRS. If there are objections to a John Doe summons, the statute of limitations for assessing tax deficiencies for investors is automatically stayed beginning six months after the service of the summons. The summons sought the identities of other taxpayers who had been involved in shelters in which the firm had participated from January 1, 1996, through the date of the petition. According to the petition, the IRS had learned that during this period Sidley had organized or sold potentially abusive tax shelters, or both, including those that were the same as or similar to various listed abusive transactions. The court granted the petition the following day. Sidley responded by providing the identities of some taxpayers covered by the summons, but withheld the names of more than 370 shelter participants on the grounds that they had not consented to disclosure.

In the midst of this controversy, Sidley learned that R. J. Ruble had a personal arrangement to receive 20 percent of the revenues from Chenery Associates' sale of the CARDS shelter. On October 27, 2003, the firm expelled Ruble from the partnership "for breaches of fiduciary duty and violations of the partnership agreement."[26] The announcement of the expulsion concluded by saying that "pursuant to our firm policy, we will not comment further on personnel matters." To avoid having the expulsion used against it as an admission that it had been involved in tax shelters, the firm took pains to explain that the expulsion "in no way relates to the substance of opinions at issue in current litigation or to any ongoing tax work for existing clients."[27]

On November 20, 2003, Ruble and former Brown & Wood managing partner Thomas Smith, who was now with the merged firm, appeared before the Senate Permanent Subcommittee on Investigations (PSI). This was the second day of hearings before the Subcommittee on the role of accountants, lawyers, and financial professionals in the U.S. tax shelter industry. The hearings were the culmination of an extensive investigation initiated in 2002 by the then-chair of the PSI, Carl Levin (D, Michigan). Accompanied by his lawyer, Ruble declined to testify, asserting his constitutional right not to incriminate himself.[28]

Smith followed with a prepared statement in which he sought to distance the firm from Ruble's tax shelter work. According to Smith, Ruble had been expelled from the firm for "accepting undisclosed compensation and for refusing to explain his conduct to the firm." Of the ten tax partners at Brown & Wood before the merger, he noted, Ruble was the only one who engaged in tax shelter practice "although he consulted with others on discrete issues." Smith explained that the firm had an opinion committee that partners were expected to consult on novel legal issues and that the firm required the approval of tax opinions by a second partner. Smith maintained, however, that "[n]o set of procedures will stop an individual from acting improperly if he or she is unwilling to abide by the rules of our profession and to engage in blatant acts of deceit and concealment."[31] Ruble, Smith said, "evaded our controls we had in place and he breached the trust we reposed in him."[29]

Senator Norm Coleman (R, Minnesota) pressed Smith during the question period about Ruble's email to KPMG partners indicating that Smith had approved an alliance with KPMG. Flushed and somewhat agitated, Smith sputtered: "[L]et me just caution, I am sure you can tell . . . I am very outraged." He continued, "The first I knew about that email was when I read it in the *Wall Street Journal* several weeks ago. I knew nothing about that. We had never been told that there was any sort of an alliance or proposed alliance with KPMG or anyone else." "I take it [Ruble was] not operating by himself?" Coleman asked. Smith responded, "Well, that is a good question. We have all of this under review. I think in large measure, what we fear most in a law firm, he was a lone wolf . . . not to mention a rogue partner, which is your greatest fear."[30]

In response to a question about the scope of Sidley's participation in KPMG transactions, Smith said the firm's understanding was that Ruble was "not involved in the design of these products, but that KPMG would come to him with the product and ask him if he could render the concurring opinion." Smith added that Ruble "would perhaps make suggestions so that he could render his opinion and perhaps he might—I guess if he saw something there to improve the product, he might have passed that on."[31]

Senator Levin was even more forceful in his questioning. He asked how the firm could justify billing clients $50,000 for "cookie-cutter" opinions and why no one at the firm asked Ruble if he had some kind of arrangement with KPMG. Smith's understanding was that KPMG would give clients a choice of two or three law firms they could use and that Ruble played no role in marketing or promoting the shelters. Levin also questioned whether any meetings had actually occurred with clients before the firm provided them with opinion letters. When Smith acknowledged that he did not know, Levin asked, "Is it possible that in most cases, there were no client consultations, you simply submitted the letter?" Smith said that he had never asked Ruble that question, but he assumed that "[t]he tax partners would have." When Levin inquired whether Smith had asked the tax partners if Ruble had any contact with clients, he acknowledged that he had not. Levin also continued to press Smith about the failure of anyone at the firm to inquire about the arrangements between KPMG and Ruble.[32]

Sidley later filed responses to supplemental questions from the Senate Permanent Subcommittee on Investigations, clarifying that Ruble's opinion letters had not been reviewed by other tax lawyers at the firm.[33] In a letter submitted on behalf of the firm, Smith explained that it was his understanding "that none of the partners in the tax department considered themselves to have functioned as a reviewing partner or 'second signer' on any opinion Mr. Ruble issued in the KPMG transactions." Smith noted that "[t]o the extent Mr. Ruble did not observe the practices, procedures, or requirements of the firm with respect to review of opinions issued by Mr. Ruble in the KPMG transactions, [he did] not know why Mr. Ruble" did not do so.[34]

One month later, the Justice Department petitioned the federal district court in Chicago to enforce the summons against Sidley. The petition included declarations from two IRS agents that elaborated on the government's information about the firm's involvement in tax shelter activities.[35] Sidley eventually disclosed the names of several hundred former shelter clients, but withheld the names of forty who objected to disclosure. After allowing these forty anonymous former clients of Sidley to intervene in the proceeding, the court granted the government's motion to enforce the summons on April 28, 2004.[36]

Targeting Tax Professionals

On December 29, 2003, the IRS announced the appointment of Cono Namorato as director of the IRS Office of Professional Responsibility (OPR). The Office oversees the activities of tax professionals under Circular 230, the Treasury Department's standards for tax practice. Namorato, a veteran tax lawyer, was a partner at the tax boutique law firm of Caplin & Drysdale where former IRS Commissioner Mortimer Caplin was a name partner. Namorato started his career as an IRS agent, attending Brooklyn Law School at night, and then went into the honors program at the Justice Department. In 1978, he left the Department to join Caplin & Drysdale, where he did mostly criminal tax work.

Namorato and Everson shared the view that tax shelter practice at the time was an abomination. Up to that point, OPR had been confined to sanctioning tax practitioners for their own personal transgressions, such as the failure to file returns. Namorato believed that the office should promote the idea that tax professionals were partners with the IRS in helping ensure compliance with the tax system. In his first public remarks after being appointed, he explained that he hoped to transform OPR from a "backwater" office working on "overaged, insignificant cases" into an office that took more initiative.[37] Under Namorato, the office's size doubled, and the number of enforcement attorneys on the staff tripled.

Namorato had to convince divisions within the IRS such as the Large and Mid-Size Business Division and CID to refer cases to OPR, since they historically had regarded the office as a "black hole" where "referrals went to die." He encouraged CID to send him cases for which they couldn't meet the criminal standard of beyond a reasonable doubt, since the standard for OPR action was lower. Namorato soon learned that OPR had no summons power because its authority was not based on the tax code but on the statute setting out the features of the Treasury Department. Undaunted, he began to use Section 10.20 of Circular 230, which provided that "[a] practitioner must, on a proper and lawful request by a duly authorized officer or employee of the Internal Revenue Service, promptly submit records or information in any matter before the Internal Revenue unless the practitioner believes in good faith and on reasonable grounds that the records or information are privileged." Some members of the tax bar protested; OPR had never done anything like this before.

In the spring, the IRS announced a new Son of BOSS settlement, which IRS Commissioner Mark Everson had identified as the most widely used and problematic shelter in circulation. This offer gave investors ninety days to disclose their use of such shelters and pay the full amount of taxes and interest due. "This is the first time we're saying, 'concede 100 cents on the dollar,'" Commissioner Everson explained. According to Everson, the IRS had obtained the names of 2,000 of the estimated 5,000 taxpayers who had engaged in versions of the shelter, avoiding more than $6 billion in taxes. In addition to back taxes and interest, taxpayers who came forward would be liable for a percentage of the applicable penalties. The offer also provided no right of appeal.

Some at the IRS privately regarded the Son of BOSS initiative as a gamble because of the insistence on penalties and the elimination of an appeal. A small response by taxpayers could hurt the credibility of the agency so officials worked hard to promote the settlement through speeches and conversations with taxpayers and tax practitioners. Addressing the ABA Section of Taxation, John Klotsche, senior advisor to Everson, emphasized that the Son of BOSS shelter was especially suitable for a global settlement offer because it had a large unknown customer base, a defined factual template, and a similar tax benefit claim.[38] Responding to criticism that the IRS should not insist that participants in the settlement pay even a percentage of applicable penalties, Klotsche underscored that the agency was confident that full 40 percent penalties without any discount would be sustained in court. The taxpayers were savvy business people, he pointed out, and their reliance on promoter opinions was questionable.

The IRS gamble paid off. On July 1, 2004, it announced a "strong turnout" by taxpayers in response to the Son of BOSS settlement offer.[39] More than 1,500 taxpayers, about 85 percent of those known to the IRS, had come forward. In addition, more than three hundred previously unknown taxpayers had accepted the offer. According to the IRS, many taxpayers were involved in transactions with reported tax losses between $10 million and $50 million and that in several cases the claimed losses were more than $500 million. IRS Chief Counsel Korb sent a warning to those taxpayers who had not come forward. "[W]e plan an aggressive litigation strategy," he said. "The word is getting out that there won't be a better deal waiting if people take these cases to court." The IRS ultimately concluded that about two-thirds of the known Son of BOSS investors took advantage of the settlement and the IRS recouped about $3.2 billion as a result.[40]

Meanwhile, the Justice Department had begun criminal investigations of the tax shelter activities of Sidley Austin and Ernst & Young. The accounting firm had settled about a year earlier with the IRS, agreeing to a $15 million payment to settle its civil liability, and said that it was fully cooperating with the investigation. Observers suggested that the government likely was examining the conduct of individuals within the firm and expressed some skepticism that the government would bring an indictment against the firm not long after similar action against Arthur Andersen had led to the collapse of that company.[41] E&Y of course hoped that its earlier settlement with the IRS would dissuade the Justice Department from indicting the company.

By the fall of 2004, a consensus had emerged that tax professionals at law and accounting firms had created an industry in abusive tax shelters and that Congress needed to act. On October 24, the American Jobs Creation Act (JOBS Act) went into effect. The Act eliminated purported ambiguities about which advisors were "promoters" of tax shelters for purposes of the registration and list-keeping requirements, imposing these requirements on all material advisors who assisted with or provided advice about reportable transactions and who received fees above certain thresholds. The statute also expanded the definition of a reportable transaction to include six categories of transactions specified in the final Treasury regulations. By broadening the registration requirements, the statute potentially imposed disclosure obligations on lawyers providing legal opinions in connection with shelters.

In addition, the statute significantly increased the penalties that applied to advisors and taxpayers for failure to disclose. For the first time, the JOBS Act imposed a penalty on a taxpayer for failure to disclose a reportable transaction, regardless of whether the transaction ultimately resulted in an understatement of tax. The JOBS Act also imposed higher penalties for understatements resulting from listed transactions and reportable transactions with a significant tax avoidance purpose. In addition, it strengthened the Office of Professional Responsibility, giving it authority over the preparation of tax opinions and law firms and empowering it to obtain injunctions against practitioners who violated Circular 230 and impose monetary penalties on individual practitioners and their firms.[42]

The Prosecutors Move In

In 2005, the IRS announced two new settlement offers. In April, it gave investors in SC2, the shelter designed and promoted by KPMG to owners of S corporations, the opportunity to resolve the agency's potential claims against them. In October, about a month after the Second Circuit summarily affirmed the trial court's disallowance of tax losses in the *Long-Term Capital* case (discussed in chapter 9),[43] the IRS announced a settlement initiative for taxpayers and five additional transactions identified by the IRS.[44]

By now, the drill was familiar. The IRS expected to recoup taxes due from a significant number of taxpayers who had participated in the shelters. It then planned to use the information it obtained to go after promoters and taxpayers who had not come forward. This would be the last global settlement initiative that the IRS offered; it saw no need for any more. The agency had finally dispelled "the generalized popular impression," which had come out of the IRS Restructuring and Reform Act of 1998, that "the IRS was no longer going to enforce the law."[45]

On August 29, 2005, the U.S. Attorney's Office in Manhattan indicted R. J. Ruble and nine other individuals in connection with KPMG's tax shelter activity. (The prosecution is described in chapter 12.) Ruble was eventually convicted on ten counts of tax evasion and was sentenced to six and a half years in prison on April 1, 2009.

Earlier, the federal prosecutor's office in Manhattan had announced that it would not seek criminal charges against Sidley Austin. The announcement noted that Ruble had done most of his work at Brown & Wood, Sidley had issued no opinions for mass-marketed shelters before the merger, and most of the opinions Ruble issued after the merger were in violation of the understanding that he would provide only a small number of opinions that he had already committed to write.[46] Simultaneously, the firm reached an agreement with the IRS to pay a penalty of $39.4 million to close the investigation of its role as a shelter promoter.[47] Sidley agreed to continue to cooperate with ongoing tax shelter investigations and declared that it had strengthened its internal procedures to prevent a recurrence of rogue activity such as Ruble's.

In addition to civil and criminal government investigations, Sidley faced several lawsuits by shelter investors whose tax losses had been disallowed by the IRS. The most comprehensive catalog of litigation, contained in an article published in 2008, counted eighteen cases in which Sidley had been named as a defendant. One prominent suit was a class action against KPMG and Sidley that eventually settled for $178 million in June 2006.[48] Sidley was expected to pay about 20 percent of this figure, or $35.6 million. Under the settlement, plaintiffs received an average pay-out of between $700,000 and $750,000.

A week after the Sidley announcement, the government indicted for-mer E&Y employees Robert Coplan, Richard Shapiro, Martin Nissen-baum, and Brian Vaughn on eight charges relating to their tax shelter work, including conspiracy to defraud the IRS, tax evasion, making false statements to the IRS, and impeding and impairing the lawful functioning of the IRS.[49] Charles Bolton, who owned investment companies that ex-ecuted E&Y shelter transactions, was also charged and pled guilty before the trial. David Smith was charged but did not appear for trial, becoming a fugitive from justice. The firm was not charged, although the govern-ment made no announcement at the time about its fate one way or the other.

At trial, former E&Y employee Belle Six took the stand against Brian Vaughn and the other VIPER participants, providing critical testimony about how the defendants had presented CDS and CDS Add-On as le-gitimate business transactions. Six had earlier pled guilty to conspiracy to defraud the government and had already paid a penalty in excess of $13 million, the amount she netted from her tax shelter activities after taxes.[50] Six's intense relationship with Vaughn had finally ended seven years ear-lier. At trial, Six told the jury, "Once I finally got him out of my head, I didn't have any emotions personally anymore."[51]

The defendants argued unsuccessfully that leaders in E&Y's national tax office had known and approved of their activities. All four were found guilty of criminal tax fraud and offenses related to their efforts to mislead the IRS. In January 2010, the judge imposed prison sentences ranging in length from one year and eight months for Vaughn to three years for Coplan. Judge Stein added an unusual provision to the terms of Coplan's and Nissenbaum's supervised release after serving their prison sentences. Both men were required to warn about the dangers of misleading the In-ternal Revenue Service in speeches to lawyers, accounting firms, and bar groups, including, possibly, the ABA Section of Taxation. Stein explained the requirement in Coplan's sentencing by saying that Coplan should "set forth his experiences and explain to these people the dangers of mislead-ing the IRS, the dangers of going along with what everyone else is doing, the dangers of thinking all you are doing is your job . . . but realizing that, at some point, it tips over into criminal liability."[52]

The convictions ultimately represented a mixed victory for the government. In late 2012, the U.S. Court of Appeals for the Second Circuit reversed the convictions of Nissenbaum and Shapiro on the grounds that there was insufficient evidence to connect them to the tax shelter activities at the firm.

In February 2013, E&Y finally entered into a non-prosecution agreement with the Justice Department in connection with its tax shelter activities. Under the agreement, which covered its involvement in CDS, COBRA, CDS Add-On, and PICO, the firm agreed to pay a $123 million fine, representing the fees from these transactions. According to the statements of facts, the firm's involvement in tax shelters was concentrated in the Strategic Individual Solutions Group (SISG), which was "primarily responsible for supervising and coordinating the marketing, implementation and defense of E&Y's tax shelter products." (The group, initially known under the acronym VIPER, is described in chapter 6.)[53]

As the statement of facts described, in 2003 the firm had disbanded the SISG and settled a penalty promoter examination with the IRS, paying a $15 million fine. Since that time, E&Y had "implemented extensive changes to its governance and compliance procedures." The firm had also substantially increased the number of its "legal and tax quality and risk management personnel." The firm also created a Quality and Integrity Program, which required all tax professionals to enter data regarding a range of tax engagement matters for monitoring and to certify compliance with the program and the listing and registration requirements in the tax code. At the time, the IRS had praised the program as a model for an effective compliance program. E&Y had also implemented a series of procedures and practices to ensure legal and ethical conduct among its tax professionals and a series of mechanisms firm-wide, including an Ethics Oversight Board and an anonymous hotline to allow employees to raise concerns.[54] The statement of facts noted the timing of these changes, which occurred in response to the Permanent Subcommittee on Investigations' investigation into the tax shelter industry in 2003.

The statement of facts emphasized that, unlike at some of the other accounting firms involved in the tax shelter industry, the senior management at E&Y did not participate in criminal wrongdoing and suggests that tax leaders were unaware of SISG's activities. For example, it describes how SISG had hidden the similarities between CDS Add-On and COBRA, which the firm had already decided to discontinue, and created a cover story to give CDS Add-On a business purpose. (This incident is described in chapter 6.) Absent from the statement is an account of what tax leaders in the firm's National Tax Department had envisioned when they created the tax shelter team in 1998 or how the group's activities, which generated substantial fees, had occurred under their watch.

Closing the Book

Beginning in early 2009, a string of BDO partners pled guilty to tax fraud in plea agreements with the U.S. Attorney's Office in Manhattan. On February 13, Michael Kerekes pled guilty to conspiring to defraud the United States and tax evasion. On March 17, Adrian Dicker pled guilty to the same two charges. On June 3, Charles Bee pled guilty to conspiracy to defraud the United States, tax evasion, and giving material false deposition testimony. Shortly after Bee's plea, on June 9, the prosecutor announced the indictment of Denis Field and Robert Greisman of BDO, along with five other people: Jenkens & Gilchrist lawyers Paul Daugerdas, Erwin Mayer, and Donna Guerin, and Deutsche Bank employees R. Craig Brubaker and David Parse. A month later, on July 9, Greisman pled guilty to conspiring to defraud the United States, tax evasion, and corruptly endeavoring to obstruct administration of the tax laws. More than a year later, on October 19, 2010, Mayer pled guilty to conspiracy and tax evasion. As part of his agreement, Mayer agreed to forfeit his two residences and various bank and investment accounts worth more than $10 million.

Just before the end of 2010, the Justice Department closed out its criminal investigation of Deutsche Bank by announcing a non-prosecution agreement under which the bank would pay more than $553 million for its involvement in tax shelter activity from 1996 to 2002. The government said that this amount reflected the fees that Deutsche Bank earned from its involvement in tax shelter activity, the amount of taxes and interest the IRS was unable to collect from taxpayers, and a penalty in connection with the IRS's examination of the bank as a shelter promoter. In return, the Justice Department agreed to refrain from prosecuting the bank for conspiracy to defraud the United States, tax evasion, and involvement in the preparation and filing of false and fraudulent tax returns.

The settlement indicated that Deutsche Bank had "participated in approximately 1,300 deals involving more than 2,100 customers, and implemented over 2,300 financial transactions related to these shelters."[55] This reflected involvement in fifteen different abusive tax shelters. According to the government, the bank had "unlawfully, willfully, and knowingly" participated in shelter activity by "assisting tax shelter promoters to structure financial transactions that would be used to generate substantial tax benefits (generally losses), by preparing financial transaction documents that would be used by others to mislead the IRS regarding the true nature of the transactions, and by executing the transactions for the taxpayer clients of the promoters."[56] Customers used the transactions in which Deutsche Bank was involved to claim $29.3 billion in unwarranted tax benefits, resulting in the evasion of $5.9 billion in taxes on ordinary income and capital gains.[57]

The trial of Denis Field and the Jenkens & Gilchrist and Deutsche Bank defendants began on March 1, 2011. (The proceedings as they relate to the Jenkens defendants are described in chapter 12.) During trial testimony, Greisman, Dicker, Bee, and Shanbrom painted a detailed portrait of Field as someone who was deeply involved in the activities of the Tax Solutions Group and who monitored it closely. They described Field's ongoing participation in important decisions regarding the group, such as its formation, its compensation structure, the approval of the Treasury short sales and short options strategy, discussions with some members of the group who expressed reservations about the shelters, the significance of Notice 2000-44, and BDO's responses to requests for information from the IRS. Bee testified that he discussed with Field in New York in late 2000 the possibility of criminal penalties for themselves and for the firm because of the shelter activity. Field had responded that the IRS didn't have the resources to handle all the cases that were arising so the firm should just stonewall the government.[58] Univer, BDO's former general counsel, also testified and described how Field had never shared the Skadden memo with the firm's board or other members of the Tax Solutions Group and how Field had represented to others at BDO that Skadden had approved the activities of the Tax Solutions Group.

In late May 2011, all the defendants except Brubaker were found guilty. A little over a year later, however, the court vacated the convictions of Field, Daugerdas, and Guerin in response to a motion for a new trial based on juror misconduct. The judge denied David Parse's motion for a new trial on the grounds that his lawyers suspected, but failed to alert the court, about problems with the juror. Donna Guerin subsequently pled guilty to one count of conspiracy and one count of tax evasion. Each count carried a maximum of five years in jail. Guerin agreed to forfeit $1.6 million. A second trial against Field and Daugerdas resulted in a mixed victory for the government. Daugerdas was found guilty, but Field was acquitted of all charges. The jury may have concluded that Field, who was busy managing the firm, was too far removed from the tax shelter activity to know that the shelters were abusive.

In June 2012, the Justice Department and IRS reached a settlement with BDO Seidman. The firm admitted that it had helped generate $6.5 billion in fraudulent tax losses through its promotion of abusive tax shelters from 1997 to 2003, for which it had earned $200 million in fees. The estimated tax loss from this activity was $1.3 billion. The firm entered into a deferred prosecution agreement with the Justice Department under which a charge of tax fraud conspiracy against it would be dismissed in December if the firm continued to cooperate in the government's criminal investigation. BDO also agreed to pay a $50 million penalty, $34.4 million of which would go to the IRS for the firm's violation of shelter registration requirements.[59]

The government also successfully concluded criminal prosecutions of several lawyers in private practice who had done work in connection with abusive tax shelters. On November 2, 2005, Graham Taylor, who had practiced at four different major law firms in San Francisco,[60] was indicted with five other people for conspiracy to commit tax fraud, wire fraud, and mail fraud, and for tax evasion in connection with a shelter that Taylor helped design known as Hybrid. The shelter involved the generation of fictitious currency transaction losses, false insurance expense deductions, and fraudulent capital losses that concealed $60 million in income and resulted in the evasion of $20 million in taxes.[61] The indictment alleged that the scheme began in April 1994 and continued through late April 2005. The other defendants included three accountants, another lawyer, and an investment broker.

On January 24, 2008, the Justice Department announced that Taylor and two other defendants had pled guilty to conspiracy to commit tax fraud. On February 13, 2008, defendant Dennis Evanson, a lawyer, was convicted in connection with the scheme of conspiring to defraud the United States and to commit mail and wire fraud. His investment banker codefendant was acquitted on all charges. Evanson was later sentenced to ten years in prison and ordered to pay $2.7 million for his role in the shelter. Meanwhile, Taylor agreed to testify on behalf of the government in the trial of the four E&Y former employees that began in New York in March 2009. He was sentenced on October 29, 2009, to three years' probation and a fine of $125,000. He resigned from the New York bar in December of that year.

In the fall of 2008 the Justice Department announced that Peter Cinquegrani, a former Arnold & Porter lawyer, had pled guilty to a criminal information charging him with conspiring to commit tax fraud, aiding and abetting tax evasion, and aiding in the submission of false and fraudulent documents to the IRS, all in connection with his work on PICO tax shelters. The government announced the same day that it had reached a settlement with Arnold & Porter, which paid a civil promoter penalty for its failure to comply with tax shelter registration requirements and its participation in the organization of listed transactions. Cinquegrani was sentenced to three years' probation.[62] Cinquegrani apologized to the court, explaining that "I think my desire to be a big shot, [to] feel that I was part of the in-crowd in the tax community, overrode my conscience."[63] In imposing the sentence, the judge noted Cinquegrani's cooperation with the government, which included explaining the PICO shelter to investigators. Earlier, Cinquegrani had been disbarred by the D.C. Court of Appeals based on his affidavit of consent to disbarment.[64]

A few months after Cinquegrani's plea, the Justice Department announced that Jay Gordon, former head of the tax practice at Greenberg Traurig, pled guilty to a two-count criminal information that charged him with conspiracy to defraud the United States in connection with the provision of shelter opinion letters, as well as with tax evasion with respect to his own tax liability. During this same period, John Campbell, formerly a lawyer at Miller Canfield, pled guilty to conspiracy to defraud the United States for his role in selling abusive tax shelters to his clients. His client, Oskar Rene Poch, pled guilty to corruptly endeavoring to obstruct the administration of the tax laws.

Campbell was sentenced to five years in prison, while Poch, who had cooperated with the government's investigation and testified at the trial of the promoters, was sentenced to one year of probation and restitution and fines totaling more than $300,000.

In June 2009, Los Angeles attorney Matthew Krane was indicted by a grand jury in Seattle, along with Jeffrey Greenstein and Charles Wilk of the investment company Quellos, for their role in an abusive tax shelter scheme on behalf of Krane's client billionaire Haim Saban.[65] He subsequently pled guilty to tax evasion in connection with a $36 million fee he received from Quellos for referring Saban to the company and to applying for a passport under a false name. In June 2011, he was sentenced to three years in prison. Krane also was ordered to return $17.9 million in fees to Saban (which Saban donated to charity) and to pay $23.1 million in back taxes.

Reinforcing Deterrence

Several important legislative initiatives occurred to strengthen the government's hand in combatting tax shelters. A number of statutes have made it financially and personally riskier for taxpayers to engage in shelter transactions, and have increased the stigma for doing so. In 2006, Congress, recognizing the role of private enforcement of tax provisions, amended the moribund tax informant program, "breath[ing] life into the statute."[66] The amendments created a centralized Whistleblower Office inside the IRS to process tips from informants about tax issues in the workplace. It also increased the awards that whistleblowers could receive for exposing tax law violations. Since 2008, the office has collected in aggregate $1,467,259,959 through the program and awarded $180,332,920 to informants.[67]

Congress also codified the economic substance doctrine in March 2010.[68] Section 7701(o) of the Internal Revenue Code now provides that a transaction will be treated for tax purposes as having economic substance if it passes a "two-part conjunctive test."[69] That test requires that a transaction "(A) . . . changes in a meaningful way (apart from Federal income tax effects) the taxpayer's economic position and (B) the taxpayer has a substantial purpose (apart from Federal income tax effects) for entering into such transaction." The statute provides that the determination of when the doctrine is relevant to a transaction "shall be made in the same manner as if [the legislation] had never been enacted." Consistent with this language, the IRS indicated at the time of the statute's enactment that it would "continue to rely on relevant case law under the common-law economic substance doctrine in applying" each part of the test.[70] There had always been significant differences of opinion as to whether codification of the doctrine would serve as a significant deterrent to abusive shelters.[71] Placement of the doctrine in the Code at least meant that its use would no longer be dependent on courts' acceptance of its legitimacy.

In addition to codifying the economic substance test, Congress amended the penalty scheme to create a "strict liability" standard when tax benefits are disallowed based on lack of economic substance. Under the new statute the penalty is 20 percent of the tax on the understatement if the relevant facts are disclosed in the return and 40 percent if no disclosure is made. The effect is to prevent taxpayers from relying on a tax opinion to avoid an accuracy-related penalty for a tax shelter transaction.[72]

The shift to strict liability, in cases where tax benefits are disallowed due to lack of economic substance, eliminated the market for legal opinions intended to function as "get out of jail free" cards. Endorsing a "strict liability" approach back in 1999, the New State Bar Association Tax Section had explained:

[A]s a result of enactment of such a regime, . . . taxpayers [are] forced to incur a real risk from entering into such transactions, and [are] induced to seek balanced, well-reasoned tax advice concerning such transactions rather than tax opinions intended principally to serve as insurance against the imposition of penalties.[73]

Other statutory initiatives have been effective in reducing the corporate appetite for shelters. These approaches shape the behavior of corporate taxpayers because they complement traditional reporting and disclosure requirements that already apply to corporations. According to one report on corporate tax planning,

there has been an environmental change in how companies approach tax planning in order to mitigate risk exposure. Companies are now more concerned than they have ever been about the diminution of their "brand value" arising from the disclosure of breakdowns in corporate governance processes, including those related to tax transactions.[74]

The result is what tax scholar Susan Morse has called "the new public corporation tax shelter compliance norm."[75] Morse notes that, in addition to IRS and Justice Department enforcement efforts, measures that have contributed to this norm include Sarbanes-Oxley (SOX), which requires publicly traded companies to institute internal control systems. SOX also limits he provision of audit and tax services by the same firm, and imposes other constraints that have expanded and altered the dynamics of the tax planning group in corporations.[76]

A second measure that has decreased the demand for aggressive shelters is Financial Accounting Standards Board Interpretation No. 48 (FIN 48), an official interpretation of accounting rules issued by the Financial Accounting Standards Board. Enacted in the wake of the corporate accounting scandals at the turn of the century, FIN 48 contains two requirements that have dampened the corporate appetite for tax shelters. First, it requires that the incorporation of a claimed tax benefit in a company's financial disclosures be premised on a conclusion that the tax position underlying the claimed benefit more likely than not will be sustained by a court. In addition, FIN 48 requires that claimed tax benefits that are not being incorporated into a company's financial statements be disclosed nonetheless. Under this second requirement, companies are obligated to disclose aggressive tax strategies that do not meet the more-likely-than-not standard.[77]

Beginning in the early 2000s, the IRS and the Justice Department effectively combined forces to identify and punish some of the major organizations and individuals involved in creating and selling abusive tax shelters. IRS administrative summonses, Justice Department enforcement actions, and John Doe summonses generated considerable information on both taxpayers and promoters. IRS settlement initiatives also provided information about shelter transactions that served as the basis for additional enforcement actions against promoters. Drawing on this information, the Justice Department launched criminal investigations of prominent accounting and law firms as well as of professionals working in them, subsequently indicting a number of individuals involved, obtaining guilty pleas and settlements, and securing a handful of convictions. All along, some commentators had insisted that the law governing tax shelters was too uncertain to support criminal prosecution. Through indictments and trials, the government succeeded in recasting the participants' actions as abetting tax fraud. As the government showed, the issue was not, in the great majority of instances, that participants had genuine doubts as to the propriety of their activities. To the contrary, the tax professionals involved were well aware that the shelters they were promoting were abusive, but went to extraordinary lengths to hide the true purpose of the transactions and create the appearance that they were legitimate investment strategies.

The government initiatives ushered in a new climate for tax shelters. As chapter 12 describes, this new climate had profound implications for KPMG and Jenkens & Gilchrist, the two firms most deeply caught up in the tax shelter industry.

12

Endgame: KPMG and Jenkens

KPMG

KPMG's extensive tax shelter operations began to catch the eye of the IRS in 2000. By the end of that year, the agency was aware that the accounting firm had been involved in both OPIS and FLIP shelters. In October 2001, the IRS informed KPMG that it was beginning an audit, and in December it issued an information document request to the firm. KPMG claimed that client confidentiality concerns prevented it from providing the documents described in the request but indicated that the firm would comply with a request for documents set forth in an administrative summons. The IRS issued summonses seeking investor lists and three different sets of documents in January, March, and May of 2002.

KPMG acknowledged that the identity of investors was not privileged but insisted that a large number of documents were protected from disclosure based on attorney-client and statutory accountant-client privileges. The firm was also slow in producing unprivileged documents that were responsive to the summonses. One internal email acknowledged that although lists of some investors in various transactions had been provided to the IRS, "not all client names were turned over for each of [the] solutions."[1] A partner who read this email, which had been widely distributed, forwarded it to Jeff Stein with a cover note explaining that she was "watching [his] back." "Given the sensitivity of this situation, should we be putting all this in print?," she wondered.[2]

In July 2002 the Department of Justice responded to KPMG's recalcitrance by filing a motion to enforce the summonses. In an accompanying declaration, the IRS agent in charge of the audit stated that an analysis of only the incomplete investor lists that KPMG had provided with respect to FLIP/OPIS and BLIPS indicated that investors had claimed $5.8 billion in phony losses.[3] He estimated the loss in revenue from BLIPS alone to be more than $1.28 billion. The agent also stated that the IRS had received a letter from a confidential source indicating that KPMG was continuing to develop and market dozens of possibly abusive shelters without registering them. "The information developed in this examination thus far," he stated, "leads me to conclude that KPMG is actively flaunting the statutes and regulations requiring transparency in the development, organization, and marketing of tax shelters."[4] The Justice Department petition and exhibits came to 376 pages and provided a detailed account of tax shelter operations inside a major accounting firm.

In the meantime, clients whose transactions were being scrutinized by the IRS were starting to bring litigation against their former advisors. In April 2002, Joseph Jacoboni filed an action alleging that KPMG had defrauded him by claiming that the FLIP shelter it sold him was a legitimate tax technique.[5] An entrepreneur, Jacoboni had grown a technical support company into a multimillion-dollar business, which he sold for more than $30 million dollars in 1997. When First Union, his long-time bank, saw the size of his gain, it immediately put Jacobini in touch with a tax partner at KPMG, who pitched him FLIP as an investment strategy that would allow him to shield the gains from his sale. Completely in the dark about how the transaction worked but repeatedly assured that it was "bullet-proof," Jacoboni paid $2.4 million to the firm to do a FLIP deal.[6] When it became clear that the IRS was going to disallow the tax benefits, Jacoboni, represented by Campbell Killefer and Damon Wright of the Venable law firm in Washington, D.C., sued KPMG and the other advisors on the transaction.

Soon afterward, the Perez brothers, founders of a health care business, brought suit against KPMG in connection with their purchase of FLIP.[7] The Perez brothers had approached Edmundo Ramirez, a trial lawyer based in McAllen, Texas, to represent them. When Ramirez first talked to tax specialists about the case, they had discouraged him from pursuing it, emphasizing that the case would turn on complex tax questions with no clear answers. Untangling the technical details of FLIP and figuring out their significance for a possible claim against the firm would be a daunting proposition. But as Ramirez thought about the story his clients had told him, he realized that KPMG and the other promoters involved had violated their obligations as trusted advisors to their clients. FLIP's marketers had failed to look out for the brothers' interests and misrepresented the legality of the transaction. Consistent with this intuition, Ramirez's complaint alleged that the accounting firm had committed fraud, malpractice, and breach of its fiduciary duties.

KPMG fought these first lawsuits aggressively, asserting initially that Jacoboni and the Perez brothers had to prove in court that the transaction didn't work before they could make a claim against the firm. As the cases progressed, the firm shifted to a different defense, contending that by purchasing the shelters their former clients were complicit in any wrongdoing by the firm.

Neither defense strategy ultimately succeeded. Since these were the first shelter lawsuits against KPMG, Ramirez and the Venable lawyers did not know what to expect and decided to collaborate, sharing information, documents, and strategies. The lawyers were particularly effective in using their different professional styles—Killefer and Wright were partners in an East Coast Am Law 100 law firm, while Ramirez was the founding partner of a small firm located just north of the Rio Grande—to obtain key documents and solicit useful admissions during depositions of KPMG witnesses. As discovery progressed, it became evident that FLIP's developers had worked closely from the outset to develop the strategy and that any claim of independence among them was a sham. It also became clear that internally the firm had had much greater doubts about the shelter's legality than it had represented to its clients.

Within a year of the first lawsuit, KPMG had been sued in at least eight other cases—a fact reported in a *Wall Street Journal* article under the headline "Lawsuits over Tax Shelters Suggest a Hard Sell by KPMG."[8] Eventually, lawyers representing the firm's former clients were successful in obtaining favorable settlements on behalf of their clients. KPMG, for its part, was able to avoid the additional negative publicity that would come from a trial.

A Whistleblower

The government's efforts and private lawsuits received a big boost with the appearance of a second whistleblower at KPMG. Unlike an earlier anonymous informer who provided information to the IRS, Michael

Hamersley eventually went public with his charges against KPMG. Even before that point, he played a critical role in helping Congress uncover details about the tax shelter industry.

A 1995 Georgetown law school graduate, Hamersley had come to KPMG after working briefly at Ernst & Young.[9] After graduation, Hamersley had accepted a position at E&Y instead of a traditional law firm because the accounting firm, with a corporate client base many times the size of a law firm, offered unique opportunities for developing high-level tax expertise. Hamersley had earned an MBA before law school, and E&Y offered him an opportunity to use his business background and develop a highly specialized tax niche. Starting salaries for lawyers at accounting firms, which had once lagged significantly behind those at law firms, were also catching up.

Hamersley joined E&Y's National Tax Department, specializing in tax issues relating to mergers and acquisitions (M&A). Soon after he started, he began to notice changes in the provision of tax services toward what he calls the "productizing" of tax. In the late 1990s, E&Y, like other major accounting firms, realized that developing standardized tax products could be an effective strategy to serve its many similarly situated clients. To Hamersley, the efficiency gains were obvious. Complex processes, such as analyzing the acquisition costs of a company, benefited from standardization. After a few years, Hamersley moved over to KPMG, where he hoped to do both product and client-based work.

As a junior person in KPMG's Washington National Tax office, Hamersley was not exposed to the discussions surrounding BLIPS and other tax shelters. He sometimes saw a Tax Product Alert about a new product or heard a description but he assumed that even the most technically aggressive products—that is, those that heavily shaded the law to reach a favorable result—could be implemented legally. It did not occur to Hamersley, who deferred to the expertise of his senior colleagues, that the firm might sign off on transactions with knowledge that material facts related to whether the transactions had economic substance were being omitted, concealed, or misrepresented.[10]

In 2000, Hamersley moved to the KPMG Los Angeles field office. He was considered a rising star at the firm and had been offered a promotion to senior management if he relocated. Higher-ups assured him that, if things continued on course, he would be made a partner within two years and would eventually take over the direction of the Los Angeles M&A tax practice.[11] Delighted, Hamersley and his wife moved across the country.

In Hamersley's new workplace, he was regularly exposed to tax shelter activity. He was surrounded by members of the firm's Stratecon practice, which had been established to develop and market tax strategies to corporate clients. As Hamersley continued to work on client service matters, he began to hear about details of corporate tax shelters being promoted by Stratecon. At first, Hamersley assumed that the aggressive salesmanship was a reflection of the "Wild West" atmosphere of the office. Over time, though, he began to realize that the focus on marketing tax shelters came from the firm's senior tax leadership.[12]

Client service tax partners in the L.A. office, who were under significant pressure to give Stratecon access to their clients, occasionally showed Hamersley the descriptions and legal opinions on tax products. Hamersley did not hesitate to voice his concerns, even though he was advised on at least one occasion not to be so vocal in his criticisms if he wanted to advance to partner. Over the next two years, he managed to avoid direct involvement in tax products, but—not one to stay quiet—persisted in raising questions about their legality.[13]

Hamersley was especially concerned about the firm's practice of selling highly aggressive tax shelters to audit clients and allowing them to include the tax benefits on their financial statements. KPMG's tax shelter promoters would team with audit partners, who received financial bonuses for facilitating sales to their clients. Frequently, audit partners would sign off on the financial statement treatment of the tax shelter based solely on a tax opinion provided by the tax partner who had developed or marketed the transaction. Hamersley was concerned that this practice compromised auditor independence since the audit partner was not relying on an objective evaluation of the tax shelter but on the opinion of the same person who was marketing the product.[14]

In 2002, Hamersley, who had always received exceptional performance evaluations, was due for partnership. His game plan was to lie low, make partner, and leave the firm as soon as possible. His wife was pregnant with their first child. That spring, he was asked to become involved in the audit of a Fortune 100 company, a former client of Arthur Andersen that had engaged KPMG to reaudit its financials to shore up investor confidence in the wake of Andersen's collapse. Hamersley was requested to review several highly aggressive tax strategies that would allow the company to claim a $450 million loss. After studying the transactions, he concluded that the strategies didn't work. Under audit standards, unless KPMG reached a "should" level of certainty—an opinion that there was at least a 70 percent likelihood that if the IRS challenged the transaction, a court would uphold the tax treatment favored by the taxpayer—the client would have to set aside reserves for a contingent liability. This meant restating its earnings without the tax benefits the aggressive transaction was supposed to produce.

As the client put pressure on KPMG to arrive at a "should" level of certainty, KPMG higher-ups insisted that Hamersley alter his analysis. After Hamersley made clear that his assessment was not going to change, he realized that his future at the firm was at risk. At the same time, he thought that he had extricated himself from the immediate problem of not being able to "get comfortable" with the client's position. His game plan was to immerse himself in his other work and start looking for an exit strategy.

Other tax partners at KPMG were able to arrive at a "should" level of certainty and signed off on the company's financial statements in the summer of 2002. Shortly afterward, the partner to whom Hamersley reported asked him to write an opinion supporting the firm's treatment of the highly aggressive tax strategy. Hamersley protested that he had arrived at a different view and showed the partner a PowerPoint presentation he had created to explain his analysis. According to Hamersley, when the partner saw the presentation, he instructed Hamersley to remove the negative information it contained.[15]

In response to Arthur Andersen's destruction of Enron audit documents, Congress had strengthened the penalties that applied to destroying audit work papers. Hamersley worried that if he followed instructions and altered his memo, he could be subject to criminal prosecution. He consulted with a private attorney and concluded that it was time to contact government officials.[16] After he watched Senator Carl Levin preside over hearings that led up to the enactment of the Sarbanes-Oxley Act, Hamersley decided to contact the staff of the Senate's Permanent Subcommittee on Investigations (PSI). When KPMG became suspicious that Hamersley was cooperating with the government, it put him on administrative leave, cut off his access to his clients, email, and files, and forbade him from coming to the office.[17] A rumor circulated in the firm that Hamersley was suffering from mental problems. While on leave during the next twelve months, Hamersley helped PSI staff members to understand the various tax strategies KPMG had promoted and to focus the investigation on the most egregious conduct.

Help from the Hill

In October 2003, a year after Hammersley contacted the PSI, he made his first public appearance at Senate Finance Committee hearings on abusive tax shelters. Hamersley testified: "A culture existed [at KPMG] in which intimidation and coercion were often used to foster the abusive tax environment. Tax professionals who 'played the game' and fully embraced the promotion of abusive tax shelters were rewarded handsomely. However," he underscored, "those who were vocal in raising concerns about abusive tax shelters were stifled and reprimanded and their opportunities for advancement were limited."[18]

As it turned out, Hamersley's testimony at the Finance Committee was a warm-up for the main event. A month later, Senators Norman Coleman and Carl Levin presided over two days of hearings of the Permanent Subcommittee on Investigations on the tax shelter industry. The PSI had been investigating the industry for over a year with Hamersley's assistance behind the scenes. After collecting thousands of pages of documents and interviewing numerous witnesses, the committee focused on shelters promoted by KPMG while also emphasizing that many other similar shelters were being marketed by major accounting firms, law firms, and investment boutiques.

The PSI heard twenty-one witnesses, six of them from KPMG. Of the KPMG witnesses, only Mark Watson, the tax partner who tried to prevent the firm from approving BLIPS, admitted to any doubt about the validity of any shelter, testifying that he "was never comfortable that BLIPS provided a reasonable opportunity to make a reasonable pre-tax profit."[19] The other KPMG witnesses, however, presented a unified front, insisting that the firm had not engaged in any wrongdoing. The thrust of their position was that "the tax laws are complicated and often ambiguous and unsettled" and that KPMG's shelters conformed to the technical requirements of the law during a period marked by a "far different regulatory and marketplace environment."[20] According to its statement, KPMG had now entered a new era in which it was guided not simply by legality but also by "whether any action could in any way risk the reputations of KPMG or our clients."[21]

Senator Levin was exasperated with KPMG's responses. At one point he asked Jeffrey Eischeid, the partner who had taken over the tax shelter group in 1999, whether FLIP, OPIS, and BLIPS weren't "primarily tax-reduction strategies that have financial transactions tied to them to give them a colorable business purpose?"[22] Eischeid denied this contention, suggesting that they were "investment strategies" that had "a significant income tax component to them."[23] Levin then proceeded to quote from several documents, including client presentations by KPMG's tax shelter team, that explicitly stated that FLIP, OPIS, and BLIPS were tax elimination techniques. Confronted with these documents, Eischeid continued to insist that these were investment strategies that had tax minimization as one "attribute."[24] Pressed to admit that the transactions were intended to eliminate taxes, Eischeid, after a moment of silence, replied that he did not know how to change his answer. "Try an honest answer," Senator Levin retorted.[25] Eischeid subsequently defended his conduct, expressing surprise that his ethics had been questioned.[26] Senator Levin did manage to obtain one concession from one of the representatives of KPMG when Richard Smith, the vice chair of Tax Services, acknowledged that the firm encouraged its professionals to design and sell tax products.[27]

At the close of the hearings, the Permanent Subcommittee on Investigations issued a Minority Staff Report that contained a discussion of the evidence that the committee had collected, a set of proposed findings, and detailed case studies of the BLIPS and SC2 shelter transactions marketed by KPMG.[28] The PSI also released thousands of pages of documents it had collected. These provided a detailed window into the activities of KPMG, Brown & Wood, and the financial advisors and banks that worked with them. In the meantime, Hamersley filed a lawsuit against KPMG, contending that the firm had retaliated against him for whistleblowing and defamed him by starting the rumors about his mental health. After the suit was settled, Hamersley joined the California Franchise Board, in a newly created department dedicated to investigating and prosecuting abusive tax shelters.

Cleaning House at KPMG

On November 18, 2003, several thousand KPMG partners were gathered in Orlando, Florida, for their annual meeting. Instead of taking advantage of the warm weather, many stayed inside to follow the PSI hearings being broadcast on C-Span. As they watched, Senators Levin and Coleman demonstrated that FLIP, OPIS, and BLIPS were not, contrary to the firm's claims, investment strategies, but transactions whose primary purpose was reducing or eliminating taxes. During the questioning, partners in the tax group, including the vice chair of Tax Services, had been exposed as liars—in front of Congress no less. As one KPMG partner described the experience, "It was like watching your own house burn down."[29]

A few weeks later, Eugene D. O'Kelly, the chair of KPMG, called a meeting of the firm's board, at which he announced that the firm was taking "a new direction." Recognizing that the firm's very survival was at stake, its highest leaders had decided, finally, to stop defying the government. As one board member noted: "We came to the party late. We drank more, and we stayed longer."[30] At the end of 2003, O'Kelly announced that Jeff Stein, who had been appointed deputy chair for Tax in 2002, was resigning. Jeffrey Eischeid, who had been in charge of Personal Financing Planning's tax products group, was removed as a partner and put on administrative leave. Richard Smith, vice chair of Tax Services, was reassigned to "unspecified new duties." Two tax partners believed not to be associated with the firm's tax shelter group, James Brasher and John Chopack, were appointed to replace, respectively, Smith and Stein.[31]

In early 2004, KPMG began to make systematic efforts to change the focus of its tax services, dismantling the organizational structure devoted to developing and mass marketing generic shelters to individuals and emphasizing the provision of advice tailored to a client's specific circumstances. It also started to disband the Innovative Strategies and Stratecon groups. Approximately half the members who had been most deeply involved in designing and marketing shelters soon left the firm. To implement more effective controls, the firm created the positions of vice chair for Risk and Regulatory Matters, which reported directly to the firm's CEO, and partner in charge of Risk and Regulatory Matters for Tax, which reported to the new vice chair. The partner in charge of Risk and Regulatory Matters for Tax was given authority to determine the parameters of acceptable tax services without interference from the business units.[32]

KPMG hoped that by cleaning house it would put its difficulties with the government behind it. It was wrong. In February 2004, it received more bad news. A grand jury was investigating its tax shelter activities, raising the specter that the firm would be indicted. The *Wall Street Journal* reported that thirty former and current employees were subjects of the criminal probe.[33] At around the same time, the IRS listed SC2, the shelter KPMG had aggressively marketed to S corporations through the Stratecon group, as abusive.[34] Meanwhile, PBS's *Frontline* aired an hour-long exposé on abusive tax shelters, which featured Joseph Jacoboni, one of the firm's clients who had bought FLIP, and Mike Hamersley, the whistleblower who had appeared before Congress in October.

As publicity mounted, KPMG became increasingly concerned about the prospect of criminal charges. Soon after the PSI hearings in November 2003, KPMG had switched lawyers, dismissing Wilkie Farr and Spalding and King, which had represented the firm in the shelter investigation by the U.S. Department of Justice and before the IRS. KPMG retained Robert Bennett of Skadden, Arps, who had a reputation for helping companies avoid prosecution.[35] Represented by Bennett, the firm began to make intense efforts to cooperate with the government.

At the urging of the government, KPMG limited the amount of legal fees that it was willing to cover for partners and employees under investigation. It had been a long-standing practice for KPMG to pay the legal fees of employees in connection with employment-related matters. In 2003, however, the government had adopted a policy, described in a memo written by then Attorney General Larry Thompson, which took into account whether a company paid legal fees in determining whether the company was cooperating fully in an investigation. Consistent with this policy, federal prosecutors in the KPMG matter emphasized that they expected the firm not to pay the fees of employees who failed to cooperate in the investigation. Eager to avoid indictment itself, the firm set a cap of $400,000 on legal fees and made clear that it would immediately cut off fees for employees who asserted their right not to incriminate themselves under the Fifth Amendment, refused to participate in interviews, "failed to be prompt, complete or truthful," or otherwise failed to cooperate in the investigation.[36] The firm also informed employees that it would cease paying legal fees for any employee indicted by the government.[37] The decision to limit attorneys' fees was a significant departure from KPMG's prior practice and that of most large companies at the time.

In the spring of 2004, KPMG's board also agreed to waive any claims of privilege and work product the firm had in connection with communications with its inside counsel related to the development and marketing of shelters. The firm's waiver was an attempt to signal cooperation, but covered only a small portion of the documents sought by the IRS's summons. KPMG continued to insist that a significant number of documents sought in the enforcement action by the Justice Department were not subject to disclosure because they were privileged communications between the firm and its clients.

In October 2003, a special master appointed by the judge in the Justice Department enforcement action against KPMG had recommended to Judge Thomas F. Hogan that the firm be ordered to disclose most of the documents it was withholding.[38] In May 2004 Judge Hogan issued a scathing opinion that invited the Justice Department to charge KPMG with obstruction of justice. In reviewing KPMG's conduct in response to the government's enforcement action, Judge Hogan found that the firm was asserting the privilege in bad faith.[39] "The Court comes to the inescapable conclusion," he wrote, "that KPMG has taken steps since the IRS investigation began that have been designed to hide its tax shelter activities."[40]

Recognizing that such a charge was not to be made lightly, the court went on to catalog each event that cumulatively showed that KPMG was intentionally attempting to avoid its legal obligations to disclose information to the IRS. The court found that KPMG falsely claimed in response to the IRS's summons that its role in the SOS tax shelter was limited to preparing tax returns, when in fact it was involved in marketing and implementing the shelter. The court also found that KPMG had delayed in providing the names of purchasers of SOS in an attempt to allow the statute of limitations to run on the IRS's claims against those clients.

The court was "most troubled" by evidence that the firm had incorrectly described documents to support "dubious claims" of privilege.[41] In particular, the firm had characterized a number of emails among members of the tax shelter group as involving particularized advice to individual clients when these documents failed to refer to any specific clients at all. The court also criticized KPMG's attempt to characterize drafts of Brown & Wood opinion letters and email discussions of the business relationship between the firm and R. J. Ruble as involving legal advice to particular clients. The court characterized the opinion letters as "boilerplate that are almost, if not completely, identical except for date, investor name, investor advisor, and dates and amounts of investment transactions."[42] According to the court, there was "little indication that these [were] independent opinion letters that reflect[ed] any sort of legal analysis, reasoned or otherwise. In fact, when examined as a group, the letters appear[ed] to be nothing more than an orchestrated extension of KPMG's marketing machine."[43]

As his opinion suggested, Judge Hogan was deeply disturbed that the firm had invoked the privilege—which is intended to protect confidential information shared between clients and their advisors—in a completely inapposite context, in an effort to mislead the government and the court. Even if the underlying shelters were arguably legitimate, KPMG's attempts to use the privilege to evade disclosure obligations that would reveal its tax activities exposed it to criminal charges for obstruction of justice.

Over the next few months, KPMG continued its efforts to demonstrate to the government and the public that it had turned over a new leaf. In the summer of 2004, Richard Rosenthal, KPMG's Chief Financial Officer since 2002, and, earlier, vice chair for Tax Services, left the firm. Known for sending emails in red eighteen-point type that instructed the recipient: "you will do this now," Rosenthal had been a protégé of Stein's. During his tenure as vice chair, he had overseen the development and marketing of the firm's most aggressive tax strategies, including SC2.[44]

Notwithstanding KPMG's efforts to get beyond its shelter activities, every week seemed to bring a new revelation or inquiry. In August 2004, the PSI released another set of exhibits, which added details about the internal apparatus the firm had developed to design and market tax shelters. In a separate development, South Carolina's Department of Revenue launched an investigation and was threatening to bring disciplinary action against the partners involved in designing and promoting shelters to customers in that state.

The trouble the firm was facing in connection with its shelter activities was not its only legal difficulty; KPMG was also defending itself in a civil case brought by the Securities and Exchange Commission arising out of a $6.1 billion restatement by Xerox Corp, a firm client.[45] A few months earlier, the firm had been censured by the SEC for improper professional conduct for its audit of Gemstar. Recognizing that its reputation was eroding, KPMG was anxious to resolve all of its outstanding legal problems as quickly as possible and move on. In early 2005, KPMG hired Sven Erik

Holmes, former chief federal judge for the Northern District of Oklahoma and earlier a partner in the Washington firm of Williams & Connolly, to assume the newly created position of vice chair for Legal Affairs. The firm brought in Holmes over Claudia Taft, its highest-ranked internal lawyer, emphasizing that it was seeking to "strengthen its legal function."[46]

After his arrival, Judge Holmes engaged in another round of house cleaning, firing several more high-level partners who were associated with KPMG's shelter activity.[47] Richard Smith, the vice chair for Tax Services from 2002 until his "reassignment" in 2004, was dismissed. David Brockway, who had headed the firm's Washington National Tax (WNT) office since the summer of 1999, and Michael Burke, a managing partner in the firm's Los Angeles office in the Statecon group, were asked to leave the firm.[48]

The Specter of Indictment

In the spring of 2005, KPMG was engaged in intense negotiations with government officials to stave off an indictment. During discussions, the firm emphasized that it had put its shelter activities behind it. It also underscored the likely collateral consequences of a prosecution. When Arthur Andersen had been indicted in 2002, its clients, worried that a criminal charge would cast doubt on the integrity of the firm's audits, had fled, leading to the firm's rapid collapse. After Andersen's failure, four major accounting firms remained to audit nearly 80 percent of publicly owned companies.[49] If KPMG was indicted, the firm emphasized, it would most likely dissolve, leaving only three major accounting firms to audit the biggest corporations. Such an outcome would have very serious implications for the financial markets. A minimum number of accounting firms with the necessary expertise and capacity were required to safeguard the quality and independence of audit services. In essence, the Big Four were "too few" for KPMG to be allowed to fail.[50] O'Kelly, the firm's chair, participated directly in discussions with the government to make the case for the importance of allowing the firm to survive. He also appealed to Bill McDonough, head of the newly created Public Company Accounting Oversight Board, and Arthur Levitt, former chair of the SEC. Meanwhile, the firm hired a public relations firm and solicited corporate audit clients to assist it in making the case for its central role in providing audit services.

The government was open to the firm's appeal. During the spring and into the summer, a vigorous debate was occurring inside the Justice Department about whether to indict the firm. On the one hand, the criminal wrongdoing—which encompassed tax fraud and obstruction of justice—was serious. It permeated the firm's tax services and had been approved at the highest levels of leadership. No one could argue that the wrongful conduct was a product of the actions of one or two rogue partners, or even—as had been the case with Arthur Andersen and Enron—the actions of an audit team captured by a single powerful client. As a federal prosecutor emphasized during negotiations, in contrast to a situation where a company engages in a corrupt action as part of the provision of a legitimate service, "the very service KPMG was providing was corrupt."[51]

On the other hand, if KPMG was indicted, it would most certainly meet the same fate as Arthur Andersen, which would have negative repercussions that rippled through the business world. The reversal of Andersen's conviction at the end of May 2005 on the grounds of defective jury instructions provided additional fodder for those arguing against indictment. In the Andersen prosecution, the Justice Department had come in for significant criticism for bringing a case that had resulted in the destruction of an important institution and the loss of tens of thousands of jobs. The Department needed to avoid a similar result.

Shortly after the debates inside the Justice Department were reported in the press, KPMG—in a highly unusual move—publicly conceded that it had engaged in wrongdoing in its tax shelter practice. According to the firm, it "took full responsibility for the unlawful conduct by former KPMG partners" and "deeply regret[ed] that it had occurred."[52] As commentators observed, the firm's public statement of responsibility was a significant admission that former clients would be able to use in lawsuits against it. Despite the statement's implications for the firm's posture in civil litigation, the firm was making an eleventh-hour attempt to stave off criminal charges.

The firm's efforts worked—in a sense. The firm was not indicted, although it did not obtain the ideal outcome it desired—an agreement from the government not to prosecute at all. In late August 2005, KPMG entered into a deferred prosecution agreement, under which the firm could still be prosecuted for its tax shelter activities if it failed to comply with the agreement's terms.[53] The firm consented to the filing of a one-count information charging it with conspiracy to commit tax evasion, which would eventually be dismissed if KPMG adhered to all the terms of the deal. The firm acknowledged assisting individuals in tax evasion, engaging in unlawful and fraudulent conduct, actively concealing shelters, and impeding the IRS—activities that were described in a detailed statement of facts to which the firm admitted. FLIP, OPIS, BLIPS, and SOS generated more than $11 billion in artificial tax losses.[54] As part of the settlement, KPMG agreed to pay a fine of $456,000,000, which represented $128,000,000 in fees earned from the shelters, $228,000,000 in restitution to the government for taxes that had gone unpaid, and $1,000,000 to settle the IRS's promoter penalty examination. At the time, the fine was by far the largest in connection with an organization's participation in the tax shelter market.

KPMG's agreement with the government contemplated that it would make substantial changes in its tax services. KPMG was required to dismantle its tax practice for high-wealth individuals; in effect, it had to disband the Personal Financial Planning group. It was also obligated to implement a firm-wide compliance program under which its professionals would receive appropriate training, violators of the firm's ethics standards and policies would be punished, and those who reported wrongdoing would be rewarded. To ensure that KPMG abided by the terms of the agreement, Richard C. Breeden, former chair of the SEC, was appointed to monitor the firm's operations. He would be involved in overseeing the implementation of the deferred prosecution agreement for a period of three years.

One aspect of the firm's shelter activity went notably unmentioned in the deferred prosecution agreement. Although the firm was apparently willing during negotiations to acknowledge wrongdoing in connection with SC2, in the end, neither that shelter, the Contested Liability Acceleration Strategy (CLAS), nor the other corporate shelters marketed by the L.A.-based Stratecon group were included. The firm had already disbanded Stratecon, and many of its members had left the firm. The IRS ultimately listed SC2 and CLAS, but, at the time of the settlement discussions, the government may have concluded that promoting corporate shelters was not as egregious as marketing shelters to individuals. Alternatively KPMG may have been more adept at keeping Stratecon's activities out of public view and protecting the partners who were members of the group.

Prosecuting Partners

In mid-August, when KPMG was finalizing the terms of the deferred prosecution agreement with the government, a lengthy anonymous memo, written by five current and former KPMG board members and three former WNT partners, was sent to KPMG's partners, the Justice Department, and several news outlets. The memo's authors decried the fact that KPMG was bowing to government pressure not to pay legal fees for individuals under investigation. In addition, the memo contended that because the tax strategies at issue had not been tested in court they could not be the basis of individual criminal liability. Emphasizing that the tax shelters had been vetted at the highest levels in the firm, the authors noted that some leaders had been fired, while others who had had a hand in approving or marketing questionable tax strategies remained at the firm.[55]

As the memo's authors further underscored, the firm's organizational culture and incentive structure had given rise to the firm's tax shelter activities, not the actions of any one or even several individuals. If the firm was responsible for wrongdoing, then all the tax leaders shared in the blame and it was unfair to single out individuals and leave them exposed to criminal liability. Organizational responsibility was inconsistent with leaving specific partners and employees to fend for themselves.

Among the individuals whom the memo identified as having been involved in tax shelter activities, but spared thus far, were James Brasher and John Chopack, the tax partners appointed a year earlier as vice chairs during the first stage of the firm's house cleaning. Within a day or so after the anonymous memo was circulated, the *Wall Street Journal* published a story describing Brasher's and Chopack's participation in the sale of tax shelters to corporate clients. As a Midwest managing partner, Brasher had urged area partners and managers to intensify their efforts in selling 401(k)Accel, a corporate shelter identified as abusive by the IRS in 2002. Chopack, for his part, had overseen the sales of CLAS, which the IRS listed in 2003.[56] A month after the article appeared, the firm announced that it had replaced Brasher and Chopack. Brasher took on other, unspecified, duties, while Chopack planned to retire in early 2006.[57]

By the time the memo appeared in mid-August 2005 word was out that some former KPMG partners and employees would be indicted. Many of the thirty individuals originally identified as subjects of the criminal investigation had rejected KPMG's offer to pay legal fees conditioned on

their cooperation and had retained their own lawyers at significant personal expense. In mid-August, the government obtained its first conviction—although not from a former KPMG employee. Domenick
DeGiorgio, a bank executive at HVB, pled guilty to conspiracy and tax
fraud in connection with KPMG's promotion of FLIP and OPIS.[58] After
the plea was announced, it was widely assumed that DeGiorgio would
provide testimony against individuals involved in designing and marketing those shelters.

Two weeks later, shortly after KPMG had entered into the deferred
prosecution agreement, an indictment was handed down against Jeff Stein,
John Lanning, Richard Smith, Jeffrey Eischeid, Philip Wiesner, John Larson, Robert Pfaff, R. J. Ruble, the former partner at Sidley Austin Brown &
Wood, and Mark Watson. While the first eight individuals had been deeply
involved in the firm's shelter activities, the charges against Watson came as
a surprise. As the technical expert in charge of the firm's review of BLIPS
in 1999, he made repeated attempts to prevent the strategy from gaining
approval. When he later testified in front of the Permanent Subcommittee
on Investigations in 2003, he was forthright about his doubts. Watson's
indictment contributed to a sense shared among observers that the government was being especially aggressive in its handling of the criminal case.

In mid-October 2004, the government filed a superseding indictment
that added counts and defendants. In total, nineteen individuals involved
in the design, approval, sale, or implementation of FLIP, OPIS, BLIPS, and
SOS were charged, including seventeen former KPMG tax partners and
managers. The scope of the indictment also covered the defendants' attempts to mislead the IRS in the firm's response to the summons. The case
was described as the biggest tax prosecution in history. Notably, as in the
case of the deferred prosecution agreement, none of the firm's corporate
tax shelter activities were involved.

Over the next few months, lawyers for the defense pooled information,
shared strategies, and filed a slew of motions together and separately that
challenged different aspects of the case. In late fall of 2005, Ron DePetris
and Marion Bachrach, who represented Wiesner, the former WNT head,
came up with the idea of fighting the indictment on the grounds that the
government had pressured KPMG into withholding legal fees from the
KPMG defendants in violation of their right to counsel. The idea seemed
far-fetched. Applicable precedents in the criminal constitutional context

define a narrow zone around state action so that the conduct of private entities cannot be easily imputed to the government. Case law also sets a very high bar for finding that a private entity's actions were involuntary and therefore the direct product of state pressure. The law is well established that the government can make all types of threats to induce defendants to waive their rights without those threats rendering the waiver involuntary.

In the KPMG context, this meant that no matter how much pressure the government put on KPMG to stop advancing fees, ultimately the decision was the firm's and was not attributable to the state for purposes of finding a violation of the defendants' right to counsel. Although DePetris and Bachrach's motion to dismiss was a long shot, the other defense lawyers signed on. Their clients had nothing to lose. One KPMG defendant, David Rivkin, who had been part of the BLIPS sales team, pled guilty, presumably to put the ordeal and expense of defending himself behind him and receiving lenient treatment if his testimony was helpful to the government.

In response to the KPMG defendants' argument that prosecutors had interfered with their right to counsel, the government's strategy was to insist that the decision to withhold legal fees had been solely the firm's, and that the government had not applied pressure on KPMG. In one memorandum, the government represented that the decision *"was KPMG's decision alone"* and added, for good measure, that "the defendants have not—and indeed cannot—point to any evidence supporting their spurious claims that the United States 'coerc[ed]' or 'bull[ied]' KPMG into its making its decision to limit the advancement of fees." In a sworn statement, Assistant U.S. Attorney Justin Weddle further declared that "we [did] not instruct or request KPMG to change its decision about paying fees, capping the payment of fees, or conditioning of fees on an employee's or partner's cooperation."[59]

When it became clear that the two sides had wholly divergent accounts of the facts, Judge Lewis Kaplan, who was presiding over the case, ordered a hearing. As the testimony and exhibits established conclusively, the government had insisted repeatedly that KPMG not pay the fees of employees and partners who refused to cooperate. Copious amounts of evidence showed that the government had been explicit in its view that the firm's payment of attorneys' fees was a factor in the government's assessment of the extent of its cooperation. The prosecution's contrary statements, made under oath to the court, were simply false.

Judge Kaplan was incensed. In a lengthy decision issued in late June 2006, he described in detail the government's successful attempts to prevent KPMG from advancing its employees' fees and the government's subsequent efforts to mislead the court. The court held that the government's actions had interfered with the fairness of the proceedings and had violated the defendants' right to counsel. Recognizing that dismissing the indictment was an extreme sanction, the court attempted to fashion a remedy short of dismissal under which KPMG would be compelled to advance the defendants' fees. If the court held that KPMG had a contractual obligation to pay attorneys' fees, this would also redress KPMG's wrongful actions against its former employees and allow the case to go forward. Even if KPMG's actions were the result of government pressure, it was ultimately the firm that had thrown its employees under the bus. When the district court attempted to resolve the question of whether KPMG was contractually required to pay the defendants' attorneys' fees, however, the Court of Appeals reversed the decision.[60] It held that the issue was beyond the district court's jurisdiction, which was limited to the criminal case. Ultimately, the only remedy available to the court to address the government's violation of the KPMG defendants' constitutional rights was dismissal of the indictment involving the thirteen KPMG defendants.[61] In August 2008, the Court of Appeals for the Second Circuit affirmed the district court's decision.[62]

Because of the government's overreaching, the biggest tax prosecution in United States history was reduced to a case against five individuals who had not been the driving force behind the firm's tax shelter activities. The remaining defendants were Larson and Pfaff, who had left KPMG to form Presidio in 1997; Amir Makov, the partner they brought on; R. J. Ruble, the outside lawyer who provided opinion letters; and a rogue KPMG partner in the L.A. office who had been terminated from the firm before discussions with the government had commenced.

In 2008, after a ten-week trial, Larson, Pfaff, and Ruble were found guilty. Makov, who had pled guilty in August 2007, offered compelling testimony against his former partners at Presidio. The evidence against the fifth defendant was weaker, and the jury acquitted him. Larson, Pfaff, and Ruble unsuccessfully appealed both to the Court of Appeals for the Second Circuit and to the Supreme Court. Larson received a ten-year prison sentence, Pfaff a nearly eight-year sentence, and Ruble a six-and-a-half-year sentence, which they were serving as of 2013.

The prosecution and conviction of individuals in connection with KPMG's involvement in abusive tax shelters—which was premised on the claim that each individual was aware that the shelters were fraudulent but promoted them anyway—was profoundly at odds with the organizational dimensions of the wrongdoing. At the firm, tax leaders implemented an incentive and reporting structure that valorized tax shelter development and sales. With increased competition in other areas in which accounting firms provide services, KPMG, like other firms, was eager to find a new source of revenue. Tax shelters, which could be sold on a value-added basis, seemed to be the solution. The focus on tax shelters created incentives to work on them. As tax leaders subtly and not so subtly communicated, promotion and career advancement were premised on involvement in the tax shelter work. In contrast, those who declined to work on shelters or raised issues about their propriety were sidelined and suffered negative career repercussions. In addition, the importance assigned tax shelter activity gave it the allure of a cutting-edge practice. For members of the tax shelter team, it must have been exciting to be among a select group chosen to participate.

As the approval process for BLIPS, described in chapter 5, suggests, the highly specialized division of expertise within the tax practice made it difficult for any one professional to grasp the centrality of economic substance in determining whether a shelter would be upheld by a court. Economic substance became a formal requirement like any other and was therefore treated technically. As a consequence, satisfying the requirement became one of technique—searching for some possible scenario in which a taxpayer might have a business reason to engage in the strategy, rather than ascertaining the economic reality that underlay the strategies they were promoting. Once evidence emerged that belied the claim that the strategies had economic substance, the momentum behind bringing the strategies to market made it very difficult to change course.

In addition, the centralized reporting structure of the firm was at odds with the idea that a core professional ideal is independent of individualized, discretionary judgment. The result was that assigning responsibility for any one decision was often difficult. Here too the BLIPS approval process is illuminating. Mark Watson, a junior partner at WNT, was assigned the task of shepherding the product through the approval process. So his judgment as a professional should have been deferred to. The reporting structure, however, made it difficult for Watson to exercise independent judgment. From the very beginning, he was under constant pressure from senior tax leaders to approve the shelters. The blending of business-generating and compliance functions up the reporting ladder to the chair of the tax practice made it impossible to separate questions of professionalism and ethics from the question of profitability. The organizational factors that shaped decision making at the firm made the assignment of responsibility to one or a handful of firm members very difficult.

Jenkens & Gilchrist

In the Crosshairs

When the IRS began to review information gathering disclosed from taxpayers in 2002 in response to the agency's amnesty offer, the name of Jenkens & Gilchrist began to appear more and more frequently. On May 21, 2002, the IRS issued twenty-two administrative summonses to the firm. The IRS requested documents and records from Jenkens to determine if it had complied with registration and list maintenance requirements with respect to certain listed or potentially abusive transactions. After reviewing its files, Jenkens concluded that 607 of the 700 client files were responsive to the summonses. The firm nevertheless refused to produce any of this material on the grounds that it was protected by the attorney-client privilege.

In the face of this resistance, the government in June 2003 took the highly unusual step of obtaining court permission to serve a John Doe summons on Jenkens to obtain the names of investors who engaged in particular transactions from January 1998 through June 15, 2003.[63] The Justice Department, the Treasury Department, and the IRS called a joint press conference to announce "the first-time issuance of a summons for the primary purpose of obtaining the identities of the investors in a technical tax shelter the IRS determined is abusive."[64] IRS Chief Counsel B. John Williams told reporters that the IRS would consider seeking John Doe summonses to preserve the statute of limitations for investors. "We will not allow investors and promoters to use stalling tactics to circumvent our compliance efforts," he emphasized.[65]

According to the IRS, the Jenkens investigation found that the firm's shelter activities involved, by a "conservative estimate," $2.4 billion in reported tax losses that should have been reported as taxable gains by 600 taxpayers.[66] The agency maintained that the attorney-client privilege did not apply to the information sought because the firm was acting as a promoter of the shelters, rather than serving as an attorney to the investors. Jenkens announced that it would not comply with the John Doe summons on the grounds that the privilege applied. "It has long been the law of this country that Americans have a right to consult with an attorney in confidence," a statement from the firm said, "and only the clients themselves can waive that right."[67]

Shortly thereafter the Justice Department petitioned the court to enforce five of the twenty-one promoter summonses and the John Doe summons. It pointed out that the Jenkens agreement with taxpayers participating in tax shelters provided that that the taxpayer and the firm "are acting solely as independent contracting parties, and neither party shall be deemed to be the agent or fiduciary of the other."[68] The Department emphasized further that even in an attorney-client relationship, the identity of the client is not privileged, except in the rare instance in which revealing the client's identity is tantamount to disclosing a confidential communication.

On April 20, 2004, the court held that the privilege did not protect the identities of Jenkens & Gilchrist's clients.[69] As the court noted, only five days earlier another federal district court in Chicago had reached the same conclusion with respect to Sidley Austin Brown & Wood's refusal to disclose the names of former clients in response to another John Doe summons by the IRS. On May 13, the court rejected the firm's other claim that the terms of the summonses were unduly ambiguous and ordered Jenkens to comply.[70] Four days later, Jenkens turned over a list of investor names to the IRS.

Meanwhile, investor lawsuits and the IRS investigation had begun to take their toll. The firm went from more than 625 lawyers in 2001 to about 460 by early 2004. William Durbin was reelected to a third term as chair of the firm at the beginning of 2004, despite significant opposition from many partners who felt he focused too narrowly on the bottom line. There was considerable unhappiness at his reelection, with some partners threatening to leave if Durbin were not replaced as chairman. Just weeks after his election, Durbin stepped down. "It was time for a change," he said. "I had initiated a lot of change within the firm that necessarily was resisted, or understandably was resisted by some."[71] Thomas Cantrill, a veteran partner who had been chair for three and a half years in the

1980s, took over. The exodus continued, however. With the departure of the firm's employee benefits practice group in the fall of that year, the firm felt it had no choice but to stop returning capital to partners who left.

The most significant investor lawsuit against Jenkens was the Denney consolidated class action in Manhattan. The suit had begun as an action filed against the firm and Ernst & Young in December 2002 by Camferdam and other COBRA investors, and eventually included 1,100 class members who had invested in various shelters. Negotiations began in November 2003 between Jenkens and David Deary, a Dallas lawyer representing the plaintiffs. The two sides negotiated during three separate sessions over the course of several days from December 2003 until early March 2004, with retired Fifth Circuit Judge Robert Parker serving as mediator. The negotiations were conducted against a backdrop of concern that the firm would go under before a settlement could be reached. Complicating matters was the resistance of Jenkens's primary insurance carrier, Executive Risk Indemnity, Inc., to covering any liability to the plaintiffs. In March 2004, the parties finally agreed to a settlement of $75 million. Jenkens would be responsible for $5.25 million; Daugerdas, Mayer, and Guerin for $6.25 million, and the firm's insurers would pay the rest.[72]

After conducting additional informal discovery as part of evaluating the settlement, however, plaintiffs' counsel insisted on an increase in the settlement amount. In addition, more than one hundred class members indicated their intention to reject the settlement and opt out of the class. This left Jenkens vulnerable to claims that could total tens of millions of dollars because the settlement had been conditioned on the firm providing a release to its insurers of any further responsibility. Jenkens had conditioned the settlement on the participation of all the plaintiffs. The firm threatened to sue its insurers if the firm went under. Eventually, the insurers agreed to provide an additional $25 million to cover any liabilities to plaintiffs who chose to opt out of the class.

In December 2004 the parties reached a final settlement, with Jenkens dropping its condition that all plaintiffs participate. The terms called for payment of $81.55 million to the plaintiff class. Jenkens, Daugerdas, Mayer, and Guerin were responsible for about $11.5 million of this and the firm's insurers for the rest. About 92 percent of the class members agreed to the terms, leaving some eighty-eight opt-out plaintiffs remaining. The court approved the settlement in February 2005.[73] With this litigation resolved, Jenkens chair Cantrill declared, "We are looking forward to putting this matter behind us and moving forward in a positive and successful direction in 2005."[74]

Cantrill hoped to put an optimistic face on the settlement, but the underlying reality was much bleaker. As the firm's settlement memo suggested, the sheer number and size of the lawsuits pending against Jenkens "[had] driven the firm to the brink."[75] As a result, "J&G's leaders [had to] spend much of their time addressing substantial and unusual competitive and business pressures on the firm's lawyers, business, and profits,"[76] and "[c]ompetitors continued to use the firm's tax-case problems to try to lure away productive shareholders, associates, and clients."[77] In the last two years, the firm had lost over 200 of its 600 lawyers. In March 2005, the firm suffered a significant additional loss with the departure of ninety-one lawyers in its New York office to Troutman Sanders.

The End of the Road

In January 2006 the *New York Times* reported that the U.S. Attorney's Office in Manhattan had impaneled a grand jury to investigate Jenkens & Gilchrist's tax shelter activity.[78] Leaders of the firm assumed that the focus was on Daugerdas, Mayer, and Guerin, but prosecutors would not rule out the firm as a target. They talked to the firm's board members and issued subpoenas to reinforce the perception that the firm might be subject to indictment. At the same time, they pushed hard for cooperation from the firm in investigating the individual lawyers. Firm management figured that the Justice Department needed to decide what to do by October 2006 to avoid having the six-year statute of limitations run on claims from 1999. It asked members of the firm to hold on until then because there was likely to be clarity by that point.

By 2006, the firm was down to 144 lawyers, compared to the 600 or so it had had in 2001. Management had done its best to keep the firm together in hopes of surviving but also to protect employees by effecting an orderly dissolution if need be. Firm leaders' approach to the Justice Department up to that point had been that the Department should not issue an indictment or take any other actions that would bring the entire firm down. Eventually, when prosecutors were unresponsive to requests for more clarity about the status of the investigation, Jenkens management told the government that the firm had no choice but to shut down. A template for an orderly dissolution was the departure of the New York office: when all its lawyers left the firm to join Troutman Sanders, the latter assumed the lease obligation for the office space.

Jenkens management did its best to keep partners from leaving immediately so that the firm could effect an orderly wind-up that involved finding people jobs elsewhere. Management tried to move offices in entire groups so that lease obligations could continue to be met. Firm chair Pat Mitchell told wavering partners that they had an obligation to the employees who had stuck with the firm rather than triggering a chaotic dissolution by jumping ship. "We're not going to survive," he emphasized, "but let's die well." In relatively short order, Jenkens lawyers in Houston, Los Angeles, Chicago, and San Antonio left for other firms. Eventually, almost a hundred lawyers went to Hunton & Williams, mostly in Dallas but also in Austin. About 95 percent of both lawyers and nonlawyers found jobs. The firm collected about 90 percent of its receivables—a high amount considering that clients knew that the firm was going under.

As negotiations proceeded, the firm brought the IRS in so that it could resolve both outstanding matters with the government. The end came swiftly. On March 29, 2007, the U.S. Attorney's Office announced that it had entered into a non-prosecution agreement with Jenkens & Gilchrist, under which the firm admitted that it had developed and marketed fraudulent tax shelters and that it had issued fraudulent opinion letters.[79] As the U.S. Attorney explained, the government's decision to enter into the agreement was based on these admissions by the firm, as well as the firm's "inability to continue practicing law as a firm"; its cooperation with the prosecutor's investigation of the tax shelter activities of the firm and its lawyers; and the firm's entry into a settlement with the IRS.[80]

According to the statement Jenkens & Gilchrist issued in connection with the agreement,

We believe that certain J&G attorneys developed and marketed fraudulent tax shelters, with fraudulent tax opinions, that wrongly deprived the US Treasury of significant tax revenues. The firm's tax shelter practice was spearheaded by tax practitioners in J&G's Chicago office who are no longer with the firm. Those responsible for overseeing the Chicago tax practice placed unwarranted trust in the judgment and integrity of the attorneys principally responsible for that practice, and failed to exercise effective oversight and control over the firm's tax shelter practice. Our prior support for the opinions adversely affected the efforts of the IRS to assess and collect tax revenues. We deeply regret our involvement in this tax practice, and the serious harm it caused to the United States Treasury.[81]

That same day, the IRS announced that it had reached a settlement with Jenkens under which the firm agreed that it was subject to a $76 million penalty due to "the firm's promotion of abusive and fraudulent tax shelters and violation of the tax law concerning tax shelter registration and maintenance and turnover to the IRS of tax shelter investor lists."[82] The agency estimated that 1,400 investors received advice from Jenkens and would owe interest and penalties for underpayment of tax. What had been the fastest growing law firm in the country nine years earlier was now out of business.

At the time of the dissolution, Henry Gilchrest, retired from the firm, was in his late seventies. A courtly southern gentleman, he had founded the firm on traditional values of providing expert advice to long-term clients and had sought to maintain a reputation for professional integrity and high standards. Now the firm that bore his name was associated with one of the biggest tax shelter scandals in U.S. history.

In June 2009, Daugerdas, Mayer, and Guerin were indicted in connection with their tax shelter activities. Former BDO officials Denis Field and Robert Greisman and Deutsche Bank employees Raymond Brubaker and David Parse were also charged.[83] The shelters named in the indictment included Treasury Short Sales, Short Options Strategy and others known under the names Swaps and HOMER.

Greisman and Mayer entered guilty pleas a year apart. Both admitted that they knew that the shelters they promoted had no reasonable possibility of making a profit because, among other reasons, the costs and fees for most of the transactions exceeded the potential profit, if any.[84] As part of his agreement, Mayer forfeited his two residences and more than $10 million.

Mayer was a key witness at the trial of the remaining defendants. He admitted that the opinion letters of Daugerdas's group all used the same template and falsely described the representations that clients ostensibly made about the reasons for entering into transactions, for engaging in trading activity, for transferring assets to partnerships and other entities, and for closing out the transactions. In addition, no client had ever articulated a nontax reason for participating in a shelter. At the time he was working on the shelters Mayer was aware that they would not be upheld under the tax law. He continued to work on them, he acknowledged, because of the enormous fees they generated. During Mayer's testimony, the prosecution asked whether Daugerdas had ever discussed his status as a taxpayer. Mayer responded that on several occasions Daugerdas had mentioned that he was briefly a taxpayer for a few years in the early 1990s.[85]

Daugerdas, Guerin, Field, and Parse were found guilty on multiple counts of tax evasion and endeavoring to obstruct and impede the internal revenue laws. Brubaker was acquitted of all the charges against him. The convictions of Daugerdas, Guerin, and Field were vacated a little over a year later on grounds of juror misconduct.[86] In September 2012 Donna Guerin pled guilty to one count of conspiracy and one count of tax evasion, each of which carried a maximum sentence of five years. She also agreed to forfeit $1.6 million as part of her plea agreement. Daugerdas and Field were retried in the fall of 2013. While Field was acquitted, Daugerdas was convicted on several counts of tax evasion, conspiracy, and mail fraud. As of December 2013, he was awaiting sentencing.

Jenkens & Gilchrist's is the story of a regional firm with national ambitions, which sought to use Paul Daugerdas to make the leap to premium billing without the need to provide customized high-end legal services. It was an aggressive firm that had grown rapidly by acquiring profitable laterals and it believed that it had learned how to manage the risks associated with them. As long as there was at least colorable legal support for Daugerdas's tax shelters, Jenkens management saw the decision as involving a business judgment about whether the rewards were worth the risk. The firm concluded they were. A major surge in tax shelter activity boosted the firm's revenues by a staggering amount and seemed to vindicate that conclusion. That same surge, however, prompted an ambitious enforcement campaign by the government that dramatically raised the stakes and eventually led to the collapse of the firm.

Jenkens & Gilchrist had lawyers responsible for ethics issues who conducted considerable training within the firm. It had a deliberative process in place that allowed opponents of hiring Paul Daugerdas to make their case at the highest level of the firm. It had a policy of requiring a second opinion on firm legal opinions that it adapted for use in monitoring Daugerdas's tax shelters. These measures reflect the laudable trend in recent years for law firms to establish a more sophisticated "ethical infrastructure,"[87] but they turned out to be inadequate to address the risks presented by Daugerdas's tax shelter practice.

The Jenkens story illustrates how organizational culture shapes the deliberations that occur within a firm's infrastructure. Culture influences whether decisions are framed as involving business risks or ethical choices, the assessment of the nature and magnitude of risks, and the determination of how well the firm can manage the risks that it assumes. Culture also determines the extent to which financial considerations subtly influence deliberation on these issues. Ultimately, at a crucial point in the history of the firm, the Jenkens culture fell short.

Conclusion

In the mid-2000s, the tax shelter industry had begun to slow down. By then a significant number of well-respected professional organizations and individuals had been drawn into the criminal justice system. To fight shelter activity, the government deployed every weapon in its regulatory arsenal—strengthening provisions in the Internal Revenue Code, enacting new regulations, challenging claims on audit, offering time-limited amnesties to taxpayers, bringing enforcement actions against firms, and ultimately launching criminal investigations and prosecutions of firms and individual tax practitioners. As evidence of the role of prestigious accounting firms and law firms mounted, the abusive tax shelter market emerged as an episode of collective wrongdoing across a major sector of professional services that historically had traded on its honesty, integrity and public-mindedness.

Using criminal prosecutions to address wrongdoing among a sector of lawyers is rare but not unprecedented. As the shelter episode suggests, the line between criminal and noncriminal conduct, especially in the white-collar context, is not always clear. Even wrongful conduct that can easily be characterized as criminal is frequently addressed through civil mechanisms. In choosing to invoke criminal processes, the government sought to communicate a clear message that the wrongdoing violated fundamental norms against assisting tax evasion. Turning to the criminal regime, however, had significant costs. The most high-profile prosecutions ended in embarrassing defeats, suggesting to observers that the government had been overly aggressive in its tactics or—of even greater concern to officials—had attempted to prosecute behavior that, even if wrongful, was arguably not criminal. The individual prosecutions that went to trial, moreover, emphasized individual culpability and obscured the organizational factors that led to the rise of the shelter industry.

By suggesting that tax shelters were the product of individual wrong-doing, the criminal cases gave a misleading account of the tax shelter episode. In the most egregious cases of wrongdoing among accounting firms, tax shelters were not the result of rogue behavior by one or a small handful of partners operating outside official organizational channels. To the contrary, shelter activity was encouraged, approved, or at the very least acquiesced in, by firm leadership, which often devoted significant organizational resources to the effort. Firms fostered internal cultures in which tax shelter development and sales were valorized. As in other cases of organizational misconduct, accounting firms socialized their constituents to engage in wrongdoing.[1] An account of the institutional dynamics serves as a necessary counterpoint to viewing the events through an individualistic lens.

In addition, the tax shelter episode holds important lessons for lawyers in general and the tax bar in particular. In spearheading the tax shelter industry, tax lawyers and accountants used their expertise to devise and sell complex transactions with neither business purpose nor economic substance. These strategies enabled taxpayers to escape billions of dollars in taxes. The tax professionals involved, moreover, did not hesitate to invoke the elite standing of the organizations in which they practiced to deflect questions about the propriety of the strategies they were promoting and investigations into their activities.

In misusing their expertise and status, tax professionals betrayed an implicit bargain between the legal and accounting professions and the state. This bargain has been at the heart of the societal understanding of the role of the legal profession in the United States since the late nineteenth century and continues to be the basis of its cultural and legal authority. Under this bargain, professionals were granted authority to regulate terms of entry, impose ethical rules, and control the institutional arrangements under which they practiced without interference from external regulators. In return, professionals would use their knowledge for the betterment of clients and society, and eschew using their expertise solely to pursue their own financial gain.

This agreement has been particularly important in the tax practice field. Given the structure of the tax code and the system's dependence on self-reporting, high-wealth individuals have available a range of mechanisms to eliminate their tax liability. They also have the resources to retain professional expertise to assist them in this goal. Tax lawyers, therefore, have been expected to advise clients against engaging in transactions whose sole or primary purpose is tax minimization. Tax advisors perform a distinctive function in the tax system, which puts them in a position to affect taxpayers' sense of civic duty to meet their tax obligations. Encouraging clients to engage in tax compliance may not only affect their specific behavior. It may also contribute to tax morale over all, fostering the view that the tax system is fair and that the burden of taxes falls equally on wealthy individuals and on salaried employees subject to automatic withholding.

Reviving professional norms that tax professionals can draw on to guide clients to engage in tax compliant behavior is no easy task. It will require lawyers to pursue new avenues of professional engagement. During much of the twentieth century, tax lawyers took for granted that formal and informal mechanisms of self-regulation—at the organized bar level and inside firms—could buffer their practice from the influence of market forces. The rise of the tax shelter industry suggests that reliance on traditional accounts of professional self-regulation is outdated. The organizations in which tax lawyers practice are too large and too vulnerable to intensified competitive forces to permit their constituents to engage in the creation and elaboration of professional ideals without regulatory and organizational support.[2] To strengthen its professional authority and independence, the tax bar may need to participate in regulatory processes that strengthen advisors' capacity to practice consistent with professional ideals. They may also need to implement organizational structures and processes that facilitate the elaboration of norms favoring compliance. We offer some suggestions along these lines, but in the end it is up to tax lawyers to identify and strengthen the sites for engagement and the norms that might animate tax practice in the twenty-first century.

Criminal Prosecution

Historically, government authorities have rarely invoked criminal sanctions against lawyers in connection with their practice of law. When they do, they seek to articulate an account of the wrongdoing that ties it to more general social norms. In the first decade of the twenty-first century, when corporate counsel engaged in backdating stock options awarded to corporate executives, authorities attempted through prosecutions to communicate their view that the behavior constituted securities fraud. In the same vein, the tax shelter prosecutions sought to communicate the view that designing and promoting tax elimination strategies was assisting clients in tax evasion. Bringing charges against the tax professionals involved connecting the dots between their hypertechnical interpretations of the tax law and the commission of tax fraud. Although there are vigorous debates in the tax community about how much economic substance a strategy needs in order for its tax benefits to be recognized, the requirement cannot simply be elided or wished away. To have economic substance, a transaction has to result in meaningful economic consequences to the client, a feature that was absent from the strategies being promoted. The prosecutions also connected the dots between aggressively promoting abusive tax strategies and involvement in a range of illegal conduct to elude detection by the IRS. This involved, in the most egregious instances, recommending that clients use grantors' trusts to hide their shelter activities, improperly resisting enforcement actions, fabricating documentation after the fact, intentionally misleading IRS examiners, and lying in formal proceedings.

Despite the powerful communicative role played by criminal prosecutions, using this tool had enormous costs. As criminal defendants, the tax professionals charged enjoyed important constitutional protections. Consequently, they had grounds to challenge the prosecutions at each step of the process. For example, the indictments of more than a dozen of the KPMG partners and managers involved in the firm's shelter activities, including tax leaders who had driven its participation, were dismissed on the ground that prosecutors had interfered with their right to counsel.

Analogous problems plagued the other prosecutions. After several months of trial, the prosecution of Paul Daugerdas and his colleague Donna Guerin, along with Denis Field of BDO and two Deutsche Bank employees, resulted in conviction of four of the five defendants. The judge was forced to set the convictions aside, however, because a juror had engaged in misconduct that affected the defendants' rights to an impartial jury and fair trial. While Daugerdas was convicted in a second trial, Field was acquitted after his lawyer argued in her summation that despite his energetic support of BDO's tax product initiatives, he was not sufficiently involved in the deployment and marketing of shelters to know that they were abusive. The prosecution and trial of four Ernst & Young employees involved in shelter promotion met a similar fate. Four months of trial resulted in their convictions, but the convictions of two were reversed on appeal because of due process violations. The appeals court ruled that the evidence was not sufficient to establish a connection between the individual defendants' deeds and the core wrongdoing that the prosecution had established.

These setbacks came at significant cost to the government, which expended substantial resources to prosecute and try the cases; they also provoked criticisms of the government's tactics and strategy, deflecting attention from the wrongful conduct underlying tax shelter activities. In the worst-case scenario, defendants whose indictments had been dismissed or convictions reversed could portray themselves as the innocent victims of overzealous prosecutors. Lost in the drawn-out processes of criminal investigations, indictments, motions to dismiss, trials, convictions, and appeals, was the idea that the tax professionals who had been most deeply involved in designing and marketing abusive tax shelters deserved the moral opprobrium that criminal sanctions were intended to communicate.

The individual prosecutions, moreover, obscured the organizational factors that contributed to the pervasiveness of the wrongdoing. It is true that KPMG and Ernst & Young—as well as Deutsche Bank—entered into deferred-prosecution and non-prosecution agreements that required them to catalog the wrongful acts in which the firms had engaged. But because the charges against these organizations were never brought to trial, details about the participants who led organizational efforts to promote tax shelter activity—and the organizational resources and structures that were diverted for that purpose—never emerged.

Instead, most of the prosecutorial energy was devoted to trying individuals for abetting tax evasion. Under the heightened constitutional requirements that apply to mens rea in tax prosecutions, the government had to establish that each defendant was aware of his or her legal obligations but acted in violation of them.[3] The government's proof, therefore, had to focus on showing what each defendant knew and did despite that knowledge. The effect was to produce a powerful narrative that individuated responsibility for wrongdoing and omitted accounts of organizational complicity.

The Dark Side of Organizations

Popular accounts portrayed the tax shelter industry as a story about individual wrongdoers—greedy tax professionals intent on hijacking their organizations to enable tax evasion. The firms involved promoted this characterization because it deflected attention from organizational complicity in the wrongdoing. The prosecution of individual wrongdoers, which served as a final exclamation point to the abusive tax shelter story, reinforced this explanation.

The preceding chapters suggest that organizational factors played an important role in shelter activities and their rapid spread. As social scientists have emphasized, organizations are more than mere collections of people. An organization's structures and dynamics shape how its constituents frame information and how they allocate responsibility for the negative effects of organizational actions. Many harmful actions are "not the volitional products of individual evildoers but rather essentially organizational products that result when complex social forces interact."[4] As sociologist Diane Vaughan notes, harms caused by organizations are often a "routine by-product of the system itself."[5] Researchers focusing on organizational crime have argued that the organizational dynamics that lead to wrongdoing are the effects of the distribution of power and division of tasks inside organizations. The very features of organizations that render them highly successful social systems—hierarchy and specialization—also give rise to the development of organizational pathologies.[6]

Vaughan proposes that exploring the interactions among three features of an organization sheds light on the "dark side of organizations." These features are the environment in which an organization functions, its structure, and the interplay of cognitive and decision-making dynamics inside the organization. An organization's environment provides the underlying conditions for the initial decision among organizational leaders and constituents to embark on wrongful conduct. External factors function to ratify and entrench this initial decision. Wrongdoing becomes institutionalized—routinized and normalized—by being embedded in an organization's structure. As Vaughan observes, "Structures, processes, and tasks are opportunity structures of misconduct because they provide a) normative support for the misconduct, b) the means for carrying out the violation and c) concealment that minimizes detection and wrongdoing."[7]

Structural features such as the allocation of authority and responsibility, the processes for decision making and review, and the division of tasks within an organization allow constituents to contribute to organizational wrongdoing while remaining ignorant of the effects of their actions and believing that they are engaged in a morally neutral or even beneficial activity. Together, environment and structure influence the cognitive and decision-making dynamics within an organization, shaping how actions and decisions are framed. According to Vaughan, "the origin of routine social non-conformity is in the connections" among the environment, organizational characteristics, and the cognitive practices of the individuals within them.[8]

The Environment
Organizations do not act in a vacuum, but react to and shape in a recursive process the economic, regulatory, and political environments in which they function. The major accounting firms that launched the shelter industry were operating in a highly competitive environment. Among the challenges they faced were the difficulty of differentiating their services and their reliance on a traditional fee structure—the hourly rate—that gave them little room to increase profits. Subject to comparable market forces, corporate law firms were in an escalating competition for clients and partners who would generate profits. Even as accounting and law firms found themselves in an increasingly competitive struggle, the economy around them was booming. In the late 1990s and 2000s, professionals at these firms compared their lot to that of professionals at financial institutions. They longed for a "Goldman-Sachs type practice"[9] that would generate substantially more income.

At the same time, firms providing tax services faced a lax regulatory environment. Among other problems, Treasury officials were preoccupied with dealing with a hostile Congress and attempting to modernize IRS operations. Limited by outdated information gathering systems, demoralized personnel, and few enforcement resources, the agency did not seem particularly eager to ferret out and challenge highly complex tax strategies. For some tax professionals involved in shelter activity, the fact that shelters were low on the government's priority list meant that they were not going to be caught if they engaged in promoting highly questionable deals. Others likely interpreted the government's inattention to shelters as a signal that shelters did not raise serious legal or ethical problems.

This second interpretation was especially plausible given the contested nature of tax law itself. As chapter 2 describes, the income tax, unlike some other areas of law, has significant gray areas that make the line between tax avoidance and evasion unclear. Because of fundamental definitional difficulties, there are a large number of scenarios about which knowledgeable and well-intentioned tax practitioners vigorously disagree. At a high level of abstraction, the requirement that tax-favored transactions have "economic substance" is uncontroversial. Nevertheless, courts, tax lawyers, and scholars are not of one mind about the most important considerations that comprise economic substance, or what amount of economic substance a tax shelter must have to be upheld by a court. Viewed after the fact, many of the shelters promoted by large accounting firms clearly lacked economic substance. At the time, however, the ambiguities inherent in tax law—magnified by organizational factors—enabled many tax professionals to convince themselves that the shelters they were promoting were legitimate.

The view among many tax professionals that shelter activity was unproblematic was reinforced by the fact that other prestigious firms were involved. For some participants "everyone else is doing it" meant that as a practical matter their firm could engage in wrongdoing without being penalized. For many others, however, the fact that other elite accounting firms—KPMG, Ernst & Young, Arthur Andersen, BDO Seidman—were marketing tax shelters was a clear indication that there was nothing illegal or unethical about the activity.

Institutionalization

At KPMG, Ernst & Young, BDO, and other firms, shelter activity became embedded in the structures and processes of the organization. Tax leaders at these firms devoted substantial organizational resources to developing and marketing tax shelters. They aligned organizational incentives, including compensation and advancement at the firm, with revenue production tied to promoting tax shelters.

On one level, the alignment of formal mechanisms with shelter activity was a signal to tax professionals at the firms that if they wanted to succeed they needed to participate in this activity. In some instances, participants believed with good reason that their positions at the firm were at stake. But the message worked at a different level too. By using the power of their positions to encourage tax shelter activity, tax leaders were communicating their view that these activities were appropriate. Tax leaders, who functioned as role models, fostered a culture in which involvement in tax shelter activity was not only not problematic but was consistent with high standards of client service and a commitment to the success of the firm. The institutionalization of shelter activity thus did more than simply dictate the terms of a rational calculus of costs and benefits, where participating in tax shelter work promoted one's career and staying clear led to career setbacks. Explicitly organizing business units around shelter work valorized it and shifted its normative valence. Tax shelter practice was no longer seen in negative terms; it was embraced as a worthwhile activity.

As tax shelter activity became intertwined with organizational processes, review mechanisms intended to prevent questionable shelters from going to market proved ineffective. In some instances, firms relied on informal processes that were deficient. At Ernst & Young, the same professionals who had designed the shelters and stood to gain from their approval conducted the review. While in hindsight this process seems highly problematic, the partners involved were well-respected tax lawyers with significant practice experience. Given their reputations as upstanding professionals who had always safeguarded the firm's interests, their judgment was presumed to be trustworthy. Under traditional professional norms, they were expected to exercise appropriate discretion to prevent clients and the firm from engaging in questionable activity.

The formal processes implemented at some firms to impose appropriate safeguards also proved to have significant weaknesses. Most obviously, they were embedded in a larger institutional structure that emphasized shelter promotion. For all that Larry DeLap, the head of the Department of Professional Practice—Tax at KPMG, tried to maintain some semblance of independence, he reported to tax leaders who did not hesitate to make their enthusiasm for tax shelters known. For his part, Mark Watson, who had been charged with steering BLIPS through the approval process at KPMG, was well aware that the product was getting some "high level attention."

A further weakness with the approval process at KPMG, illustrated by the BLIPS review, was the division of substantive issues among subject matter experts. Whether BLIPS had economic substance became a narrow technical question. Those assigned the task of resolving the issue struggled to create a scenario, however implausible, where a client might actually purchase the strategy to make money. Economic substance was resolved by recourse to some imagined set of facts. Treated as a technical question, the economic substance problem became decoupled from the

334   Conclusion

broader question of whether the strategy would perpetrate tax fraud by allowing clients to claim losses for transactions that did not reflect economic reality.

As participants struggled to resolve this issue, responsibility for the problem moved from one participant to the next. Eventually the question of whether BLIPS had economic substance was "deferred to implementation." As the process unfolded and responsibility shifted, other participants could reasonably believe that they no longer were responsible for deciding the issue. Despite Mark Watson's grave reservations about BLIPS, he repeatedly assured himself that more senior tax partners with greater expertise were accountable for the final decision. He also believed he could rely on Deutsche Bank and its law firm Shearman & Sterling, which, he assumed, would never participate in activities that helped clients engage in tax evasion. Steven Rosenthal, who shared Watson's concerns, repeatedly insisted during the review process that he was not opining on the question of economic substance.

Later, as the implementation process moved forward, Rosenthal and Watson saw Deutsche Bank documents that made clear that the loan in BLIPS was a loan in name only. After their efforts to persuade David Brockway to revisit the decision to approve BLIPS proved unsuccessful, they saw no choice but to give up. Each believed, with good reason, that the decision to market BLIPS had been made at a higher level at the firm, and that they had done all they could.

Organizational dynamics also contributed to a diffusion of responsibility for the decision to market BLIPS. KPMG's review process allowed participants to lose sight of the bigger question of whether their actions were implicated in tax fraud and to convince themselves that they bore no responsibility for the outcome. This phenomenon is consistent with frequently observed processes in organizations that engage in misconduct. As social psychologist John Darley notes, the diffusion and fragmentation of information and responsibility in an organization, which are by-products of the division of labor and specialization in organizational settings, will often lead to wrongdoing. These processes have often been observed in organizations whose actions end up harming others. They include Ford's decision to continue marketing the Pinto model even after internal revelations that the car's fuel tank had a potentially fatal design defect,[10] and NASA's disastrous decision to launch the *Challenger* space shuttle despite warnings that some components had not been proven safe in a launch at cold temperature.[11] The pervasive presence of these dynamics in professional firms—ostensibly organized as partnerships in which members are expected to grasp and be accountable for the bigger picture—underscores the importance of understanding how information becomes disaggregated and responsibility is diffused.

If disaggregation and diffusion marked the review process at KPMG, different informational dynamics were at the core of the review process implemented at Jenkens & Gilchrist. Once the decision was made to have Daugerdas open a branch office in Chicago, the firm instituted a review process in which a tax lawyer in Texas would sign off on opinions emanating from Chicago. This system was consistent with similar review processes already instituted at the firm. The assumption was that it would be sufficient to protect the firm from the risks associated with Daugerdas's tax practice.

Some tax lawyers at the firm suggested to management that effective oversight required someone familiar with the highly technical subject of tax shelters in general and with the specific transactions for which opinions were being issued. One problem was that no one in the firm had worked on tax shelters. Michael Cook, who agreed to review Daugerdas's strategies, was presented with opinions that were based on representations about transactions and clients' motivation for entering into them. He was not in a position, however, to determine if those representations accurately described a client's genuine intentions. The client's purpose was crucial in assessing whether tax losses from the transaction were likely to be upheld, since clients had to be motivated by a legitimate business purpose or reasonable hope of economic gain. While Cook could review the technical aspects of the strategies, he did not have access to the very information he needed to distinguish legitimate tax strategies from abusive ones.

Like Mark Watson at KPMG, Cook was assigned a nearly impossible task. The firm had already implicitly endorsed Daugerdas's shelter practice by deciding to hire him after a debate on its propriety. Daugerdas likely assumed that he would routinely receive approval for transactions that followed this template. In addition, Cook effectively stood between his partners and a projected additional $6 million to divide among themselves (including himself, of course). The structure that was implemented, in which a single lawyer with limited authority inside the firm was asked to review dozens of complex potentially lucrative transactions, was a recipe for failure.

In both the KPMG and Jenkens cases, geographic distance coupled with communication technologies exacerbated the weaknesses of the process. Mark Watson was acutely aware that tax leaders of his firm were monitoring his decision-making process. Many of them, including Jeff Stein and John Lanning, the vice chair of Tax Services, were not located at Washington National Tax, where Watson worked, but in KPMG's New York office. During the review, they remained largely invisible, announcing their presence occasionally by email to urge approval. Emails, like other communication technologies, provide only an incomplete account of the sender's intent. KPMG tax leaders used them to augment their power by turning them into communications by disembodied and omniscient overseers.[12] When the time came time to approve BLIPS, Larry DeLap wrote Watson an email, copying the tax leaders, pressing him to sign off. Because DeLap was in California, Watson did not have the opportunity to voice his concerns in a face-to-face conversation or to determine whether DeLap had similar hesitations. Had their offices been in close proximity, they might have talked informally and developed a strategy to push back against senior tax leadership. At KPMG, email functioned to rally the converted and to isolate and weaken those who had reservations or counseled a more cautious approach.

At Jenkens & Gilchrist, the geographic isolation of the Chicago office from the main office in Dallas, coupled with the failure to have a long-term Jenkens lawyer in the same office as Daugerdas, created similar challenges. In the modern age, Daugerdas's location in Chicago, far from the firm's Dallas headquarters, would present no obstacle to effectively practicing as a member of the firm. It would, however, mean that Daugerdas would not be subject to the kind of informal norms that people can impose in regular face-to-face relationships with one another. For all intents and purposes, Daugerdas ran his own practice just as he had before; only the name of the law firm on the door was different. This may have reinforced his sense that he could operate more or less in an unfettered fashion. Reviewing Daugerdas's tax strategies back in Austin, Cook was significantly hampered by his inability to gauge Daugerdas's aggressiveness and his lack of any contact with the clients who purchased them.

At both KPMG and Jenkens, opportunities for face-to-face conversations during the review process might have opened up avenues for different choices and courses of action.

Organizational Commitment Bias

As these examples suggest, environment and organizational structure interacted to shape the interpretations, decisions, and actions of the tax professionals who participated in the tax shelter market. Two other types of cognitive and decision-making dynamics occurred repeatedly as firms became invested in participating in the tax shelter industry. These dynamics, which have been observed in individuals, are intensified in the organizational context.

The first is a phenomenon described among economists as the "sunk cost" problem. Once an individual invests resources in a course of action, it is very difficult to reverse course, even when continuing will likely result in harmful or costly outcomes. The problem of sunk costs is exacerbated in the organizational context. As Darley notes, "[i]t is hard enough for an individual to reserve a personal decision, even when no one else knows of the decision. In organizational settings, the decisions are far harder to reverse."[13] The employee who originally advocated for the decision is likely to suffer adverse reputational and career-related consequences; the organization risks embarrassment because costly resources have been wasted in implementing the decision.

The difficulty of altering course came up frequently at the firms involved in the tax shelter industry. KPMG, Ernst & Young, and other firms routinely continued to sell a particular shelter, even after a decision had been made that promotion of the shelter should cease. The continued sales were justified on the grounds that clients had already signed a retainer agreement. Only PwC, responding to intense public embarrassment from the exposure of its tax shelter activities on Capitol Hill, decided to exit the shelter market, unwind the transactions, and refund fees to clients.

The cognitive dynamics associated with the problem of reversing the decision to market shelters are reflected in the interpretative gloss that Michael Kerekes, a member of the tax shelter group at BDO, gave to Notice 2000-44, which was issued by the IRS in August of 2000. The notice made clear that the agency intended to challenge the tax benefits claimed from Son of BOSS transactions. In analyzing the notice, Kerekes correctly recognized that it applied to the transactions then being marketed by BDO. His memo focused exclusively, however, on the effective date of the listing requirements that applied to BDO. It failed to address the heart of the notice, which was the IRS's position that Son of BOSS shelters did not have economic substance. As the memo emphasized, "it does not discuss whether the Notice should be viewed as having any effect on the substantive law relating to the transactions."[14]

A more complete reading of the notice would have concluded that it raised a serious question about all the Son of BOSS transactions that BDO had already sold. It also would have addressed the further question of whether the firm should consider unwinding the transactions, or, at the very least inform clients who had already bought the strategy that there was a significant risk of challenge. Not only did Kerekes's memo not consider these issues, it went so far as to argue that the memo did not apply to future transactions for which the firm already had an engagement letter. This gave the firm a green light to implement transactions that were already in the works without listing them with the IRS. Coupled with the failure to discuss the central issue raised by the notice, the strained logic of Kerekes's memo suggests that he was so wedded to promoting Son of BOSS shelters that he was incapable of revisiting the question of whether they were legitimate tax reduction strategies.

Jenkens & Gilchrist also exhibited a stubborn commitment to an ultimately disastrous course of action despite gaining information that should have led it at least to consider whether to reverse course. Paul Daugerdas had projected revenues of about $6 million a year when he was negotiating moving to the firm. In 1999, however, his practice produced about $28 million in income, or almost five times the amount that the firm anticipated. This figure was more than 13 percent of the firm's total revenues. In 2000, he generated almost $91 million in income, or almost a third of Jenkens's revenues.

This vast increase in expected revenues raised two potential issues. First, could a tax practice relying on mass products and standard routines legitimately generate such massive revenues, or did this order of magnitude suggest that the firm should look more closely at Daugerdas's practice? Second, if the firm continued to support the practice, transactions of this volume would require a much more extensive oversight process than the firm had established. Jenkens management never confronted either issue. Reexamining the propriety of Daugerdas's practice and the effectiveness of the firm's monitoring system would have required admission that the firm may have erred in its initial decisions. In addition, of course, it could have jeopardized the substantial flow of income from tax shelter practice. While the need to revisit the firm's earlier decisions may seem obvious from the outside, not doing so seemed reasonable to those immersed in the situation.

Beyond illuminating the organizational dimensions of professional activity, the shelter industry has implications for the status and authority of tax advisors in the American tax system. In particular, it raises the question whether tax lawyers can advise clients consistent with the professional norms to which they have traditionally claimed adherence, given that the organizations in which professionals practice tend to magnify rather than buffer the competitive forces to which they are prey. Allegiance to these ideals is not simply a reflection of a self-serving ideology that rationalizes the material benefits and social status that lawyers enjoy—although lawyers have certainly invoked these ideals for this purpose. The assumption that tax professionals will encourage lawful conduct by their clients is incorporated into the fabric of the American tax system.

The Role of Tax Advisors in Promoting Compliance

The elite American bar has long justified the prerogatives it has been granted by society by invoking the conception of the independent counselor. Under this ideal, articulated by the legal philosopher Lon Fuller more than half a century ago, in the lawyer's office "the lawyer's quiet counsel *takes the place* of force."[15] For Fuller, as for elite lawyers who espoused this view, a lawyer's capacity to counsel clients to engage in law-abiding behavior promoted freedom in a democratic society. This was particularly true for wealthy clients with the strongest incentives and greatest resources to evade legal requirements. Rather than rely on intrusive oversight and enforcement mechanisms to elicit their compliance with legal norms, society could rely on wealthy individuals voluntarily to obey legal mandates in accordance with their lawyers' advice. As the Supreme Court emphasized three decades later, the role of a lawyer in encouraging legal compliance was the rationale for giving the attorney-client privilege a wide scope in the realm of client counseling.[16]

In tax practice, the importance of advice in promoting compliance is reflected in the function of tax opinions to abate penalties that taxpayers would otherwise be required to pay for understatement of taxes. Under the applicable standards, the IRS prohibits an opinion author from advising a client about the likelihood of audit or detection of the strategy. Instead, the lawyer is required to opine that more likely than not a court would uphold the tax benefits of the transaction were it challenged by the IRS. In other words, the lawyer is expected to give his or her expert opinion as to whether the tax treatment favored by the client is consistent with the law. Moreover, the provision that a taxpayer can avoid penalties by reasonably relying on a more-likely-than-not opinion assumes that tax lawyers are motivated to advise clients against engaging in abusive tax strategies.

In addition to securing their clients' compliance, tax advisors have a role in promoting positive tax morale—the belief that citizens should meet their tax obligations because others are paying their share. A distinctive feature of the tax regime is that taxpayers' sense of obligation is especially sensitive to expectations of how other taxpayers will behave. Research indicates that high rates of compliance with tax obligations are significantly correlated with what is called high "tax morale": "the intrinsic motivation to pay taxes based on citizens' sense of obligation to their state." This sense of obligation is quite fragile, because it is not simply an internally derived attitude. Rather, it is highly sensitive to the attitudes and behavior of others, as well as influenced by perceptions of government.[17]

As one researcher puts it, tax compliance is "a social act." A sense of intrinsic obligation is the product of "conditional cooperation." Research indicates that if a taxpayer perceives that there is a high percentage of other taxpayers who avoid paying their fair share, she is less likely to comply with her own obligations. In those circumstances, she doesn't want to be a "sucker" who incurs the cost of helping support a cooperative scheme for free riders who benefit from it without contributing to it. In addition, less tangibly, lower compliance in this situation may reflect the desire to conform to norms of social behavior. In any event, tax morale, and thus compliance, decreases as people believe tax evasion to be more common. Research on tax morale, in other words, suggests a certain paradox: a taxpayer's sense of *categorical* obligation to pay taxes is *conditioned* on the perception that a critical mass of other people share the same attitude.

Taxpayers' sensitivity to others' behavior can create a particular challenge for tax law because research suggests that most people believe that other taxpayers are less committed to paying their fair share of taxes than they are. As a result, any given taxpayer contemplating compliance may begin with an attitude of suspicion that potentially could disrupt conditional cooperation. As one scholar describes it, "The systematic misperception that other people hold norms and views that are less supportive of honest taxpaying could lead to a vicious cycle of people adapting their own ethics and behavior to these perceived norms and thus contributing themselves to the invidious culture."[18]

In this respect, tax compliance can be likened to an assurance game, in contrast to a prisoner's dilemma. In the prisoner's dilemma, noncooperation is the dominant strategy for an individual regardless of what other people do. A prisoner's dilemma scenario reflects the following preference ordering: "(I) I do not contribute, but enough others do; (II) we all contribute; (III) no one contributes; (IV) I contribute, but not enough others do."[19] The absence of communication or enforceable agreements to cooperate, reflected in the prisoner's dilemma, leads a participant to reason that if sufficient people cooperate to provide a common benefit, it is preferable not to cooperate and to free-ride on their efforts. Alternatively, if not enough people cooperate, it's best not to do so, thereby avoiding the cost of participating without receiving the benefits of shared participation. In the first instance, we can analogize a participant's reasoning to greed, in the second to fear, both born of self-interest.

As the scholar Daphna Lewinsohn-Zamir suggests, failure to cooperate in some cases may be due neither to greed nor to fear but to what she calls "hopelessness."[20] In this scenario, a person's highest-ranked preference may be that everyone contributes so that all will enjoy a common benefit. This person may not cooperate, however, because "[b]oth the knowledge that one's own contribution will have a miniscule effect on the desired outcome and the fear that not enough others will contribute may create a feeling of hopelessness: People reason that, regardless of what they choose to do, the collective goal will not be achieved."[21] If they somehow had assurance that others would cooperate, they would, too.

In an assurance game, an individual's preference ordering is as follows: "(I) everyone contributes; (II) no one contributes; (III) I do not contribute, but others do; (IV) I contribute, but others do not."[22] In contrast to a prisoner's dilemma, there is no dominant strategy in an assurance game. That is, an individual's choice is dependent upon what others do. If others cooperate, the individual will also do so, because, unlike the preference ordering in a prisoner's dilemma, the individual prefers mutual cooperation. If others do not cooperate, she will not, because she would incur the cost of cooperating without achieving the common benefit. Either alternative is an equilibrium, since no one has an incentive to change her behavior when she knows what other people will do.

The likelihood of cooperation in an assurance game "depends to a great extent on the existence and quality of information regarding the action that is likely to be taken by others (or likely to be expected by everyone to be taken by others)."[23] Thinking of tax compliance as an assurance game thus underscores that in this area of law compliance rests on a basic norm of obligation that is highly susceptible to being overridden by the perception of noncompliance by others.

A tax advisor can play a critical role in this assurance game, serving as both an explicit and implicit source of information for the client about other taxpayers' behavior. Clients reasonably assume that a lawyer who is a tax specialist is familiar with a large number of other taxpayers. The lawyer may expressly tell the client that most people are taking advantage of certain tax provisions. Or she may communicate the idea that others treat tax law as rules that define the terms of a contest with the IRS. She also may implicitly convey such information through the way she discusses the tax code and the remarks she makes about the IRS. If the lawyer fosters the perception that other taxpayers lack a sense of civic obligation, she can lead the client to adopt a similar attitude in self-defense. By contrast, conveying a sense of respect for the tax law and of the good faith of other taxpayers can help secure the cooperation necessary for the tax system to work.[24]

Historically, it was assumed that professional norms that encouraged tax lawyers to advise their clients to comply with tax laws were imparted informally through the organizations in which tax professionals worked and the organized tax bar activities in which they participated. This view was of a piece with the traditional account of professional self-regulation, under which lawyers were given broad discretion to determine the rules and conditions of practice that would foster their capacity to exercise their expert judgment to further societal aims. As the tax shelter episode illustrates, the organizations in which tax lawyers practice can no longer be trusted to buffer lawyers from competitive market forces or instill professional norms.

The Limits of Traditional Professional Self-Regulation

In the traditional account of professionalism, each profession was an island of self-regulation, which enjoyed a measure of insulation from both market pressures and state supervision. This insulation gave lawyers and accountants the freedom of action necessary to act consistent with professional ideals. Freed from subservience to market imperatives and government control, a profession, it was claimed, generated its own distinctive normative order. Law firms and accounting firms ostensibly served as the vehicle for socializing lawyers into that order, relying principally on informal organizational norms to regulate their members' behavior. For most of the twentieth century, tax lawyers in elite law firms were especially effective in developing and sustaining a shared sense of the boundaries of ethical tax practice. Norm enforcement relied not so much on specific rules that a practitioner consulted when deciding how to behave, but on the cultivation of a certain expertise and orientation to tax practice.

As chapter 3 describes, several forces have undermined belief in the continued viability of the implicit professional bargain. Intensified market pressures have made financial performance an increasingly important consideration in law and accounting firms. Of necessity, lawyers must attend more to economic self-interest in their deliberations, creating the risk that traditional professional values will be subordinated or displaced. In tax practice, this development has led respectable mainstream organizations to provide more aggressive advice to clients and become involved in abusive shelter work. In addition, the tax practice community has become more fragmented, and there is less consensus about the norms that should guide practice. The result is increasing skepticism about relying on the legal and accounting professions to police themselves and to ensure that professionals act ethically. This raises doubts about the extent to which law and accounting firms can serve as sites in which shared professional ideals are articulated and enacted in daily practice. If tax lawyers are to revive the norms that animated their traditional counseling role, they will have to explore alternative avenues of engagement with the tax regime.

Hybrid Regulation

What Ted Schneyer has called "bar corporatism" may elicit the revival of professional norms by providing a middle ground between traditional self-regulation and outside regulation of tax practitioners.[25] Under this approach, a regulatory agency with expertise in the field oversees practice in a specialized area, guided by dialogue and negotiation with practitioners. Schneyer suggested that such a regime emerged twenty years ago with respect to banking practice in the wake of the collapse of the savings and loan industry. When questions arose about the conduct of lawyers that had represented failing savings and loans, the federal Office of Thrift Supervision (OTS) did not wait for bar disciplinary authorities to act. Rather, the agency itself undertook aggressive enforcement action under interpretations of the ethics rules it regarded as applicable to banking lawyers.

As part of its response, the OTS worked closely with the private bar in establishing remedies and standards of conduct. Some firms, for instance, negotiated consent agreements with the agency that set forth detailed procedures for representing banking clients. The agency worked closely with the American Bar Association (ABA) Business Section to establish standards for preparing third-party legal opinions and reform other areas of banking practice. Reflecting on the OTS approach, Schneyer comments, "If the regulators are unwilling to defer to the traditional regime of professional self-regulation, they seem equally reluctant to dictate standards for lawyers unilaterally, such as through their own rulemaking proceedings. Instead, informal dialogue with a designated bar representative—the ABA—is the order of the day."[26]

Bar corporatism holds promise as a form of regulation that can include both outside oversight and participation by the bar in setting practice standards. While the bar is not completely self-governing, it has the opportunity to participate in shaping the rules that will govern practitioners. The regulatory agency welcomes such participation because it operates on the assumption that individuals are motivated to some degree by a desire to fulfill their professional obligations, not simply to avoid incurring penalties. This approach also accepts the possibility that this desire can lead professionals to establish and informally enforce norms of behavior that further compliance with regulations.

The tax shelter crisis, however, suggests that the tax bar's efforts to engage in a bar corporatist approach have been too narrow. Since Circular 230 was first enacted, the tax bar has collaborated with the IRS to articulate standards governing practice before the agency.[27] When the Treasury Department has considered revising these standards, it has solicited the views of the tax bar and given it an influential role in the process. On occasion, the tax bar has taken the initiative to propose more stringent requirements. At the height of the tax shelter crisis, for example, the organized tax bar mounted a vigorous campaign to strengthen regulations to deter shelter activity.[28]

Historically, however, the bar and IRS have emphasized controlling the conduct of individual tax professionals. Regulatory efforts have not given attention to the organizational influences that shape the conduct of tax professionals working in firms. As the rise of the shelter industry illustrates, wrongdoing by professional firms is a product of interactions among its environment, structure, and the cognitive and decision-making dynamics generated by the specialization and diffusion of responsibility. In exploring new regulatory directions, tax lawyers and the IRS might focus on developing approaches that limit professional organizations' incentives to engage in tax shelter activity. Such an approach would pay attention to the less visible organizational influences that gave rise to the shelter market. It would also empower law and accounting firms to resist client pressures. The current period of low demand for shelters is an opportune moment for the tax bar to explore initiatives that will permit them to resist client pressure when the demand for shelters arises again.

The tax bar might, for example, engage with the IRS to develop an amendment to Circular 230 that would render firms liable for involvement in abusive tax shelter by their members. One such approach would be to extend firm liability to any instance in which there is failure to take reasonable steps to ensure compliance with Circular 230 provisions. A second measure, which would create even more incentive to develop an adequate compliance program, would provide that a firm is presumptively vicariously liable for any of its practitioners' violations of Circular 230. The firm, however, could either assert a defense or receive lenient treatment if it had in place an effective compliance system.

This second proposal mirrors the Organizational Sentencing Guidelines, which have prompted the development of extensive compliance programs in corporations. As two practitioners have observed, "Without question, the Guidelines' greatest practical effect thus far is to raise the business community's awareness of the need for effective compliance programs."[29] The rules could also require certification of the effectiveness of a compliance program from the head of tax practice and managing partner of the firm, similar to the certifications currently required by top management of internal control systems.

Consistent with responsive regulatory approaches, the IRS would not dictate the procedures that firms used, but would focus on outcomes.[30] Firms would be able to establish whatever procedures they believed were effective in ensuring compliance with Circular 230. This independence would provide the opportunity for the exercise of professional discretion, and would encourage the involvement of tax practitioners and other lawyers in the firm in establishing and enforcing practice norms. Some firms might choose to share the details of their compliance programs with the IRS, which could publicize those that it believed reflected best practices. The result ideally would be an evolving set of evidence-based compliance procedures.

The different structures of accounting firms and law firms would require different organizational approaches. As the previous chapters suggest, accounting firms engaged in coordinated shelter strategies that received an imprimatur of legitimacy from high-level executives. Transforming organizational incentives in accounting firms to discourage tax shelter activity would require attending to the hierarchical reporting structure of accounting firms and their historical tendency to meld revenue-generating and compliance functions.

One possible model might be the firm-wide changes E&Y implemented in response to the adverse publicity it received in 2003 as a result of the Permanent Subcommittee on Investigations' investigation into the firm's tax shelter activities. According to the nonprosecution agreement the firm entered into in 2013, E&Y had "implemented extensive changes to its governance and compliance procedures, and also substantially increased the number of its legal and tax quality and risk management personnel." Its software-based Quality and Integrity Program, which monitored data entered by members of its tax practice regarding a range of tax engagement matters, was praised by the IRS as a model for an effective compliance program. E&Y also instituted a series of procedures and practices to ensure legal and ethical conduct among its tax professionals and firm-wide.[31]

Expanding the reach of Circular 230 would also create an incentive for law firms to respond to the challenges posed by their structures, which are less integrated and centralized than those of accounting firms. At law firms, the risk of individual lawyers' involvement in tax shelters is exacerbated by a reluctance to establish constraints on profitable individuals and practices and the uneven distribution of management skills in firms. Work on abusive shelters by lawyers in corporate firms was likely to result from a combination of pressures for individual performance, the opportunity to avoid close firm oversight, and competitive pressures on firms that led them to look the other way when they suspected that high revenues might be the product of questionable activity. The prospect of firm liability could serve as one incentive for firms to take more robust steps to monitor behavior in the face of these tendencies.

Broadening the scope of Circular 230 to encompass firm liability for wrongdoing by members of a firm's tax practice is one possible approach to address firms' roles in causing misconduct, but there are others to be explored. Regulatory and professional initiatives that give attention to organizational factors would complement and enhance existing measures to discourage tax shelter activity, including enforcement of regulatory requirements and, in the most egregious circumstances, recourse to the criminal process. These approaches would seek to deter misbehavior by tax professionals who take a calculating approach to compliance with professional standards. Organizational approaches developed collaboratively by the tax bar and the IRS might also encourage the articulation of professional norms and elicit informal efforts to enforce them. They might also prompt interpretation of sanctions as expressions of support for and commitment to professional ideals and practices.

Conclusion

Lawyers' and accountants' involvement in the tax shelter crisis at the turn of the century differs from culpable professionals' roles in other corporate scandals in recent years. Participants in shelter activity did not simply play a supporting role in the wrongdoing of others; they were major protagonists in the commission of fraud. Tax professionals developed hypertechnical interpretations of obscure provisions of the tax code, designed and marketed highly complex shelters, and sold lengthy opinions to purchasers claiming that the shelters would be upheld in court. This recent shelter episode also differs from earlier ones because accountants and lawyers were not sketchy salesmen trying to sell partnerships in dubious real estate deals to generate phony tax losses. They were partners in Big Five accounting firms and prestigious law firms, whose reputations gave shelter transactions a patina of respectability. Professionals at the heart of the tax system, in other words, were actively working to undermine it.

For the moment tax shelter activity abetted by elite professional firms in the United States appears to have declined. But, if the past is any indication, it is unlikely that the industry has been shut down for good. The tax code is likely to become more complex, and financial instruments more complicated. Avenues to evade tax liability have moved and flourished off-shore. Competitive pressures on accounting and law firms almost certainly will continue to intensify, and the IRS is never a favorite of budgetary committees on Capitol Hill. For these reasons, while it is not possible to know what form they will take or what provisions of the Internal Revenue Code they will seek to exploit, there is a risk that at some point in the future a new wave of abusive shelters is likely to emerge. With current demand for shelters ebbing, professional organizations have an opportunity to put in place robust procedures that insulate them from the temptation to pursue abusive shelter work, and their members from organizational pressures to engage in it. If they can do this effectively, the next wave of abusive shelters may not be as severe, and accountants and lawyers may succeed in steering clear of wrongdoing.

The stakes for tax professionals are substantial. Across almost every area of specialization, lawyers and other professionals are becoming increasingly subject to external regulatory mandates, and their authority to regulate their practice is eroding. The vulnerability of the organizations in which lawyers practice creates risks of increasing external oversight and encroachment. As the shelter episode illustrates, one danger is that a handful of professionals will engage in wrongdoing and subject themselves and their firms to criminal liability. A more pervasive concern is that the public will become increasingly skeptical of claims by the accounting and legal professions that they are capable of regulating themselves to serve the public good, and will conclude that firms in which tax professionals practice are "professional service" firms in name only. At that point, the public is likely to demand a more intrusive regulatory response that could eliminate meaningful opportunities for the exercise of professional judgment at elite firms. Moreover, the professional ideals that once drew lawyers and accountants to sophisticated tax practice will no longer have much traction. If tax professionals are concerned about such developments, it behooves them to reinvigorate the commitments that have traditionally animated tax practice.

Notes

Introduction

1. John D. McKinnon, "Written Off: How New Tax Shelter Promised Big Savings but Finally Fell Apart—For PricewaterhouseCoopers, Complex Plan Proved an Embarrassment—the Old Paper-Clip Trick," *Wall Street Journal*, August 21, 2000, A1.

2. Ibid.

3. Janet Novack and Laura Sanders, "The Hustling of X Rated Tax Shelters," *Forbes*, December 14, 1998.

4. See U.S. Senate Committee on Governmental Affairs, Permanent Subcommittee on Investigations, *U.S. Tax Shelter Industry: The Role of Accountants, Lawyers, and Financial Professionals*, hearings, November 18 and 20, 2003 (Washington, D.C.: Government Printing Office, 2004), 4 vols.

5. Ibid., vol. 1, 255.

6. Ibid., 147.

7. Sheldon D. Pollack and Jay A. Soled, "Tax Professionals Behaving Badly," 105 *Tax Notes* 201 (October 11, 2004).

8. "Selected Exhibits Relating to BDO Seidman Enforcement Action," 2002 *TNT* 136-8 (July 16, 2002).

9. See Upjohn v. United States, 449 U.S. 383 (1981).

10. Robert W. Gordon and William H. Simon, "The Redemption of Professionalism?," in *Lawyers' Ideals/Lawyers' Practices: Transformations in the American Legal Profession*, ed. Robert L. Nelson, David M. Trubek, and Rayman L. Solomon (Ithaca: Cornell University Press, 1992), 230–231; Christine Parker and Tanina Rostain, "Law Firms, Global Capital, and the Sociological Imagination," *Fordham Law Review* 80 (2011–2012): 2347.

Chapter 1

1. "Practices and Procedures of the Internal Revenue Service," hearings before the Senate Finance Committee, 105th Cong. 190 (September 23, 24, and 25, 1997), 2.

2. "IRS Oversight," hearings before the Senate Finance Committee, 105th Cong. 598 (April 28, 29, 30, and May 1, 1998), 7.

3. See Ryan J. Donmoyer, "Inspector General Deems IRS Witness Allegations 'Unfounded,'" 1998 *TNT* 80-1 (April 27, 1998).

4. John D. McKinnon, "Highly Publicized Horror Story That Led to Curbs on IRS Quietly Unravels in Virginia Civil Court," *Wall Street Journal*, December 9, 1999, A28; Ryan J. Donmoyer, "News Analysis: 'Jackbooted IRS Thugs' Face Bigger Weapons Than They Carry," 1998 *TNT* 90-4 (May 11, 1998).

5. Barbara Kirchheimer, "Business-Related Portions of Contract Could Change," 1995 *TNT* 30-1 (February 14, 1995).

6. Sheldon D. Pollack, *Refinancing America: The Republican Antitax Agenda* (Albany: SUNY Press, 2002), 83.

7. Internal Revenue Service, "IT Modernization Vision and Strategy" (October 2006), 5, available at http://www.irs.gov/pub/irs-news/mvs-10-06.pdf (accessed December 12, 2013).

8. General Accounting Office (GAO), "IRS Does Not Adequately Manage Its Operating Funds" (February 1994), reprinted in 1994 *TNT* 28-80. In 2004, the General Accounting Office's name was changed to the Government Accountability Office.

9. GAO, "IRS Results of Fiscal Year 1998 Financial Statement Audit" (1998), 1.

10. GAO, "Report to the Commissioner of Internal Revenue, Custodial Financial Weaknesses," General Accounting Office (1999), 2, available at www.gao.gov/assets/230/227768.pdf.

11. Ibid.

12. Isaac William Martin, *The Permanent Tax Revolt: How the Property Tax Transformed American Politics* (Stanford: Stanford University Press, 2008), 2.

13. Ibid., 12.

14. Ibid., 15.

15. Thomas Byrne Edsall and Mary D. Edsall, *Chain Reaction* (New York: W. Norton, 1991), 131.

16. Ibid., 116–131.

17. Jacob S. Hacker and Paul Pierson, "Tax Politics and the Struggle over Activist Government," in *The Transformation of American Politics: Activist Government and the Rise of Conservatism*, ed. Paul Pierson and Theda Skocpol (Princeton: Princeton University Press, 2007), 256, 262.

18. Romain Huret, *A Republic without Taxpayers? Tax Resisters in the United States from the Civil War to the Present* (Cambridge, Mass.: Harvard University Press, forthcoming 2014), 279 (manuscript on file with authors).

19. Hacker and Pierson, "Tax Politics," 263–265.

20. Contract with America (1994), http://www.nationalcenter.org/ContractwithAmerica.html (accessed September 19, 2013).

21. David Cay Johnston, "Behind I.R.S. Hearings, a G.O.P. Plan to End Tax Code," *New York Times*, May 4, 1998, A16.

22. See Michael J. Graetz, *100 Million Unnecessary Returns: A Simple, Fair, and Competitive Tax Plan for the United States* (New Haven: Yale University Press, 2008), 39.

23. Alison Mitchell, "Leaders of G.O.P. Seek to Overhaul Federal Tax Code," *New York Times*, September 28, 1997, 36–37.

24. http://www.atr.org/userfiles/Congressional_pledge(1).pdf (accessed October 9, 2013).

25. In 1997, only 16 percent of individual returns were electronically filed. By 2000, it was finally above 25 percent. See Tracey Anderson, Mark Fox, and Bill N. Schwartz, "History and Trends in E-filing: A Survey of CPA Practitioners," *CPA Journal Online*, http://www.nysscpa.org/cpajournal/2005/1005/essentials/p66.htm (accessed September 19, 2013).

26. See Carol Steinberg, "Raking In Taxes Is Hard Work for the I.R.S., Too," *New York Times*, April 16, 2000.

27. David Cay Johnston, *Perfectly Legal* (New York: Portfolio, 2003), 157–158; David Cay Johnston, "Computers Clogged, I.R.S. Seeks to Hire Outside Processors," *New York Times*, January 31, 1997. See also Steinberg, "Raking In Taxes."

28. David Cay Johnston, "Your Taxes: Some New Tricks to Help Filers Avoid an Old Audit Trap," *New York Times*, February 25, 1996, A1.

29. Charles O. Rossotti, *Many Unhappy Returns: One Man's Quest to Turn Around the Most Unpopular Organization in America* (Boston: Harvard Business Review Press, 2005), 3.

30. Johnston, *Perfectly Legal*, 158; David C. Johnston, "End of the I.R.S. Pipeline: Tax Returns of '90s Meet I.R.S. Technology of '60s," *New York Times*, April 15, 1995, 31.

31. Johnston, *Perfectly Legal*, 158–159; Johnston, "Computers Clogged."

32. Johnston, "End of the I.R.S. Pipeline."

33. Johnston, *Perfectly Legal*, 160.

34. David Cay Johnston, "I.R.S. Puts Off Plan for Detailed Audits of Random Returns," *New York Times*, October 24, 1995, 1.

35. Johnston, "Your Taxes: Some New Tricks," 26.

36. Johnston, *Perfectly Legal*, 160–161.

37. Johnston, "I.R.S. Puts Off Plan."

38. GAO, "IRS' Partnership Compliance Activities Could Be Improved" (June 1995), 6. http://www.gpo.gov/fdsys/pkg/gaoreports-ggd-95-151/pdf/gaoreports -ggd-95-151.pdf (accessed October 9, 2013).

39. Johnston, *Perfectly Legal*, 177–178.

40. Ryan J. Donmoyer, "Executive Brain Drain Leaves IRS Searching for Leadership," 1995 *TNT* 163-1 (August 21, 1995).

41. Johnston, *Perfectly Legal*, 151, 132.

42. GAO, "Tax Administration: IRS' Partnership Compliance Activities Could Be Improved"; GAO, "Tax Administration: Tax Requirements of Small Businesses" (August 1999), www.gpo.gov/fdsys/pkg/GAOREPORTS-GGD-99-133/html/GAOREPORTS-GGD-99-133.htm (accessed October 9, 2013).

43. Department of the Treasury, "The Problem of Corporate Tax Shelters: Discussion, Analysis, and Legislative Proposals" (July 1999), www.treasury.gov/resource-center/tax-policy/Documents/CTSwhite.pdf (accessed October 9, 2013).

44. Ibid.

45. Johnston, *Perfectly Legal*, 166–168.

46. "IRS Oversight," hearings before the Senate Finance Committee, 1.

47. Rossotti, *Many Unhappy Returns*, 7–13.

48. Senator Frank Murkowski quoted in Johnston, *Perfectly Legal*, 14.

49. Rossotti, *Many Unhappy Returns*, 12–13.

50. "Infernal Revenue Disservice," *Newsweek*, October 13, 1997, www.highbeam.com/doc/1G1-19856453.html (accessed October 9, 2013).

51. The Honorable William H. Webster, Review of the Internal Revenue Service's Criminal Investigation Division, April 1999, available at 1999 *TNT* 71-40.

52. Johnston, *Perfectly Legal*, 148.

53. Ibid.

54. Ibid., 148–149.

55. Richard W. Stevenson, "Senate Votes 97–0 to Overhaul I.R.S. after Complaints," *New York Times*, May 8, 1998, A1.

56. U.S. Code, Title 26, §7525(a)(1). Communications regarding tax shelters, however, were not protected by the statutory privilege; see ibid., §7525(b)(2).

57. Robert Manning and David F. Windish, "The IRS Restructuring and Reform Act: An Explanation," 1998 *TNT* 128-104 (July 6, 1998).

58. "Report of the Joint Committee on Taxation Relating to the Internal Revenue Service as Required by the IRS Reform and Restructuring Act of 1998," 1999 *TNT* 99-23 (May 24, 1999).

59. Rossotti, *Many Unhappy Returns*, 2.

60. Ibid., 15.

61. David Cay Johnston, "Senate Panel Applauds Changes at I.R.S.," *New York Times*, April 15, 1999, C8.

62. Archie Ingersoll, "IRS Campaign Stresses Warm, Cuddly Side," *Wall Street Journal*, August 1, 2000, B2.

63. George Guttman, "The Interplay of Enforcement and Voluntary Compliance," 1999 *TNT* 118-9 (June 18, 1999).

64. Amy Hamilton, "Rossotti Gives Risky Speech on State of IRS Reform," 1999 *TNT* 146-3 (July 29, 1999).

65. Amy Hamilton, "Lawmakers Track IRS Reform One Year Later," 1999 *TNT* 141-2 (July 22, 1999).

66. Manning and Windish, "The IRS Restructuring and Reform Act."

67. David Cay Johnston, "White House Seeks to Ease Rules Put on I.R.S. Workers," *New York Times*, February 12, 2002, C4.

68. Johnston, *Perfectly Legal*, 175.

69. David Cay Johnston, "I.R.S. Workers Face More Investigations by Treasury Agents," *New York Times*, November 18, 1999, A1.

70. Johnston, "White House Seeks to Ease Rules"; David Cay Johnston, "Court Is Asked to Block False Complaints Against I.R.S.," *New York Times*, December 9, 2003, C4.

71. Ibid.

72. Hamilton, "Lawmakers Track IRS Reform."

73. Johnston, *Perfectly Legal*, 152.

74. Ibid.

75. Ibid., 151.

76. Ibid., 151–152; David Cay Johnston, "Job Fears Push I.R.S. Workers to Relax Effort," *New York Times*, May 18, 1999, A1; McKinnon, "Highly Publicized Horror Story," A28.

77. Karen Hube, "The Aftermath—Return to Sender: The IRS Is Auditing Fewer People These Days but Trying to Guess the Red Flags Isn't Easy," *Wall Street Journal*, February 28, 2000, R19.

78. "Report of the Joint Committee on Taxation Relating to the Internal Revenue Service as Required by the IRS Reform and Restructuring Act of 1998," 2000 *TNT* 84-67 (May 3, 2000).

79. David Cay Johnston, "I.R.S. More Likely to Audit the Poor and Not the Rich," *New York Times*, April 16, 2000, 11.

Chapter 2

1. Michael J. Graetz, *100 Million Unnecessary Returns: A Simple, Fair, and Competitive Tax Plan for the United States* (New Haven: Yale University Press, 2008), 116.

2. Knetsch v. United States, 364 U.S. 361 (1960).

3. In 1954 the Code was amended to exclude prospectively the deduction of any indebtedness incurred to purchase "a single premium life insurance, endowment, or annuity contract."

4. Knetsch v. United States, 364 U.S. at 362; 364 U.S. at 366 (quoting Gilbert v. Commissioner, 248 F.2d 399, 411 (dissenting opinion)).

5. Ibid.

6. 293 U.S. 465, 470 (1935).

7. 293 U.S. 465, 469 (1935).

8. Leandra Lederman, "W(h)ither Economic Substance?," *Iowa Law Review* 389 (2010): 95.

9. United Parcel Service of America, Inc. v. Commissioner, 254 F.3d 1014, 1019 (11th Cir. 2001).

10. Horn v. Commissioner, 968 F.2d 1229, 1230 (D.C. Cir. 1992).

11. Bail Bonds by Marvin Nelson, Inc. v. Commissioner, 820 F.2d 1543, 1549 (9th Cir. 1987).

12. David Weisbach, "Formalism in the Tax Law," *University of Chicago Law Review* 66 (1999): 867–868.

13. Ibid., 868.

14. Ibid., 869.

15. Ibid., 863 (footnote omitted).

16. Ibid., 864 (footnote omitted).

17. Ibid., 869.

18. Ibid., 869–871.

19. Ibid., 871.

20. Kristin E. Hickman and Claire Hill, "Concepts, Categories, and Compliance in the Regulatory State," *Minnesota Law Review* 94 (2010): 1151–1154.

21. Joseph Bankman, "The Tax Shelter Battle," in *The Crisis in Tax Administration*, ed. Henry J. Aaron and Joel Slemrod (Washington, D.C.: Brookings Institution Press, 2004), 9, 12.

22. Ibid.

23. James S. Eustice, "Abusive Corporate Tax Shelters: Old 'Brine' in New Bottles," *Tax Law Review* 55, no. 2 (2002): 141.

24. Daniel N. Shaviro, "The Story of Knetsch v. United States and Judicial Doctrines Combating Tax Avoidance," in *Tax Stories: An In-Depth Look at Ten Leading Federal Income Tax Cases*, ed. Paul L. Caron (New York: Foundation Press, 2002), 327.

25. Ibid., 369.

26. Michael Doran, "Tax Penalties and Tax Compliance," *Harvard Journal on Legislation* 46 (2009): 142.

27. Ibid.

28. See, e.g., IRS Form 1040, U.S. Individual Income Tax Return 2 (2012).

29. "Substantial Understatement of Income Tax," Treasury Reg. §1.6662-4(d).

30. "Definitions and Special Rules," U.S. Code, Title 26, §6664(d).

31. "Imposition of Accuracy-Related Penalty on Underpayments," U.S. Code, Title 26, §6662(a) (1999).

32. Shaviro, "The Story of Knetsch v. United States."

33. Ibid., 316.

34. Weisbach, "Formalism in the Tax Law," 220–221.

35. Gregory v. Helvering, 293 U.S. 465, 469 (1935).

36. Lederman, "W(h)ither Economic Substance?," 4.

37. Shaviro, "The Story of Knetsch v. United States," 369; David Weisbach, "Ten Truths about Tax Shelters," *Tax Law Review* 55 (2002): 222–225.

38. Interview with former government official.

39. Henry Ordower, "The Culture of Tax Avoidance," *Saint Louis University Law Review* 55 (2010): 53.

40. Ibid., 66.

41. Alan Murray and Jeffrey Birnbaum, *Showdown at Gucci Gulch: Lawmakers, Lobbyists, and the Unlikely Triumph of Tax Reform* (New York: Random House, 1988), 10.

42. Ordower, "The Culture of Tax Avoidance," 57.

43. Ibid., 70.

44. Dennis J. Ventry, Jr., "Tax Shelter Opinions Threatened the Tax System in the 1970s," 2006 *TNT* 99-30 (May 23, 2006).

45. George K. Yin, "Getting Serious about Corporate Tax Shelters: Taking a Lesson from History," *SMU Law Review* 54 (2001): 213.

46. Ventry, "Tax Shelter Opinions."

47. A subchapter S corporation is one with 100 shareholders or fewer whose profits and losses pass through to shareholders rather than being recorded on a tax return of the corporation. "S Corporation Defined," U.S. Code, Title 26, §1361.

48. Yin, "Getting Serious about Corporate Tax Shelters," 210–211.

49. Ibid., 211.

50. "Passive Activity Losses and Credits Limited," U.S. Code, Title 26, §469.

51. "Deductions Limited to Amount at Risk," U.S. Code, Title 26, §465.

52. Yin, "Getting Serious about Corporate Tax Shelters," 212.

Chapter 3

1. Robert B. Reich, *Supercapitalism: The Transformation of Business, Democracy, and Everyday Life* (New York: Vintage Press, 2007), 51.

2. L. G. Thomas, "The Two Faces of Competition: Dynamic Resourcefulness and the Hypercompetitive Shift," *Organization Science* 7 (May–June 1996): 221.

3. Ibid.

4. Ibid.

5. Reich, *Supercapitalism*, 30.

6. Ibid., 30, 60.

7. Ibid., 64.

8. Richard A. D'Aveni, *Hypercompetition* (New York: Free Press, 1994); L. G. Thomas and Richard A. D'Aveni, "The Changing Nature of Competition in the U.S. Manufacturing Sector, 1950–2002," *Strategic Organization* 7 (2009): 387.

9. D'Aveni, *Hypercompetition*, 217–218.

10. Reich, *Supercapitalism*, 51.

11. Ibid., 52.

12. Ibid., 65.

13. Diego Comin and Thomas Philippon, "The Rise in Firm-Level Volatility: Causes and Consequences," Working Paper 11388, National Bureau of Economic Research (May 2005), http://www.nber.org/papers/w11388.pdf (accessed December 18, 2013); Thomas, "The Two Faces of Competition," 225.

14. Neil Fligstein, *The Transformation of Corporate Control* (Cambridge, Mass.: Harvard University Press, 1990), 215.

15. Ibid., 239.

16. Ibid.

17. Edward D. Kleinbard, "Corporate Tax Shelters and Corporate Tax Management," *Tax Executive* 51 (1999): 238.

18. John R. Robinson, Stephanie Sikes, and Connie D. Weaver, "Performance Measurement of Corporate Tax Departments," *Accounting Review* 85 (2010): 1062.

19. Joel Slemrod, "The Economics of Corporate Tax Selfishness," Working Paper 10858, National Bureau of Economic Research (September 2004), 11.

20. Tracy Hollingsworth, *Manufacturers Alliance/MAPI Survey of Corporate Tax Departments*, 4th ed. (Arlington, Va.: Manufacturers Alliance/MAPI, 2002, copy on file with author), 67–68.

21. Clark, Martire & Bartolomeo, "A Study of Fortune 1000 Tax Directors," prepared for KPMG (December 2000).

22. Kleinbard, "Corporate Tax Shelters," 238.

23. The World Top Incomes Database, http://topincomes.g-mond .parisschoolofeconomics.eu (accessed September 25, 2013).

24. Ibid.

25. Ibid.

26. Ibid.

27. Lucian Bebchuk and Jesse Fried, *Pay without Performance: The Unfulfilled Promise of Executive Compensation* (Cambridge, Mass.: Harvard University Press, 2004), 1.

28. Carola Frydman and Raven E. Saks, "Historical Trends in Executive Compensation 1936–2003," http://eh.net/eha/system/files/eha-meeting-2006/pdf/session_2c_frydman_and_saks.pdf (accessed September 25, 2013).

29. Roger Lowenstein, *Origins of the Crash: The Great Bubble and Its Undoing* (New York: Penguin, 2004), 113.

30. Ibid., 124.

31. John Cassidy, *Dot.con: How America Lost Its Mind and Money in the Internet Era: The Greatest Story Ever Sold* (New York: HarperCollins, 2002), 85–86.

32. Ibid., 196–197.

33. Ibid., 244.

34. Ibid., 220.

35. Ibid., 120.

36. William M. Sullivan, *Work and Integrity: The Crisis and Promise of Professionalism in America* (San Francisco: Jossey-Bass, 2005); Eliot Freidson, *Professionalism: The Third Logic* (Chicago: University of Chicago Press, 2001).

37. Marc Galanter and William Henderson, "The Elastic Tournament: A Second Transformation of the Big Law Firm," *Stanford Law Review* 60 (2008).

38. Charles W. Wootton and Carel M. Wolk, "The Development of 'The Big Eight' Accounting Firms in the United States, 1900 to 1990," *Accounting Historians Journal* 1, no. 4 (1992): 16–17.

39. Michael Chatfield, *A History of Accounting Thought*, rev. ed. (New York: Krieger Publishing, 1977), 207–208.

40. Wootton and Wolk, "The Development of 'The Big Eight,'" 19.

41. Ibid., 7.

42. Paul D. Montagna, *Certified Public Accounting: A Sociological View of a Profession in Change* (Houston: Scholars Book Co., 1974).

43. Richard Susskind, *The End of Lawyers? Rethinking the Nature of Legal Services* (New York: Oxford University Press, 2009), 29.

44. Gary J. Previts and Barbara D. Merino, *A History of Accountancy in the United States: The Cultural Significance of Accounting* (Columbus: Ohio State University Press, 1998), 338–340.

45. Erwin O. Smigel, *The Wall Street Lawyer: Professional Organization Man?* (Glencoe, Ill.: Free Press, 1964); Montagna, *Certified Public Accounting*, 212.

46. Ibid.

47. United States v. Simon, 425 F.2d 796 (2d Cir. 1969), *cert. denied*, 397 U.S. 1006 (1970) (*"Continental Vending"*); Susan E. Squires et al., *Inside Arthur Andersen: Shifting Values, Unexpected Consequences* (Upper Saddle River, N.J.: Financial Times Prentice Hall, 2003), 68.

48. Squires et al., *Inside Arthur Andersen*, 69–70.

49. Montagna, *Certified Public Accounting*.

50. Ibid.; Stephen A. Zeff, "How Accounting Firms Got Where They Are Today," *Accounting Horizons* 17 (2003): 267.

51. Arthur Levitt, Jr., *Take on the Street: What Wall Street and Corporate America Don't Want You to Know* (New York: Pantheon Books, 2002).

52. Squires et al., *Inside Arthur Andersen*.

53. John Phillips and Richard C. Sansing, "Contingent Fees and Tax Compliance," *Accounting Review* 73 (1998): 2.

54. AICPA Code of Conduct Rulings 24 and 25, http://www.aicpa.org/Research/Standards/CodeofConduct/Pages/et_391.aspx (accessed October 8, 2013).

55. U.S. Senate Committee on Governmental Affairs, Permanent Subcommittee on Investigations, *U.S. Tax Shelter Industry: The Role of Accountants, Lawyers, and Financial Professionals*, hearings, November 18 and 20, 2003 (Washington, D.C.: Government Printing Office, 2004), www.gpo.gov/fdsys/pkg/CHRG.../pdf/CHRG-108shrg91043.pdf (accessed October 7, 2013).

56. John T. Lanning, "KPMG Recruiting Pitch: Practice Tax," *Legal Times* (September 6, 1999); Geanne Rosenberg, "Big Five Pays Top Dollar for Tax Partners—Especially KPMG," *National Law Journal* (November 6, 2000).

57. *Bowman's Accounting Report* 14 (March 2000): 2; Minority Staff Report, "Four KPMG Case Studies: FLIP, OPIS, BLIPS, and SC2," in Permanent Subcommittee on Investigations, *U.S. Tax Shelter Industry*, vol. 1, 166–167.

58. Ronald Gilson and Robert Mnookin, "Sharing among the Human Capitalists: An Economic Inquiry into the Corporate Law Firm and How Partners Split Profits," *Stanford Law Review* 37 (1985): 313.

59. Milton C. Regan, Jr., *Eat What You Kill: The Fall of a Wall Street Lawyer* (Ann Arbor: University of Michigan Press, 2005), 24–26.

60. Ibid., 27–29.

61. Jerome Carlin, *Lawyers' Ethics: A Survey of the New York City Bar* (New York: Russell Sage, 1966).

62. Tanina Rostain, "Self-Regulatory Authority, Markets and the Ideology of Professionalism," in *The Oxford Handbook of Regulation*, ed. Robert Baldwin et al. (Oxford: Oxford University Press, 2010), 182–184.

63. Carlin, *Lawyers' Ethics*.

64. Robert L. Nelson, *Partners with Power: The Social Transformation of the Large Law Firm* (Berkeley: University of California Press, 1988).

65. Michael Hatfield, "Legal Ethics and Federal Taxes, 1945–1965: Patriotism, Duties, and Advice," *Florida Tax Review* 12 (2012): 55.

66. American Bar Association Standing Committee on Ethics and Professional Responsibility, Formal Opinion 314 (1965), Westlaw: ABA Formal Op. 314

67. ABA Section of Taxation, "Proposed Revision to Formal Opinion 314," reprinted in Bernard Wolfman and James Holden, *Ethical Problems in Federal Taxation*, 2nd ed. (Charlottesville: Michie, 1985), 71.

68. Seymour Mintz in "What Is Good Tax Practice: A Panel Discussion," New York University, Proceedings of the 31st Institute on Federal Taxation (1963), 24.

69. Randolph W. Thrower, "Preserving the Integrity of the Federal Tax System," New York University, Proceedings of the 33rd Institute on Federal Taxation (1975), 707, 708.

70. Henry Sellin, "Professional Responsibility of the Tax Practitioner," *Taxes* 52 (1974): 585.

71. Ibid., 606.

72. Randolph Paul, "The Responsibilities of the Tax Adviser," *Harvard Law Review* 63 (1950): 385.

73. Ibid., 384.

74. Sellin, "Professional Responsibility of the Tax Practitioner," 608.

75. "Does not the citizen owe his government and his neighbors the duty of pay-ing his share of taxes as required by law?" Jerome Hellerstein, "Ethical Problems in Office Counseling," *Tax Law Review* 8 (1952–1953): 9.

76. Merle Miller, "A Taxpayer's Duty to His Fellow Taxpayers," *NYU Annual Institute on Federal Taxation* 19 (1961): 2.

77. H. Brian Holland in "What Is Good Tax Practice," 34.

78. Merle Miller, "Morality in Tax Planning," *NYU Annual Institute on Federal Taxation* 10 (1952): 1081, 1083.

79. Peter Canellos, "A Tax Practitioner's Perspective on Substance, Form, and Business Purpose in Structuring Business Transactions and in Tax Shelters," *SMU Law Review* 54 (2001): 52, 55. While this article was published in 2001, it is an especially good expression of the perspective of the traditional elite tax bar.

80. Ibid., 53 (footnote omitted).

81. Ibid., 56; George Cooper, "The Avoidance Dynamic: A Tale of Tax Planning, Tax Ethics, and Tax Reform," *Columbia Law Review* 80 (1980): 1581 (distin-guishing between two types of advice: "(1) advice on how best from a tax stand-point to carry out a non-tax-motivated transaction that the client has already determined to pursue, and (2) advice on how to save taxes as an end in itself, without any particular transactional objectives in mind").

82. Cooper, "The Avoidance Dynamic," 1582.

83. Tanina Rostain, "Sheltering Lawyers: The Organized Bar and the Tax Shelter Industry," *Yale Journal on Regulation* 23 (2006): 114.

84. Ibid.

85. Canellos, "A Tax Practitioner's Perspective," 55.

86. Ibid., 49.

87. Jacob Rabkin, remarks in "Ethical Problems of Tax Practitioners," *Tax Law Review* 8 (1952): 28–29.

88. Cooper, "The Avoidance Dynamic."

89. Ibid., 1567.

90. Ibid., 1578.

91. Ibid.; Frederic Corneel, "Guidelines for Tax Practice Second," *Tax Law Re-view* 43 (1989–1990): 313.

92. "Inside the DuPont Legal Model," *New Legal Review* (May 11, 2010), http://www.cpaglobal.com/newlegalreview/4377/inside_dupont_legal_model (accessed October 8, 2013).

93. Joel Henning, "Strategic Planning," in *Hildebrandt Handbook of Law Firm Management* (New York: Hildebrandt International, 2012), chapter 1.

94. David Maister, *Managing the Professional Service Firm* (New York: Simon and Schuster, 1993).

95. Nelson, *Partners with Power*, 224.

96. Ibid.

97. David Jargiello and Phyllis Gardner, "Free Agent Dysfunction: Management Realpolitik for U.S. Law Firms" (August 16, 2010), 17, http://www.jargiellolaw.com/White_Paper_Series_-_Free_Agent_Dysfunction_-_Print_v3.2_-_COPY.pdf (accessed October 8, 2013).

98. Joseph Bankman, "The Business Purpose Doctrine and the Sociology of Tax," *SMU Law Review* 54 (2001): 154.

99. Rostain, "Sheltering Lawyers," 89 n. 50.

100. John Lanning, "A Tug-of-War over New Law Students," *Legal Times* (September 6, 1999), S42.

101. "E&Y First of Big Five in U.S. Market to Ally with Law Firm," *Journal of Accountancy* (January 2000).

102. Richard Lavoie, "Subverting the Rule of Law: The Judiciary's Role in Fostering Unethical Behavior," *University of Colorado Law Review* 75 (2004): 147–148.

103. Bankman, "The Business Purpose Doctrine and the Sociology of Tax," 151.

104. Ibid.

105. Ibid., 152.

Chapter 4

1. Mike Brewster, *Unaccountable: How Accounting Firms Forfeited the Public Trust* (Hoboken, N.J.: John Wiley & Sons, 2003), 112.

2. Michael Chatfield and Richard Vangermeersch, *The History of Accounting: An International Encyclopedia* (New York: Garland Publishing, 1996), 75; U.S. Senate Committee on Governmental Affairs, Permanent Subcommittee on Investigations, *U.S. Tax Shelter Industry: The Role of Accountants, Lawyers, and Financial Professionals*, hearings, November 18 and 20, 2003, vol. 1 (Washington, D.C.: Government Printing Office, 2004), 166.

3. Brewster, *Unaccountable*, 176.

4. *Bowman's Accounting Report* 14 (March 2000): 2. In 2000, KPMG separately incorporated its management consulting services group and sold off a 20 percent interest. Randall S. Thomas et al., "Megafirms," *North Carolina Law Review* 80 (2001): 166.

5. Jacoboni v. KPMG, et al., Case No. 6:02-CV-510-On1-22DAB, Richard (Larry) DeLap deposition (July 18, 2003), 203–204, SCDOR-License-029053. (Sources with SCDOR numbers refer to documents obtained by the South Carolina Department of Revenue in connection with an investigation into possible violations of South Carolina revenue regulations. These documents were obtained through a state Freedom of Information Act request.)

6. Ibid.

7. Jacoboni v. KPMG, Gregg W. Ritchie deposition (June 16, 2003), 31, SCDOR-License-026649.

8. Perez, et al., v. KPMG, et al., C2593-02-A, District Court, 92nd Judicial District, Hidalgo County, Robert A. Pfaff deposition (October 7, 2003), 15–16, SCDOR-License-026581.

9. Calvin Johnson, "Tales from the KPMG Skunk Works: The Basis-Shift or Defective-Redemption Shelter," 2005 *TNT* 142-30 (July 2005).

10. Perez, et al., v. KPMG, et al., Pfaff deposition (October 7, 2003), 15–16, SCDOR-License-026581.

11. Johnson, "Tales from the KPMG Skunk Works."

12. Geraldine Fabrikant, "The MCA Sale: The Deal; Seagram Puts the Finishing Touches on Its $5.7 Billion Acquisition of MCA," *New York Times*, April 10, 1995.

13. Lee A. Sheppard, "Can Seagram Bail Out of Dupont without Capital Gain," 1995 *TNT* 75-4 (April 18, 1995); Lee A. Sheppard, "Attention K Mart Shoppers: Tax Shelters in Aisle 6," 1998 *TNT* 182-6 (September 21, 1998).

14. Perez, et al., v. KPMG, et al., John Larson deposition (October 1, 2003), 19–21, SCDOR-License-026455.

15. Ibid., at 66, SCDOR-License-026473.

16. Treasury Regulation 1.302-2(c).

17. Johnson, "Tales from the KPMG Skunk Works." Our discussion draws heavily from this article.

18. Ibid., 439.

19. R. J. Ruble, "The Professional Responsibilities of a Tax Lawyer in the Context of Corporate Tax Shelters," Practicing Law Institute, Tax Law and Estate Planning Course Handbook Series, Tax Law and Practice, PLI Order No. J0-001E (October–November 1999).

20. United States v. John Larson, Robert Pfaff, and Raymond J. Ruble, 05 CR 888 (LAK) (S.D.N.Y.), government exhibit FO-99.

21. U.S. Senate Committee on Governmental Affairs, Permanent Subcommittee on Investigations, "The Role of Professional Firms in the U.S. Tax Shelter Industry," report, April 13, 2005, 50. This report updates the Permanent Subcommittee on Investigations' original report (see note 2 above) to reflect developments and new information that had emerged since it conducted hearings on the tax shelter industry in 2003.

22. Perez, et al., v. KPMG, et al., Larson deposition (October 1, 2003), 38.

23. Ibid., Jeffrey Eischeid deposition, exhibit 41, SCDOR-License-027049.

24. Complaint in Jacoboni v. KPMG, et al., Case No. 6:02-CV-510-On1-22DAB, reprinted in "Justice Releases Petitions, Exhibits Relating to KPMG Enforcement Actions," 2002 *TNT* 159-23, part 1 of 2 (August 16, 2002).

25. Jacoboni v. KPMG, DeLap deposition (July 18, 2003), 35–36, SCDOR-License-029011.

26. Ibid., 38-41, SCDOR-License-029012.

27. Permanent Subcommittee on Investigations, *U.S. Tax Shelter Industry*, testimony of Richard (Larry) DeLap, vol. 1, 45.

28. ACM Partnership v. Commissioner, T.C. Memo 1997-115, *aff'd in part and rev'd in part*, 157 F.3d 231 (3d Cir. 1998).

29. Perez, et al., v. KPMG, et al., DeLap deposition (August 28, 2003), 35–36, SCDOR-License-029011; ibid., Eischeid deposition, exhibit 39, SCDOR-License-027043.

30. Ibid., plaintiff's exhibit 47, SCDOR-License-027071.

31. Ibid., plaintiff's exhibit 57, SCDOR-License-027104.

32. Permanent Subcommittee on Investigations, *U.S. Tax Shelter Industry*, vol. 1, 167; and exhibit 97t, vol. 3, 2068–2069.

33. Ibid., exhibit 97z, vol. 3, 2121–2130.

34. Ibid., exhibit 97a, vol. 3, 1951–1956.

35. John Lanning, "A Tug-of-War over New Law Students," *Legal Times* (September 6, 1999); Geanne Rosenberg, "Big Five Pays Top Dollar for Tax Partners—Especially KPMG," *National Law Journal*, November 6, 2000, B8.

36. *ABA Journal*, July 1998.

37. Lanning, "A Tug-of-War over New Law Students."

38. Permanent Subcommittee on Investigations, *U.S. Tax Shelter Industry*, exhibit 97jj, vol. 3, 2174–2179; exhibit 97ll, vol. 3, 2189–2209; exhibit 97nn, vol. 3, 2210–2220.

39. Ibid., exhibit 97kk, vol. 3, 2180–2188.

40. Jacoboni v. KPMG, et al., DeLap deposition (August 28, 2003), 45–46, SCDOR-License-029019.

41. Jacoboni v. KPMG, et al., Ritchie deposition (June 16, 2003), 118, SCDOR-License-026671.

42. Permanent Subcommittee on Investigations, *U.S. Tax Shelter Industry*, exhibit 137, vol. 3, 2735–2744.

43. Ibid., 2740.

44. Ibid., 2735–2744.

45. Ibid.

46. Jacoboni v. KPMG, et al., Ritchie deposition (June 16, 2003), 85–86, SCDOR-License-026662.

47. Ibid., 88; Permanent Subcommittee on Investigations, *U.S. Tax Shelter Industry*, exhibit 38, vol. 1, 528.

48. Jacoboni v. KPMG, et al., Ritchie deposition (June 16, 2003), 31, SCDOR-License-026649.

49. Ibid., 119, SCDOR-License-026671.

50. Jacoboni v. KPMG, et al., Ritchie deposition (cont.) (November 16, 2003), exhibit 30, SCDOR-License-03025.

51. Ibid., 183–184, SCDOR-License-026687.

52. Ibid., exhibit 48, SCDOR-License-030297.

53. Permanent Subcommittee on Investigations, *U.S. Tax Shelter Industry*, exhibit 38, vol. 1, 528–531.

54. Jacoboni v. KPMG, et al., Ritchie deposition (June 16, 2003), 286, SCDOR-License-026713; Permanent Subcommittee on Investigations, *U.S. Tax Shelter Industry*, exhibits 94i and 94j, vol. 2, 887–898.

55. Jacoboni v. KPMG, et al., Ritchie deposition (June 16, 2003), exhibit 1, SCDOR-License-030038.

56. Ibid.

57. Ibid., Robert Simon deposition (January 9, 2004), exhibit 20, SCDOR-License-030766.

58. Ibid., exhibit 144, SCDOR-License-029282.

59. KPMG Deferred Prosecution Agreement, 1:05-crim-00903-LAP, statement of facts, ¶6, http://www.justice.gov/usao/nys/pressreleases/August05/kpmgstatementoffacts.pdf (accessed September 28, 2013).

60. Jacoboni v. KPMG, et al., Ritchie deposition (November 12, 2003), 461, SCDOR-License-030806.

61. Ibid., Stein deposition (June 6, 2003), SCDOR-License-028865.

62. Ibid., Ritchie deposition, exhibit 45 (November 12, 2003) (emphasis in original), SCDOR-License-331772.

63. Permanent Subcommittee on Investigations, *U.S. Tax Shelter Industry*, exhibit 94k, vol. 2, 905–909.

64. Jacoboni v. KPMG, et al., Ritchie deposition, plaintiff's exhibit 47 (November 12, 2003), SCDOR-License-331523.

65. Jacoboni v. KPMG, et al., Simon deposition, plaintiff's exhibit 23 (January 9, 2004), SCDOR-License-331514.

66. Permanent Subcommittee on Investigations, *U.S. Tax Shelter Industry*, exhibit 94k, vol. 2, 905–909.

67. Ibid.

68. Jacoboni v. KPMG, et al., Ritchie deposition, plaintiff's exhibit (November 12, 2003), 507, SCDOR-License-030220.

69. Ibid., plaintiff's exhibit 47, 482–483, SCDOR-License-030214.

70. Ibid.

71. Permanent Subcommittee on Investigations, *U.S. Tax Shelter Industry*, exhibit 155, vol. 4, 3245–3247.

72. Ibid.

73. Jacoboni v. KPMG, et al., Ritchie deposition, exhibit 14 (July 18, 2003), SCDOR-License-030038.

74. Ibid., exhibit 18, SCDOR-License-030121.

75. Ibid. (capital letters in original).

76. Ibid., Ritchie deposition, plaintiff's exhibit (November 12, 2003), 507, SCDOR-License-030220.

77. Ibid., Ritchie deposition, 461, SCDOR-License-030806.

78. Jacoboni v. KPMG, et al., DeLap deposition (July 18, 2003), 231, SCDOR-License-029060; Permanent Subcommittee on Investigations, *U.S. Tax Shelter Industry*, exhibit 15, vol. 1, 452.

79. KPMG Deferred Prosecution Agreement, statement of facts, ¶6.

80. Lee A. Sheppard, "Dissecting Partnership Gambits for Rich People," 2002 *TNT* 126-3 (July 1, 2002).

81. Ibid.

82. Sheppard, "Dissecting Partnership Gambits for Rich People"; Karen C. Burke and Grayson M. P. McCouch, "Cobra Strikes Back: Anatomy of a Tax Shelter," *Tax Lawyer* 62 (2008); IRS Rev. Rul. 88-77 and IRS Rev. Rul. 95-26.

83. Sheppard, "Dissection Partnership Gambits"; Burke and McCouch, "Cobra Strikes Back."

84. Diversified Group Inc. v. Paul Daugerdas and Jenkens & Gilchrist, Raymond J. Ruble affidavit, exhibit P, in "Justice Releases Petition in Sidley Enforcement Action," 2003 *TNT* 202-13 (October 20, 2003).

85. KPMG Deferred Prosecution Agreement, statement of facts, ¶20.

86. Ibid.

Chapter 5

1. U.S. Senate Committee on Governmental Affairs, Permanent Subcommittee on Investigations, *U.S. Tax Shelter Industry: The Role of Accountants, Lawyers, and Financial Professionals*, hearings, November 18 and 20, 2003 (Washington, D.C.: Government Printing Office, 2004), exhibit 98kk, vol. 3, 2341–2361.

2. Ibid., 2342–2343.

3. Ibid., exhibit 10, vol. 1, 428–438, 429.

4. Ibid., exhibit 98kk, vol. 3, 2341.

5. IRS Notice 2000-44, Internal Revenue Bulletin 2000-36 (August 14, 2000), 1.

6. U.S. Senate Committee on Governmental Affairs, Permanent Subcommittee on Investigations, "The Role of Professional Firms in the U.S. Tax Shelter Industry," report, April 13, 2005, 85.

7. Ibid., 88.

8. Karen C. Burke and Grayson M. P. McCouch, "Cobra Strikes Back: Anatomy of a Tax Shelter," *Tax Lawyer* 62 (2008): 59.

9. See Permanent Subcommittee on Investigations, *U.S. Tax Shelter Industry*, exhibit 73, vol. 1, 654.

10. Ibid.

11. Ibid.

12. Ibid., exhibit 95ii, vol. 2, 1405–1487.

13. Ibid., exhibit 85, vol. 1, 669.

14. Ibid.

15. Ibid., exhibit 174, vol. 1.

16. United States v. John Larson, Robert Pfaff, and Raymond J. Ruble, RS1 05 CR 888 (LAK) (November 13, 2008), transcript, 3079.

17. Permanent Subcommittee on Investigations, *U.S. Tax Shelter Industry*, exhibit 95l, vol. 2, 1267.

18. Ibid., exhibit 95m, vol. 2, 1268–1269.

19. Ibid.

20. United States v. Larson, 3100–3104.

21. Permanent Subcommittee on Investigations, *U.S. Tax Shelter Industry*, exhibit 95k, vol. 2, 1263.

22. Ibid., exhibit 95h, vol. 2, 1261.

23. Ibid., exhibit 95j.

24. Ibid.

25. Ibid.

26. Ibid.

27. Ibid., exhibit 95n, vol. 2, 1270.

28. Permanent Subcommittee on Investigations, *U.S. Tax Shelter Industry*, vol. 1, 178.

29. United States v. Larson, 729–732.

30. Permanent Subcommittee on Investigations, *U.S. Tax Shelter Industry*, exhibit 95p, vol. 2, 1273.

31. United States v. Larson, 3175.

32. Ibid., 3176, 1432.

33. Permanent Subcommittee on Investigations, *U.S. Tax Shelter Industry*, exhibit 64, vol. 1, 622.

34. Ibid., exhibit 95q, vol. 2, 1283.

35. Ibid., exhibit 77, vol.1, 661.

36. Ibid., exhibit 65, vol. 1, 623, 626.

37. Ibid., exhibit 81, vol. 1, 665.

38. United States v. Larson, 3094–3097.

39. Jonathan D. Glater, "Former Banker Pleads Guilty in Tax Shelter Case," *New York Times*, August 12, 2005, C1.

40. Permanent Subcommittee on Investigations, *U.S. Tax Shelter Industry*, exhibit 65, vol. 1, 623, 626.

41. Ibid., exhibit 12, vol. 1, 448.

42. Ibid., exhibit 65, vol. 1, 623, 626.

43. Amy Boardman and Carrie Johnson, "Accounting for Competition," *Legal Times*, February 3, 1997.

44. Permanent Subcommittee on Investigations, *U.S. Tax Shelter Industry*, exhibit 155-fn 98, vol. 4, 3468.

45. Ibid., exhibit 65, vol. 1, 623, 625.

46. Ibid.

47. Ibid.

48. Ibid., exhibit 65, vol. 1, 623, 624.

49. Ibid.

50. Ibid., exhibit 39, vol. 1 532.

51. Ibid. (italics in original).

52. Ibid.

53. Ibid.

54. Permanent Subcommittee on Investigations, *U.S. Tax Shelter Industry*, exhibit 95dd, vol. 2, 1386.

55. Alan Murray and Jeffrey Birnbaum, *Showdown at Gucci Gulf: Lawyers, Lobbyists, and the Unlikely Triumph of Tax Reform* (New York: Random House, 1988), 213–220.

56. United States v. Larson, government exhibit B-129.

57. Ibid., government exhibit B-315.

58. Permanent Subcommittee on Investigations, *U.S. Tax Shelter Industry*, exhibit 82, vol. 1, 666.

59. Ibid., exhibit 13, vol. 1, 450.

60. United States v. Larson, government exhibit B-140.

61. Ibid.

62. Permanent Subcommittee on Investigations, *U.S. Tax Shelter Industry*, exhibit 110, vol. 1, 2657.

63. Ibid., exhibit 95oo, vol. 2, 72.

64. Ibid.

65. Ibid., exhibit 95pp, vol. 2, 1501.

66. Permanent Subcommittee on Investigations, "The Role of Professional Firms in the U.S. Tax Shelter Industry," 106–107.

67. Permanent Subcommittee on Investigations, *U.S. Tax Shelter Industry*, exhibit 95ss, vol. 2, 1507.

68. Ibid., exhibit 95ccc, vol. 2, 1526; Permanent Subcommittee on Investigations, "The Role of Professional Firms in the U.S. Tax Shelter Industry," 107–108.

69. United States v. Larson, testimony of Amir Makov, 3327.

70. Glater, "Former Banker Pleads Guilty."

71. United States v. Larson, 3325; exhibit B-184.

72. Ibid., 3339.

73. Complaint in Allan Abrams, et al., v. KPMG (Superior Court of New Jersey, Law Division, Bergen County Docket # L-4191-05; United States v. Larson, 1821–1835.

74. Permanent Subcommittee on Investigations, *U.S. Tax Shelter Industry*, exhibit 30, vol. 1, 500.

75. KPMG Deferred Prosecution Agreement, 1:05-crim-00903-LAP, statement of facts, ¶6, http://www.justice.gov/usao/nys/pressreleases/August05/kpmgstatementoffacts.pdf (accessed September 28, 2013).

76. Ibid., exhibit 19, 460, 462.

77. IRS Notice 99-36, Internal Revenue Bulletin 1999-26 (June 14, 1999), 1.

78. Santa Clara Valley Housing Group Inc., and Kristen Bowes v. United States, C08-05-097 (LHK-HRL), deposition, exhibit 204, filed in support of United States' Motion for Summary Adjudication of the Issues (April 21, 2011).

79. Ibid., exhibit 172.

80. Permanent Subcommittee on Investigations, *U.S. Tax Shelter Industry*, exhibit 155-fn 121, vol. 4, 3482, 3489.

81. Ibid., exhibit 6, vol. 1, 412.

82. Ibid., exhibit 59, vol. 1, 604, 607.

83. Ibid., exhibit 43, vol. 1, 545–554.

84. Ibid., exhibit 21, vol. 1, 464, 483–485.

85. Ibid., 485.

86. Permanent Subcommittee on Investigations, "The Role of Professional Firms in the U.S. Tax Shelter Industry," 201.

87. Permanent Subcommittee on Investigations, *U.S. Tax Shelter Industry*, exhibit 155-fn 163, vol. 4, 3596, 3599.

88. Ibid.

89. Ibid.

90. Permanent Subcommittee on Investigations, *U.S. Tax Shelter Industry*, appendix B, Case Study of S-Corporation Charitable Contribution Strategy, vol. 1, 266.

91. Jonathan Weil, "IRS Puts Shelter Sold by KPMG on 'Abusive List,'" *Wall Street Journal*, April 2, 2004, C6.

92. Jonathan Weil, "KPMG Shelter Shaved $1.7 Billion off Taxes of 29 Large Companies," *Wall Street Journal*, June 16, 2004, A1.

93. Permanent Subcommittee on Investigations, *U.S. Tax Shelter Industry*, exhibit 38, vol. 1, 528.

94. Ibid.

95. Ibid., exhibit 89, vol. 1, 680–683.

96. Ibid., exhibit 147a, vol. 3, 2878, 2907–2909; Permanent Subcommittee on Investigations, "The Role of Professional Firms in the U.S. Tax Shelter Industry," 76.

97. KPMG Deferred Prosecution Agreement, statement of facts, ¶6.

Chapter 6

1. Janet Novack and Laura Saunders, "The Hustling of X-Rated Shelters," *Forbes*, December 14, 1998.

2. United States v. Robert Coplan, et al., 07 CR 00453 (SHS), transcript, 1070.

3. Ibid., 541–542, 2135.

4. Ibid., 2139.

5. Ibid., 2117–2122

6. Ibid., 2126.

7. Ibid., government exhibit 2; transcript at 2142.

8. Ibid., 1789.

9. Ibid., 1798–1799.

10. U.S. Senate Committee on Governmental Affairs, Permanent Subcommittee on Investigations, "The Role of Professional Firms in the U.S. Tax Shelter Industry," report, April 13, 2005, 88.

11. Sala v. United States, 552 F.Supp. 2d 1167. (2008); Williams v. Brown & Wood, 841 N.Y.S. 2d 222 (2007).

12. Permanent Subcommittee on Investigations, "The Role of Professional Firms in the U.S. Tax Shelter Industry," 81–82.

13. United States v. Coplan, government exhibit 66 (emphasis in original).

14. Ibid.

15. Ibid.

16. Ibid., 2271.

17. Ibid.

18. Permanent Subcommittee on Investigations, "The Role of Professional Firms in the U.S. Tax Shelter Industry," 84.

19. Ibid, 82, 84.

20. United States v. Coplan, 2202–2203.

21. Ibid., government exhibit 19.

22. Ibid.

23. Email from Robert B. Coplan, October 22, 1999, re: Cobra Pricing (on file with authors).

24. Murfam Farms v. United States, 06-245T (before the U.S. Court of Federal Claims), April 22, 2010, transcript, 1825–1827.

25. Ibid., 1771; defendant's exhibit D-959.

26. Ibid., defendant's exhibit D-782.

27. Ibid.

28. Ibid., 1827; defendant's exhibit D-802.

29. Ibid., 1841–1842.

30. Ibid., 1769–1775; defendant's exhibit D-959.

31. Ibid., 1809–1810; defendant's exhibit D-707.

32. Ibid., defendant's exhibit D-754.

33. Ibid., defendant's exhibit D-799.

34. Ibid., defendant's exhibit D-595.

35. Ibid., defendant's exhibit D-956.

36. United States v. Coplan, government exhibit 175.

37. Murfam Farms v. United States, 1741.

38. Ibid., defendant's exhibit D-199.

39. Ibid.

40. Ibid.

41. Ibid., defendant's exhibit D-956.

42. United States v. Coplan, government exhibit 107.

43. Ibid.

44. Ibid.

45. Ibid., government exhibit 111.

46. Murfam Farms v. United States, defendant's exhibit D-808. The reference to "ACM" is to ACM Partnership v. Commissioner, 157 F.3d 231 (3d Cir. 1998), which struck down a tax shelter on the grounds of what was interpreted as a newly invigorated economic substance doctrine.

47. United States v. Coplan, government exhibit 879.

48. Ibid., 718–719.

49. Ibid.

50. Murfam Farms v. United States, defendant's exhibit D-1017.

51. Ibid., defendant's exhibit D-1018.

52. Ibid., defendant's exhibit D-1017.

53. Ibid., defendant's exhibit D-1023.

54. Ibid.

55. Ibid.

56. United States v. Coplan, government exhibit 206.

57. Ibid., 2430.

58. Ibid., 3734.

59. Ibid., 3997.

60. Lynnley Browning, "Four Men, but not Ernst & Young Are Charged in Tax Shelter Case," *New York Times*, May 31, 2007.

61. United States v. Coplan, 2310; government exhibit 413.

62. Ibid.

63. Ibid., government exhibit 278.

64. Ibid., 1193–1201; government exhibit 859.

65. Ibid.

66. Ibid., government exhibits 534 and 535.

67. Ibid., 1226–1227; government exhibits 552 and 554.

68. Ibid., 1228.

69. Ibid., government exhibit 555.

70. Ibid., 1231–1232.

71. Ibid., 754.

72. Ibid., 755.

73. Ibid., 756.

74. United States v. Robert Coplan, et al., indictment 1:06-cv-00245-EJD.

75. Ibid.; Carlisle, et al. v. Curtis, Mallet-Prevost, et al., Case: 2:05-cv-00059 -DLB-JGW (E.D.Ky., March 3, 2005).

76. Candyce Martin 1999 Irrevocable Trust v. United States, No. C 08-5150 (PJH) (N.D.Calif., October 6, 2011) (order denying petition and entering findings of fact and conclusions of law).

77. Maguire Partners, United States of America's Post-trial Proposed Findings of Act and Conclusions of Law (August 12, 2008).

78. Maguire Partners Master Invs., LLC v. United States, 2009 U.S. Dist., LEXIS 130704 (2009).

79. KPMG Production to South Carolina Department of Revenue, SCDOR-License-034808.

80. Permanent Subcommittee on Investigations, "The Role of Professional Firms in the U.S. Tax Shelter Industry," 89.

81. Candyce Martin 1999 Irrevocable Trust v. United States.

Chapter 7

1. United States v. Daugerdas, et al., 09 CR 581 (WHP) (S.D.N.Y. 2011), transcript, 4307.

2. Ibid., 6337.

3. Ibid., 4307.

4. Ibid., 4040.

5. Ibid., 6855–6856.

6. Ibid., government exhibit 301-12.

7. Ibid., 1199.

8. Ibid., 1586.

9. Ibid., 1240.

10. Ibid., 1218.

11. Jones v. BDO Complaint, 3:06-CV-115, Judge Echols (D.C.M.D. Tenn. March 27, 2007), §54.

12. United States v. Daugerdas, 1230.

13. Ibid., 1493–1494.

14. Ibid., 1217–1218; government exhibit 301-269.

15. "Selected Exhibits Relating to BDO Seidman Enforcement Actions," 2002 *TNT* 136-8 (July 10, 2002), at 7.

16. Ibid., 8.

17. Ibid.

18. Ibid.

19. Ibid., 11.

20. United States v. Daugerdas, 1100.

21. Ibid., government exhibit 301-216.

22. Ibid., 4087, Revenue Ruling 95-26.

23. Ibid., 1137.

24. Ibid., 1148.

25. Ibid., 1262.

26. Ibid., 1212.

27. Ibid., 6359.

28. Ibid., 6366.

29. Ibid., 1282; ibid., government exhibit 300-65.

30. Ibid., government exhibits 300-74 and 300-173.

31. Ibid., 6373.

32. Ibid., government exhibit 300-131.

33. Ibid., 1233–1234.

34. Ibid., 1234.

35. Ibid., 1235.

36. Ibid., 1244.

37. Ibid., 1246.

38. Ibid., 1252.

39. Ibid., 4401.

40. Ibid., 4091–4093; government exhibit 301-216.

41. Ibid., 4093.

42. Ibid., 6911–6913.

43. Ibid., 6912 (emphasis in original).

44. Ibid., government exhibit 300-117.

45. IRS Notice 2000-44, Internal Revenue Bulletin 2000-36 (August 14, 2000), 1, 4.

46. Ibid., 4–5.

47. Ibid., 5–6.

48. United States v. Daugerdas, 4117.

49. Ibid., 4112.

50. Memorandum from Michael Kerekes to David Dreier, Esq., Re: IRS notice and amended regulations, August 11, 2000 (on file with authors).

51. Ibid., 6387.

52. Ibid., 4517.

53. Ibid., 6384.

54. Ibid., government exhibit 301-81.

55. Ibid.

56. Ibid.

57. Ibid.

58. Ibid.

59. Ibid.

60. Ibid.

61. Ibid.

62. Ibid.

63. Ibid.

64. Ibid.

65. Ibid.

66. Ibid.

67. Ibid., government exhibit 301-292.

68. Ibid., government exhibit 301-83.

69. Ibid., 6384.

70. Ibid., 4176.

71. Ibid., 4181.

72. "Selected Exhibits Relating to BDO Seidman Enforcement Actions," 2002 *TNT* 136-8 (July 16, 2002), at 1.

73. Ibid.

74. Ibid.

75. Ibid., 2.

76. Ibid.

77. Ibid.

78. Ibid., 4178.

79. Ibid., 6390.

80. Ibid., 1348.

81. Ibid.

82. Ibid., 1363.

83. Ibid., 6392.

84. United States v. Daugerdas, government exhibit 302-81.

85. Health Integrated E-Release, "Health Integrated Welcomes Denis Field, CPA, JD, LLM and David Friend, MD, MBA to Board of Directors," May 29, 2007, http://www.ereleases.com/pr/health-integrated-welcomes-denis-field-cpa-jd-llm-and-david-friend-md-mba-to-board-of-directors-9972 (accessed October 8, 2013).

86. Caleb Newquist, "BDO's Tax Shelter Team Was Known as the Wolf Pack," *Going Concern*, March 8, 2011, http://goingconcern.com/2011/3/bdos-tax-shelter-team-was-known-as-the-wolf-pack (accessed October 8, 2013).

87. Vidya Devaiah, "Embattled Ex-Head of 5th Largest Accounting Firm Turns to Indian Legal Outsourcing," *Law without Borders*, July 7, 2010, http://lawwithoutborders.typepad.com/legaloutsourcing/2010/07/denis-field-hires-indian-legal-outsourcing-company-embattled-exchairmanceo-of-fifth-largest-accounti.html (accessed October 8, 2013).

Chapter 8

1. Chris Klein, "A Texas Firm Leads Nation in Growth," *National Law Journal*, January 12, 1998, A1, A11.

2. Ibid., 1.

3. Ibid., 11.

4. Ibid.

5. Ibid.

6. The book will continue to use the term "partner" to refer to the owners of the firm because this common term makes it easier to discuss comparisons with other firms, the vast majority of which are organized as partnerships.

7. Michael Granberry, "Directions Change, but the Highway Man Is Driven to Succeed," *Dallas Morning News* (May 7, 2000).

8. "Merger Mania: The Texas Shuffle," *American Lawyer* (July 1999).

9. Nathan Koppel, "Fatal Vision: How a Bid to Boost Profits Led to a Law Firm's Demise," *Wall Street Journal*, May 17, 2007.

10. Ibid.

11. United States v. Daugerdas, et al., 09 CR 581 (WHP) (S.D.N.Y. 2011), 2291.

12. United States v. Daugerdas, government exhibit 201-34.

13. Professional Services Agreement between Jenkens & Gilchrist, Texas Professional Corporation, and Jenkens & Gilchrist, Illinois Professional Corporation, December 20, 1999 (on file with authors).

14. Ibid.

15. Ibid., government exhibit 201-34.

16. Ibid.

17. Ibid.

18. Ibid., government exhibit 201-33.

19. Ibid., government exhibit 201-246.

20. Paul Braverman, "Helter Shelter," *American Lawyer*, December 2003.

21. 34 T.C.M. (CCH) 727 (1975).

22. Letter from Grady P. Dickens, Scheef & Stone LLP to Paul Daugerdas, Jenkens & Gilchrist, PC, September 24, 1999 (on file with authors).

23. Internal Revenue Service, Notice 2000-44: "Tax Avoidance Using Artificially High Basis," August 11, 2000 (on file with authors).

24. Letter from Donna M. Guerin, Jenkens & Gilchrist, PC, to shelter participant, September 13, 2000.

25. Camferdam, et al., v. Ernst & Young, et al., Plaintiffs' Second Amended Complaint and Original Class Action Complaint, No. 02 Civ. 10100 (BSJ) (S.D.N.Y.).

26. United States v. Daugerdas, 30.

27. Ibid.

28. Ibid.

29. Ibid., 31.

30. Ibid., government exhibit 201-273, at 9.

31. Ibid., 10.

32. Ibid., 2357.

33. Ibid., 2494.

34. Ibid., 2363.

35. Ibid., 2358.

36. Enforcement Action, Johnson Second Declaration (March 9, 2004).

37. Unites States v. Daugerdas, 3663–3664.

38. Koppel, "Fatal Vision," A1.

39. Email from Patrick O'Daniel to Donna M. Guerin, January 12, 2000 (on file with authors).

40. Ibid., 3570.

41. Ibid., 3572.

42. Ibid., 3577.

43. Koppel, "Fatal Vision."

44. Memo from Paul Daugerdas to Jenkens & Gilchrist Board of Directors, May 28, 2001 (on file with authors).

45. Ibid., 2602.

46. The Diversified Group, Inc. v. Paul Daugerdas, 00 Civ. 0771 (SAS), February 2, 2000, complaint.

47. Ibid. at 3.

48. Ibid. at 4.

49. Ibid. at 4–5.

50. The Diversified Group, Inc. v. Paul Daugerdas, 139 F.Supp. 2d 445 (S.D.N.Y. 2001).

51. Indemnity agreement between Jenkens & Gilchrist Illinois; Paul M. Daugerdas and Paul M. Daugerdas, Chartered; and Jenkens & Gilchrist Texas (on file with authors).

52. Braverman, "Helter Shelter," 71.

53. David Laney memorandum to Jenkens & Gilchrist Board (on file with authors).

54. Unites States v. Daugerdas, government exhibit 203-28.

Chapter 9

1. Those who were convicted were R. J. Ruble, Sidley Austin Brown & Wood; Dennis Evanson, Utah attorney; William Bradley, Louisiana attorney; Robert Pfaff, Presidio; John Larson, Presidio; Robert Coplan, Ernst & Young; and John Ohle, Bank One. Those who pled guilty are Donna Guerin, Jenkens & Gilchrist; Erwin Mayer, Jenkens & Gilchrist; Peter Cinquegrani, Arnold & Porter; Graham Taylor, San Francisco attorney; Jay Gordon, Greenberg Traurig; John Campbell, Miller Canfield; Matthew Krane, Los Angeles attorney; Adrian Dicker, BDO Seidman, Michael Kerekes, BDO Seidman; Robert Greisman, BDO Seidman; and Charles Wilk, Quellos.

The convictions of Martin Nissenbaum and Richard Shapiro of Ernst & Young were reversed on appeal. A new trial was granted after the convictions of Paul Daugerdas of Jenkens & Gilchrist and Denis Field of BDO Seidman. After the second trial Daugerdas was convicted and Field was acquitted. KPMG's termination of coverage of attorneys' fees resulted in dismissal of the indictments of Jeffrey Stein, Richard Smith, Philip Wiesner, Steven Gremminger, and Carl Hasting. Raymond Craig Brubaker, of Deutsche Bank was acquitted. Finally, David (Lippman) Smith of Private Capital Management Group and Bolton Capital Management is a fugitive from justice.

2. United States v. John Larson, Robert Pfaff, Raymond J. Ruble, and David Greenberg, RS1 05 CR 888 (LAK), 3065.

3. RLP Holdings v. Bayerische Hypo- und Vereinsbank, et al., Fulton County Superior Court, Georgia, Civil Action 2006CV127554 (December 12, 2006). Among the defendants named in the lawsuit are Ruble and Michael G. Wolfson of Sidley Austin Brown & Wood.

4. Summons Enforcement against Sidley Austin Brown & Wood (December 29, 2003), Kan Declaration, reprinted in 2003 *TNT* 202-2.

5. U.S. Senate Committee on Governmental Affairs, Permanent Subcommittee on Investigations, *U.S. Tax Shelter Industry: The Role of Accountants, Lawyers, and Financial Professionals*, hearings, November 18 and 20, 2003 (Washington, DC: Government Printing Office, 2004), exhibit 120, vol. 3, 2699.

6. Ibid.

7. U.S. Senate Committee on Governmental Affairs, Permanent Subcommittee on Investigations, "The Role of Professional Firms in the U.S. Tax Shelter Industry," report, April 13, 2005, 50.

8. Permanent Subcommittee on Investigations, *U.S. Tax Shelter Industry*, exhibit 120, vol. 3, 2699.

9. Ibid.

10. United States v. Larson, et al., government exhibit FO-99.

11. Summons Enforcement Action, exhibit D.

12. Ibid., exhibit E.

13. Ibid., exhibit G.

14. United States v. Larson, et al., government exhibit FO-116.

15. Ibid., government exhibit FO-116-002.

16. Ibid.

17. Summons Enforcement Action, Kan Declaration, §43.

18. Permanent Subcommittee on Investigations, *U.S. Tax Shelter Industry*, exhibit 118, vol. 3, 2693.

19. Ibid., exhibit 128, vol. 3, 2720.

20. Ibid., exhibit 118, vol. 3, 2693.

21. Ibid.

22. Ibid.

23. Ibid., exhibit 91, vol. 3, 857–864.

24. Ibid.

25. Ibid.

26. Permanent Subcommittee on Investigations, "The Role of Professional Firms in the U.S. Tax Shelter Industry," 104.

27. Permanent Subcommittee on Investigations, *U.S. Tax Shelter Industry*, exhibit 131, vol. 3, 2723.

28. Ibid.

29. Ibid., exhibit 100d, vol. 3, 2544.

30. Ibid.

31. Ibid., exhibit 100g, vol. 3, 2548.

32. Ibid., exhibit 100i, vol. 3, 2551.

33. Ibid., exhibit 100c, vol. 3, 2546.

34. Ibid., exhibit 35, vol. 1, 522.

35. Ibid., exhibit 152, vol. 3, 3002.

36. Ibid., exhibit 100k, vol. 3, 2553–2556.

37. Permanent Subcommittee on Investigations, "The Role of Professional Firms in the U.S. Tax Shelter Industry," 106.

38. United States v. Larson, et al., Makov testimony, 3239–3242.

39. Ibid., 3242.

40. United States v. John Larson, Robert Pfaff, Raymond J. Ruble, and David Greenberg, RS1 05 CR 888 (LAK) (S.D.N.Y. 2008), indictment §52.

41. Justice Petition in Sidley Enforcement Action—Exhibit 25, Licensing Agreement, reprinted in 2004 *TNT* 2-37 (January 5, 2004).

42. International Air Leases, Inc. v. United States, US Bankr. Ct., ¶¶41–42 (S.D.Fla. August 27, 2003), reprinted in 2004 *TNT* 3-20.

43. Lukens Law Group v. Jones, et al., Case No. C 04 5357 WHA (N.D.Cal. February 7, 2005), first amended complaint, ¶43.

44. United States v. Larson, et al., government exhibit FO-531.

45. Ibid.

46. Permanent Subcommittee on Investigations, *U.S. Tax Shelter Industry*, vol. 1, 83.

47. Summons Enforcement, exhibit M, reprinted in 2003 *TNT* 202-16 (October 20, 2003).

48. "Brown & Wood Opinion Letter on Investment Strategies Available," 2003 *TNT* 238-54 (December 11, 2003).

49. United States v. Larson, et al., government exhibit B-389.

50. Ibid., government exhibit S-81.

51. Permanent Subcommittee on Investigations, *U.S. Tax Shelter Industry*, testimony of Thomas Smith, vol. 1, 78.

52. United States v. Robert Coplan, et al., indictment 1:06-cv-00245-EJD.

53. Peter Lattman, "More Law Firms Touched by Tax Shelter Investigation," *Wall Street Journal Law Blog*, July 3, 2007.

54. Coplan indictment at ¶24(f).

55. United States v. Robert Coplan, et al., 07 CR 00453 (SHS) (S.D.N.Y. 2009), transcript at 2194.

56. Joel Rosenblatt, "Locke, Lord Settles Lawsuit over Tax-Shelter Letters (Update 2)," *Bloomberg News*, July 2, 2009.

57. Ibid.

58. Permanent Subcommittee on Investigations, "The Role of Professional Firms in the U.S. Tax Shelter Industry," 87.

59. Ibid.

60. Jonathan Weisman, "Senators Question Tax Shelter Letters; Miers's Law Firm Sold Documents Backing Arrangement the IRS Criticized," *Washington Post*, October 27, 2005.

61. Ibid.

62. Fidelity International Currency Advisor A Fund, LLC v. United States, No. 4:05-cv-40151.

63. United States v. Coplan, et al., 1855, 1887–1889.

64. Ibid., 1788.

65. Ibid., 1789.

66. Ibid., 1849–1852, 1885.

67. Ibid., 1890.

68. U.S. Attorney for the Southern District of New York, "Attorney Pleads Guilty to Criminal Tax Fraud Related to Tax Shelters," press release, September 11, 2008.

69. Lynnley Browning, "Lawyer Tied to Kickbacks Quits the Bar," *New York Times*, November 16, 2006.

70. In the Matter of Jay I. Gordon, an Attorney, Respondent, Departmental Disciplinary Committee for the First Judicial Department, Petitioner, November 9, 2006.

71. Long-Term Capital Holdings v. United States, 330 F. Supp. 2d 122 (D.Conn. 2004).

72. Kara Scannell, "Nobel Winner Stiglitz Says Deals at LTCM Had No Economic Value," *Wall Street Journal*, July 18, 2003, C14.

73. Roger Lowenstein, *When Genius Failed* (New York: Random House, 2001).

74. Long-Term Capital Holdings v. United States, 146.

75. Ibid.

76. Ibid., 151.

77. Ibid., 149.

78. Ibid.

Chapter 10

1. Interview with former IRS official.

2. "IRS Enforcement Drops Sharply," 1999 *TNT* 69-3 (April 12, 1999). This article is the source of the figures in this paragraph.

3. See U.S. Code, Title 26, §6112 (1984) (amended in 2004); the legislation was the Deficit Reduction Act of 1984, PL 98-369.

4. 293 U.S. 495 (1935).

5. ACM Partnership v. Comm'r, 157 F.3d 231 (3d Cir. 1998).

6. Ibid. at 247.

7. Randall Smith, "Collection Drive: IRS Battles Colgate Over an Arcane Deal That Cut Its Tax Bill—Merrill-Designed Partnership Is Part of 'Vibrant' Genre: The Corporate Shelter—Paper Losses and Paper Gains," *Wall Street Journal*, May 3, 1996, A1.

8. Janet Novack and Laura Saunders, "The Hustling of X-Rated Shelters," *Forbes*, December 14, 1998.

9. This development is discussed in chapter 3.

10. Novack and Saunders, "The Hustling of X-Rated Shelters," 3.

11. Ibid., 4.

12. Joseph Bankman, "The New Market in Corporate Tax Shelters," *Tax Notes* 83 (June 21, 1999): 1775.

13. Ibid., 1776.

14. Ibid., 1782.

15. Ibid., 1784, 1785.

16. U.S. Department of the Treasury, *The Problem of Corporate Tax Shelters: Discussion, Analysis, and Legislative Proposals*, July 1999, http://www.treasury.gov/resource-center/tax-policy/Documents/ctswhite.pdf (accessed October 6, 2013).

17. Ibid., i.

18. The Treasury report acknowledged that differences between accounting and tax income can result from factors other than reliance on tax shelters, such as the operation of accelerated depreciation rules. The difference nonetheless had been steadily increasing in the last several years. For instance, the ratio between book and tax income was 1.08 in 1990 and 1.86 in 1996, which was the highest since 1985; ibid., 32.

19. Ibid., 28–29.

20. Ibid., 28.

21. Revenue Provisions in President's Fiscal Year 2000 Budget, Written Testimony of Ken Kies in Hearings before the Committee on Ways and Means, House of Representatives, One Hundred Sixth Congress, First Session, March 10, 1999, reprinted in 1999 *TNT* 47-69 (March 10, 1999).

22. Ibid.

23. Ibid., transcript, 227.

24. Ibid., 228.

25. Ibid.

26. Ibid., 73.

27. Ibid., 75.

28. Ibid., 77.

29. Ibid., 80.

30. "IRS Oversight," hearings before the Senate Finance Committee (April 22, 1999), http://www.finance.senate.gov/library/hearings/download/?id=28acef51-4e7c-4389-b196-12ea9086ee19 (accessed October 6, 2013).

31. William V. Roth, *The Power to Destroy* (New York: Atlantic Monthly Press, 1999), 185–206.

32. William H. Webster, Review of the Internal Revenue Service's Criminal Investigation Division (United States, Internal Revenue Service 1999), 3.

33. Ibid., 2.

34. Amy Hamilton, "IRS to Launch Corporate Tax Shelter Initiative," 1999 *TNT* 207-4 (October 27, 1999).

35. Internal Revenue Service, "Matthews to Head Criminal Investigation," 1999 *TNT* 230-13 (December 1, 1999).

36. Transcript of Hearings on Corporate Tax Shelters, before the Committee on Ways and Means, House of Representatives, One Hundred Sixth Congress, First Session, November 10, 1999, 102, reprinted in 1999 *TNT* 223-28 (November 19, 1999).

37. Ibid., 144.

38. Ibid., 145.

39. Ibid.

40. Ibid., 145–146.

41. "Doggett Release on Shutdown of 'Boss' Tax Shelter," 1999 *TNT* 237-18 (December 10, 1999).

42. John McKinnon, "Written Off: How New Tax Shelter Promised Big Savings But Finally Fell Apart—For PricewaterhouseCoopers, Complex Plan Ultimately Proved an Embarrassment—The Old Paper-Clip Trick," *Wall Street Journal,* August 21, 2000.

43. Ibid.

44. U.S. Senate Committee on Governmental Affairs, Permanent Subcommittee on Investigations, *U.S. Tax Shelter Industry: The Role of Accountants, Lawyers, and Financial Professionals*, hearings, November 18 and 20, 2003 (Washington, D.C.: Government Printing Office, 2004), vol. 1, 54.

45. Sala v. United States, No. 05-cv-00636-LTB-KLM (April 22, 2008).

46. "Kiss That Tax Shelter Goodbye?," *Business Week*, November 14, 1999.

47. Interview with former Treasury official.

48. "Summers Speech on Tax Shelters," 2000 *TNT* 40-34 (February 29, 2000).

49. Ibid.

50. "IRS Issues Temporary and Proposed Regs on Corporate Tax Shelter Registration," 2000 *TNT* 40-19 (February 19, 2000).

51. "IRS Issues Temporary and Proposed Regs on Customer List Requirement," 2000 *TNT* 40-18 (February 29, 2000).

52. IRS Bulletin No. 2000-12, "Disclosure Requirements for Corporate Tax Shelters," March 20, 2000, at 835, 836–837.

53. IRS Notice 2000-44, "Tax Avoidance Using Artificially High Basis," August 11, 2000.

54. Jacoboni v. KPMG, et al., Case No. 6:02-CV-510-On1-22DAB, Richard (Larry) DeLap deposition (July 18, 2003), 51.

55. Lee Shepard, "Should We Have Tax Shelter Legislation," 2000 *TNT* 220-30 (November 13, 2000).

56. For a history of the U.S. corporate income tax and an account of the debate, see Steven A. Bank, *From Sword to Shield: The Transformation of the Corporate Income Tax, 1861 to Present* (New York: Oxford University Press, 2010).

57. Shepard, "Should We Have Tax Shelter Legislation."

58. "Grassley-Baucus Release on Draft Tax Shelter Bill," 2001 *TNT* 151-64 (August 6, 2001).

59. "IRS Publishes Proposed Circular 230 REGS," 2001 *TNT* 14-120 (January 22, 2001).

60. "Senior Counsel Warns of Vigorous Enforcement of Tax Shelter Cases," 2001 *TNT* 43-7 (March 5, 2001).

61. "IRS, Merrill Lynch Reach Settlement over Tax Shelter," 2001 *TNT* 182-24 (August 30, 2001).

62. IES Industries Inc. v. United States, 253 F.3d 350 (8th Cir. 2001); United Parcel Service v. Commissioner, 254 F.3d 1014 (11th Cir. 2001).

63. Boca Investerings Partnership v. United States, 314 F.3d 625 (D.C. Cir. 2003).

64. Saba Partnership v. Commissioner, 273 F.3d 1135 (D.C. Cir. 2001); Compaq Computer Corp. Commissioner 277 F.3d. 778 (5th Cir. 2001).

65. "Kies Seeks Meeting with Treasury on Leasing Transaction," 2001 *TNT* 139-37 (July 19, 2001).

66. "IRS Tax Shelter Analysis," 2001 *TNT* 250-11 (December 18, 2001).

67. "IRS, Treasury Officials Promote Shelter Disclosure Initiative," 2002 *TNT* 17-4 (January 25, 2000).

68. "Disclosure Initiative for Accuracy-Related Penalties Announced," 2001 *TNT* 247-3 (December 24, 2001).

69. "ABA Tax Section Meeting: LMSB Official Reviews Corporate Tax Shelter Disclosure Initiative," 2002 *TNT* 14-5 (January 22, 2002).

70. "IRS, Treasury Officials Promote Shelter Disclosure Initiative."

71. "ABA Tax Section Meeting: LMSB Official Reviews."

72. "Privilege Waiver Agreement for Shelter Disclosure," 2002 *TNT* 37-66 (February 25, 2002).

73. "More Shelters Being Disclosed in Amnesty Initiative," 2002 *TNT* 48-5 (March 12, 2001).

74. Ibid.

75. Ibid.

76. "Treasury's Enforcement Proposals for Abusive Tax Avoidance Transactions," 2002 *TNT* 55-28 (March 21, 2002).

77. Ibid., 92–93.

78. Ibid. The regulations also altered the definition of "reportable transaction" to consist of any transaction that met at least one of a list of criteria.

79. "Rossotti Testimony at Finance Committee Hearing on Tax Scams," 2001 *TNT* 67-49 (April 6, 2001).

80. Ibid.

81. "Rossotti Testimony at Finance Committee Hearing on Fraudulent Tax Schemes," 2002 *TNT* 71-30 (April 12, 2002).

82. "GAO Testimony at JCT Joint Review of IRS," 2002 *TNT* 94-17 (May 15, 2002).

83. Ibid.

84. "JCT Reports on Progress in IRS Reform," 2002 *TNT* 93-18 (May 14, 2002).

85. John D. McKinnon, "Bush Administration Appears to Ease Curbs on Tax Shelters," *Wall Street Journal*, March 4, 2002.

86. Report of Investigation by the Special Investigative Committee of the Board of Directors of Enron Corp. February 1, 2002, http://i.cnn.net/cnn/2002/LAW/02/02/enron.report/powers.report.pdf (accessed October 9, 2013).

87. "Grassley Release on Enron Tax Shelters," 2002 *TNT* 13-26 (January 18, 2002).

88. John McKinnon, "Former Critics of IRS in Congress Now Clamor for Tough Enforcement," *Wall Street Journal*, April 8, 2002, A28.

89. "Finance Presses for Enron's Opinion Letters," 2002 *TNT* 123-5 (June 26, 2002).

90. McKinnon, "Former Critics of IRS in Congress Now Clamor for Tough Enforcement."

91. Lee A. Sheppard, "Dissecting Partnership Gambits For Rich People," 2002 *TNT* 126-3 (July 1, 2002); "Fishtail, Bacchus, Sundance, and Slapshot: Four Enron Transactions Funded and Facilitated by U.S. Financial Institutions," S. Prt. 107-82 (107th Congress, January 2, 2003), http://www.gpo.gov/fdsys/pkg/CPRT-107SPRT83559/pdf/CPRT-107SPRT83559.pdf (accessed October 9, 2013); "Report of Investigation of Enron Corporation and Related Entities Regarding Federal Tax and Compensation Issues, and Policy Recommendations," Joint Committee on Taxation Staff, http://www.jct.gov/s-3-03-vol1.pdf (accessed October 9, 2013).

92. "Corporate Tax Shelters: The Slippery Slope to Enron?," 2002 *TNT* 58-26; see also Victor Fleischer, "Options Backdating, Tax Shelters, and Corporate Culture," *Virginia Tax Review* 24 (2007): 103.

93. "Senate Panel Gives IRS Shelter Crackdown $ 10 Million Boost," 2002 *TNT* 137-1 (July 17, 2002).

Chapter 11

1. John D. McKinnon, "Enron May Use IRS Amnesty Program to Seek Relief from Tax-Shelter Fines," *Wall Street Journal*, February 28, 2002, A1.

2. "Examination of Books and Witness," U.S. Code, Title 26, §7602(a).

3. Ibid., §7602(b).

4. Internal Revenue Service, IR-2002-82, June 27, 2002; U.S. Senate Committee on Governmental Affairs, Permanent Subcommittee on Investigations, "The Role

of Professional Firms in the U.S. Tax Shelter Industry," report, April 13, 2005, 100.

5. U.S. Petition to Enforce Summonses against Arthur Andersen (Civil Action No. 02C 6790), reprinted in 2002 *TNT* 186-14 (September 25, 2002).

6. Ibid.

7. "Poe Intervenors Assert Section 7525 Privilege," reprinted in 2003 *TNT* 132-31 (July 10, 2003). Taxpayer brief in support of motion to intervene in Arthur Andersen Enforcement Action.

8. "Justice Department Petition Relating to BDO Seidman Enforcement Actions," reprinted in 2002 *TNT* 136-6 (July 16, 2002).

9. Camferdam, et al., v. Ernst & Young, et al., complaint, sec. 5, reprinted in 2002 *TNT* 248-4 (December 26, 2002).

10. Lee A. Sheppard, "News Analysis: Dissecting the Compensatory Option Sale Shelter," 2003 *TNT* 27-6 (February 10, 2003).

11. Editorial, "Unbridled Greed," *New York Times*, February 24, 2003, A16.

12. David Cay Johnston, "Wall St. Firms Are Faulted in Report on Enron's Taxes," *New York Times*, February 13, 2003.

13. "IRS Issues Final Regs on Tax Shelter Reporting, List Maintenance Rules," 2003 *TNT* 40-10 (February 28, 2003).

14. "Chief Counsel Sees Work on Guidance and Shelters Pay Off," 2003 *TNT* 47-2 (March 11, 2003).

15. Prepared Testimony of Commissioner of Internal Revenue Mark W. Everson before the Senate Finance Committee Hearing on Corporate Tax Shelters, October 21, 2003, 114, www.irs.gov/pub/irs-utl/sfc-oct19-03.pdf (accessed October 9, 2013); http://www.finance.senate.gov/imo/media/doc/102103etest.pdf (accessed October 6, 2013).

16. "Senate Confirms Everson as New IRS Commissioner," 2003 *TNT* 86-7 (May 5, 2003).

17. "Everson Testimony at House Appropriations Panel Hearing on IRS Compliance Efforts," reprinted in 2003 *TNT* 89-36 (May 8, 2003).

18. "Matthews Named IRS Deputy Commissioner for Services and Enforcement," 2003 *TNT* 143-4 (July 25, 2003).

19. Ibid.

20. Internal Revenue Service, IR-2003-84, July 2, 2003, http://www.irs.gov/uac/IR-2003-84 (accessed October 6, 2013).

21. United States v. BDO Seidman, 337 F.3d 802 (7th Cir. 2003).

22. United States v. BDO Seidman, 2004 U.S. Dist. LEXIS 12145 (N.D.Ill. East. Div. 2004).

23. United States v. Arthur Andersen, 2003 U.S. Dist. LEXIS 14228 (N.D.Ill. 2003).

24. "Everson Says IRS Will Resort to Summons Enforcement Where Necessary," 2003 *TNT* 181-30 (September 18, 2003).

25. "U.S. Petition to Enforce Summonses against Arthur Andersen."

26. "Sidley Austin Says Expulsion of Partner Not Due to Shelter Opinions," 2003 *TNT* 210-6 (October 30, 2003).

27. Ibid.

28. U.S. Senate Committee on Governmental Affairs, Permanent Subcommittee on Investigations, *U.S. Tax Shelter Industry: The Role of Accountants, Lawyers, and Financial Professionals*, hearings, November 18 and 20, 2003 (Washington, D.C.: Government Printing Office, 2004), vol. 1, 76.

29. Ibid., 77.

30. Ibid., 82.

31. Ibid., 83.

32. Ibid., 88.

33. "Responses to Supplemental Questions for the Record Submitted by Senator Carl Levin for Thomas R. Smith, Jr.," ibid., exhibit 152, vol. 3, 2999.

34. Ibid., 3004.

35. Declaration of Richard E. Bosch, Justice Department Enforcement Petition, reprinted in 2003 *TNT* 201-18 (October 15, 2003).

36. United States v. Sidley Austin Brown & Wood, 2004 U.S. Dist. LEXIS 7355 (N.D.Ill. 2004).

37. ABA Section of Taxation Meeting: "IRS Office of Professional Responsibility Director Outlines Changes," 2004 *TNT* 90-8 (May 10, 2004).

38. "IRS and Practitioners Wrestle over Son-of-Boss Settlement Offer," 2004 *TNT* 91-2 (May 11, 2004).

39. "Strong Response to 'Son of Boss' Settlement Initiative," Internal Revenue Service, IR-2004-87, July 1, 2004, http://www.irs.gov/uac/Strong-Response-to -"Son-of-Boss"-Settlement-Initiative (accessed October 6, 2013).

40. "Son-of-Boss Settlement Nets $ 3.2 Billion for IRS," 2005 *TNT* 57-1 (March 25, 2005).

41. "Grand Jury Investigating Ernst & Young Tax Shelter Sales," *Accountingweb*, May 25, 2004, http://www.accountingweb.com/topic/firm-news/grand-jury -investigating-ernst-young-tax-shelter-sales (accessed October 6, 2013).

42. Permanent Subcommittee on Investigations, "The Role of Professional Firms in the U.S. Tax Shelter Industry," 87.

43. Long-Term Capital Holdings v. United States, 330 F. Supp. 2d 122 (D.Conn. 2004), reprinted in 2004 *TNT* 169-15 (August 31, 2004); aff'd in unpublished opinion, 2005 U.S. App. Lexis 20988 (2nd Cir. 2005).

44. Internal Revenue Service, Announcement 2005-80, reprinted in 2005 *TNT* 208-11 (October 28, 2005).

45. News analysis, "Two Minutes to Midnight: Settle Your Shelter Case," 2006 *TNT* 34-4 (February 21, 2006).

46. U.S. Attorney's Office, Southern District of New York, "Manhattan United States Attorney Announces Decision Not to Prosecute Sidley Austin LLP," May 23, 2007.

47. "Sidley Austin to Pay $39.4 Million Tax Shelter Penalty," 2007 *TNT* 101-3 (May 24, 2007).

48. "Court Approves Amended Settlement between Shelter Investors, KPMG (Marvin Simon Et Al. V. KPMG LLP et al.)," court order, reprinted at 2006 *TNT* 107-23 (June 5, 2006).

49. Lynnley Browning, "Four Men, but Not Ernst & Young, Are Charged in Tax Shelter Case," *New York Times*, May 31, 2007.

50. Trial transcript in United States v. Coplan, et al. (07 CR 00453 (SHS)), 2108–2109.

51. Ibid., 2538.

52. Mark Hamblett, "Tax Lawyers' Sentences Include 'Explaining Dangers of Misleading IRS,'" *New York Law Journal*, January 22, 2010.

53. Non-prosecution agreement between Department of Justice and Ernst & Young (February 26, 2013), statement of facts, http://www.justice.gov/usao/nys/pressreleases/March13/EYNPAPR/EY%20NPA.pdf (accessed October 8, 2013).

54. Ibid.

55. "DOJ Says It Will Not Prosecute Deutsche Bank AG for Tax Crimes," 2010 *TNT* 245-25 (December 22, 2010) (non-prosecution agreement).

56. Ibid., 7.

57. Ibid.

58. United States v. Daugerdas, et al., 09 CR 581 (WHP) (S.D.N.Y. 2011), transcript, 6385–6390.

59. Janet Novack, "BDO Admits Generating $6.5 Billion in Phony Tax Shelter Losses, Pays $50 Million," *Forbes*, June 13, 2012.

60. Taylor at one time practiced at what were then Pillsbury, Madison, & Sutro; LeBouef, Lamb, Greene, & MacRae; Altheimer & Gray; and Seyfarth Shaw. There is no evidence that anyone else at these firms was aware of his involvement in promoting abusive tax shelters.

61. Indictment, United States v. Evanson, et al., Case 2:05-cr-00805-TC-DON (C.D.Utah), November 2, 2005; "Six Indicted for $20 Million Conspiracy to Defraud the U.S. Government," Department of Justice press release, November 3, 2005.

62. "Former Arnold Porter Partner Gets Probation for Tax Scheme," *JD Journal*, March 30, 2010, http://www.jdjournal.com/2010/03/30/former-arnold-porter-partner-gets-probation-for-tax-scheme/ (accessed October 6, 2013).

63. Mark Hamblett, "Former Arnold & Porter Partner Gets Probation in Tax Shelter Fraud Case," *Law.Com*, March 31, 2010, http://www.law.com/jsp/law/LawArticleFriendly.jsp?id=1202447152661 (accessed October 6, 2013).

64. "Former Arnold & Porter Partner Disbarred in D.C.," *Legal Times*, April 16, 2009, http://legaltimes.typepad.com/blt/2009/04/former-arnold-porter-partner-disbarred-in-dc.html.

65. Indictment, United States v. Jeffery Greenstein, et al., case no. CR08-0296RSM (W.D.Wash.), June 4, 2009, http://online.wsj.com/public/resources/documents/greensteinidictment.pdf.

66. Dennis J. Ventry, Jr., "Whistleblowers and *Quitam* for Tax," *Tax Lawyer* 61 (2008): 357, 361.

67. IRS Whistleblower Office, 2012 Annual Report to Congress, reprinted in 2013 *TNT* 31-14 (February 14, 2013).

68. The doctrine is codified at U.S. Code, Title 26, §7701(o) (2012).

69. IRS, "Guidance for Examiners and Managers on the Codified Economic Substance Doctrine and Related Penalties," http://www.irs.gov/Businesses/Guidance-for-Examiners-and-Managers-on-the-Codified-Economic-Substance-Doctrine-and-Related-Penalties, July 15, 2011.

70. IRS Notice 2010-62, "Interim Guidance under the Codification of the Economic Substance Doctrine and Related Provisions in the Health Care and Education Reconciliation Act of 2010," 5.

71. Scholars have taken different views of the value of codifying the economic substance doctrine. See Marvin A. Chirelstein and Lawrence A. Zelenak, "Tax Shelters and the Search for a Silver Bullet," *Columbia Law Review* 105 (2005): 1839; Bret Wells, "How Codification Changes Decided Cases," *Florida Tax Review* 10 (2011): 411.

72. U.S. Code, Title 26, §§6662(b)(6), 6662(i).

73. "New York State Bar Association Tax Section Applauds Some Anti-Corporate Tax Shelter Proposals, Rejects Others. Tax Section, Report on Corporate Tax Shelters," 1999 *TNT* 82-29 (April 23, 1999), at sec. 10.

74. "Ernst & Young Analyzes Tax Transparency Dynamics," 2006 *TNT* 69-10 (April 1, 2006).

75. Susan Cleary Morse, "The How and Why of the New Public Corporation Tax Shelter Compliance Norm," *Fordham Law Review* 75 (2006–2007): 961.

76. Ibid., 964–973.

77. Financial Accounting Standards Board, FASB Interpretation No. 48: "Accounting for Uncertainty in Income Taxes," June 2006, http://www.fasb.org/cs/BlobServer?blobcol=urldata&blobtable=MungoBlobs&blobkey=id&blobwhere=1175820931560&blobheader=application/pdf (accessed October 6, 2013).

Chapter 12

1. U.S. Senate Committee on Governmental Affairs, Permanent Subcommittee on Investigations, *U.S. Tax Shelter Industry: The Role of Accountants, Lawyers, and Financial Professionals*, hearings, November 18 and 20, 2003 (Washington, D.C.: Government Printing Office, 2004), exhibit 98yy, vol. 3, 2388.

2. Ibid.

3. IRS Agent Declaration in Support of Justice Department's KPMG Enforcement Actions, reprinted in 2002 *TNT* 136-10 (July 16, 2002).

4. Ibid.

5. Jacoboni v. KPMG, Case No. 6:02-CV-510 (M.D.Fla. April 29, 2002).

6. *Frontline*, "Tax Me if You Can," PBS documentary, http://www.pbs.org/wgbh/pages/frontline/shows/tax/etc/script.html (accessed January 14, 2014).

7. Perez, et al., v. KPMG, et al., C2593-02-A, District Court, 92nd Judicial District, Hidalgo County (November 19, 2003).

8. Cassell Bryan-Low, "Lawsuits over Tax Shelters Suggest a Hard Sell by KPMG," *Wall Street Journal*, May 21, 2003, C1.

9. Michael Hamersley, Written Testimony before the United States Senate Finance Committee, October 21, 2003, reprinted in 2003 *TNT* 204-35 ("Hamersley Senate Testimony").

10. *Frontline*, "Tax Me if You Can."

11. Michael Hamersley v. KPMG, LLP, et al., Case No. BC 297905, complaint, ¶9, Superior Court of the California (L.A. County), reprinted in 2003 *TNT* 124-5 (June 27, 2003).

12. Hamersley v. KPMG, complaint, ¶17.

13. Ibid., ¶18.

14. Ibid.

15. Ibid., ¶¶46, 50.

16. Hamersley v. KPMG, written testimony, 1–2, 8.

17. Hamersley v. KPMG, complaint, ¶¶58, 60, 62, 63.

18. "Tax Shelters: Who's Buying, Who's Selling, and What's the Government Doing About It?," Hearing before the Committee on Finance, United States Senate, 108th Cong., First Session (October 21, 2003), 128–129.

19. Permanent Subcommittee on Investigations, *U.S. Tax Shelter Industry*, vol. 1, 18–19.

20. Ibid., 33, 32.

21. Ibid., 57.

22. Ibid., 39.

23. Ibid.

24. Ibid., 40.

25. Ibid., 44.

26. David Cay Johnston, "Changes at KPMG after Criticism of Its Tax Shelters," *New York Times*, January 13, 2004, C1.

27. Permanent Subcommittee on Investigations, *U.S. Tax Shelter Industry*, vol. 1, 67.

28. Ibid., 145, appendix: "Four KPMG Case Studies: FLIP, OPIS, BLIPS, and SC2."

29. Lynnley Browning, "How an Accounting Firm Went from Resistance to Resignation," *New York Times*, August 28, 2005, 11.

30. Ibid.

31. Johnston, "Changes at KPMG."

32. U.S. Senate Committee on Governmental Affairs, Permanent Subcommittee on Investigations, "The Role of Professional Firms in the U.S. Tax Shelter Industry," report, April 13, 2005, 75–76.

33. Jonathan Weil, "KPMG Wins Dismissal of a Suit by Ex-Client Who Claimed Fraud," *Wall Street Journal*, March 15, 2004, C5.

34. IRS, Notice 2004-30, 2004-1 C.B. 828, 2004 IRB LEXIS 142, 2004-17 I.R.B. 828 (I.R.S. 2004).

35. "In the Crossfire: Prosecutors' Tough New Tactics Turn Firms against Employees—as Sentencing Rules Stiffen, KPMG Axes Tax Partners, Won't Pay Their Legal Costs—What 'Cooperation' Entails," *Wall Street Journal*, June 4, 2004, A1.

36. United States v. Stein, 435 F.Supp.2d 330 (2006).

37. Ibid.

38. United States v. KPMG, initial report and recommendations, January 27, 2003 (D.D.C.), reprinted in 2003 *TNT* 52-18 (March 18, 2003).

39. United States v. KPMG, 316 F.Supp.2d 30 (D.D.C. 2004).

40. Ibid., 37.

41. Ibid., 38.

42. Ibid., 40.

43. Ibid.

44. Browning, "How an Accounting Firm Went from Resistance to Resignation"; Jonathan Weil, "KPMG's Chief of Finance Quits as Probes Go On," *Wall Street Journal*, July 7, 2004, A3.

45. Carrie Johnson and Brooke A. Masters, "KPMG Hires Federal Judge; Firm Facing Investigation, Civil Charges," *Washington Post*, January 21, 2005, E1.

46. Ibid.

47. Browning, "How an Accounting Firm Went from Resistance to Resignation."

48. Diya Gullapalli, "KPMG Ousts Executive, Partners; Steps Tied to Tax-Shelter Scrutiny," *Wall Street Journal*, April 28, 2005, C2.

49. Deborah Solomon and Diya Gullapalli, "SEC Weighs a 'Big Three' World," *Wall Street Journal*, June 22, 2005, C1.

50. Joseph Nocera, "Auditors: Too Few to Fail," *New York Times*, June 25, 2005, C1.

51. Statement of David Kelley, quoted in Joseph L. Barloon Memorandum to KPMG March 3, 2005 Re: March 2, 2005 Meeting with SDNY, 3 (on file with authors).

52. Diya Gullapalli, "KPMG's Flynn Takes the Helm at a Stormy Time," *Wall Street Journal*, June 17, 2005, C1.

53. Department of Justice, U.S. Attorney's Office, Southern District of New York, Re: KPMG—Deferred Prosecution Agreement, August 26, 2005, http://www.justice.gov/usao/nys/pressreleases/August05/kpmgdpagmt.pdf (accessed 10/8/2013).

54. KPMG Statement of Facts, August 26, 2005, http://www.justice.gov/usao/nys/pressreleases/August05/kpmgstatementoffacts.pdf (accessed 10/8/2013).

55. Anonymous Memo to WSJ et al. re: KPMG and DOJ Investigation of Tax Shelter Activity: Is Anyone Interested in the Truth?, August 10, 2005 (on file with authors).

56. Jonathan Weil, "KPMG Tax Duo Tied to Shelters," *Wall Street Journal*, August 10, 2005, C1.

57. "KPMG Shifts Tax Managers," *New York Times*, September 13, 2005, C19 (Reuters).

58. "Banker Pleads Guilty to Fraud Charges for Blips Scheme," 2005 *TNT* 155-1 (August 12, 2005).

59. See United States v. Stein, superseding indictment (October 2004), reprinted in 2005 *TNT* 200-14 (October 17, 2005).

60. United States v. Stein, 435 F.Supp.2d 330, 351 (S.D.N.Y. 2006); United States v. Stein, 486 F.3d 753 (2nd Cir. 2007).

61. United States v. Stein, 495 F.Supp.2d 390 (S.D.N.Y. 2007).

62. United States v. Stein, 541 F.3d 130 (2nd Cir. 2008).

63. John W. Darrah, "Court Order in Jenkens & Gilchrist Enforcement Action. (John Does)," 2003 *TNT* 127-23 (July 2, 2003).

64. Sheryl Stratton, "Privilege Sidelines Shelter Actions, Gov't Changes Tack," 2003 *TNT* 140-7 (July 22, 2003).

65. Ibid.

66. Ibid.

67. Kathy Kristof, "IRS Demands List of Law Firm's Tax-Shelter Clients," *Sun-Sentinel*, July 1, 2003.

68. Justice Petition in Jenkens & Gilchrist Enforcement Action—Exhibit B, reprinted in 2003 *TNT* 127-36 (July 2, 2003).

69. United States v. Jenkens & Gilchrist, 2004 U.S. Dist. LEXIS 6919 (N.D.Ill. 2004).

70. United States v. Jenkens & Gilchrist, 2004 U.S. Dist. LEXIS 8645 (N.D.Ill. 2004).

71. Brenda Sapino Jeffreys and Miriam Rozen, "Taxing Times," *Texas Lawyer*, March 15, 2004, 19.

72. Cassell Bryan-Low, "Moving the Market: Jenkens & Gilchrist Agrees to Pay $75 Million in Tax Shelter Case," *Wall Street Journal*, March 8, 2004, C3.

73. Class Certification, Jenkens & Gilchrist Settlement Approved (Thomas Denney et al. v. Jenkens & Gilchrist et al.) (230 F.R.D. 317) (No. 03 Civ. 5460 (SAS)) (D.C.N.Y.), reprinted in 2005 *TNT* 34-11 (February 22, 2005).

74. "Law Firm to Settle Suits over Tax Advice," *Bloomberg News*, January 4, 2005.

75. Denney, et al., v. Jenkens & Gilchrist, et al., No. 03-CV-5460 (SAS), Jenkens & Gilchrist's Brief in Support of the Settlement, January 18, 2005, at 8.

76. Ibid., 9.

77. Ibid., 8.

78. Lynnley Browning, "Tax Shelter Inquiry Expands," *New York Times*, January 25, 2006.

79. Paul Davies, David Reilly, and Nathan Koppel, "Law Firm's Work on Tax Shelters Leads to Demise—Litigation, Penalty Fell Jenkens & Gilchrist; 'An Orderly Transition,'" *Wall Street Journal*, March 30, 2007, A1.

80. "U.S. Enters Non-Prosecution with Jenkens & Gilchrist in Connection with Its Fraudulent Tax Shelter Activity," press release, Department of Justice, U.S. Attorney's Office, Southern District of New York, March 29, 2007, http://www.irs .gov/pub/irs-news/jenkins__gilchrist_np_pr.pdf (accessed October 8, 2013).

81. Jenkens & Gilchrist, Statement of Jenkens & Gilchrist re: Non-Prosecution Agreement, reprinted in 2007 *TNT* 62-50 (March 30, 2007).

82. "Jenkens & Gilchrist Admits It Is Subject to $76 Million IRS Penalty," IR-2007-71, March 29, 2007, http://www.irs.gov/uac/Jenkens-&-Gilchrist-Admits -It-Is-Subject-to-$76-Million-IRS-Penalty (accessed October 8, 2013).

83. United States v. Daugerdas, et al., indictment, 09 CR (S.D.N.Y. 2009), at 9.

84. "Former Accounting Firm Partner Pleads Guilty to Tax Fraud, " press release, U.S. Department of Justice, U.S. Attorney's Office, Southern District of New York, July 9, 2009, http://www.justice.gov/usao/nys/pressreleases/July09/ greismanrobertpleapr.pdf (accessed October 8, 2013); "Former Jenkens & Gilchrist Attorney Pleads Guilty in Manhattan Federal Court to Creating and Implementing Illegal Tax Shelters That Generated Billions of Dollars in Fraudulent Tax Losses," press release, U.S. Department of Justice, U.S. Attorney's Office, Southern District of New York, October 19, 2010, http://www.justice.gov/usao/nys/ pressreleases/October10/mayererwinpleapr.pdf (accessed October 5, 2013).

85. United States v. Daugerdas, et al., 09 CR 581 (WHP) (S.D.N.Y. 2011), transcript, 2829.

86. The court denied Parse's request for a new trial on the grounds that his attorneys had suspected, but failed to notify the court, that the juror was concealing the relevant information.

87. Elizabeth Chambliss and David B. Wilkins, "Promoting Effective Ethical Infrastructure in Large Law Firms: A Call for Research and Reporting," *Hofstra Law Review* 30 (2002): 691; Ted Schneyer, "A Tale of Four Systems: Reflections on How Law Influences the 'Ethical Infrastructure' of Law Firms," *South Texas Law Review* 39 (1998): 245.

Conclusion

1. John Darley, "How Organizations Socialize Individuals into Evildoing," in *Codes of Conduct: Behavior Research into Business Ethics*, ed. D. M. Messick and A. E. Tenbrunsel (New York: Russell Sage Foundation, 1996), 13.

2. Christine Parker and Tanina Rostain, "Law Firms, Global Capital, and the Sociological Imagination," *Fordham Law Review* 80 (2012): 2347.

3. Cheek v. United States, 498 U.S. 192 (1991).

4. Darley, "How Organizations Socialize Individuals," 13.

5. Diane Vaughan, "The Dark Side of Organizations: Mistake, Misconduct and Disaster," *Annual Review of Sociology* 25 (1999): 271–305.

6. Neil Fligstein, "Organizations: Theoretical Debates and the Scope of Organizational Theory," in *The Sage Handbook of Sociology*, ed. Craig Calhoun, Chris Rojek, and Brian Turner (London: Sage Publications, 2005).

7. Vaughan, "The Dark Side of Organizations," 289.

8. Ibid., 274.

9. Jacoboni v. KPMG, et al., Robert Simon deposition (January 9, 2004), exhibit 9, SCDOR-License-030607.

10. Dennis A. Gioia, "Pinto Fires and Personal Ethics: A Script Analysis of Missed Opportunities," *Journal of Business Ethics* 11 (1992): 379.

11. Diane Vaughan, *The Challenger Launch Decision: Risky Technology, Culture, and Deviance at NASA* (Chicago: University of Chicago Press, 1996).

12. Sherry Turkle, *Alone Together: Why We Expect More from Technology and Less from Each Other* (New York: Basic Books, 2011).

13. Darley, "How Organizations Socialize Individuals," 21

14. Memorandum from Michael Kerekes to David Dreier, Esq., Re: IRS notice and amended regulations, August 11, 2000 (on file with authors).

15. Lon L. Fuller and John D. Randall, "Professional Responsibility: Report of the Joint Conference," *American Bar Association Journal* 44 (1958): 1161 (emphasis in original).

16. Upjohn v. United States, 449 U.S. 383 (1981).

17. Benno Torgler, *Tax Compliance and Tax Morale* (Cheltenham: Edward Elgar Publishing, 2007); Erich Kirchler, *The Economic Psychology of Tax Behavior* (New York: Cambridge University Press, 2007).

18. Michael Wenzel, "Misperceptions of Social Norms about Tax Compliance: From Theory to Intervention," *Journal of Economic Psychology* 26 (2005): 881.

19. Michael Wenzel, "Motivation or Rationalization: Causal Relations between Ethics, Norms, and Tax Compliance," *Journal of Economic Psychology* 26 (2005): 387 (footnote omitted).

20. Daphna Lewinsohn-Zamir, "Consumer Preferences, Citizen Preferences, and the Provision of Public Goods," *Yale Law Journal* 108 (1998): 379.

21. Ibid., 392.

22. Ibid. (footnote omitted).

23. Ibid., 393 (footnote omitted).

24. Tanina Rostain, "Ethics Lost: Limitations of Current Approaches to Lawyer Regulation," *Southern California Law Review* 71 (1997–1998): 1273, 1336–1337.

25. Ted Schneyer, "From Self-Regulation to Bar Corporatism: What the S&L Crisis Means for the Regulation of Lawyers," *South Texas Law Review* 35 (1994): 639.

26. Ibid., 673–674 (footnote omitted).

27. Treasury Department, "Rules Governing Authority to Practice," Code of Federal Regulations, Title 31, Subtitle A, Part 10; Treasury Department Circular 230, 4-1600A C.B. (1921), 412.

28. Tanina Rostain, "Sheltering Lawyers: The Organized Tax Bar and the Tax Shelter Industry," *Yale Journal of Regulation* 23 (2006): 77.

29. Dan K. Webb and Steven F. Molo, "Some Practical Considerations in Developing Effective Compliance Programs: A Framework for Meeting the Requirements of the Sentencing Guidelines," *Washington University Law Quarterly* 71 (1993): 375.

30. Tahlia Gordon, Steven Mark, and Christine Parker, "Regulating Law Firm Ethics Management: An Empirical Assessment of the Regulation of Incorporated Legal Practices in NSW," *Journal of Law and Society* 37, no. 3 (September 2010).

31. Non-Prosecution Agreement between Department of Justice and Ernst & Young (February 26, 2013), Statement of Facts, http://www.justice.gov/usao/nys/pressreleases/March13/EYNPAPR/EY%20NPA.pdf (accessed October 8, 2013).

Index